UNDERSTANDING AND USING
ENGLISH GRAMMAR
Second Edition

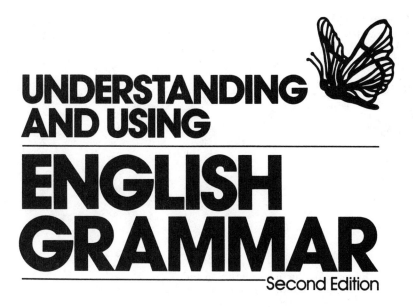

UNDERSTANDING AND USING
ENGLISH GRAMMAR
Second Edition

Betty Schrampfer Azar

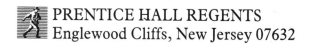 PRENTICE HALL REGENTS
Englewood Cliffs, New Jersey 07632

Library of Congress Cataloging-in-Publication Data

Azar, Betty Schrampfer, (date)
  Understanding and using English grammar / by Betty Schrampfer
Azar. -- 2nd ed.
    p. cm.
  Includes index.
  ISBN 0-13-943614-6
  1. English language--Textbooks for foreign speakers. 2. English
language--Grammar--1950- I. Title.
 [PE1128.A97 1989]   88-31425
                                                          CIP
  428.2'4--dc19

Editorial/production supervision and
   interior design: *Ros Herion Freese*
Cover design: *Joel Mitnick Design*
Manufacturing buyer: *Laura Crossland*

 © 1989 by Prentice-Hall, Inc.
A Simon & Schuster Company
Englewood Cliffs, New Jersey 07632

Printed in the United States of America

10 9 8

ISBN 0-13-943614-6

ISBN 0-13-943663-4 {VOL. A}

ISBN 0-13-943671-5 {VOL. B}

Prentice-Hall International (UK) Limited, *London*
Prentice-Hall of Australia Pty. Limited, *Sydney*
Prentice-Hall Canada Inc., *Toronto*
Prentice-Hall Hispanoamericana, S.A., *Mexico*
Prentice-Hall of India Private Limited, *New Delhi*
Prentice-Hall of Japan, Inc., *Tokyo*
Simon & Schuster Asia Pte. Ltd., *Singapore*
Editora Prentice-Hall do Brasil, Ltda., *Rio de Janeiro*

To my mother,
   FRANCES NIES SCHRAMPFER
and my father,
   WILLIAM H. SCHRAMPFER

Contents

Chapter 5 SINGULAR AND PLURAL 197

Chapter 6 ADJECTIVE CLAUSES 238

Chapter 10 CONDITIONAL SENTENCES 347

Appendix 1 SUPPLEMENTAL GRAMMAR UNITS A1

Preface to the Second Edition

The second edition of *Understanding and Using English Grammar* contains changes directed primarily toward clarification of structure presentations in the charts and improvements in the exercises. The revisions are based in large part upon the many wonderful and graciously offered suggestions from teachers and students familiar with the original text. A few new short grammar units have been included. One grammar area (comparisons) has been moved from *Understanding and Using English Grammar* to the second edition of *Fundamentals of English Grammar.* Additional notes on structure differences between American and British English have been included in the second edition.

The text remains a developmental skills text for students of English as a second or foreign language. While focusing on grammar, it promotes the development of all language skills in a variety of ways.

As in the original edition, the charts consist of examples accompanied by explanations and are intended to be easily understood by the students. Terminology is kept to a minimum.

The exercises reflect an eclectic approach, not only because there are many effective ways of teaching language, but also because certain structures simply tend to lend themselves to one approach rather than another. The exercises may be directed toward listening skills, oral production, writing skills, or reading comprehension—or any combination thereof. Some of the exercises have a straightforward, controlled concentration on form and meaning. These are followed by other more complicated and challenging exercises that engender creative, independent use of target structures. The exercise contexts reflect realistic, typical language use and are relevant to the students' concerns, daily lives, and life experiences. Items in the exercises are variously designed to encourage students to talk about themselves and their activities, to promote vocabulary development, to be informative, to engender cross-cultural comparisons, to be thought-provoking, to cause a smile or a chuckle, or to stimulate short discussions on a variety of topics.

In order to meet the needs of different teachers in different teaching situations, the revision of *Understanding and Using English Grammar* is available in two formats: in a single volume or in split volumes. The restructuring of the organization was designed principally to accommodate splitting the text into two volumes, with Volume A focusing on verb forms and Volume B focusing on complex structures. As in the original edition, each chapter is a self-contained unit; the teacher may present the chapters in the given order or rearrange the order of presentation to suit his/her needs and purposes.

Appendix 1 (*Supplementary Grammar Units*) has been expanded and now includes exercises. Information about parts of speech and basic structures such as questions and negatives is in the appendix so that students may have these units available whether using the single-volume text or the split volumes. The teacher can fit these units in as s/he deems appropriate in the syllabus. A teacher may, for example, choose to teach the question unit either prior to or in the course of teaching the verb tense chapter, may teach it in conjunction with the noun clause chapter, or may simply refer to it as needed in connection with tenses, modals, the passive, or any other unit. Much of the material in Appendix 1 is review from the other two texts in the series, but not all. As with any other grammar units in the text, the Appendix 1 material seeks to consolidate previous understandings as the basis upon which to expand usage ability.

Understanding and Using English Grammar (blue cover) is intended for upper-level students. It is part of a series of three grammar books. *Fundamentals of English Grammar* (black) is directed toward mid-level students, and *Basic English Grammar* (red) is designed for lower-level students.

WORKBOOKS

The second edition is accompanied by student workbooks: *Understanding and Using English Grammar—Workbooks A and B*. They contain not only Self-study Practices (answers given) for independent out-of-class work by the students, but also Guided Study Practices (answers not given) for classwork, homework, and individualized instruction as the teacher sees the need. In addition, there are suggestions for oral and/or writing activities, an emphasis on vocabulary development, and two practice tests for each chapter.

TEACHER'S GUIDE

The second edition of *Understanding and Using English Grammar* is also accompanied by a much expanded *Teacher's Guide* that contains: presentation suggestions; specific techniques for handling the varied types of exercises; background grammar notes; item notes on cultural content, vocabulary, and structure usage; problems to anticipate; suggestions for oral and written student-centered activities; and answers to the exercises.

ACKNOWLEDGMENTS

First of all, I would like to express my appreciation to Donald A. Azar for his irreplaceable encouragement, partnership, good humor, and computer expertise. He is the co-author of the *Workbooks* and also has served as an advisor on the revision. A person of myriad skills, he has eased the way through a demanding project during a busy time in our lives, making the work I enjoy even more enjoyable.

I wish also to express my great appreciation to Barbara Matthies, the writer of the accompanying *Teacher's Guide*, for her continuing support both as a colleague and a friend—and for a wonderful time in Kathmandu, where we spent hours tossing around ideas. To me, there is nothing better than a good friend/colleague who likes to talk about English grammar and the teaching of ESL/EFL.

I wish to express my gratitude to the following colleagues for their suggestions, interest, keen perceptions, and cheerful repartee: Irene Juzkiw, Rachel Spack (Shelley) Koch, Jeanie Francis, Susan Jamieson, Phyllis Mithin, Larry Francis, Barbara Leonhard, Nancy Price, Maureen Burke, Steve Molinsky, Bill Bliss, and Candace Matthews. An additional special thanks goes to Shelley, Jeanie, Susan, and Barbara Andrews for their wonderful contributions to and interest in the workbook project.

The many other colleagues I have spoken with about the revision are too numerous to name, but I thank all of them for sharing their ideas with me. I would like to say a special thank you to the teachers I met in Puerto Rico. And to all of those who so conscientiously and scrupulously responded to the questionnaire on revising the text, my heartfelt thanks.

The reviewers of the revised manuscript have been exceptionally helpful. In particular, I wish to thank Mr. Richard Eisman; Ms. J. Rajah; Ms. Mohana K. Nambiar; Dr. Dagmar Buhring Acuna, Universidad Interamericana de Puerto Rico; Mr. James E. Purpura, Institute for North American Studies, Barcelona, Spain; Ms. Teresa Pica, University of Pennsylvania, Graduate School of Education; Prof. Habibah HJ. Ashari, Coordinator, TESL Program, Center of Preparatory Education, MARA Institute of Technology, Malaysia; Mr. Richard L. Coe, State University of New York at Buffalo, Cooperative Education Program in Malaysia; Ms. Lynne Sarkisan Cresitello; Mr. Nicholas J. Dimmitt, University of Bahrain, Isa Town, Bahrain; Ms. Cheryl Engber, Indiana University; Ms. Linda A. Moody, Associate Director, The English Center for International Women, Mills College; Mr. William R. Slager, Department of English, University of Utah; and Ms. Shirley Wu, Singapore.

I must say a special thank you to Lilian and Leonard Feinberg, who graciously made available to me language teaching materials they had written. They are much appreciated as friends and mentors.

My gratitude also goes to Tina Carver, editor and friend, and to Ed Stanford, Andy Martin, Gil Muller, Noel Carter, Ros Herion Freese, Sylvia

Moore, Don Martinetti, and all of the others with Prentice Hall Regents who made this project possible and enjoyable.

I wish to thank Chelsea Parker for her willing, cheerful, and able office assistance. She is also a great joy and delight in my life.

Finally, I thank my mother for inputting and editing, my father for being a veritable wellspring of ideas for entries, and both of them for helping with the tedious job of reading proof. Throughout my life, they have been and still are ever ready to assist me in my various endeavors—for which I am truly grateful.

BETTY S. AZAR
Langley, Washington

UNDERSTANDING AND USING
ENGLISH GRAMMAR
Second Edition

CHAPTER *1*
Verb Tenses

☐ **EXERCISE 1—ORAL:** Interview another student in the class. Take notes during the interview, and then introduce this student to the rest of the class. Possible topics for the interview follow. As a class, discuss what questions you might ask to elicit this information.

1. name
2. spelling of name
3. country of origin
4. residence at present
5. length of time in (*this city or country*), both past and future
6. reason for coming here
7. field of study or work
8. spare-time activities and interests
9. general well-being and adjustment to living here
10. comments on living here

☐ **EXERCISE 2—WRITTEN:** Write a short autobiographical paragraph telling who you are, what you have done in the past two years, and what your plans are for the next two years.

☐ **EXERCISE 3—ORAL (BOOKS CLOSED):** Ask a classmate a question using ***what*** *+ a form of* ***do*** (e.g., *What are you doing? What did you do? What have you done?*). Use the given time expressions.

Example: every morning
Student A: What do you do every morning?
Student B: I (go to classes/eat breakfast/etc.) every morning.

1. every day before you come to school
2. last night
3. since you got up this morning
4. right now
5. at (*this exact time*) yesterday
6. for the past five minutes
7. tomorrow
8. at (*this exact time*) tomorrow
9. by the time you got to class this morning
10. by the time you go to bed tonight

***AN OVERVIEW OF ENGLISH VERB TENSES FOLLOWS IN CHARTS 1-1
THROUGH 1-5.*** The diagram shown below will be used in the tense descriptions:

1-1 THE SIMPLE TENSES

TENSE	EXAMPLES	MEANING
SIMPLE PRESENT	(a) It *snows* in Alaska. (b) I *watch* television every day.	In general, the simple present expresses events or situations that *exist always*, *usually*, *habitually*; they exist now, have existed in the past, and probably will exist in the future.
SIMPLE PAST	(c) It *snowed* yesterday. (d) I *watched* television last night.	*At one particular time in the past*, this happened. It began and ended in the past.
SIMPLE FUTURE	(e) It *will snow* tomorrow. (f) I *will watch* television tonight.	*At one particular time in the future*, this will happen.

1-2 THE PROGRESSIVE TENSES*

<table>
<tr>
<td colspan="3">Form: be + -ing (present participle)
Meaning: The progressive tenses give the idea that an action is in progress during a particular time. The tenses say that an action begins before, is in progress during, and continues after another time or action.</td>
</tr>
<tr>
<td>PRESENT PROGRESSIVE
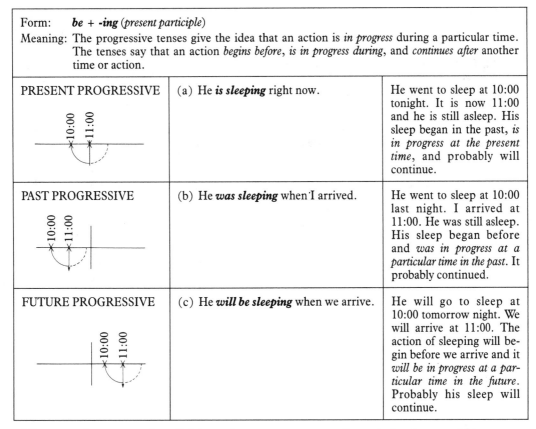</td>
<td>(a) He is sleeping right now.</td>
<td>He went to sleep at 10:00 tonight. It is now 11:00 and he is still asleep. His sleep began in the past, is in progress at the present time, and probably will continue.</td>
</tr>
<tr>
<td>PAST PROGRESSIVE</td>
<td>(b) He was sleeping when I arrived.</td>
<td>He went to sleep at 10:00 last night. I arrived at 11:00. He was still asleep. His sleep began before and was in progress at a particular time in the past. It probably continued.</td>
</tr>
<tr>
<td>FUTURE PROGRESSIVE</td>
<td>(c) He will be sleeping when we arrive.</td>
<td>He will go to sleep at 10:00 tomorrow night. We will arrive at 11:00. The action of sleeping will begin before we arrive and it will be in progress at a particular time in the future. Probably his sleep will continue.</td>
</tr>
</table>

*The progressive tenses are also called the continuous tenses: *present continuous*, *past continuous*, and *future continuous*.

1-3 THE PERFECT TENSES

Form:	**have** + *past participle*	
Meaning: The perfect tenses all give the idea that one thing *happens before* another time or event.		

PRESENT PERFECT eat — now (time?)	(a) I **have** already **eaten**.	I *finished* eating sometime *before now*. The exact time is not important.
PAST PERFECT eat — arrive	(b) I **had** already **eaten** when they arrived.	First I finished eating. Later they arrived. My eating was completely *finished before another time in the past.*
FUTURE PERFECT eat — arrive	(c) I **will** already **have eaten** when they arrive.	First I will finish eating. Later they will arrive. My eating will be completely *finished before another time in the future.*

1-4 THE PERFECT PROGRESSIVE TENSES

Form:	**have** + **been** + **-ing** (*present participle*)	
Meaning:	The perfect progressive tenses give the idea that one event is *in progress immediately before, up to, until another time or event.* The tenses are used to express the *duration* of the first event.	

PRESENT PERFECT PROGRESSIVE	(a) I **have been studying** for two hours.	Event in progress: studying. When? *Before now, up to now.* How long? For two hours.
PAST PERFECT PROGRESSIVE	(b) I **had been studying** for two hours before my friend came.	Event in progress: studying. When? *Before another event in the past.* How long? For two hours.
FUTURE PERFECT PROGRESSIVE	(c) I **will have been studying** for two hours by the time you arrive.	Event in progress: studying. When? *Before another event in the future.* How long? For two hours.

1-5 SUMMARY CHART OF VERB TENSES

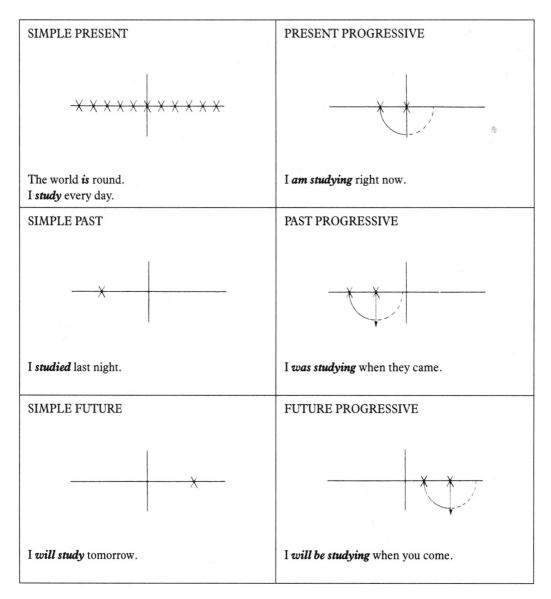

SIMPLE PRESENT

The world *is* round.
I *study* every day.

PRESENT PROGRESSIVE

I *am studying* right now.

SIMPLE PAST

I *studied* last night.

PAST PROGRESSIVE

I *was studying* when they came.

SIMPLE FUTURE

I *will study* tomorrow.

FUTURE PROGRESSIVE

I *will be studying* when you come.

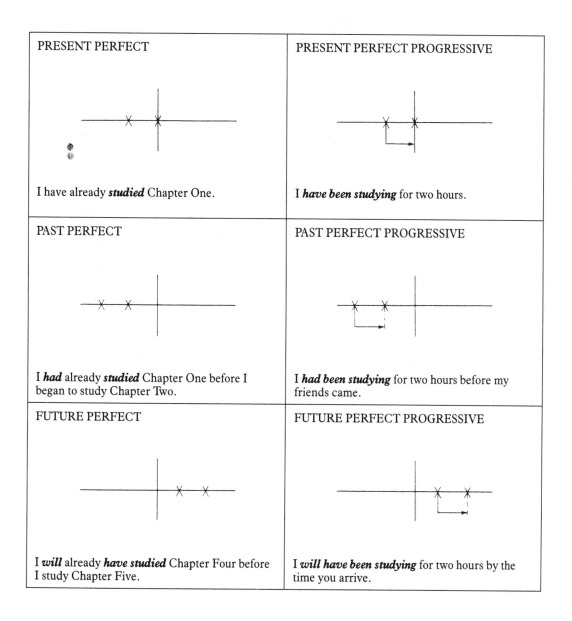

PRESENT PERFECT

I have already **studied** Chapter One.

PRESENT PERFECT PROGRESSIVE

I **have been studying** for two hours.

PAST PERFECT

I **had** already **studied** Chapter One before I began to study Chapter Two.

PAST PERFECT PROGRESSIVE

I **had been studying** for two hours before my friends came.

FUTURE PERFECT

I **will** already **have studied** Chapter Four before I study Chapter Five.

FUTURE PERFECT PROGRESSIVE

I **will have been studying** for two hours by the time you arrive.

□ **EXERCISE 4—ORAL (BOOKS CLOSED):** Practice using tenses by answering the questions in complete sentences.

1. What do you do every day?
2. What did you do yesterday?
3. What will you do tomorrow?
4. What are you doing right now?
5. What were you doing at this time yesterday?
6. What will you be doing at this time tomorrow?
7. What have you done since you got up this morning?
8. What had you done before you went to bed last night?
9. What will you have done by the time you go to bed tonight?
10. What are you doing? How long have you been doing that?
11. What were you doing before I walked into the classroom today? How long had you been doing that?
12. What will you be doing before I walk into the classroom tomorrow? How long will you have been doing that?

□ **EXERCISE 5—SPELLING PRETEST (BOOKS CLOSED):** You will be using many verbs in their *-ing* and *-ed* forms in this chapter. Use this pretest to check yourself on spelling rules. On another piece of paper, write the words that your teacher says.

Example: (cry + -ed)
Teacher: Cried. I cried because I was sad. Cried.
Written Response: cried

1. (hope + -ed)
2. (dine + -ing)
3. (stop + -ed)
4. (plan + -ing)
5. (rain + -ed)
6. (wait + -ing)
7. (listen + -ing)
8. (happen + -ed)
9. (begin + -ing)
10. (occur + -ed)
11. (start + -ing)
12. (warn + -ed)
13. (enjoy + -ed)
14. (play + -ing)
15. (study + -ing)
16. (worry + -ed)
17. (die + -ed)
18. (lie + -ing)

1-6 SPELLING OF -*ING* AND -*ED* FORMS

(1) VERBS THAT END IN -*E*	(a) hope date injure	hoping dating injuring	hoped dated injured	-*ING* FORM: If the word ends in -*e*, drop the -*e* and add -*ing*.* -*ED* FORM: If the word ends in -*e*, just add -*d*.
(2) VERBS THAT END IN A VOWEL AND A CONSONANT	ONE-SYLLABLE VERBS			
	(b) stop rob beg	stopping robbing begging	stopped robbed begged	*1 vowel* → *2 consonants*******
	(c) rain fool dream	raining fooling dreaming	rained fooled dreamed	*2 vowels* → *1 consonant*
	TWO-SYLLABLE VERBS			
	(d) listen offer open	listening offering opening	listened offered opened	*1st syllable stressed* → *1 consonant*
	(e) begin prefer control	beginning preferring controlling	(began) preferred controlled	*2nd syllable stressed* → *2 consonants*
(3) VERBS THAT END IN TWO CONSONANTS	(f) start fold demand	starting folding demanding	started folded demanded	If the word ends in two consonants, just add the ending.
(4) VERBS THAT END IN -*Y*	(g) enjoy pray buy	enjoying praying buying	enjoyed prayed (bought)	If -*y* is preceded by a vowel, keep the -*y*.
	(h) study try reply	studying trying replying	studied tried replied	If -*y* is preceded by a consonant: -*ING* FORM: keep the -*y*, add -*ing*. -*ED* FORM: change -*y* to -*i*, add -*ed*.
(5) VERBS THAT END IN -*IE*	(i) die lie tie	dying lying tying	died lied tied	-*ING* FORM: Change -*ie* to -*y*, add -*ing*. -*ED* FORM: Add -*d*.

*Exception: If a verb ends in -*ee*, the final -*e* is not dropped: *seeing, agreeing, freeing*.
**Exception: -*w* and -*x* are not doubled: *plow* → *plowed*; *fix* → *fixed*.

☐ **EXERCISE 6**: Give the correct *-ing* form for the following.

1. hold → *holding*
2. hide
3. run
4. ruin
5. come
6. write
7. eat
8. sit
9. act
10. pat
11. open
12. begin
13. earn
14. fry
15. die
16. employ

☐ **EXERCISE 7**: Give the correct *-ing* and *-ed* forms for the following.

1. boil → *boiling, boiled*
2. try
3. stay
4. tape
5. tap
6. offer
7. prefer
8. gain
9. plan
10. tie
11. help
12. study
13. admit
14. visit
15. hug
16. rage

☐ **EXERCISE 8**: Give the correct *-ed* form for the following.

1. bore
2. jar
3. jeer
4. intensify
5. sob
6. loot
7. point
8. ripen
9. refer
10. destroy

☐ **EXERCISE 9**: Give the correct *-ing* form for the following.

1. raid
2. ride
3. bid
4. bury
5. lie
6. argue
7. tame
8. teem
9. trim
10. harm

1-7 SIMPLE PRESENT

	(a) Water *consists* of hydrogen and oxygen. (b) Most animals *kill* only for food. (c) The world *is* round.	The simple present says that something was true in the past, is true in the present, and will be true in the future. It is used for *general statements of fact*.
✗✗✗✗✗✗✗✗✗✗	(d) I *study* for two hours every night. (e) My classes *begin* at nine. (f) He always *eats* a sandwich for lunch.	The simple present is used to express *habitual or everyday activity*.
	(g) I *have* only a dollar right now. (h) I *don't recognize* that man. (i) He *needs* a pen right now.	Certain verbs are not used in the progressive tenses. (See Chart 1-9.) With these verbs, the simple present may indicate a situation that exists right now, at the moment of speaking.

1-8 PRESENT PROGRESSIVE

start / now / finish? in progress	(j) John *is sleeping* right now. (k) I need an umbrella because it *is raining*. (l) John and Mary *are talking* on the phone.	The present progressive expresses an activity that is *in progress at the moment of speaking*. It began in the recent past, is continuing at present, and will probably end at some point in the future.
	(m) I *am taking* five courses this semester. (n) John *is trying* to improve his work habits. (o) She *is writing* another book this year.	Often the activity is of a general nature: something generally in progress this week, this month, this year. Note (o): The sentence means that writing a book is a general activity she is engaged in at present, but it does not mean that at the moment of speaking she is sitting at her desk with pen in hand.

□ **EXERCISE 10:** Use either the SIMPLE PRESENT or the PRESENT PROGRESSIVE of the verbs in parentheses.

1. Diane can't come to the phone because she (*wash*)_____*is washing*_____ her hair.

2. Diane (*wash*)_____ her hair every other day or so.

3. Kathy (*sit, usually★*)_____ in the front row during class, but today she (*sit*)_____ in the last row.

4. Please be quiet. I (*try*)_____ to concentrate.

5. (*Lock, you, always★*)_____ the door to your apartment when you leave?

6. I wrote to my friend last week. She hasn't answered my letter yet. I (*wait, still★*)_____ for a reply.

7. After three days of rain, I'm glad that the sun (*shine*)_____ again today.

8. Every morning, the sun (*shine*)_____ in my bedroom window and (*wake*)_____ me up.

9. A: Look! It (*snow*)_____.

   B: It's beautiful! This is the first time I've ever seen snow. It (*snow, not★*)_____ in my country.

10. Mike is a student, but he (*go, not★*)_____ to school right now because it's summer. He (*attend*)_____ college from September to May every year, but in the summers he (*have, usually★*)_____ a job at the post office. In fact, he (*work*)_____ there this summer.

□ **EXERCISE 11—ORAL:** On a piece of paper, write one direction that you want a classmate to follow. Examples: *Stand up. Smile. Open the door. Sneeze.*

(To the teacher: Collect and then redistribute the directions. Ask each student in turn to perform the required action, and have another student use the present progressive to describe this action.)

★See Appendix 1 for usual placement of midsentence adverbs (Chart A-4), for question forms (Chart B-1), and for negative forms (Chart C-1).

1-9 NONPROGRESSIVE VERBS

NONPROGRESSIVE (a) Ali **knows** this grammar.	Some verbs are *nonprogressive*: they are not used in any of the progressive tenses. These verbs describe states (i.e., conditions that exist); they do not describe activities that are in progress. In (a): "Ali knows" describes a mental state that exists.
PROGRESSIVE (b) Kim **is reading** about this grammar.	COMPARE: In (b): "Kim is reading" is an activity in progress. Progressive tenses can be used with the verb **read** but not with the verb **know**.

COMMON NONPROGRESSIVE VERBS				
(1) MENTAL STATE	*know* *realize* *understand* *recognize*	*believe* *feel* *suppose* *think★*	*imagine* *doubt* *remember* *forget*	*want* *need* *prefer* *mean*
(2) EMOTIONAL STATE	*love* *like* *appreciate*	*hate* *dislike*	*fear* *envy*	*mind* *care*
(3) POSSESSION	*possess*	*have★*	*own*	*belong*
(4) SENSE PERCEPTIONS	*taste★* *smell★*	*hear* *feel★*	*see★*	
(5) OTHER EXISTING STATES	*seem* *look★* *appear★*	*cost* *owe* *weigh★*	*be★* *exist*	*consist of* *contain* *include*

★Verbs with an asterisk are also commonly used as progressive verbs, with a difference in meaning, as in the following examples:

	NONPROGRESSIVE (*existing state*)	PROGRESSIVE (*activity in progress*)
think	I **think** he is a kind man.	I **am thinking** about this grammar.
have	He **has** a car.	I **am having** trouble. She **is having** a good time.
taste	This food **tastes** good.	The chef **is tasting** the sauce.
smell	These flowers **smell** good.	Don **is smelling** the roses.
see	I **see** a butterfly. **Do** you **see** it?	The doctor **is seeing** a patient.
feel	The cat's fur **feels** soft.	Sue **is feeling** the cat's fur.
look	She **looks** cold. I'll lend her my coat.	I **am looking** out the window.
appear	He **appears** to be asleep.	The actor **is appearing** on the stage.
weigh	A piano is heavy. It **weighs** a lot.	The grocer **is weighing** the bananas.
be	I **am** hungry.	Tom **is being** foolish.★★

★★COMPARE:

(a) *Bob is foolish.* = Foolishness is one of Bob's usual characteristics.

(b) *Tom is being foolish.* = Right now, at the moment of speaking, Tom is doing something that the speaker considers foolish.

The verb **be** (+ *an adjective*) is used in the progressive to describe a temporary characteristic. Very few adjectives are used with **be** in the progressive; some of the most common are: *foolish, nice, kind, lazy, careful, patient, silly, rude, polite, impolite.*

☐ **EXERCISE 12:** Use either the SIMPLE PRESENT or the PRESENT PROGRESSIVE of the verbs in parentheses.

1. I can't afford that ring. It (*cost*) _____ *costs* _____ too much.

2. Look. It (*begin*) _____ to rain. Unfortunately, I (*have, not**) _____ my umbrella with me. Tom is lucky. He (*wear*) _____ a raincoat.

3. I (*own, not*) _____ an umbrella. I (*wear*) _____ a waterproof hat on rainy days.

4. Right now I (*look*) _____ around the classroom. Yoko (*write*) _____ in her book. Carlos (*bite*) _____ his pencil. Wan-Ning (*scratch*) _____ his head. Ahmed (*stare*) _____ out the window. He (*seem*) _____ to be daydreaming, but perhaps he (*think*) _____ hard about verb tenses. What (*think, you*) _____ Ahmed (*do*) _____?

---
*A form of **do** is usually used in the negative when the main verb is **have** (especially in American English but also commonly in British English); e.g., *I don't have a car.* Using **have** without a form of **do** is also possible but less common: *I haven't a car.*

5. There's a book on my desk, but it (*belong, not*) _____ _____ to me.

6. Dennis (*fix*) _____ the roof of his house today, and he (*need*) _____ some help. Can you help him?

7. Barbara (*tutor, often*) _____ other students in her math class. This afternoon she (*help*) _____ Steve with his math assignment because he (*understand, not*) _____ the material they (*work*) _____ on in their class this week.

8. Right now I (*look*) _____ at Janet. She (*look*) _____ angry. I wonder what's the matter. She (*have*) _____ a frown on her face. She certainly (*have, not*) _____ any fun right now.

9. A: Who is that woman who (*stand*) _____ next to the window?

   B: Which woman? (*Talk, you*) _____ about the woman who (*wear*) _____ the blue and gold dress?

   A: No, I (*talk, not*) _____ about her. I (*mean*) _____ the woman who (*wear*) _____ the blue suit.

   B: Oh. I (*know, not*) _____. I (*recognize, not*) _____ her.

10. A: Close your eyes. Now listen carefully. What (*hear, you*) _____ _____? What (*do, I*) _____?

    B: I (*believe*) _____ you (*rub*) _____ the top of your desk with your hand.

    A: Close, but not exactly right. Try again. (*Listen, you*) _____ _____ carefully?

    B: Aha! You (*rub*) _____ your hands together.

    A: Right!

☐ **EXERCISE 13—WRITTEN:** Go to a place where there are many people (or imagine yourself to be in such a place). Describe the activities you observe. Let your reader see what you see; draw a "picture" by using words.

Use present tenses. Begin your writing with a description of your own immediate activities; e.g., *I am sitting on a bench at the zoo.*

1-10   USING THE PRESENT PROGRESSIVE WITH *ALWAYS*

(a) Mary **always leaves** for school at 7:45.	In sentences referring to present time, usually the simple present is used with **always** to describe habitual or everyday activities, as in (a).
(b) Mary **is always leaving** her dirty socks on the floor for me to pick up! Who does she think I am? Her maid?	In special circumstances, a speaker may use the present progressive with **always** to complain, i.e., to express annoyance or anger, as in (b).*
(c) I **am always/forever/constantly picking** up Mary's dirty socks!	In addition to **always**, the words **forever** and **constantly** are used with the present progressive to express annoyance.

*COMPARE: "*Mary **is always leaving** her dirty socks on the floor*" expresses annoyance.
"*Mary **always leaves** her dirty socks on the floor*" is a statement of fact in which the speaker is not necessarily expressing an attitude of annoyance. Annoyance may, however, be included in the speaker's tone of voice.

☐ **EXERCISE 14—ORAL:** Assume you have a roommate named Jack who has many bad habits. These bad habits annoy you. Pretend you are speaking to a friend and complaining about Jack. Use the present progressive. Use *always, constantly*, or *forever* in each sentence. Say your sentence aloud with some annoyance, impatience, or anger in your voice.

Here is a list of some of Jack's bad habits:

1. He messes up the kitchen. → *He's always messing up the kitchen!*
2. He leaves his dirty dishes on the table.
3. He borrows my clothes without asking me.
4. He brags about himself.
5. He tries to show me that he's smarter than I.
6. He cracks his knuckles while I'm trying to study.

7. I like fresh air and like to have the windows open, but he closes the windows.

8. *Complete the following with your own words.*

A: I really don't know if I can stand to have Sue for a roommate one more day. She's driving me crazy.

B: Oh? What's wrong?

A: Well, for one thing she's always _____.

B: Really?

A: And not only that. She's forever _____.

B: That must be very inconvenient for you.

A: It is. And what's more, she's constantly _____.

Can you believe that? And she's always _____.

B: I think you're right. You need to find a new roommate.

1-11 REGULAR AND IRREGULAR VERBS

REGULAR VERBS: The simple past and past participle end in *-ed*.				English verbs have four principal parts:
SIMPLE FORM	SIMPLE PAST	PAST PARTICIPLE	PRESENT PARTICIPLE	(1) simple form
hope	*hoped*	*hoped*	*hoping*	(2) simple past
stop	*stopped*	*stopped*	*stopping*	(3) past participle
listen	*listened*	*listened*	*listening*	(4) present participle
study	*studied*	*studied*	*studying*	
start	*started*	*started*	*starting*	
IRREGULAR VERBS: The simple past and past participle do not end in *-ed*.				Some verbs have irregular past forms. Most of the irregular verbs in English are given in the following alphabetical list.
SIMPLE FORM	SIMPLE PAST	PAST PARTICIPLE	PRESENT PARTICIPLE	
break	*broke*	*broken*	*breaking*	
come	*came*	*come*	*coming*	
find	*found*	*found*	*finding*	
hit	*hit*	*hit*	*hitting*	
swim	*swam*	*swum*	*swimming*	

AN ALPHABETICAL LIST OF IRREGULAR VERBS

SIMPLE FORM	SIMPLE PAST	PAST PARTICIPLE	SIMPLE FORM	SIMPLE PAST	PAST PARTICIPLE
arise	arose	arisen	forbid	forbade	forbidden
be	was, were	been	forecast	forecast	forecast
bear	bore	borne/born	forget	forgot	forgotten
beat	beat	beaten/beat	forgive	forgave	forgiven
become	became	become	forsake	forsook	forsaken
begin	began	begun	freeze	froze	frozen
bend	bent	bent	get	got	gotten★
bet	bet	bet★	give	gave	given
bid	bid	bid	go	went	gone
bind	bound	bound	grind	ground	ground
bite	bit	bitten	grow	grew	grown
bleed	bled	bled	hang	hung	hung
blow	blew	blown	have	had	had
break	broke	broken	hear	heard	heard
breed	bred	bred	hide	hid	hidden
bring	brought	brought	hit	hit	hit
broadcast	broadcast	broadcast	hold	held	held
build	built	built	hurt	hurt	hurt
burst	burst	burst	keep	kept	kept
buy	bought	bought	know	knew	known
cast	cast	cast	lay	laid	laid
catch	caught	caught	lead	led	led
choose	chose	chosen	leave	left	left
cling	clung	clung	lend	lent	lent
come	came	come	let	let	let
cost	cost	cost	lie	lay	lain
creep	crept	crept	light	lit/lighted	lit/lighted
cut	cut	cut	lose	lost	lost
deal	dealt	dealt	make	made	made
dig	dug	dug	mean	meant	meant
do	did	done	meet	met	met
draw	drew	drawn	mislay	mislaid	mislaid
eat	ate	eaten	mistake	mistook	mistaken
fall	fell	fallen	pay	paid	paid
feed	fed	fed	put	put	put
feel	felt	felt	quit	quit	quit★
fight	fought	fought	read	read	read
find	found	found	rid	rid	rid
fit	fit	fit★	ride	rode	ridden
flee	fled	fled	ring	rang	rung
fling	flung	flung	rise	rose	risen
fly	flew	flown	run	ran	run

SIMPLE FORM	SIMPLE PAST	PAST PARTICIPLE	SIMPLE FORM	SIMPLE PAST	PAST PARTICIPLE
say	said	said	sting	stung	stung
see	saw	seen	stink	stank/stunk	stunk
seek	sought	sought	strive	strove	striven
sell	sold	sold	strike	struck	struck/stricken
send	sent	sent	string	strung	strung
set	set	set	swear	swore	sworn
shake	shook	shaken	sweep	swept	swept
shed	shed	shed	swim	swam	swum
shine	shone/shined	shone/shined	swing	swung	swung
shoot	shot	shot	take	took	taken
show	showed	shown/showed	teach	taught	taught
shrink	shrank/shrunk	shrunk	tear	tore	torn
shut	shut	shut	tell	told	told
sing	sang	sung	think	thought	thought
sit	sat	sat	throw	threw	thrown
sleep	slept	slept	thrust	thrust	thrust
slide	slid	slid	understand	understood	understood
slit	slit	slit	undertake	undertook	undertaken
speak	spoke	spoken	upset	upset	upset
speed	sped/speeded	sped/speeded	wake	woke/waked	woken/waked
spend	spent	spent	wear	wore	worn
spin	spun	spun	weave	wove	woven
spit	spit/spat	spit/spat	weep	wept	wept
split	split	split	win	won	won
spread	spread	spread	wind	wound	wound
spring	sprang/sprung	sprung	withdraw	withdrew	withdrawn
stand	stood	stood	wring	wrung	wrung
steal	stole	stolen	write	wrote	written
stick	stuck	stuck			

*The following are some differences in verb forms between American English and British English:

American	**British**
bet-bet-bet	*bet-bet-bet* OR *bet-betted-betted*
fit-fit-fit	*fit-fitted-fitted*
get-got-gotten	*get-got-got*
quit-quit-quit	*quit-quitted-quitted*

American: *burn, dream, kneel, lean, leap, learn, smell, spell, spill, spoil* are usually regular: *burned, dreamed, kneeled, leaned, leaped, etc.*

British: simple past and past participle forms of these verbs can be regular but more commonly end with **-t**: *burnt, dreamt, knelt, leant, leapt, learnt, smelt, spelt, spilt, spoilt.*

□ **EXERCISE 15—ORAL:** Practice pronouncing the following past forms of regular verbs.

> **GROUP A:** Final *-ed* is pronounced /*t*/ after voiceless sounds:
>
> 1. looked
> 2. asked
> 3. helped
> 4. laughed
>
> 5. pushed
> 6. watched
> 7. dressed
> 8. boxed

> **GROUP B:** Final *-ed* is pronounced /*d*/ after voiced sounds:
>
> 9. sobbed
> 10. believed
> 11. filled
> 12. poured
>
> 13. roamed
> 14. judged
> 15. enjoyed
> 16. dried

> **GROUP C:** Final *-ed* is pronounced /əd/ after *-d* and *-t*:
>
> 17. needed
> 18. defended
> 19. added
> 20. loaded
>
> 21. waited
> 22. rested
> 23. counted
> 24. halted

Practice the following sentences aloud.

25. My friend jumped up and down and shouted when she heard the news.
26. The concert lasted for two hours.
27. With the coming of spring, the river flooded and inundated several villages.
28. She tapped the top of her desk.
29. He described his house.
30. They demanded to know the answer.
31. The airplane departed at six and landed at eight.
32. Alice pushed and I pulled.
33. He handed me his dictionary.
34. Jack tooted his horn.
35. They asked us to help them.

□ **EXERCISE 16—ORAL (BOOKS CLOSED):** This and the following three exercises are quick oral reviews of irregular verbs. In this exercise, answer with "yes" and a complete sentence.★

---

*Usually a short answer is given to a yes/no question. *Example:*
    A: *Did you sit down?*
    B: *Yes, I did. (short answer)*
In this exercise you are asked to give a full answer so that you can review the simple past of irregular verbs. Which irregular verbs come easily for you? Which ones are a little more troublesome? Which ones don't you know?

Example: Did you sit down?

Response: Yes, I sat down.

1. Did you drink some coffee before class?
2. Did you bring your books to class?
3. Did you forget your briefcase?
4. Did you shake your head?
5. Did you catch the bus this morning?
6. Did you drive to school?
7. Did you lose your book?
8. Did you find your book?
9. Did you wind your watch this morning?
10. Did you understand what I said?
11. Did you tell your friend the news?
12. Did you spread the news?
13. Did you fall on the ice?
14. Did you hurt yourself when you fell?
15. Did you fly to (*this city*)?
16. Did you wear a coat to class?
17. Did you hang your coat on a hook?
18. Did you eat lunch?
19. Did you take chemistry in high school?
20. Did you ride the bus to school?
21. Did you swear to tell the truth?
22. I made a mistake. Did you forgive me?
23. Did you write a letter to your family?
24. Did you bite the dog???

□ **EXERCISE 17—ORAL (BOOKS CLOSED):** Answer, ''No, Someone else . . . .''

Example: Did you shut the door?

Response: No, someone else shut the door.

1. Did you make a mistake?
2. Did you break that window?
3. Did you steal my wallet?
4. Did you take my piece of paper?
5. Did you draw that picture?
6. Did you sweep the floor this morning?
7. Did you teach class yesterday?
8. Did you dig that hole in the garden?
9. Did you feed the cat?
10. Did you hide my book from me?
11. Did you blow that whistle?
12. Did you throw a piece of chalk out the window?
13. Did you tear that piece of paper?
14. Did you build that house?
15. Did you speak to (. . .)?

☐ **EXERCISE 18—ORAL (BOOKS CLOSED):** Answer with "yes."

> *Example:* Did you sit down?
> *Response:* Yes, I sat down.

1. Did you give me some money?
2. Did you stand at the bus stop?
3. Did you choose the blue pen?
4. Did you run to class this (*morning*)?
5. Did you sleep well last night?
6. Did you hear that noise outside the window?
7. Did you withdraw some money from the bank?
8. Did you wake up at seven this morning?
9. Did you swim in the ocean?
10. Did you go home after class yesterday?
11. Did you bend your elbow?
12. Did you send a letter?
13. Did you sing a song?
14. Did you stick your hand in your pocket?
15. Did you grind the pepper?
16. Did you strike the desk with your hand?
17. Did you light a match?
18. Did you mean what you said?
19. Did you hold your hand up?
20. Did you speak to (. . .)?

☐ **EXERCISE 19—ORAL (BOOKS CLOSED):** Answer with "yes."

> *Example:* Did the students come to class?
> *Response:* Yes, they came to class.

1. Did class begin at (*nine*)?
2. Did the sun rise at six this morning?
3. Did you cut your finger?
4. Did it bleed when you cut it?
5. Did the grass grow after the rain?
6. Did a bee sting you?
7. Did the telephone ring?
8. Did the water freeze?
9. Did your friend quit school?
10. Did the soldiers fight?
11. Did the thief creep into the room?
12. Did the policeman shoot at the thief?

13. Did the thief flee?

14. Did your team win the game yesterday?

15. Did your car slide on the ice?

16. Did the door swing open?

17. Did the children blow up some balloons?

18. Did the balloons burst?

19. Did the radio station broadcast the news?

20. Did you know all of the irregular verbs?

☐ **EXERCISE 20:** Some of the verbs in the irregular verb list can be troublesome. Many native speakers find some of these verbs troublesome, too, especially *lay* and *lie*. Study the examples. (See Appendix 1, Chart A-1 for more information about transitive and intransitive verbs.)

TRANSITIVE (followed by an object)	INTRANSITIVE (not followed by an object)
(a) *raise, raised, raised* Tom raised his head.	(b) *rise, rose, risen* The sun rises in the east.
(c) *set, set, set* I will set the book on the desk.	(d) *sit, sat, sat* I sit in the front row.
(e) *lay, laid, laid* I am laying the book on the desk.	(f) *lie,* ★ *lay, lain* He is lying on his bed.
(g) *hang, hung, hung* I hung my clothes in the closet. (h) *hang, hanged, hanged* They hanged the criminal by the neck until he was dead.	

★Lie is a regular verb (*lie, lied*) when it means "not tell the truth": *He lied to me about his age.*

Choose the correct word in parentheses.

1. The student (raised, rose) his hand in class.

2. Hot air (raises, rises).

3. Ann (set, sat) in a chair because she was tired.

4. I (set, sat) your dictionary on the table a few minutes ago.

5. Hens (lay, lie) eggs.

6. Al is (laying, lying) on the grass in the park right now.

7. Jan (laid, lay) the comb on top of the dresser a few minutes ago.

8. If you are tired, you should (lay, lie) down and take a nap.

9. San Francisco (lay, lies) to the north of Los Angeles.

10. We (hanged, hung) the picture on the wall.

1-12 SIMPLE PAST

	(a) I **walked** to school yesterday. (b) He **lived** in Paris for ten years, but now he is living in Rome. (c) I **bought** a new car three days ago.	The simple past indicates that an activity or situation *began and ended at a particular time in the past.*
	(d) I **stood** under a tree *when it began to rain.* (e) *When she* **heard** *a strange noise*, she **got** up to investigate. (f) *When I* **dropped** *my cup*, the coffee **spilled** on my lap.	If a sentence contains **when** and has the simple past in both clauses, the action in the "**when** clause" happens first. In (d): 1st: The rain began. 2nd: I stood under a tree.

1-13 PAST PROGRESSIVE

	(g) I **was walking** down the street when it began to rain. (h) While I **was walking** down the street, it began to rain. (i) I **was standing** under a tree when it began to rain.	In (g): 1st: I was walking down the street. 2nd: It began to rain. In other words, both actions occurred at the *same* time, but *one action began earlier and was in progress when the other action occurred.*
	(j) At eight o'clock last night, I **was studying**. (k) Last year at this time, I **was attending** school.	In (j): My studying began before 8:00, was in progress at that time, and probably continued.
	(l) While I **was studying** in one room of our apartment, my roommate **was having** a party in the other room.	Sometimes the past progressive is used in both parts of a sentence when two actions are in progress simultaneously.
	(m) It **rained** this morning. (n) It **was raining** this morning.	In some cases, the simple past and the past progressive give almost the same meaning, as in (m) and (n).

☐ **EXERCISE 21:** Use the SIMPLE PAST or the PAST PROGRESSIVE in the following.

1. I am sitting in class right now. I (*sit*) _____was sitting_____ in class at this exact same time yesterday.

2. I don't want to go to the zoo today because it is raining. The same thing happened yesterday. I (*want, not*) _____ to go to the zoo because it (*rain*) _____.

3. I (*call*) _____ Roger at nine last night, but he (*be, not*) _____ at home. He (*study*) _____ at the library.

4. I (*hear, not*) _____ the thunder during the storm last night because I (*sleep*) _____.

5. It was beautiful yesterday when we went for a walk in the park. The sun (*shine*) _____. A cool breeze (*blow*) _____. The birds (*sing*) _____.

6. My brother and sister (*argue*) _____ about something when I (*walk*) _____ into the room.

7. I got a package in the mail. When I (*open*) _____ it, I (*find*) _____ a surprise.

8. Tommy went to his friends' house, but the boys (*be, not*) _____ there. They (*play*) _____ soccer in the vacant lot down the street.

9. Stanley (*climb*) _____ the stairs when he (*trip*) _____ and (*fall*) _____. Luckily, he (*hurt, not*) _____ himself.

10. While Mrs. Emerson (*read*) _____ the little boy a story, he (*fall*) _____ asleep, so she (*close*) _____ the book and quietly (*tiptoe*) _____ out of the room.

11. I really enjoyed my vacation last January. While it (*snow*) _____ in Iowa, the sun (*shine*) _____ in Florida. While you (*shovel*) _____ snow in Iowa, I (*lie*) _____ on the beach in Florida.

12. While Ted (*shovel*) _____ snow from his driveway yesterday, his wife (*bring*) _____ him a cup of hot chocolate.

□ **EXERCISE 22**: Use the SIMPLE PAST or the PAST PROGRESSIVE.

1. I (*have, almost*) _____ a car accident last night. I
   (*drive*) _____ down Washington Avenue when
   suddenly I (*see*) _____ a car in my lane. It (*come*)
   _____ right at my car. I (*step*) _____
   on the brakes and (*swerve*) _____ to the right. The
   other car (*miss, just*) _____ my car by about an inch.

2. Ten years ago, the government (*decide*) _____ to
   begin a food program. At that time, many people in the rural areas of the
   country (*starve*) _____ due to several years of
   drought.

3. It was my first day of class. I (*find, finally*) _____
   the right room. The room (*be, already*) _____ full of
   students. On one side of the room, students (*talk, busily*) _____
   _____ to each other in Spanish. Other students
   (*speak*) _____ Japanese, and some (*converse*) _____
   _____ in Arabic. It sounded like the United
   Nations. Some of the students, however, (*sit, just*) _____
   quietly by themselves. I (*choose*) _____ an empty
   seat in the last row and (*sit*) _____ down. In a few
   minutes, the teacher (*walk*) _____ into the room
   and all the multilingual conversation (*stop*) _____.

4. A: (*Hear, you*) _____ what she just said?
   B: No, I (*listen, not*) _____. I (*think*) _____
   _____ about something else.

5. A: Why weren't you at the meeting?
   B: I (*wait*) _____ for an overseas call from my
   family.

6. A: I'm sure you met Carol Jones at the party last night.
   B: I don't remember her. What (*wear, she*) _____?

7. A: What's wrong with your foot?

   B: I (step) _____ on a bee while I (run) _____

   _____ barefoot through the grass. It (sting) _____

   _____ me.

8. A: How (break, you) _____ your arm?

   B: I (slip) _____ on the ice while I (cross) _____

   _____ the street in front of the dorm.

1–14 USING EXPRESSIONS OF PLACE WITH PROGRESSIVE TENSES

(a) Kay *is studying* **in her room**. (b) Kay *is* **in her room** *studying*. (c) Jack *was* **in bed** *reading* a book when I came.	An expression of place can sometimes come between the auxiliary **be** and the **-ing** verb in a progressive tense, as in (b) and (c).

☐ **EXERCISE 23:** In the following, change the position of the expression of place.

1. Sally is listening to music in her room. → *Sally is in her room listening to music*.
2. Roy is taking a nap on the couch.
3. Anita was attending a conference in England last month.
4. The teacher is correcting papers at her desk.
5. Some of the students were late to class because they were playing soccer at the park.

Complete the following: Use the PRESENT PROGRESSIVE or the PAST PROGRESSIVE. Use the expression of place in parentheses.

6. A: Where's Joan? (*at the library*)

    B: _____ *She's at the library studying for a test.* _____

7. A: Is Mark here? (*upstairs*)

    B: Yes. _____

8. A: Have you seen Professor Marx? (*in her office*)

    B: Yes. _____

9. A: Where's your mother, Jimmy? (*in the kitchen*)

    B: _____

10. A: Ahmed was absent yesterday. Where was he? (*at home*)

    B: _____

11. A: Was Mr. Rivera out of town last week? (*in New York*)

    B: Yes. _____

*Add expressions of place between **be** and the **-ing** verb.*

12. My sister is visiting some relatives. → *My sister is in Chicago visiting some relatives.*
13. I'm back to work now, but a month ago I was lying in the sun.
14. We are studying English grammar.
15. No one could see the thief because he was hiding from the police.
16. When I saw Diana, she was trying to find out what she was supposed to do.

☐ **EXERCISE 24:** Come to class prepared to do a pantomime. While you are doing your pantomime, the rest of the class will try to determine what you are doing and then, when you are finished, will describe what you did, step by step.

Examples of subjects for a pantomime:

(a) threading a needle and sewing on a button
(b) washing dishes, and perhaps breaking one
(c) bowling
(d) reading a newspaper while eating breakfast

(To the teacher: Suggested time limit for each pantomime: two minutes. In all, each pantomime and the oral description should take no more than four or five minutes. The intention is that a few pantomimes be presented each day for the rest of the time spent working on verb tenses.)

☐ **EXERCISE 25—WRITTEN:** In writing, describe one or more of the pantomimes that are performed by your classmates. Give a title to the pantomime, and identify the pantomimist. Use a few "time words" to show the order in which the actions were performed; e.g., *first, next, then, after that, before, when, while.*

1–15 PRESENT PERFECT

(time?)	(a) They *have moved* into a new apartment. (b) *Have* you ever *visited* Mexico? (c) I *have* already *seen* that movie. (d) I *have* never *seen* snow.	The present perfect expresses the idea that something happened (or never happened) *before now, at an unspecified time in the past.* The exact time it happened is not important. If there is a specific mention of time, the simple past is used: *I saw that movie last night.*
	(e) We *have had* four tests so far this semester. (f) I *have written* my wife a letter every other day for the last two weeks. (g) I *have met* many people since I came here in June. (h) I *have flown* on an airplane many times.	The present perfect also expresses the *repetition of an activity before now.* The exact time of each repetition is not important.

	(i) I *have been* here *since seven o'clock.*
	(j) We *have been* here *for two weeks.*
	(k) I *have had* this same pair of shoes *for three years.*
	(l) I *have liked* cowboy movies ever *since I was a child.*
	(m) I *have known* him *for many years.*
		The present perfect also, when used with *for* or *since*, expresses a situation that *began in the past and continues to the present.*
		In the examples, notice the difference between *since* and *for*:
		    since + *a particular time*
		    for + *a duration of time*

□ **EXERCISE 26:** Use the SIMPLE PAST or the PRESENT PERFECT. In some sentences, either tense is possible but the meaning is different.

1. I (*attend, not*) ___*haven't attended*___ any parties since I came here.

2. Al (*go*) _____ to a party at Sally's apartment last Saturday night.

3. Bill (*arrive*) _____ here three days ago.

4. Bill (*be*) _____ here since the 22nd.

5. Try not to be absent from class again for the rest of the term. You (*miss, already*) _____ too many classes. You (*miss*) _____ two classes just last week.

6. Last January, I (*see*) _____ snow for the first time in my life.

7. In her whole lifetime, Anna (*see, never*) _____ snow.

8. I (*know*) _____ Greg Adams for ten years.

9. So far this week, I (*have*) _____ two tests and a quiz.

10. Up to now, Professor Williams (*give*) _____ our class five tests.

□ **EXERCISE 27—ORAL (BOOKS CLOSED):** Answer the question in a complete sentence.

Example: How many tests have you taken since the beginning of the (*semester*)?

Response: I have taken (*three, several, many*) tests since the beginning of the (*semester*). OR: I haven't taken any tests since the beginning of the (*semester*).

1. How many books have you bought since the beginning of the (*semester*)?
2. How many letters have you gotten so far this month/week?
3. How many letters have you written since the beginning of the month/week?
4. How many questions have I asked so far?
5. How many times have you flown in an airplane?
6. How many people have you met since you came here?

7. How many classes have you missed since the beginning of the (*semester*)?

8. How many cups of coffee have you had since you got up this morning?

9. How many classes have you had so far today?

10. How many times have you eaten (*your native*) food/eaten at a restaurant since you came here?

☐ **EXERCISE 28:** Complete the sentences with any appropriate time expressions.

1. Today is _____*the 14th of June*_____. I bought this book _____*two weeks*_____ ago.

   I have had this book since _____*June 1*_____.

   I have had this book for _____*two weeks*_____.

2. I have a pen. I bought it _____ ago.

   I have had this pen for _____.

   I have had this pen since _____.

3. Today is _____. I moved to this city _____

   _____.

   I have been in this city since _____.

   I have been here for _____.

4. It is 19____. I started going to school in 19____.

   I have been a student for _____.

   I have been a student since _____.

5. I first met our teacher _____.

   I have known her/him for _____.

   I have known her/him since _____.

☐ **EXERCISE 29—ORAL (BOOKS CLOSED):** Answer the questions in complete sentences.

To the teacher: Following is an example of a possible exchange.

To Student **A:** *When did you come to (this city/country)?*
  --I came here on June 2nd.

To Student **B:** *How long has (Student A) been here?*
  --He/she has been here for two weeks.
  Or, using **since**?
  --He/she has been here since June 2nd.

1. **A.** When did you arrive (*in this city/country*)? **B.** How long has (. . .) been here?

2. **A:** When did you get to class today? **B:** How long has (. . .) been in class?

3. **A:** What time did you get up this morning? **B:** How long has (. . .) been up?

4. Who in this class owns a car/bicycle? **A:** When did you buy it? **B:** How long has (. . .) had a car/bicycle?

5. Who is wearing a watch? **A:** When did you get it? **B:** How long has (. . .) had his/her watch?

6. Who is married? **A:** When did you get married? **B:** How long has (. . .) been married?

7. **A:** Do you know (. . .)? When did you meet him/her? **B:** How long has (. . .) known (. . .)?

8. **A:** Is that your pen/notebook/pencil sharpener? When did you buy it? **B:** How long has (. . .) had his/her pen/notebook/pencil sharpener?

☐ **EXERCISE 30—ORAL (BOOKS CLOSED):** To practice irregular past participles, begin your response with ''I have never . . . .''

Example: see that movie
Response: I've never seen that movie.

1. drive a truck
2. buy an airplane
3. read that book
4. break a window
5. draw a picture of yourself
6. ride a horse
7. eat paper
8. teach English
9. catch a butterfly
10. make apple pie
11. win a lottery
12. fly an airplane
13. sleep in a tent
14. write a letter to the President of the United States
15. lose your wallet
16. have a car accident
17. speak to (*a local personage*)
18. steal anything
19. fall off a mountain
20. bring a friend to class
21. hold a snake
22. feed a lion
23. build a house
24. forget your name
25. wear a kimono
26. drink Turkish coffee
27. understand Einstein's theory of relativity
28. leave your umbrella at a restaurant

☐ **EXERCISE 31—ORAL (BOOKS CLOSED):** *Student A:* Ask a question beginning with "Have you ever . . . ." *Student B:* Answer the question.

Example: break your arm.
Student A: Have you ever broken your arm?
Student B: Yes, I have. OR: No, I haven't.

1. climb a mountain
2. write a book
3. be in (*Japan*)
4. tell a lie
5. smoke a cigar
6. ride a motorcycle
7. teach (*a particular subject*)
8. see a ghost
9. meet (. . .)'s parents
10. give a speech in English
11. eat (*Thai*) food
12. study biology
13. play a violin
14. go to (*a particular landmark in this city*)
15. walk on the moon
16. watch (*a particular TV show*)
17. take a course in chemistry
18. drive (*a particular kind of car*)
19. fall asleep during class
20. have (*a particular kind of food*)

☐ **EXERCISE 32—ORAL:** *Have* and *has* (used as auxiliary verbs, not as main verbs) are usually contracted with personal pronouns in both speaking and informal writing. *Have* and *has* are often contracted with nouns and other words in informal speaking but not in writing. (See Appendix 1, Chart A-8.) Practice pronouncing contracted *have* and *has* in the following sentences.

1. You've been there. They've been there. She's been there. We've all been there.
2. Mary has never been there. → *"Mary's" never been there.*
3. The weather has been nice lately.
4. My neighbors have asked me over for dinner.
5. The teacher has never eaten hot Vietnamese food.
6. The teacher has a red tie. (*No contraction; **has** is the main verb.*)
7. My parents have lived in the same house for over thirty years.
8. My parents have a house.
9. Where have you been?
10. What have you done with my books?

☐ **EXERCISE 33:** Use the SIMPLE PAST or the PRESENT PERFECT.

1. What (*learn, you*) _____ since you (*come*) _____
   here? How many new friends (*make, you*) _____?
   I hope you (*meet, already*) _____
   a lot of interesting people.

2. Since classes began, I (*have, not*) _____ much free time. I
   (*have*) _____ several big tests to study for.

3. Last night my roommate and I (*have*) _____ some free
   time, so we (*go*) _____ to a show.

4. I admit that I (*get★*) _____ older since I last (*see*) _____
   you, but with any luck at all, I (*get, also*) _____
   wiser.

5. The science of medicine (*advance*) _____ a great
   deal in the nineteenth century.

6. Since the beginning of the twentieth century, medical scientists (*make*)
   _____ many important discoveries.

7. Libraries today are different from those in the 1800s. For example, the
   contents of libraries (*change*) _____ greatly through
   the years. In the 1800s, libraries (*be*) _____ simply
   collections of books. However, today most libraries (*become*) _____
   _____ multimedia centers that contain tapes, computers,

★COMPARE:

(a) I **have gotten** (British: **have got**) four letters so far this week.	In (a): **have gotten** (**have got**) is present perfect.
(b) I **have got** a problem.	In (b): **have got** is NOT present perfect. In (b), **have got** means **have**: *I've got a problem.* = *I have a problem.* The expression **have got** is common in informal spoken English. Its meaning is present; it has no past form.

disks, films, magazines, music, and paintings. The role of the library in society (*change, also*) _____. In the 1800s, libraries (*be*) _____ open only to certain people, such as scholars or the wealthy. Today libraries serve everyone.

8. A: Are you taking Chemistry 101 this semester?

   B: No, I (*take, already*) _____ it. I (*take*) _____ it last semester. This semester I'm in 102.

9. A: Hi, Judy. Welcome to the party. (*Meet, you, ever*) _____ _____ my cousin?

   B: No, I _____.

10. A: Do you like lobster?

    B: I don't know. I (*eat, never*) _____ it.

11. A: Do you do much traveling?

    B: Yes. I like to travel.

    A: What countries (*visit, you*) _____?

    B: Well, I (*be*) _____ in India, Turkey, Afghanistan, and Nepal, among others.

    A: I (*be, never*) _____ in any of those countries. When (*be, you*) _____ in India?

    B: Two years ago. I (*visit, also*) _____ many of the countries in Central America. I (*take*) _____ a tour of Central America about six years ago.

    A: Which countries (*visit, you*) _____?

    B: Guatemala, El Salvador, Honduras, and Nicaragua.

    A: I (*want, always*) _____ to travel to other countries, but I (*have, not*) _____ the opportunity to travel extensively. I (*go*) _____ to England six years ago, but I (*go, not*) _____ _____ anywhere since then.

1–16 PRESENT PERFECT PROGRESSIVE

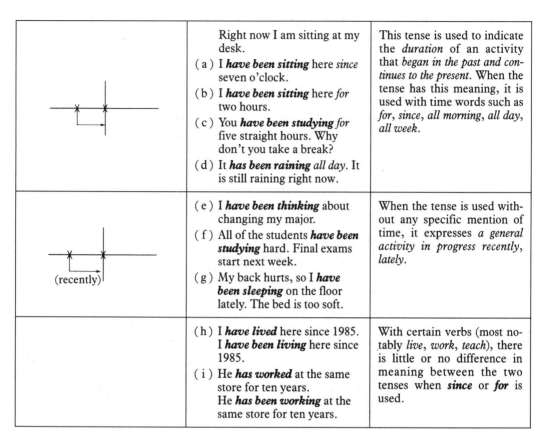

	Right now I am sitting at my desk. (a) I **have been sitting** here *since* seven o'clock. (b) I **have been sitting** here *for* two hours. (c) You **have been studying** *for* five straight hours. Why don't you take a break? (d) It **has been raining** *all day*. It is still raining right now.	This tense is used to indicate the *duration* of an activity that *began in the past and continues to the present.* When the tense has this meaning, it is used with time words such as *for, since, all morning, all day, all week.*
(recently)	(e) I **have been thinking** about changing my major. (f) All of the students **have been studying** hard. Final exams start next week. (g) My back hurts, so I **have been sleeping** on the floor lately. The bed is too soft.	When the tense is used without any specific mention of time, it expresses *a general activity in progress recently, lately.*
	(h) I **have lived** here since 1985. I **have been living** here since 1985. (i) He **has worked** at the same store for ten years. He **has been working** at the same store for ten years.	With certain verbs (most notably *live, work, teach*), there is little or no difference in meaning between the two tenses when **since** or **for** is used.

□ **EXERCISE 34:** Use the PRESENT PERFECT PROGRESSIVE in the following.

1. The boys are playing soccer right now. They (*play*) *have been playing* for almost two hours. They must be getting tired.

2. Alex is talking on the phone. He (*talk*) _____ on the phone for over a half an hour. He should hang up soon. Long distance is expensive.

3. I'm trying to study. I (*try*) _____ to study for the last hour, but something always seems to interrupt me. I think I'd better go to the library.

Complete the following by writing two sentences. Use the PRESENT PERFECT PROGRESSIVE in the first sentence; then make another sentence that might typically follow in this situation.

4. The baby is crying. She . . . *has been crying for almost ten minutes. I wonder what's wrong.*

5. It's raining. It . . . .

6. I'm studying. I . . . .

7. I'm waiting for my friend. I . . . .

8. Bob is sitting in the waiting room. He . . . .

☐ **EXERCISE 35:** Use the PRESENT PERFECT or the PRESENT PERFECT PROGRESSIVE. In some sentences, either tense may be used with little or no change in meaning.

1. It (*snow*) _____ all day. I wonder when it will stop.

2. We (*have*) _____ three major snowstorms so far this winter. I wonder how many more we will have.

3. It's ten P.M. I (*study*) _____ for two hours and probably won't finish until midnight.

4. I (*write*) _____ them three times, but I still haven't received a reply.

5. I (*live*) _____ here since last March.

6. The telephone (*ring*) _____ four times in the last hour, and each time it has been for my roommate.

7. The telephone (*ring*) _____ for almost a minute. Why doesn't someone answer it?

8. The little boy is dirty from head to foot because he (*play*) _____ _____ in the mud.

□ **EXERCISE 36:** Use the PRESENT PROGRESSIVE or the PRESENT PERFECT PROGRESSIVE.

1. A: (*Be, you*) _____ able to reach Bob on the phone yet?

   B: Not yet. I (*try*) _____ for the last twenty minutes, but the line (*be*) _____ busy.

2. A: Hi, Jenny. I (*see, not*) _____ you for weeks. What (*do, you*) _____ lately?

   B: Studying.

3. A: What are you going to order for dinner?

   B: Well, I (*have, never*) _____ pizza, so I think I'll order that.

4. A: What's the matter? Your eyes are red and puffy. (*Cry, you*) _____ _____?

   B: No. I just finished peeling some onions.

5. A: Dr. Jones is a good teacher. How long (*be, he*) _____ at the university?

   B: He (*teach*) _____ here for twenty-five years.

□ **EXERCISE 37—ORAL/WRITTEN:** Complete the following with your own words.

1. . . . since 8 o'clock this morning.
   → *I have been sitting in class since 8 o'clock this morning.*
     I have had three classes since 8 o'clock this morning.
2. . . . since I came to . . . .
3. . . . since 19 . . . (*year*).
4. . . . since (*month*).
5. . . . since (*day*).
6. . . . since . . . o'clock this morning/afternoon/evening.
7. . . . since the beginning of the 20th century.
8. . . . since . . . .

1–17 PAST PERFECT

	(a) My parents **had** already **eaten** by the time I got home. (b) Until yesterday, I **had** never **heard** about it. (c) The thief simply walked in. Someone **had forgotten** to lock the door.	The past perfect expresses an activity that was *completed before another activity or time in the past.*
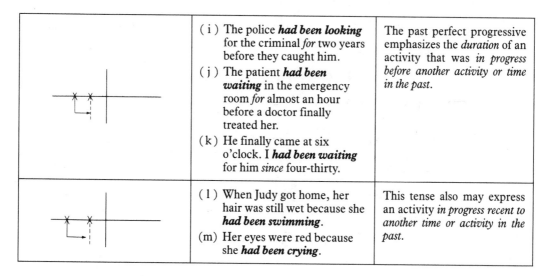	(d) Sam **had** already **left** *when* we got there. (e) Sam **had left** *before* we got there. (f) Sam **left** *before* we got there. (g) *After* the guests **had** *left*, I went to bed. (h) *After* the guests **left**, I went to bed.	In (d): *First*: Sam left. *Second*: We got there.* If either **before** or **after** is used in the sentence, the past perfect is often not necessary because the time relationship is already clear. The simple past may be used, as in (f) and (h). Note: (e) and (f) have the same meaning; (g) and (h) have the same meaning.

*COMPARE: Sam *left* *when* we got there. = *First*: We got there.
                                                    Second: Sam left.

1–18 PAST PERFECT PROGRESSIVE

	(i) The police **had been looking** for the criminal *for* two years before they caught him. (j) The patient **had been waiting** in the emergency room *for* almost an hour before a doctor finally treated her. (k) He finally came at six o'clock. I **had been waiting** for him *since* four-thirty.	The past perfect progressive emphasizes the *duration* of an activity that was *in progress before another activity or time in the past.*
	(l) When Judy got home, her hair was still wet because she **had been swimming**. (m) Her eyes were red because she **had been crying**.	This tense also may express an activity *in progress recent to another time or activity in the past.*

□ **EXERCISE 38—ORAL:** *Had* (used as an auxiliary verb, not a main verb) is usually contracted with personal pronouns in both speaking and informal writing. *Had* is often contracted with nouns and other words in informal speaking but not in writing. (See Appendix 1, Chart A-8.) Practice pronouncing contracted *had* in the following sentences.

1. We'd never seen it before. He'd never seen it. They'd never seen it.
2. I'd never seen it before. I'd like to see it again.*
3. We got home late. The children had already fallen asleep.
4. My roommates had finished dinner by the time I got home.
5. My roommates had dinner early.
6. We couldn't cross the river. The flood had washed away the bridge.
7. You were at Jim's at eight. Where had you been before that?
8. Who had been there before you?

□ **EXERCISE 39:** Use the SIMPLE PAST or the PAST PERFECT. Are there some blanks where either tense is possible?

1. He (*be*) _____ a newspaper reporter before he (*become*)

   _____ a businessman.

2. I (*feel*) _____ a little better after I (*take*) _____

   the medicine.

3. I was late. The teacher (*give, already*) _____

   a quiz when I (*get*) _____ to class.

4. The anthropologist (*leave*) _____ the village when she

   (*collect*) _____ enough data.

5. It was raining hard, but by the time class (*be*) _____

   over, the rain (*stop*) _____.

□ **EXERCISE 40:** Use the SIMPLE PAST or the PAST PERFECT.

1. Class (*begin, already*) _____ by the time I

   (*get*) _____ there, so I (*take, quietly*) _____ a

   seat in the back.

---

*COMPARE: *I'd been* = *I had been* ('d + past participle = past perfect)
         I'd like = *I would like* ('d + simple form = *would*)

2. Millions of years ago, dinosaurs (*roam*) _____ the earth, but they (*become*) _____ extinct by the time humankind first (*appear*) _____.

3. I (*see, never*) _____ any of Picasso's paintings before I (*visit*) _____ the art museum.

4. I almost missed my plane. All of the other passengers (*board, already*) _____ by the time I (*get*) _____ there.

5. Yesterday at a restaurant, I (*see*) _____ Pam Donnelly, an old friend of mine. I (*see, not*) _____ her in years. At first, I (*recognize, not*) _____ her because she (*lose*) _____ at least fifty pounds.

□ **EXERCISE 41:** Use the PRESENT PERFECT PROGRESSIVE or the PAST PERFECT PROGRESSIVE.

1. It is midnight. I (*study*) _____ for five straight hours. No wonder I'm getting tired.

2. It was midnight. I (*study*) _____ for five straight hours. No wonder I was getting tired.

3. Jack suddenly realized that the teacher was asking him a question. He couldn't answer because he (*daydream*) _____ for the last ten minutes.

4. Wake up! You (*sleep*) _____ long enough. It's time to get up.

5. At least two hundred people were waiting in line to buy tickets to the game. Some of them (*stand*) _____ in line for more than four hours. We decided not to try to get tickets for ourselves.

☐ **EXERCISE 42:** Discuss the meaning of the verb forms by reading the following pairs of sentences and then answering the question.

1. a. Dan was leaving the room when I walked in.
   b. Sam had left the room when I walked in.
   QUESTION: *Who did I run into when I walked into the room?*
   (ANSWER: Dan)

2. a. When the rain stopped, Gloria was riding her bicycle to work.
   b. When the rain stopped, Paul rode his bicycle to work.
   QUESTION: *Who got wet on the way to work?*

3. a. Dick went to the store because he was running out of food.
   b. Ann went to the store because she had run out of food.
   QUESTION: *Who is better at planning ahead?*

4. a. Ms. Lincoln taught at this school for nine years.
   b. Mr. Sanchez has taught at this school for nine years.
   QUESTION: *Who is teaching at this school now?*

5. a. Alice was walking to the door when the doorbell rang.
   b. George walked to the door when the doorbell rang.
   QUESTION: *Who expected the doorbell to ring?*

6. a. When I got there, Marie had eaten.
   b. When I got there, Joe ate.
   QUESTION: *Who was still hungry when I got there?*

7. a. Don lived in Chicago for five years.
   b. Carlos has been living in Chicago for five years.
   QUESTION: *Who still lives in Chicago?*

8. a. Jane put some lotion on her face because she had been lying in the sun.
   b. Sue put some lotion on her face because she was lying in the sun.
   QUESTION: *Who put lotion on her face after she stood up?*

9. a. I looked across the street. Mr. Fox was waving at me.
   b. I looked across the street. Mrs. Cook waved at me.
   QUESTION: *Who began to wave at me before I looked across the street?*

☐ **EXERCISE 43—ORAL (BOOKS CLOSED):** From the given situation, make up a "chain story." One person begins the story; then others continue the story in turn using certain cue words.

Example: (Pierre) had a terrible day yesterday. The trouble began early in the morning. His alarm clock rang at 7:00.

Cue: *when*

Student A: When his alarm clock rang, he got out of bed and stepped on a snake. He was nearly frightened to death, but the snake slithered away without biting him.

Cue: *after*

Student B: After the snake left, Pierre got dressed in a hurry and ran downstairs to have breakfast.

Cue: *while*

Student C: While he was running downstairs, he fell and broke his arm.

etc.

Possible situations to begin chain stories.

1. (. . .) had a terrible day yesterday.
2. (. . .) had a great vacation last summer.
3. (. . .) got into a lot of trouble a couple of days ago.
4. (. . .) had a really interesting experience last week.
5. (*Make up the beginning of a story.*)

Cue words (which may be used in any order):

1. when
2. after
3. before
4. while
5. by the time
6. as soon as
7. already
8. never
9. then
10. next
11. after that

12. later
13. for (*a length of time*)
14. since
15. because

□ **EXERCISE 44—WRITTEN:** Break into groups and sit in a circle. Take out a piece of paper and write the following sentence, using the name of the person sitting to your right in place of (. . .).

(. . .) *had a strange experience yesterday.*

Then write one or two additional sentences, and pass your paper to the person sitting to your left, who will continue the story. Continue to pass the papers to the left until everyone in the group has had a chance to write part of the story.

Then decide which of the stories in your group is the most entertaining or the most interesting. As a group, make any necessary corrections in grammar or spelling. Read it aloud to the rest of the class.

(Note: You may wish to establish a time limit for each contribution to the story. When the time limit is up, each person must pass his/her paper even if it contains an unfinished sentence. The next person will then have to finish the sentence and continue writing the story.)

1-19 SIMPLE FUTURE/*BE GOING TO*

——————|—×——————	(a) He ***will finish*** his work tomorrow.	***Will*** or ***be going to*** is used to express future time.*
	(b) He ***is going to finish*** his work tomorrow.	In speech, ***going to*** is often pronounced "gonna."

*The use of ***shall*** with *I* or *we* to express future time is possible but uncommon in American English. ***Shall*** is used much more frequently in British than in American English.

□ **EXERCISE 45—ORAL:** ***Will*** is usually contracted with personal pronouns in both speaking and informal writing. ***Will*** is often contracted with nouns and with other pronouns in speaking but not in writing. Practice pronouncing contracted ***will*** in the following sentences.

1. I'll come. He'll come. You'll come.
2. She'll help us. They'll help us too.
3. I'm sure we'll do well on the test.
4. It'll probably rain tomorrow.
5. Bob will (*Bob'll*) be here soon.
6. The weather will be hot in August.
7. Mary will come tomorrow.
8. Bill will be here too.
9. The children will be home at 3:00.
10. Who will be at the meeting?
11. Where will you be around five?
12. How long will Tom be here?
13. Nobody will recognize you in that wig.
14. That will be a lot of fun.
15. What will you do?

1–20 WILL VERSUS *BE GOING TO*

To express a PREDICTION—either *WILL* or *BE GOING TO* is used:	
(a) According to the weather report, it ***will be*** cloudy tomorrow. (b) According to the weather report, it ***is going to be*** cloudy tomorrow. (c) Be careful! You***'ll hurt*** yourself! (d) Watch out! You***'re going to*** hurt yourself!	When the speaker is making a prediction (a statement about something s/he thinks will be true or will occur in the future), either ***will*** or ***be going to*** is possible. There is no difference in meaning between (a) and (b). There is no difference in meaning between (c) and (d).

To express a PRIOR PLAN—only *BE GOING TO* is used:	
(e) A: Why did you buy this paint? B: I***'m going to paint*** my bedroom tomorrow.	When the speaker is expressing a prior plan (something the speaker intends to do in the future because in the past s/he has made a plan or decision to do it), only ***be going to*** is used.★ In (e): Speaker B has made a prior plan. She decided to paint her bedroom last week. She intends to paint her bedroom tomorrow.
(f) I talked to Bob yesterday. He is tired of taking the bus to work. He***'s going to buy*** a car. That's what he told me.	In (f): The speaker knows Bob's intention to buy a car. Bob made the decision in the past and he intends to act on this decision in the future. ***Will*** is not appropriate in (e) and (f).

To express WILLINGNESS—only *WILL* is used:	
(g) A: The phone's ringing. B: I***'ll get*** it.	In (g): Speaker B is saying: "I am willing, I am happy to get the phone." He is not making a prediction. He has made no prior plan to answer the phone. He is, instead, volunteering to answer the phone and uses ***will*** to show his willingness.
(h) A: I don't understand this problem. B: Ask your teacher about it. She***'ll help*** you.	In (h): Speaker B feels sure about the teacher's willingness to help. ***Be going to*** is not appropriate in (g) and (h).

★COMPARE:

Situation 1: A: *Are you busy this evening?*
      B: *Yes. **I'm going to meet** Jack at the library at seven. **We're going to study** together.*

In situation 1, only ***be going to*** is possible. The speaker has a prior plan, so he uses ***be going to***.

Situation 2: A: *Are you busy this evening?*
      B: *Well, I really haven't made any plans. **I'll eat/I'm going to eat** dinner, of course. And then **I'll probably watch/I'm probably going to watch** TV for a little while.*

In situation 2, either ***will*** or ***be going to*** is possible. Speaker B has not planned his evening. He is "predicting" his evening (rather than stating any prior plans), so he may use either ***will*** or ***be going to***.

☐ **EXERCISE 46:** Use *WILL* and/or *BE GOING TO* with the verb in parentheses.

PART I: EXPRESSING PREDICTIONS

1. Sue (*graduate*) _will graduate/is going to graduate_ in June. After that, she (*begin*) _will begin/is going to begin_ work at an electronics firm.

2. Fred (*be*) _____ at the meeting tomorrow. I think Jane (*come*) _____ too.

3. A: Can you give Ed a message for me?

   B: Sure. I (*see, probably*) _____

   him at the meeting this evening.

4. The damage we do to our environment today (*affect*) _____

   _____ the quality of life of future generations.

5. A: Mr. Swan (*be, not*) _____ here next term. He has resigned. Who (*be*) _____ the new teacher? Do you know?

   B: Yes. Mary Jefferson. Ms. Jefferson (*teach*) _____

   _____ the same courses Mr. Swan taught: English, algebra, and geometry. I (*be*) _____ in her algebra class. Do you know which algebra class you (*be*) _____

   in next term?

PART II: EXPRESSING PRIOR PLAN VS. WILLINGNESS:
Use *be going to* if you think the speaker is expressing a prior plan. If you think there is no prior plan, use *will*.

6. A: This letter is in French, and I don't speak a word of French. Can you help me?

   B: Sure. I (*translate*) _will translate_ it for you.

7. A: Do you want to go shopping with me? I(*go*) _am going to go_

   to the shopping mall downtown.

   B: Sure. What time do you want to leave?

8. A: This light doesn't work. The bulb is probably burned out. Where are the new light bulbs?

    B: I (*get*) _____ one for you.

9. A: It's cold in here.

    B: I agree. I (*turn*) _____ the heater on.

    A: That's a good idea.

10. A: I (*enroll*) _____ in the community college next spring.

    B: Oh? I didn't know you wanted to go back to school.

    A: I need to sharpen my skills so I can get a better job. I (*take*) _____ _____ a course in word processing.

11. A: Brrr. Who turned up the air conditioner? It's really cold in here. My nose is cold and my fingers are cold.

    B: I (*make*) _____ you a hot cup of tea.

    A: Thanks. That sounds good.

12. A: Oh, oh! I've spilled coffee on my shirt.

    B: Just a minute. I (*get*) _____ a damp cloth for you.

13. A: What do you want to be when you grow up?

    B: I (*be*) _____ an astronaut.

    A: Good for you!

14. A: Do you mind if I turn the TV off? I (*place*) _____ _____ a long distance call, and it's hard to hear if the TV is on.

    B: No, that's fine. I wasn't watching it anyway.

15. A: Who wants to erase the board? Are there any volunteers?

    B: I (*do*) _____ it!

    C: I (*do*) _____ it!

    D: No, no! I (*do*) _____ it!

16. A: Why do you have an eraser in your hand?

    B: I (*erase*) _____ the board.

1–21 EXPRESSING THE FUTURE IN TIME CLAUSES

(a) Bob will come soon. *When Bob **comes**, we will see him.* (b) Linda is going to leave soon. *Before she **leaves**, she is going to finish her work.* (c) I will get home at 5:30. *After I **get** home, I will eat dinner.* (d) The taxi will arrive soon. *As soon as it **arrives**, we'll be able to leave for the airport.* (e) They are going to come soon. I'll wait here *until they **come**.*	In (a): "When Bob comes" is a time clause.* ***when + subject + verb = a time clause*** **Will** or **be going to** is NOT used in a time clause. The meaning of the clause is future, but the simple present tense is used.

	A time clause begins with such words as ***when, before, after, as soon as, until*** and includes a subject and a verb. The time clause can come either at the beginning of the sentence or in the second part of the sentence:
	     When he comes, we'll see him.
	     OR:
	     We'll see him *when he comes*.

(f) I will go to bed *after I **finish** my work.* (g) I will go to bed *after I **have finished** my work.*	Occasionally, the present perfect is used in a time clause, as in (g). Examples (f) and (g) have the same meaning. The present perfect stresses the completion of the act in the time clause before the other act occurs in the future.

*A "time clause" is an adverb clause. See Chart 8-5 for more information.

☐ **EXERCISE 47:** Use *WILL/BE GOING TO* or the SIMPLE PRESENT. (In this exercise, both *will* and *be going to* are possible when a future tense is necessary, with little or no difference in meaning.)

1. Peter is going to leave in half an hour. He (*finish*) _____*will finish /*_____ _____*is going to finish*_____ all of his work before he (*leave*) _____*leaves*_____.

2. I'm going to eat lunch at 12:30. After I (*eat*) _____, I (*take, probably*) _____ a nap.

3. I'll get home around six. When I (*get*) _____ home, I (*call*) _____ Sharon.

4. I'm going to watch a TV program at nine. Before I (*watch*) _____ _____ that program, I (*write*) _____ a letter to my parents.

5. Gary will come soon. I (wait) _____
   here until he (come) _____.

6. I'm sure it will stop raining soon. As soon as the rain (stop) _____
   _____, I (walk) _____ to the drugstore
   to get some film.

7. Right now I'm a junior in college. After I (graduate) _____
   with a B.A., I (intend) _____ to enter graduate school and
   work for an M.A. Perhaps I (go) _____ on for a Ph.D. after I
   (get) _____ my Master's degree.

8. A: How long (stay, you) _____ in this country?

   B: I (plan) _____ to be here for about
      one more year. I (hope) _____ to graduate a year from this
      June.

   A: What (do, you) _____ after you
      (leave) _____?

   B: I (return) _____ home and (get)
      _____ a job. How about you?

   A: I (be) _____ here for at least two more years
      before I (return) _____ home and (get) _____
      a job.

☐ **EXERCISE 48—ORAL:** Complete the following with your own words. Use *WILL/BE
GOING TO* and the SIMPLE PRESENT, as appropriate.

1. When I . . . this afternoon, I . . . .
   → *When I go downtown this afternoon, I'm going to go to the bank and the post
   office.*
2. After I . . . tomorrow morning, I . . . .
3. Tomorrow, I . . . before I . . . .
4. I . . . when . . . next year.
5. As soon as class . . . , I . . . .
6. I . . . until my friend . . . .
7. When I . . . tomorrow, I . . . .

1–22 USING THE PRESENT PROGRESSIVE AND THE SIMPLE PRESENT TO EXPRESS FUTURE TIME

PRESENT PROGRESSIVE (a) My wife has an appointment with a doctor. She *is seeing* Dr. North *next Tuesday*. (b) Sam has already made his plans. He *is leaving at noon tomorrow*. (c) A: What are you going to do this afternoon? B: *After lunch* I *am meeting* a friend of mine. We *are going* shopping. Would you like to come along?	The present progressive may be used to express future time when the idea of the sentence concerns a planned event or definite intention. (COMPARE: A verb such as *rain* is not used in the present progressive to indicate future time because rain is not a planned event.) A future meaning for the present progressive tense is indicated either by future time words in the sentence or by the context.
SIMPLE PRESENT (d) The museum *opens at ten tomorrow morning*. (e) Classes *begin next week*. (f) John's plane *arrives at 6:05 P.M. next Monday*.	The simple present can also be used to express future time in sentences that concern events that are on a definite schedule or timetable. These sentences usually contain future time words. Only a few verbs are used in this way: e.g., *open, close, begin, end, start, finish, arrive, leave, come, return*.

□ **EXERCISE 49:** Indicate the meaning expressed by the italicized verbs by writing ***in the future***, ***now***, or ***habitually*** in the blanks.

1. I *am taking* four courses next semester.   *in the future*

2. I *am taking* four courses this semester.   *now*

3. Students usually *take* four courses every semester.   *habitually*

4. I'll mail this letter at the corner when I *take* Susan home.   _____

5. My brother's birthday is next week. I *am giving* him a sweater.   _____

6. Shhh. The broadcaster *is giving* the latest news about the crisis in England. I want to hear what she's saying.   _____

7. When I *graduate*, I'm going to return home.   _____

8. When students *graduate*, they receive diplomas.   _____

9. I'm tired. I *am going* to bed early tonight.   _____

10. When I *am* in New York, I'm going to visit the Museum of Modern Art.   _____

11. When I *am* home alone in the evening, I like to read or watch television. _____

12. A: Are you busy?
    B: Not really.
    A: What *are* you *doing*? A: _____

    B: I'm *writing* a letter to my folks. B: _____

    A: When you *finish* your letter, do you want to play a game of chess? A: _____

13. A: What *are* you *doing* after class? A: _____

    B: I'm *eating* at the cafeteria with Cindy. Do you want to join us? B: _____

14. Tony *will arrive* at eight tomorrow evening. _____

15. Tony *is going to arrive* at eight tomorrow evening. _____

16. Tony *is arriving* at eight tomorrow evening. _____

17. Tony *arrives* at eight tomorrow evening. _____

18. When Tony *arrives*, we'll have a party. _____

1–23 FUTURE PROGRESSIVE

	(a) I will begin to study at seven. You will come at eight. I **will be studying** when you come. (b) Right now I am sitting in class. At this same time tomorrow, I **will be sitting** in class.	The future progressive expresses an activity that will be *in progress at a time in the future*.
	(c) Don't call me at nine because I won't be home. I **am going to be studying** at the library.	The progressive form of *be going to*: *be going to + be + -ing*
	(d) Don't get impatient. She **will be coming** soon. (e) Don't get impatient. She **will come** soon.	Sometimes there is little or no difference between the future progressive and the simple future, especially when the future event will occur at an indefinite time in the future, as in (d) and (e).

☐ **EXERCISE 50:** Use the FUTURE PROGRESSIVE or the SIMPLE PRESENT.

1. Right now I am attending class. Yesterday at this time, I was attending class. Tomorrow at this time, I (*attend*) _____ class.

2. Tomorrow I'm going to leave for home. When I (*arrive*) _____ _____ at the airport, my whole family (*wait*) _____ _____ for me.

3. When I (*get*) _____ up tomorrow morning, the sun (*shine*) _____, the birds (*sing*) _____ _____, and my roommate (*lie, still*) _____ _____ in bed fast asleep.

4. A: When do you leave for Florida?

   B: Tomorrow. Just think. Two days from now I (*lie*) _____ _____ on the beach in the sun.

   A: Sounds great! I (*think*) _____ about you.

5. A: How can I get in touch with you while you're out of town?

   B: I (*stay*) _____ at the Pilgrim Hotel. You can reach me there.

6. Next year at this time, I (*do*) _____ exactly what I am doing now. I (*attend*) _____ school and (*study*) _____ hard next year.

7. Look at those dark clouds. When class (*be*) _____ over, it (*rain, probably*) _____.

8. A: Are you going to be in town next Saturday?

   B: No. I (*visit*) _____ my aunt in Chicago.

1–24 FUTURE PERFECT

<table>
<tr>
<td>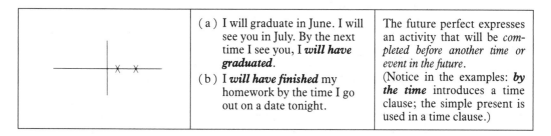</td>
<td>(a) I will graduate in June. I will see you in July. By the next time I see you, I will have graduated.

(b) I will have finished my homework by the time I go out on a date tonight.</td>
<td>The future perfect expresses an activity that will be completed before another time or event in the future.
(Notice in the examples: by the time introduces a time clause; the simple present is used in a time clause.)</td>
</tr>
</table>

1–25 FUTURE PERFECT PROGRESSIVE

<table>
<tr>
<td></td>
<td>(c) I will go to bed at ten P.M. He will get home at midnight. At midnight I will be sleeping. I will have been sleeping for two hours by the time he gets home.</td>
<td>The future perfect progressive emphasizes the duration of an activity that will be in progress before another time or event in the future.</td>
</tr>
<tr>
<td></td>
<td>(d) When Professor Jones retires next month, he will have taught for 45 years.

(e) When Professor Jones retires next month, he will have been teaching for 45 years.</td>
<td>Sometimes the future perfect and the future perfect progressive give the same meaning, as in (d) and (e). Also, notice that the activity expressed by either of these two tenses may begin in the past.</td>
</tr>
</table>

☐ **EXERCISE 51:** Use any appropriate tense.

1. Ann and Andy got married on June 1st. Today is June 14th. Ann and Andy (*be*) _____ married for two weeks. By June 7th, they (*be*) _____ married for one week. By June 28th, they (*be*) _____ married for four weeks.

2. This traffic is terrible. We're going to be late. By the time we (*get*) _____ to the airport, Bob's plane (*arrive, already**) _____, and he'll be wondering where we are.

---

*With the future perfect, **already** has two possible positions: *I will already have finished. I will have already finished.*

3. The traffic was very heavy. By the time we (*get*) _____ to the airport, Bob's plane (*arrive, already*) _____.

4. This morning I came to class at 9:00. Right now it is 10:00, and I am still in class. I (*sit*) _____ at this desk for an hour. By 9:30, I (*sit*) _____ here for a half an hour. By 11:00, I (*sit*) _____ here for two hours.

5. I'm getting tired of sitting in the car. Do you realize that by the time we arrive in Phoenix, we (*drive*) _____ for twenty straight hours?

6. Margaret was born in 1950. By the year 2000, she (*live*) _____ _____ on this earth for 50 years.

7. Go ahead and leave on your vacation. Don't worry about this work. By the time you (*get*) _____ back, we (*take*) _____ _____ care of everything.

8. I don't understand how those marathon runners do it! The race began over an hour ago. By the time they reach the finish line, they (*run*) _____ _____ steadily for more than two hours. I don't think I can run more than two minutes!

9. What? He got married again? At this rate, he (*have*) _____ a dozen wives by the time he (*die*) _____.

10. We have been married for a long time. By our next anniversary, we (*be*) _____ married for 43 years.

☐ **EXERCISE 52—ORAL/WRITTEN:** What do you think the world will be like a hundred years from now? What changes will have occurred between then and now? Use your imagination and make some predictions. Following are some topics to think about:

1. means of transportation
2. sources of energy
3. population growth
4. food sources
5. extinction of animal species
6. exploration of the oceans; of the earth's interior
7. space exploration; contact with beings from outer space
8. weapon technology
9. role of computers in daily life
10. long-term solutions to today's political crises
11. architecture

12. clothing styles
13. international language
14. international world government

15. international television; international communication via communication satellites

Note: You may wish to make comparisons among the past, the present, and the future. For example: *A hundred years ago, the automobile hadn't been invented. Today it is one of the most common means of transportation and has greatly changed the way people lead their lives. By the year _____, the automobile will have become obsolete. A hundred years from now, people will use small, jet-propelled, wingless flying machines in place of cars.*

☐ **EXERCISE 53**: Discuss the differences (if any) in meaning in the following groups of sentences. Some of the sentences need to be completed to make their meaning clear.

1. a. He watches television.
   b. He is watching television.
2. a. I am sitting in class . . . .
   b. I was sitting in class . . . .
   c. I will be sitting in class . . . .
3. a. I have finished my homework.
   b. I had finished my homework . . . .
   c. I will have finished my homework . . . .
4. a. The students had left before the teacher arrived.
   b. The students left before the teacher arrived.
   c. The students had left when the teacher arrived.
   d. The students left when the teacher arrived.
   e. The students were leaving when the teacher arrived.
5. a. I have been waiting for her for two hours.
   b. I had been waiting for her for two hours . . . .
   c. I will have been waiting for her for two hours . . . .
6. a. Ali has been studying Chapter Three.
   b. He has studied Chapter Two.
   c. He studied Chapter Two . . . .
7. a. She has been doing a lot of research on that project.
   b. She has done a lot of research on that project.
8. a. I will study when you come.
   b. I am going to study when you come.
   c. I will be studying when you come.
   d. I am going to be studying when you come.
   e. I will have studied by the time you come.
   f. I will have been studying for two hours by the time you come.
9. a. He worked for that company for two years.
   b. He has been working for that company for two years.

10. a. The train will leave at 10:00 tomorrow morning.
   b. The train is going to leave at 10:00 tomorrow morning.
   c. The train leaves at 10:00 tomorrow morning.
   d. The train is leaving at 10:00 tomorrow morning.

☐ **EXERCISE 54—ORAL (BOOKS CLOSED):** In order to practice verb tenses, answer the questions in complete sentences.

1. What have we been studying? What is one tense we have studied since the beginning of the term? When, to the best of your recollection, did we study it?
2. What else will we have studied in this class by the time the term ends?
3. This class began on (*date*). Had you studied verb tenses before that?
4. We're going to finish studying Chapter 1 on (*day or date*). How long will we have been studying Chapter 1 by that time?
5. What were you doing at this time yesterday? What did you do after that?
6. What are you doing right now? How long have you been doing that?
7. What are you going to be doing at this time tomorrow?
8. What will you be doing tonight at midnight? What were you doing last night at midnight?
9. Where will you be living three years from now? Where were you living three years ago? Can you name one specific thing you did three years ago? Can you name one specific thing you will do three years from now?
10. What places have you been to since you came to (*this city*)? When?
11. Make some generalizations about things you do.
12. What are some things you have done many times since you came here?
13. What are some of the things you have done in your lifetime? When?
14. What have you done that no one else in this class (or in the world?) has ever done?
15. What is the exact place you are sitting right now?
    How long have you been sitting there today?
    How long will you have been sitting there by the time class is over?
    How often do you sit there during class?
    How many times have you sat there?
    Before today, when did you last sit there?
    Had you sat there before that?
    Where were you sitting at this time yesterday?
    Where are you going to be sitting at this time tomorrow?

☐ **EXERCISE 55:** Use any appropriate tense for the verbs in parentheses.

1. John is in my English class. He (*study*) _____

   English this semester. He (*take, also*) _____ some other

   classes. His classes (*begin*) _____ at 9:00 every day.

2. Yesterday John ate breakfast at 8:00. He (*eat, already*) _____ _____ breakfast when he (*leave*) _____ for class at 8:45. He (*eat, always*) _____ breakfast before he (*go*) _____ to class. I (*eat, not, usually*) _____ _____ breakfast before I (*go*) _____ to class. But I (*get, usually*) _____ hungry about midmorning. Tomorrow before I (*go*) _____ to class, I (*eat*) _____ _____ breakfast.

3. John is in class every morning from 9:00 to 12:00. Two days ago, I (*call*) _____ him at 11:30, but I could not reach him because he (*attend*) _____ class at that time.

4. Don't try to call John at 11:30 tomorrow morning because he (*attend*) _____ class at that time.

5. Yesterday John took a nap from 1:00 to 2:00. I came at 1:45. When I (*get*) _____ there, John (*sleep*) _____. He (*sleep*) _____ for 45 minutes by the time I came.

6. Right now John (*take*) _____ a nap. He (*fall*) _____ asleep an hour ago. He (*sleep*) _____ for an hour.

7. Three days ago, John (*start*) _____ to read *A Farewell to Arms*, a novel by Ernest Hemingway. It is a long novel. He (*finish, not*) _____ reading it yet. He (*read*) _____ it because his English teacher assigned it.

8. Since the beginning of the semester, John (*read*) _____ three novels. Right now he (*read*) _____ *A Farewell to Arms*. He (*read*) _____ that novel for the past three days. He (*intend*) _____ to finish it next week. In his lifetime, he (*read*) _____ many novels, but this is the first Hemingway novel he (*read, ever*) _____.

9. Tomorrow, after he (*eat*) _____ dinner, John (*go*) _____ to a movie. In other words, he (*eat*) _____ dinner by the time he (*go*) _____ to the movie.

☐ **EXERCISE 56—ORAL:** Pair up with another student in the class.

STUDENT A:

(1) Use the questions in this exercise to initiate conversation with Student B.

(2) Do not simply read the questions. Look at the text briefly, then look directly at Student B each time you ask a question.

(3) If Student B does not answer fully or if you are interested in getting more information, ask your own questions in addition to those which are suggested.

(4) Pay special attention to verb tense usage in both the questions and the responses.

STUDENT B:

(1) Do not look at the written questions in this exercise. Only Student A should look at the text.

(2) Answer the questions fully. Often your response will consist of more than one sentence.

(3) Answer in complete sentences in order to practice using verb tenses.

1. What is happening in this room?
   What else is happening?
2. What was happening in this room when you walked in today?
   What else was happening?
3. What did you do yesterday? (*Student A: Listen carefully for past tense verbs*
   What else did you do?   *in the responses.*)
   And what else did you do?
4. How long have you been living in (*this city*)?
   How long will you have been living here by the end of (*the semester/term, etc.*)?
5. Where did you eat dinner last night?
   What did you have?
   How was it?
   What did you do after you had eaten?
6. What were you doing at 8 o'clock last night?
   What will you be doing at 8 o'clock tomorrow night?
7. Are you taking any classes besides English?
   How is everything going?
   What are you doing in one of your classes?
8. How long have we been talking to each other?
   What have we been talking about?
9. How do you like living here?
   Have you had any interesting experiences since you came here?
   Have you met any interesting people?
10. What do you think the world will be like when you are seventy years old?

☐ **EXERCISE 57—ORAL:** Same as the preceding exercise.

1. What are you doing right now?
    What are you going to be doing for the next ten minutes or so?
2. What did you do last weekend? (*Student A: Listen carefully for past tense*
    What else did you do?   *verbs in the response.*)
    And what else did you do?
3. What is the teacher doing?
    How long has he/she been (*doing that*)?
4. What are you going to do for the rest of today?
    What will you be doing at midnight?
5. What will you have done by the time you go to bed tonight?
6. How long have you been studying English at this school?
    How long had you studied English before you came here?
    What have you been doing outside of class to improve your English?
7. What have we been doing for the past ten minutes or so?
    Why have we been (*doing that*)?
8. What are some of the things you have done since you came to (*this city*)?
9. Have you read a newspaper lately?
    What is happening in the world?
10. What countries have you visited?
    When did you visit (*a particular country*).
    Why did you go there?
    What did you like about that country?
    What did you dislike about that country?
    Are you planning to go back there again someday?

☐ **EXERCISE 58—ORAL/WRITTEN:** Before you come to class, think of an interesting, dangerous, or amusing experience you have had. You will then tell that story to a classmate, who will report that experience in a composition.

☐ **EXERCISE 59—ORAL:** In a short speech (two or three minutes), summarize an article in a recent newspaper. You may speak from notes if necessary, but your notes should contain no more than fifteen words. Use your notes only for a very brief outline of important information.

☐ **EXERCISE 60:** Use any appropriate tense for the verbs in parentheses. In some instances, more than one tense is possible.*

1. A: There is something I have to tell you.

   B: Go ahead. I (*listen*) _____.

---

*Your teacher can tell you if one tense is more idiomatic, i.e., more likely to be used by a native speaker.

2. A: Hi, Ann. (*Meet, you*) _____ my friend, George
   Smith?

   B: No, I (*have, never*) _____ the pleasure.

   A: Then let me introduce you.

3. A: Stop! What (*you, do*) _____?

   B: I (*try*) _____ to get this piece of toast out of the
   toaster. It's stuck.

   A: Well, don't use a knife. You (*electrocute*) _____
   yourself!

   B: What do you suggest I do?

   A: Unplug it first.

4. A: There's Jack.

   B: Where?

   A: He (*lie*) _____ on the grass under that tree over
   there.

   B: Oh yes. I (*see*) _____ him. He (*look, certainly*)
   _____ comfortable. Let's go talk to him.

5. A: (*Take, you*) _____ Econ 120 this semester?

   B: No, I _____.

   A: (*Take, you, ever*) _____ it?

   B: Yes, I _____.

   A: When (*take, you*) _____ it?

   B: Last semester.

   A: Who (*be*) _____ your professor?

B: Dr. Lee.

A: Oh, I have the same professor. What (*be, he*) _____ like?

B: He (*be*) _____ very good.

6. A: What's wrong with Chris?

B: While he (*yawn*) _____, a fly (*fly*) _____ into his mouth.

A: I (*believe, not*) _____ that! You (*kid*) _____

_____!

7. A: I (*go*) _____ to a play last night.

B: (*Be, it*) _____ any good?

A: I thought so. I (*enjoy*) _____ it a lot.

B: What (*see, you*) _____?

A: *Arsenic and Old Lace.* I (*see, never*) _____ it before.

B: Oh, I (*see*) _____ that play too. I (*see*) _____ it a couple of years ago. It (*be*) _____ good, (*be, not*) _____ it?

8. A: I was in your hometown last month. It looked like a nice town. I (*be, never*) _____ there before.

B: What (*do, you*) _____ in that part of the country?

A: My wife and I (*drive*) _____ to Washington, D.C. to visit her family.

9. A: May I borrow some money? My check (*be*) _____ supposed to arrive yesterday, but I still (*receive, not*) _____

_____ it. I (*need*) _____ to buy a book for one of my classes, but I (*have, not*) _____

_____ any money.

B: Sure. I'd be happy to lend you some. How much (*need, you*) _____

_____?

A: How about five dollars? Thanks. I (*pay*) _____ you back as soon as I (*get*) _____ my check.

10. A: Hello?

    B: Hello. May I speak to Sue?

    A: She (*be, not*) _____ in right now. May I take a message?

    B: Yes. This is Art O'Brien. Would you please ask her to meet me at the library this afternoon? I (*sit*) _____ at one of the study booths on the second floor.

☐ **EXERCISE 61:** Use any appropriate tense for the verbs in parentheses.

1. My grandfather (*fly, never*) _____ in an airplane, and he has no intention of ever doing so.

2. Jane isn't here yet. I (*wait*) _____ for her since noon, but she still (*arrive, not*) _____.

3. In all the world, there (*be*) _____ only 14 mountains that (*reach*) _____ above 8,000 meters (26,247 feet).

4. I have a long trip ahead of me tomorrow, so I think I'd better go to bed. But let me say good-bye now because I won't see you in the morning. I (*leave, already*) _____ by the time you (*get*) _____ up.

5. Right now we (*have*) _____ a heat wave. The temperature (*be*) _____ in the upper 90s for the last six days.

6. Last night I (*go*) _____ to a party. When I (*get*) _____ there, the room was full of people. Some of them (*dance*) _____ and others (*talk*) _____. One young woman (*stand*) _____ by herself. I (*meet, never*) _____ her, so I (*introduce*) _____ myself to her.

7. About three yesterday afternoon, Jessica (*lie*) _____ in bed reading a book. Suddenly she (*hear*) _____ a

loud noise and (get) _____ up to see what it was.

She (look) _____ out the window. A truck (back,

just) _____ into her new car!

8. Next month I have a week's vacation. I (plan) _____

to take a trip. First, I (go) _____ to Madison,

Wisconsin, to visit my brother. After I (leave) _____

Madison, I (go) _____ to Chicago to see a friend

who (study) _____ at a university there. She (live)

_____ in Chicago for three years, so she

(know) _____ her way around the city. She (promise)

_____ to take me to many interesting places. I (be,

never) _____ in Chicago, so I (look) _____

_____ forward to going there.

9. Yesterday while I (sit) _____ in class, I (get) _____

the hiccups. The person who (sit) _____ next to me

told me to hold my breath. I (try) _____ that, but it

didn't work. The instructor (lecture) _____, and I

didn't want to interrupt him, so I just sat there trying to hiccup quietly.

Finally, after I (hiccup) _____ for almost five

minutes, I (raise) _____ my hand and (excuse)

_____ myself from the class to go get a drink of

water.

10. The weather has been terrible lately. It (rain) _____

off and on for two days, and the temperature (drop) _____

at least twenty degrees. It (be) _____ in the low 40s right now.

Just three days ago, the sun (shine) _____ and the

weather was pleasant. The weather certainly (change) _____

_____ quickly here. I never know what to expect.

Who knows? When I (wake) _____ up tomorrow

morning, maybe it (snow) _____.

□ **EXERCISE 62:** Use any appropriate tenses.

    A: Hi, my name is Jose.
    B: Hi, my name is Ali.

(1) JOSE: (*You, study*) _____ at this university?

(2) ALI: Yes, I _____. _____ you?

(3) JOSE: Yes, I (*be*) _____ here since last September. Before that
         I (*study*) _____ English at another school.

(4) ALI: What (*you, take*) _____?

(5) JOSE: I (*take*) _____ chemistry, math, psychology, and
         American history. What (*take, you*) _____?

(6) ALI: I (*study*) _____ English. I (*need*) _____
         to improve my English before I (*take*) _____ regular
         academic courses next semester.

(7) JOSE: How long (*you, be*) _____ here?

(8) ALI: I (*be*) _____ here since the beginning of this semester.
         Actually, I (*arrive*) _____ in the United States six
         months ago, but I (*study*) _____
         English at this university only since January. Before that I (*live*) _____
         _____ with my brother in Washington, D.C.

(9) JOSE: You (*speak*) _____ English very well. (*You, study*) _____
         _____ a lot of English before you (*come*)
         _____ to the United States?

(10) ALI: Yes. I (*study*) _____ English for ten years
         in my own country. And also, I (*spend*) _____ some
         time in Canada a couple of years ago. I (*pick*) _____ up
         a lot of English while I (*live*) _____ there.

(11) JOSE: You (*be*) _____ lucky. When I (*come*) _____
         to the United States, I (*study, never*) _____
         any English at all. So I had to spend a whole year studying nothing but
         English before I (*start*) _____ school.

(12) ALI: How long (_you, plan_) _____ to be in the U.S.?

(13) JOSE: I (_be, not_) _____ sure. Probably by the time I (_return_)

_____ home, I (_be_) _____

here for at least five years. How about you?

(14) ALI: I (_hope_) _____ to be finished with all my work in two

and a half years.

□ **EXERCISE 63**: Use any appropriate tenses.

(1) Dear Ann,

(2)   I (_receive_) _____ your letter about two weeks ago

(3) and (_try_) _____ to find time to write you back ever

(4) since. I (_be_) _____ very busy lately. In the past two

(5) weeks, I (_have_) _____ four tests, and I have another

(6) test next week. In addition, a friend (_stay_) _____ with

(7) me since last Thursday. She wanted to see the city, so we (_spend_) _____

(8) a lot of time visiting some of the interesting places here. We (_be_) _____

(9) _____ to the zoo, the art museum, and the botanical gardens.

(10) Yesterday we (_go_) _____ to the park and (_watch_) _____

(11) a balloon race. Between showing her the city and studying for my exams, I

(12) (_have, barely_) _____ enough time to breathe.

(13)   Right now it (_be_) _____ 3 A.M. and I (_sit_) _____

(14) at my desk. I (_sit_) _____ here five hours doing my

(15) studying. My friend's plane (_leave_) _____ at 6:05, so I

(16) (_decide_) _____ not to go to bed. That's why I (_write_)

(17) _____ to you at such an early hour in the day. I

(18) (_get_) _____ a little sleepy, but I would rather stay up. I

(19) (_take_) _____ a nap after I (_get_) _____

(20) back from taking her to the airport.

(21)   How (_get, you_) _____ along? How (_go, your_

(22) _classes_) _____? Please write soon.

☐ **EXERCISE 64—WRITTEN:** Write a letter to a friend or family member. Discuss your activities, thoughts, feelings, adventures in the present, past, and future. The purpose of this exercise is for you to use every possible tense.

Write about what you *do, are doing, have done, have been doing, did, were doing, had done, had been doing, will do, are going to do, will be doing, will have done,* and *will have been doing.* Include appropriate time expressions: *today, every day, right now, already, so far, since, next week,* etc.

Use the verb tenses in any order you wish and as many times as necessary. Try to write a natural-sounding letter.

☐ **EXERCISE 65—ERROR ANALYSIS:** All of the following sentences are adapted from student writing and contain typical errors. See how many of these errors you can find and correct.

Example: I visit my uncle home many time when I was a child.
Corrections: I *visited* my *uncle's* home many *times* when I was a child.

1. I am living at 3371 grand avenue since last september.

2. I have been in New York city two week ago.

3. My country have change its capital city five time.

4. Dormitory life is not quiet. Everyone shouted and make a lot of noise in the halls.

5. My friends will meet me when I will arrive at the airport.

6. Hasn't anyone ever tell you to knock on the door before you enter someone else's room? Didn't your parents taught you to do that?

7. When I was a child, I viewed thing from a much lower height. Many physical objects around me appear very large. When I want to move something such as a chair, I need help.

8. I will intend to go back home when I will finish my education.

9. The phone rung while I doing the dishes. I dry my hands and answer it. When I am hear my husband voice, I very happy.

10. I am in the United States for the last four months. During this time, I had done many thing and saw many place.

11. When the old man started to walk back to his cave, the sun has already hided itself behind the mountain.

12. While I am writing my composition last night, someone knocks on the door.

□ **EXERCISE 66—PREPOSITIONS:** Supply an appropriate preposition for each of the following expressions of time.

1. I'll meet you _____*in*_____ the morning.

2. I'll meet you _____ the afternoon.

3. I'll meet you _____ the evening.

4. I usually stay home _____ night.

5. I get out of class _____ noon.

6. I'll call you _____ six o'clock.

7. She came _____ Monday.*

8. She came _____ March.

9. I was born _____ 1970.

10. I was born _____ March 15th.

11. I was born _____ March 15th, 1970.

12. He played a trick on me _____ April Fool's Day.

13. I'll help you _____ a minute, just as soon as I finish this work.

14. I'll help you _____ a moment, just as soon as I finish this work.**

15. _____ the moment, I'm doing an exercise.

16. I'm living in the dorm _____ present.

17. I like to go swimming _____ the summer.

18. I like to go skiing _____ the winter.

---

*__On__ is used for a particular day or date. __In__ is used for a month or year.

**__In a moment__ means __soon__. __At the moment__ means __at this time__ (or __at that time__).

CHAPTER 2
Modal Auxiliaries and Similar Expressions

2–1 INTRODUCTION

The modal auxiliaries in English are: *can*, *could*, *had better*, *may*, *might*, *must*, *ought to*, *shall*, *should*, *will*, *would*.

Modal auxiliaries generally express a speaker's attitudes, or "moods." For example, modals can express that a speaker feels something is necessary, advisable, permissible, possible, or probable; and, in addition, they can convey the strength of these attitudes.

Each modal has more than one meaning or use. (See Chart 2-23.)

(a) MODAL AUXILIARIES	Modals do not take a final *-s*, even when the subject is *he*, *she*, or *it*.
I We You They He She It $\Big\} +$ $\begin{cases} \textit{can } do \text{ it.} \\ \textit{could } do \text{ it.} \\ \textit{had better } do \text{ it.} \\ \textit{may } do \text{ it.} \\ \textit{might } do \text{ it.} \\ \textit{must } do \text{ it.} \\ \textit{ought to } do \text{ it.} \\ \textit{shall } do \text{ it.} \\ \textit{should } do \text{ it.} \\ \textit{will } do \text{ it.} \\ \textit{would } do \text{ it.} \end{cases}$	CORRECT: *He can do it.* INCORRECT: *He cans do it.*
	Modals are followed immediately by the simple form of a verb. CORRECT: *He can do it.* INCORRECT: *He can to do it./He can does it./He can did it.* The only exception is *ought*, which is followed by an infinitive (*to* + the simple form of a verb). CORRECT: *She ought to go to the meeting.*
(b) SIMILAR EXPRESSIONS *be able to* do it *be going to* do it *be supposed to* do it *be to* do it *have to* do it *have got to* do it *used to* do it	In (b) is a list of some common expressions whose meanings are similar to those of some of the modal auxiliaries. For example, *be able to* is similar to *can*; *be going to* is similar to *will*. An infinitive (*to* + the simple form of a verb) is used in these similar expressions.

☐ **EXERCISE 1—ERROR ANALYSIS:** All of the following contain errors in the forms of modals. Point out and correct the errors.

1. *INCORRECT: She can to see it.*

2. *INCORRECT: She cans see it.*

3. *INCORRECT: She can sees it.*

4. *INCORRECT: She can saw it.*

5. *INCORRECT: Can you please to pass the rice?*

6. *INCORRECT: Do you can see it?★*

7. *INCORRECT: They don't can go there.★★*

2–2 POLITE REQUESTS WITH "I" AS THE SUBJECT

MAY I COULD I	(a) *May I* (please) *borrow* your pen? (b) *Could I borrow* your pen (please)?	*May I* and *could I* are used to request permission. They are equally polite.★ Note in (b): In a polite request, *could* has a present or future meaning, not a past meaning.
CAN I	(c) *Can I borrow* your pen?	*Can I* is used informally to request permission, especially if the speaker is talking to someone s/he knows fairly well. *Can I* is usually not considered as polite as *may I* or *could I*.
	TYPICAL RESPONSES: Certainly. Yes, certainly. Of course. Yes, of course. Sure. *(informal)*	Often the response to a polite request consists of an action, a nod or shake of the head, or a simple "uh-huh."

★Might is also possible: *Might I borrow your pen. Might I* is quite formal and polite; it is used much less frequently than *may I* or *could I*.

★See Appendix 1, Chart B-1 for question forms with modals.
★★See Appendix 1, Chart C-1 for negative forms with modals.

2-3 POLITE REQUESTS WITH "YOU" AS THE SUBJECT

WOULD YOU WILL YOU	(a) *Would you pass* the salt (please)? (b) *Will you* (please) *pass* the salt?	The meaning of *would you* and *will you* in a polite request is the same. *Would you* is more common and is often considered more polite. The degree of politeness, however, is often determined by the speaker's tone of voice.
COULD YOU	(c) *Could you pass* the salt?	Basically, *could you* and *would you* have the same meaning. The difference is slight: *would you* = *Do you want to do this please?* *could you* = *Do you want to do this please, and is it possible for you to do this?* *Could you* and *would you* are equally polite.
CAN YOU	(d) *Can you pass* the salt?	*Can you* is often used informally. It usually sounds less polite than *could you* or *would you*.
	TYPICAL RESPONSES: Yes, I'd (I would) be happy to. Yes, I'd be glad to. Certainly. Sure. (*informal*)	A person usually responds in the affirmative to a polite request. If a negative response is necessary, a person might begin by saying, "I'd like to, but . . ." (e.g., "I'd like to pass the salt, but I can't reach it. I'll ask Tom to pass it to you.").

☐ **EXERCISE 2—ORAL (BOOKS CLOSED):** Ask and answer polite questions.

> **STUDENT A:** Make a polite request for the given situation.
> **STUDENT B:** Give a typical response.

1. You and (. . .) are sitting at the dinner table. You want the butter.
   → *Student A: (Anna), would you please pass me the butter?*
   Student B: Certainly, I'd be glad to. Here you are.
2. You want to ask your teacher a question.
3. You're at your friend's apartment. You want to use the phone.
4. You're speaking on the phone to your brother. You want him to pick you up at the airport when you arrive home.
5. You want to leave class early. You're speaking to your instructor.

6. You want (. . .) to meet you in front of the library at three this afternoon.

7. You knock on your professor's half-open door. He's sitting at his desk. You want to go in.

8. You want to make an appointment to see Dr. North. You're speaking to her secretary.

9. You are at a gas station. You want the attendant to check the oil.

10. You are in your chemistry class. You're looking at your textbook. On page 100 there is a formula which you do not understand. You want your professor to explain this formula to you.

11. You call your friend. Her name is (. . .). Someone else answers the phone.

12. You want to see (. . .)'s dictionary for a minute.

13. You want a stranger in an airport to keep her eye on your luggage while you get a drink of water.

14. You want (. . .) to tape something on the VCR tonight while you're away at a meeting.

2–4 POLITE REQUESTS WITH *WOULD YOU MIND*

ASKING PERMISSION (a) *Would you mind if I closed the window?* (b) *Would you mind if I used the phone?*	Notice in (a): ***would you mind if I*** is followed by the simple past.★ The meaning in (a): *May I close the window? Is it all right if I close the window? Will it cause you any trouble or discomfort if I close the window?*
TYPICAL RESPONSES No. Not at all. No, of course not. No, that would be fine.	Another typical response might be "unh-unh," meaning *no*.
ASKING SOMEONE ELSE TO DO SOMETHING (c) *Would you mind closing the window?* (d) Excuse me? *Would you mind repeating that?*	Notice in (c): ***would you mind*** is followed by ***-ing*** (a gerund). The meaning in (c): *I don't want to cause you any trouble, but would you please close the window? Would that cause you any inconvenience?*
TYPICAL RESPONSES No. I'd be happy to. Not at all. I'd be glad to.	

★Sometimes in informal spoken English, the simple present is used: *Would you mind if I close the window?* (Note: The simple past does not refer to past time after *would you mind*; it refers to present or future time. See Chart 10-3 for more information.)

☐ **EXERCISE 3:** Using the verb in parentheses, fill in the blank either with *if I* + *the past tense* or with *the -ing form of the verb*. In some of the sentences, either response is possible but the meaning is different.

1. I'm getting tired. I'd like to go home and go to bed. Would you mind (*leave*) ___*if I left*___ early?

2. I'm sorry. I didn't understand what you said. Would you mind (*repeat*) ___*repeating*___ that?

3. A: Are you going to the post office?

   B: Yes.

   A: Would you mind (*mail*) _____ this letter for me?

   B: Not at all.

4. A: Are you coming with us?

   B: I know I promised to go with you, but I'm not feeling very good. Would you mind (*stay*) _____ home?

   A: Of course not.

5. A: I still don't understand how to work this algebra problem. Would you mind (*explain*) _____ it again?

   B: Not at all. I'd be happy to.

6. A: It's getting hot in here. Would you mind (*open*) _____ the window?

   B: No.

7. A: This is probably none of my business, but would you mind (*ask*) _____ you a personal question?

   B: It depends.

8. A: Would you mind (*smoke*) _____?

   B: I'd really rather you didn't.

9. A: Excuse me. Would you mind (*speak*) _____ a little more slowly? I didn't catch what you said.

   B: I'd be happy to.

10. A: I don't like this TV program. Would you mind (*change*) _____ the channel?

    B: Unh-unh.

2-5 USING IMPERATIVE SENTENCES TO MAKE POLITE REQUESTS

(a) **Shut** the door. (b) **Be** on time. (c) **Don't shut** the door. (d) **Don't be** late.	An imperative sentence has an understood subject (*you*), and the verb (e.g., *shut*) is in the simple form. *Shut the door. = (You) shut the door. Be on time. = (You) be on time.* In the negative, **don't** precedes the simple form of the verb.
(e) **Turn** right at the corner. (f) **Shut** the door. (g) **Please shut** the door. **Shut** the door, **please**.	An imperative sentence can be used to give directions, as in (e). An imperative sentence can be used to give an order, as in (f). It can also be used to make a polite request, as in (g), when the word ***please*** is added.*

*Sometimes ***would you/could you*** is added as a tag question (almost as an afterthought) to turn an imperative into a polite request; e.g., *Shut the door, would/could you?* Sometimes, usually in a formal situation, ***won't you*** is added to an imperative as a tag question to make a polite request; e.g., *Have a seat, won't you?* (See Appendix 1, Chart B-4 for information about tag questions.)

☐ **EXERCISE 4—ORAL (BOOKS CLOSED):** Turn the following imperative sentences into polite requests.

Example: Open the window.

Possible responses: Please open the window. Could you please open the window? Would you mind opening the window?

Example: Give me a cup of coffee.

Possible responses: May I please have a cup of coffee? Could you get me a cup of coffee?

1. Turn on the light.
2. Give me that book.
3. Sit down.
4. Say that again.
5. Give me your pen.
6. Pass me the butter.
7. Give me a ride home in your car.
8. Tell me what time it is.
9. Mail these letters if you go to the post office.
10. Close the window and turn on the air conditioner.
11. Let me out of the elevator.

☐ **EXERCISE 5—ORAL (BOOKS CLOSED):** Ask polite questions in the following situations. Use any appropriate modal (***may, could, would,*** *etc.*) or polite imperative.

1. Your plane leaves at six P.M. tomorrow. You want your friend to take you to the airport.
2. You're sitting at your friend's house. A bowl of fruit is sitting on the table. You want an apple.
3. You're in class. You're hot. The window is closed.

4. You're in a car. Your friend's driving. You want her to stop at the next mailbox so you can mail a letter.

5. You're trying to study. Your roommate is playing his music tapes very loudly, and this is bothering you.

6. You call your friend. Someone else answers and tells you that he's out. You want to leave a message.

7. You want your pen. You can't reach it, but your friend can. You want her to hand it to you.

8. You're at a restaurant. You want some more coffee.

9. You're at your friend's house. You want to help her set the dinner table.

10. You're the teacher. You want a student to shut the door.

11. You want to make a telephone call. You're in a store and have to use a pay phone, but you don't have any change. All you have is (*a one-dollar bill*). You ask a clerk for change.

12. You're at a restaurant. You've finished your meal and are ready to leave. You ask the waiter for the check.

13. You call your boss's house. His name is Mr. Smith. You want to talk to him. His wife answers the phone.

14. You're giving a dinner party. Your guests have just arrived. You want to get them something to drink.

15. Your guests have arrived. You want them to sit down.

16. You're walking down the hall of the classroom building. You need to know what time it is. You ask a student you've never met.*

17. You're in the middle of the city. You're lost. You're trying to find the bus station. You stop someone on the street to ask for directions.

18. You call the airport. You want to know what time Flight 62 arrives.

19. You're in a department store. You find a sweater that you like, but you can't find the price tag. You ask the clerk to tell you how much it costs.

20. It's your first day on campus. You're supposed to be at the library for a meeting, but you can't find the library. You ask for information from another student you meet on the sidewalk.

☐ **EXERCISE 6—ORAL/WRITTEN:** What are some common polite requests you have heard or have said in the following places?

1. in this classroom
2. at a restaurant
3. at a clothing store
4. at an airport
5. on the telephone
6. at a service station ➤

---

*The responses to 16 through 20 may include noun clauses. For word order in noun clauses, see Chapter 7.

2-6 EXPRESSING NECESSITY: *MUST, HAVE TO, HAVE GOT TO*

(a) All applicants *must take* an entrance exam. (b) All applicants *have to take* an entrance exam.	*Must* and *have to* both express necessity. In (a) and (b): It is necessary for every applicant to take an entrance exam. There is no other choice. The exam is required.
(c) I'm looking for Sue. I *have to talk* to her about our lunch date tomorrow. I can't meet her for lunch because I *have to go* to a business meeting at 1:00. (d) Where's Sue? I *must talk* to her right away. I have an urgent message for her.	In everyday statements of necessity, *have to* is used more commonly than *must*. *Must* is usually stronger than *have to* and can indicate urgency or stress importance. In (c): The speaker is simply saying, "I need to do this and I need to do that." In (d): The speaker is strongly saying, "This is very important!"
(e) I *have to* ("hafta") be home by eight. (f) He *has to* ("hasta") go to a meeting tonight.	Note: *have to* is usually pronounced "hafta"; *has to* is usually pronounced "hasta."
(g) I *have got to go* now. I have a class in ten minutes. (h) I *have to go* now. I have a class in ten minutes.	*Have got to* also expresses the idea of necessity: (g) and (h) have the same meaning. *Have got to* is informal and is used primarily in spoken English. *Have to* is used in both formal and informal English.
(i) I *have got to go* ("I've gotta go/I gotta go") now.	Usual pronunciation of *got to* is "gotta." Sometimes *have* is dropped in speech: "I gotta do it."
(j) PRESENT or FUTURE I *have to/have got to/must study* tonight. (k) PAST: I *had to study* last night.	The idea of past necessity is expressed by *had to*. There is no other past form for *must* (when it means necessity) or *have got to*.

☐ **EXERCISE 7—ORAL (BOOKS CLOSED):** Answer the questions. Practice pronouncing the usual spoken forms of *have to* and *have got to*.

1. What are some of the things you have to do today or tomorrow?
2. What does (. . .) have to do today?
3. What have you got to do after class?
4. What has (. . .) got to do after class?
5. Can you think of something very important that you must do today or tomorrow?
6. What is something that you had to do yesterday?
7. Ask a classmate a question using *have to* and *what time/where/how often/why*.*

---

*A form of *do* is used with *have to* in questions: e.g., *When does he have to leave?*

2-7 LACK OF NECESSITY AND PROHIBITION: *HAVE TO* AND *MUST* IN THE NEGATIVE

LACK OF NECESSITY (a) Tomorrow is a holiday. We ***don't have to go*** to class. (b) I can hear you. You ***don't have to shout.****	When used in the negative, ***must*** and ***have to*** have different meanings.
	do not have to = *lack of necessity.* In (a): It is not necessary for us to go to class tomorrow because there is a holiday.
PROHIBITION (c) You ***must not look*** in the closet. Your birthday present is hidden there. (d) You ***must not tell*** anyone my secret. Do you promise?	***must not*** = *prohibition* (DO NOT DO THIS!) In (c): Do not look in the closet. I forbid it. Looking in the closet is prohibited.
	Negative contraction: ***mustn't***. (The first "t" is not pronounced: "muss-ənt.")

*Lack of necessity may also be expressed by ***need not*** + *the simple form of a verb:* You ***needn't shout***. The use of ***needn't*** as an auxiliary is chiefly British other than when it is used in certain common expressions such as "You needn't worry."

☐ **EXERCISE 8:** Use ***must not*** or ***do not have to*** in the following.

1. I've already finished all my work, so I ___*don't have to*___ study tonight. I think I'll read for a while.

2. I ___*must not*___ forget to take my key with me.

3. You _____ introduce me to Dr. Gray. We've already met.

4. A person _____ become rich and famous in order to live a successful life.

5. In order to be a good salesclerk, you _____ be rude to a customer.

6. I _____ go to the doctor. I'm feeling much better.

7. A person _____ get married in order to lead a happy and fulfilling life.

8. Johnny! You _____ play with sharp knives.

9. We _____ go to the concert if you don't want to, but it might be good.

10. An entering freshman _____ declare a major immediately. The student may wait a few semesters before deciding upon a major.

11. Bats _____ see in order to avoid obstacles. They can navigate in complete darkness.

12. This is an opportunity that comes once in a lifetime. We _____ _____ let it pass. We must act.

13. If you encounter a growling dog, you _____ show any signs of fear. If a dog senses fear, it is more likely to bite a person.

14. Tigers are magnificent animals. We _____ allow them to become extinct.

15. The class trip to the art museum is optional. You _____ _____ go, but you might enjoy it.

☐ **EXERCISE 9—ORAL (BOOKS CLOSED):** Complete the sentences with your own words.

Example: Students don't have to . . . .
Possible response: Students in elementary school don't have to pay tuition.
Example: Students must not . . . .
Possible response: Students must not cheat during tests.

1. Children must not . . . .
2. Children don't have to . . . .
3. Drivers must not . . . .
4. Drivers don't have to . . . .
5. We don't have to . . . .
6. We must not . . . .
7. (. . .) doesn't have to . . . .
8. (. . .) must not . . . .
9. Waiters must not . . . .
10. Waiters don't have to . . . .
11. I don't have to . . . .
12. I must not . . . .

2-8 ADVISABILITY: *SHOULD, OUGHT TO, HAD BETTER*

(a) You ***should study*** harder. You ***ought to study*** harder. (b) Drivers ***should obey*** the speed limit. Drivers ***ought to obey*** the speed limit.	***Should*** and ***ought to*** have the same meaning: they express advisability. The meaning ranges in strength from a suggestion ("This is a good idea.") to a statement about responsibility or duty ("This is a very important thing to do."). In (a): "This is a good idea. This is my advice." In (b): "This is an important responsibility."
(c) You ***shouldn't leave*** your keys in the car.	Negative contraction: ***shouldn't.*** *
(d) I ***ought to*** ("otta") ***study*** tonight, but I think I'll watch TV instead.	***Ought to*** is sometimes pronounced "otta" in informal speaking.
(e) The gas tank is almost empty. We ***had better stop*** at the next service station. (f) You ***had better take*** care of that cut on your hand soon, or it will get infected.	In meaning, ***had better*** is close to ***should/ought to***, but ***had better*** is usually stronger. Often ***had better*** implies a warning or a threat of possible bad consequences. In (e): If we don't stop at a service station, there will be a bad result. We will run out of gas. Notes: ***Had better*** has a present or future meaning. It is followed by the simple form of a verb. It is more common in speaking than writing.
(g) You***'d better*** take care of it. (h) You ***better*** take care of it. (i) You***'d better not*** be late.	Contraction: ***'d better***, as in (g). Sometimes in speaking, ***had*** is dropped, as in (h). Negative form: ***had better*** + ***not***.

****Ought to*** is not commonly used in the negative. If it is used in the negative, the ***to*** is often dropped: *You **oughtn't (to) leave** your keys in the car.*

☐ **EXERCISE 10—ORAL:** Complete the following sentences.

1. I should study tonight because . . . .
2. I ought to study tonight because . . . .
3. I had better study tonight. If I don't, ...
4. I should wash my clothes today, but . . . .
5. I'd better wash my clothes today, or . . . .
6. It's a beautiful day. We ought to . . . .
7. It looks like rain. If you're going out, you'd better . . . .
8. You'd better obey the speed limit. If . . . .
9. You shouldn't stay up late tonight because . . . .
10. You'd better not stay up late tonight. If you do . . . .

☐ **EXERCISE 11—ORAL (BOOKS CLOSED):** Give advice in the following situations by using **should, ought to,** or **had better**.

Example: I have a test tomorrow.
Response: You should (ought to, had better) study tonight.

1. I'm writing a composition, and there is a word I don't know how to spell.
2. I don't feel good. I think I'm catching a cold.
3. I can't see the blackboard when I sit in the back row.
4. I'm cold.

5. My foot is asleep.
6. I'm homesick.
7. I have a problem with my student visa.
8. My roommate snores and I can't get to sleep.
9. I need to improve my English.
10. I can't stop yawning.
11. My library book is due today.
12. There's no food in my house, and some guests are coming to dinner tonight.
13. I have only twenty-five cents in my pocket, but I need some money to go out tonight.
14. My apartment is a mess, and my mother is coming to visit me tomorrow.
15. I'm about to leave on a trip, but the gas gauge in my car is on empty.
16. I have a toothache.
17. I have the flu.
18. My friend is arriving at the airport this evening. I'm supposed to pick him up, but I've forgotten what time his plane gets in.
19. I have the hiccups.

☐ **EXERCISE 12—ORAL:** Which sentence in the following pairs is stronger? Discuss situations in which a speaker might say these sentences.

1. a. You *should go* to a doctor.
   b. You*'d better go* to a doctor.
2. a. Mary *should go* to work today.
   b. Mary *must go* to work today.
3. a. We*'ve got to go* to class.
   b. We *ought to go* to class.

4. a. I *have to go* to the post office.
   b. I *should go* to the post office.
5. a. We *shouldn't go* into that room.
   b. We *must not go* into that room.
6. a. You*'d better not go* there alone.
   b. You *shouldn't go* there alone.

☐ **EXERCISE 13:** Use either ***should*** or ***must/have to*** in the following. In some sentences either is possible, but the meaning is different.

1. A person _____ eat in order to live.

2. A person _____ eat a balanced diet.

3. If you want to become a doctor, you _____ go to medical school for many years.

4. We _____ go to Colorado for our vacation.

5. According to my academic advisor, I _____ take another English course.

6. I _____ write to my folks tonight, but I think I'll wait and do it tomorrow.

7. You _____ have a passport if you want to travel abroad.

8. Everyone _____ have certain goals in life.

9. Rice _____ have water in order to grow.

10. I _____ go to class, but I don't feel good. I think I'd better stay home.

11. If a door is locked, you _____ use a key to open it.

12. I don't have enough money to take the bus, so I _____ walk home.

13. If you don't know how to spell a word, you _____ look it up in the dictionary.

14. This pie is very good. You _____ try a piece.

15. This pie is excellent! You _____ try a piece.*

2-9 THE PAST FORM OF *SHOULD*

(a) I had a test this morning. I didn't do well on the test because I didn't study for it last night. I **should have studied** last night.	Past form: **should have** + *past participle.* *
(b) You were supposed to be here at 10 P.M., but you didn't come until midnight. We were worried about you. You **should have called** us. (You did not call.)	In (a): "I should have studied" means that studying was a good idea, but I didn't do it. I made a mistake.
	Usual pronunciation of **should have**: "should-of" or "shoulda."
(c) I hurt my back. I **should not have carried** that heavy box up two flights of stairs. (I carried the box and now I am sorry.)	In (c): "I should not have carried" means that I carried something, but it turned out to be a bad idea. I made a mistake.
(d) We went to the movie, but it was a bad movie. We wasted our time and money. We **should not have gone** to the movie.	Usual pronunciation of **should not have**: "shouldn't-of" or "shouldn't'a."

*The past form of **ought to** is **ought to have** + *past participle*. (*I ought to have studied.*) It has the same meaning as the past form of **should**. In the past, **should** is used more commonly than **ought to**. **Had better** is only rarely used in a past form (e.g., *He* **had better have taken** *care of it.*) and usually only in speaking, not writing.

☐ **EXERCISE 14—ORAL:** Make sentences based on the following situations. Use **should have** + *past participle*.

1. Tom made a mistake yesterday. He left the door to his house open, and a bird flew in. He had a terrible time catching the bird.
   → *Tom shouldn't have left the door open.*
2. There was an important meeting yesterday afternoon, but you decided not to go. That was a mistake.
3. Ann didn't feel good a couple of days ago. I told her to see a doctor, but she didn't. That was a mistake. Now she is very sick.
4. I didn't invite Sam to my party. That made him feel bad. I'm sorry I didn't invite him.

———————
*Sometimes in speaking, **must** has the meaning of a very enthusiastic **should**.

5. Mary sold her car. That was a mistake because now she can't take trips to see her friends and relatives.

6. Alex signed a contract to buy some furniture without reading it thoroughly. Now he has discovered that he is paying a lot more money than he expected. He made a mistake.

☐ **EXERCISE 15—ORAL (BOOKS CLOSED):** Use *should have* + *past participle* in your response.

Example: You failed the test because you didn't study.
Response: I should have studied.
Example: You didn't study because you went to a movie.
Response: I shouldn't have gone to a movie.

1. You are cold because you didn't wear a coat.
2. You misspelled a word because you didn't look it up in the dictionary.
3. Your friend is upset because you didn't write him a letter.
4. You are broke now because you spent all your money foolishly.
5. The room is full of flies because you opened the window.
6. You don't have any food for dinner because you didn't go to the grocery store.
7. You overslept this morning because you didn't set your alarm clock.
8. Your friends went to (*New Orleans*) over vacation. They had a good time. You didn't go with them, and now you are sorry.
9. John loved Mary, but he didn't marry her. Now he is unhappy.
10. John loved Mary, and he married her. But now he is unhappy.
11. You didn't have a cup of coffee. Now you are sleepy.
12. You didn't stop for gas, and then you ran out of gas on the highway.
13. You were sick yesterday, but you went to class anyway. Today you feel worse.
14. The weather was beautiful yesterday, but you stayed inside all day.
15. You bought your girlfriend a box of candy for her birthday, but she doesn't like candy.
16. The little girl told a lie. She got into a lot of trouble.
17. You have a stomach ache because you ate (*five hamburgers*).
18. You had to pay a fine because your library book was overdue.
19. You lent your car to (. . .), but s/he had an accident because s/he was driving on the wrong side of the road.
20. When (. . .) fell asleep on the overnight train from (*place name*) to (*place name*), her purse was stolen.

2-10 EXPECTATIONS: *BE SUPPOSED TO* AND *BE TO*

(a) The game *is supposed to begin* at 10:00. (b) The game *is to begin* at 10:00. (c) The committee *is supposed to meet* tomorrow. (d) The committee *is to meet* tomorrow.	*Be supposed to* and *be to* (a form of *be* followed immediately by an infinitive, e.g., *is to begin*) express the idea that someone (I, we, they, the teacher, lots of people, my father, etc.) expects something to happen. *Be supposed to* and *be to* often express expectations about scheduled events or correct procedures. In (a) and (b): The speaker expects the game to begin at 10:00 because that is the schedule. *Be to* is stronger, more definite, than *be supposed to*.
COMPARE: (e) I *should go* to the meeting. I can get some information if I go. Going to the meeting is a good idea.	*Be supposed to* and *be to* also express expectations about behavior; often they give the idea that someone expects a particular person to do something.
(f) I *am supposed to go* to the meeting. My boss told me that he wants me to attend.	*Be supposed to* is close in meaning to *should*, but *be supposed to*, as in (f), gives the idea that someone else expects (requests or requires) this behavior.
COMPARE: (g) I *must be* at the meeting. The meeting can't occur without me because I'm the only one who has certain information.	*Be to* is close in meaning to *must*, but *be to*, as in (h), includes the idea that someone else strongly expects (demands or orders) this behavior.
(h) I *am to be* at the meeting. My boss ordered me to be there. He will accept no excuses.	*Be to* is used to state strong expectations: e.g., rules, laws, instructions, demands, orders.

☐ **EXERCISE 16—ERROR ANALYSIS:** Find and correct the errors in the following sentences.

1. The building custodian supposed to unlock the classrooms every morning.

2. You're not suppose to open that door.

3. Where are we suppose to meet?

4. I have a meeting at seven tonight. I suppose to be there a little early to discuss the agenda.

5. When we go to the store, Annie, you do not suppose to handle the glassware. It might break, and then you'd have to pay for it out of your allowance.

□ **EXERCISE 17—ORAL:** Restate the following rules in sentences with *be to*.

1. NO SMOKING. → *You are not to smoke.*
2. KEEP OFF THE GRASS.
3. NO EATING OR DRINKING IN THIS ROOM.
4. MOVE TO THE REAR OF THE BUS.
5. DO NOT JOKE WITH AIRPORT PERSONNEL WHILE YOUR HAND LUGGAGE IS BEING INSPECTED.
6. USE THE STAIRS IN CASE OF FIRE. DO NOT USE THE ELEVATOR.
7. NO LITTERING.
8. SLOWER TRAFFIC KEEP RIGHT.

□ **EXERCISE 18—ORAL (BOOKS CLOSED):** Practice using *be to*. Make up several sentences using *be to* for each of the following situations.

Example:　　　　The teacher gave the students a writing assignment. Tell us what the students are to do.

Possible response: They are to write a composition./They are to write it about a person they admire./They are to hand it in next Tuesday./They are to write it in ink./They are not to write it in pencil.

1. Jack's back hurt, so he went to a doctor. She gave him some instructions. Tell us what he is to do and what he is not to do.
2. This is your assignment for the next class. (*Supply an assignment.*) Can you repeat to me what you are to do?
3. Your son has some jobs to do before he can go outside and play. What is he to do?
4. You have a new job as a cook. Your boss told you what she expects of you. Can you tell us what she expects of you?
5. You are on a committee to make rules for this school. The committee is writing a list of rules. What does this list include?
6. All of us use the library. What behavior is expected of us? ("*We are to . . . .*")
7. You are in charge of some children at a playground. You want to make sure they understand the rules you set. Tell them the rules. ("*Children, you are to . . . .*")
8. Who lives in an apartment building or dormitory? What is expected of its residents?

□ **EXERCISE 19—ORAL:** Which sentence in each pair is stronger?

1. a. You *have got to wear* your seatbelt.
   b. You *should wear* your seatbelt.
2. a. You *are to wear* your seatbelt.
   b. You *ought to wear* your seatbelt.
3. a. You *must wear* your seatbelt.
   b. You *had better wear* your seatbelt.
4. a. You *have to wear* your seatbelt.
   b. You *are supposed to wear* your seatbelt.
5. a. We *are to bring* our own pencils to the test.
   b. We *are supposed to bring* our own pencils.
6. a. We *are supposed to bring* our own pencils.
   b. We *have to bring* our own pencils.
7. a. We *ought to bring* our own pencils.
   b. We *have got to bring* our own pencils.
8. a. We *had better bring* our own pencils.
   b. We *should bring* our own pencils.

□ **EXERCISE 20—ORAL:** Complete the following and discuss the meaning you wish to express by giving reasons for your statement.

Example: I'd better . . . .
Possible response: I'd better write my mother a letter. (*Reason:* If I don't, there will be a bad result: she'll be angry or start worrying about me or feel hurt.)

1. I should . . . .
2. I'm supposed to . . . .
3. I ought to . . . .
4. I'd better . . . .
5. I have to . . . .
6. I've got to . . . .
7. I am to . . . .
8. I must . . . .
9. I shouldn't . . . .
10. I'm not supposed to . . . .
11. I'd better not . . . .
12. I don't have to . . . .
13. I am not to . . . .
14. I must not . . . .

2–11 MAKING SUGGESTIONS: *LET'S, WHY DON'T, SHALL I/WE*

(a) ***Let's go*** to a movie. (b) ***Let's not go*** to a movie. ***Let's stay*** home instead.	***Let's*** = ***let us***. ***Let's*** is followed by the simple form of a verb. Negative form: ***let's*** + ***not*** + *simple verb*. The meaning of ***let's***: "I have a suggestion for us."
(c) ***Why don't we go*** to a movie? (d) ***Why don't you come*** around seven? (e) ***Why don't I give*** Mary a call?	***Why don't*** is used primarily in spoken English to make a friendly suggestion. In (c): *why don't we go = let's go*. In (d): I suggest that you come around seven. In (e): Should I give Mary a call? Do you agree with my suggestion?
(f) ***Shall I open*** the window? Is that okay with you? (g) ***Shall we leave*** at two? Is that okay? (h) Let's go, ***shall we***? (i) Let's go, ***okay***?	When ***shall*** is used with "I" or "we" in a question, the speaker is usually making a suggestion and asking another person if s/he agrees with this suggestion. Sometimes "shall we?" is used as a tag question after ***let's***. More informally, "okay?" is used as a tag question, as in (i).

□ **EXERCISE 21—ORAL:** Pair up with another student. Together make up a short dialogue (5 to 10 lines) that includes the given sentence(s) and ***why don't***. (Include ***let's***, too, if you wish.) Then present your dialogue to the class.

Example: I don't feel very good.

Dialogue: A: Is something the matter, Carlos?
　　　　　B: *I don't feel very good.*
　　　　　A: Oh? What's wrong?
　　　　　B: My stomach feels a little upset.
　　　　　A: Maybe it's something you ate. *Why don't you go home and rest for a while?*
　　　　　B: I think I will.

1. I don't feel good.
2. I'm hungry.
3. Where should we go for our vacation?
4. I'm sleepy.
5. What a beautiful day it is! We shouldn't stay inside all day.
6. It's hot in here.
7. I don't know what this word means.
8. There's a meeting tonight, but I really don't want to go.

9. I'd like to eat out tonight.

10. The children are bored.

11. I don't like my job.

12. What do you feel like doing tonight?

2-12 MAKING SUGGESTIONS: *COULD*

--What should we do tomorrow? (a) Why don't we go on a picnic? (b) We **could go** on a picnic.	**Could** can be used to make suggestions. (b) is similar to (a) in meaning; i.e., the speaker is suggesting a picnic.
--I'm having trouble in math class. (c) You **should talk** to your teacher.	**Should** gives definite advice. In (c), the speaker is saying: "I believe it is important for you to do this. This is what I recommend."
--I'm having trouble in math class. (d) You **could talk** to your teacher. Or you **could ask** Ann to help you with your math lessons. Or I **could try** to help you.	**Could** offers suggestions or possibilities. In (d), the speaker is saying: "I have some possible suggestions for you. It is possible to do this. Or it is possible to do that."*
--I failed my math class. (e) You **should have talked** to your teacher and gotten some help from her during the term.	**Should have** gives "hindsight advice."** In (e), the speaker is saying: "It was important for you to talk to the teacher, but you didn't do it. You made a mistake."
--I failed my math class. (f) You **could have talked** to your teacher. Or you **could have asked** Ann to help you with your math. Or I **could have tried** to help you.	**Could have** offers "hindsight possibilities."** In (f), the speaker is saying: "You had the chance to do this or that. It was possible for this or that to happen. You missed some good opportunities."

*__Might__ (but not __may__) can also be used to make suggestions (*You __might talk__ to your teacher.*), but the use of __could__ is more common.
**"Hindsight" refers to looking at something after it happens.

☐ **EXERCISE 22:** Discuss Speaker B's use of *should* and *could* in the following dialogues. In your own words, what is Speaker B saying?

1. A: Ted doesn't feel good. He has a bad stomach ache.
   B: He *should see* a doctor.

2. A: Ted doesn't feel good. He has a bad stomach ache. What do you think he should do?
   B: Well, I don't know. He *could see* a doctor. He *could see* Dr. Smith. Or he *could see* Dr. Jones. Or he *could* simply *stay* in bed for a day and hope he feels better tomorrow.

3. A: I need to get to the airport.
   B: You *should take* the airport bus. It's cheaper than a taxi.

4. A: I need to get to the airport.
   B: Well, you *could take* the airport bus. Or you *could take* a taxi. Maybe Fred *could take* you. He has a car.

5. A: I took a taxi to the airport, and it cost me a fortune.
   B: You *should have taken* the airport bus.

6. A: I took a taxi to the airport, and it cost me a fortune.
   B: You *could have taken* the airport bus. Or maybe Fred *could have taken* you.

☐ **EXERCISE 23—ORAL (BOOKS CLOSED):** Answer the questions. Use *could* to suggest possibilities. Use *should* only if you want to give strong, definite advice.

Example: I need to get to the airport. Any suggestions?
Possible response: You could take a taxi or the airport bus. Or I could take you if I can borrow my brother's car.
Possible response: In my opinion, you should take the airport bus.

1. I don't have any plans for this weekend. I need some suggestions.

2. (. . .) and I want to go to a nice restaurant for dinner tonight. Any suggestions?

3. I need to get from here to (*name of a place in this city/town*). Any suggestions?

4. (. . .) needs to buy an umbrella, but s/he doesn't know where to go. S/he needs some suggestions.

5. I'm hungry. I'm going to eat an egg. Give me some suggestions on how to cook it. What are the possibilities?

6. I need to get a car, but it can't be very expensive. Any suggestions?

7. I bought a (*name of a car*), but I'm unhappy with it. In hindsight, can you suggest other possibilities for a kind of car I could have bought?

8. I went to the food store yesterday and bought some bread. That's all. But then when it came time for me to fix myself some dinner, all I had was some bread and butter. Suggest some possibilities of other things I could have bought.

9. I went to (*name of a place*) for my vacation last summer, but I didn't enjoy it. In hindsight, can you suggest some other possibilities that I didn't think of? (I had only five days and a limited amount of money.)

10. (. . .) went to (*name of a restaurant*) for dinner last night, but the food was terrible. Do you have any hindsight suggestions?

2-13 EXPRESSING DEGREES OF CERTAINTY: PRESENT TIME

--Why isn't John in class? **100% sure:** He **is** sick. **95% sure:** He **must be** sick. **less than 50% sure:** $\begin{cases}\text{He } \textbf{\textit{may be}} \text{ sick.} \\ \text{He } \textbf{\textit{might be}} \text{ sick.} \\ \text{He } \textbf{\textit{could be}} \text{ sick.}\end{cases}$	"Degree of certainty" refers to how sure we are—what we think the chances are—that something is true. If we are sure something is true in the present, we don't need to use a modal. For example, if I say, "John is sick," I am sure; I am stating a fact that I am sure is true. My degree of certainty is 100%.
--Why isn't John in class? (a) He **must be** sick. (Usually he is in class every day, but when I saw him last night, he wasn't feeling good. So my best guess is that he is sick today. I can't think of another possibility.)	**Must** is used to express a strong degree of certainty about a present situation, but the degree of certainty is still less than 100%. In (a): The speaker is saying: "Probably John is sick. I have evidence to make me believe that he is sick. That is my logical conclusion, but I do not know for certain."
--Why isn't John in class? (b) He **may be** sick. (c) He **might be** sick. (d) He **could be** sick. (I don't really know. He may be at home watching TV. He might be at the library. He could be out of town.)	**May**, **might**, and **could** are used to express a weak degree of certainty. In (b), (c), and (d): The speaker is saying: "Perhaps, maybe,* possibly John is sick. I am only making a guess. I can think of other possibilities." (b), (c), and (d) have the same meaning.

***Maybe** (spelled as one word) is an adverb: **Maybe** *he is sick*. **May be** (spelled as two words) is a verb form: *He* **may be** *sick*.

☐ **EXERCISE 24—ORAL (BOOKS CLOSED):** From the given information, make your "best guess" by using **must**.

> *Example:* Alice always gets the best grades in the class. Why?
> *Response:* She must study hard./She must be intelligent.

1. (. . .) is yawning. Why?
2. (. . .) is sneezing and coughing. Why?
3. (. . .) is wearing a wedding ring. Why?
4. (. . .) is shivering and has goose bumps. Why?
5. (. . .)'s stomach is growling. Why?
6. (. . .) is scratching his arm. Why?
7. (. . .) is going to get married in five minutes. His/her hands are shaking. Why?

8. (. . .) has already had two glasses of water, but now he/she wants another. Why?
9. (. . .) is smiling. Why?
10. (. . .) is crying. Why?
11. You just picked up a telephone receiver, but there is no dial tone. Why?
12. There is a restaurant in town that is always packed (full). Why?
13. I am in my car. I am trying to start it, but the engine won't turn over. I left my lights on all day. What's wrong?
14. Every night there is a long line of people waiting to get into (*a particular movie*). I wonder why.
15. Don't look at your watch. What time is it?

□ **EXERCISE 25—ORAL (BOOKS CLOSED):** Respond by using "I don't know" + *may/might/could.*

Example: (. . .)'s grammar book isn't on her desk. Where is it?
Response: I don't know. It may/might/could be in her book bag.

1. (. . .) isn't in class today. Where is s/he? (*I don't know. S/he . . . .*)
2. Where does (. . .) live? (*I don't know. S/he . . . .*)
3. What do you think I have in my briefcase/pocket/purse?
4. What kind of watch is (. . .) wearing?
5. I can't find my pen. Do you know where it is?
6. How old do you think (*someone famous*) is?

□ **EXERCISE 26:** Complete the sentences by using ***must*** or ***may/might/could*** with the expressions in the list or with your own words.

be about ten	*be very proud*	✔ *like green*
be at a meeting	*feel terrible*	*miss them very much*
be crazy	*fit Jimmy*	
be rich	*have the wrong number*	

1. A: Have you noticed that Professor Adams wears something green every day?
   B: I know. He ___*must like green.*___

2. A: Ed just bought his wife a diamond necklace with matching earrings.
   B: That's expensive! He _____
   A: He is.

3. A: Look at the man standing outside the window on the fifteenth floor of the building.

   B: He _____

   A: I agree. Only a nut would do something like that.

4. A: Where's Ms. Adams? She's not in her office.

   B: I don't know. She _____

   A: If you see her, would you tell her I'm looking for her?

   B: Certainly, Mr. French.

5. A: Hello?

   B: Hello. May I speak to Ron?

   A: I'm sorry. You _____

      There's no one here by that name.

6. A: I've heard that your daughter recently graduated from law school and that your son has gotten a scholarship to the state university. You _____

      _____

   B: We are.

7. A: You're coughing and sneezing, blowing your nose, and running a fever. You _____

   B: I do.

8. A: This winter jacket is still in good shape, but Tommy has outgrown it.
   Do you think it would fit one of your sons?

   B: Well, it's probably too small for Johnny, too, but it _____

   _____

9. A: How long has it been since you last saw your family?

   B: Over a year.

   A: You _____

   B: I do.

10. A: How old is their daughter now?

    B: Hmmm. I think she was born around the same time our daughter was
    born. She _____

2-14 DEGREES OF CERTAINTY: PRESENT TIME NEGATIVE

100% sure: Sam **isn't** hungry.	
99% sure: { Sam **couldn't be** hungry. / Sam **can't be** hungry. }	
95% sure: Sam **must not be** hungry.	
less than 50% sure: { Sam **may not be** hungry. / Sam **might not be** hungry. }	

(a) Sam doesn't want anything to eat. He **isn't** hungry. He told me his stomach is full. He says he isn't hungry. I believe him.	In (a): The speaker is sure that Sam is not hungry.
(b) Sam **couldn't/can't be** hungry! That's impossible! I just saw him eat a huge meal. He has already eaten enough to fill two grown men. Did he really say he'd like something to eat? I don't believe it.	In (b): The speaker believes that there is no possibility that Sam is hungry (but the speaker is not 100% sure). Notice the negative use: **couldn't** and **can't** forcefully express the idea that the speaker believes something is impossible.
(c) Sam isn't eating his food. He **must not be** hungry. That's the only reason I can think of.	In (c): The speaker is expressing a logical conclusion, a "best guess."
(d) I don't know why Sam isn't eating his food. He **may/might not be** hungry right now. Or maybe he doesn't feel well. Or perhaps he ate just before he got here. Who knows?	In (d): The speaker uses **may not/might not** to mention a possibility.

□ **EXERCISE 27—ORAL:** Complete the sentences by giving your "best guess."

1. A: Sally has flunked every test so far this semester.
   B: She must not . . . *study very hard.*
2. A: Who are you calling?
   B: Dick. The phone is ringing, but there's no answer.
   A: He must not . . . .
3. A: I'm trying to be a good host. I've offered Alice a glass of water, a cup of coffee or tea, a soft drink. She doesn't want anything.
   B: She must not . . . .
4. A: I offered Mr. Chang some nuts, but he refused them. Then I offered him some candy, and he accepted.
   B: He must not . . . .
5. A: Jack seems very lonely to me.
   B: I agree. He must not . . . .
6. A: I've been trying to get Timmy into bed for the past hour, but he's still playing with his toys.
   B: He must not . . . .

□ **EXERCISE 28—ORAL:** Give possible reasons for Speaker B's conclusions.

1. A: Someone is knocking at the door. It might be Mary.
   B: It couldn't be Mary. (*Reason? Mary is in Moscow./Mary went to a movie tonight.*)
2. A: Someone left this wool hat here. I think it belongs to Alex.
   B: It couldn't belong to him. (*Reason?*)
3. A: Someone told me that Fred is in Norway.
   B: That can't be right. He couldn't be in Norway. (*Reason?*)
4. A: Look at that big bird. Is it an eagle?
   B: It couldn't be an eagle. (*Reason?*)
5. A: Someone told me that Jane quit school.
   B: You're kidding! That can't be true. (*Reason?*)

□ **EXERCISE 29—ORAL:** Discuss the meaning of the italicized verbs in the following.

1. **SITUATION:** Anna looks at some figures in her business records:
   $3456 + $7843 = $11,389.

   a. At first glance, she says to herself, "Hmmm. That *may not be* right."
   b. Then she looks at it again and says, "That *must not be* right. 6 + 3 is 9, but 5 + 4 isn't 8."
   c. So she says to herself, "That *couldn't be* right!"
   d. Finally, she adds the figures herself and says, "That *isn't* right."

2. **SITUATION:** Some people are talking about Ed.

   a. Tim says, "Someone told me that Ed quit his job, sold his house, and moved to an island in the Pacific Ocean."

   b. Lucy says, "That *may not be* true."

   c. Linda says, "That *must not be* true."

   d. Frank says, "That *can't be* true."

   e. Don says, "That *isn't* true."

3. **SITUATION:** Tom and his young son hear a noise on the roof.

   a. Tom says, "I wonder what that noise is."

   b. His son says, "It *may be* a bird."

   c. Tom: "It *can't be* a bird. It's running across the roof. Birds don't run across roofs."

   d. His son: "Well, some birds do. It *could be* a big bird that's running fast."

   e. Tom: "No, I think it *must be* some kind of animal. It *might be* a mouse."

   f. His son: "It sounds much bigger than a mouse. It *may be* a dragon!"

   g. Tom: "Son, it *couldn't be* a dragon. We don't have any dragons around here. They exist only in story books."

   h. His son: "It *could be* a little dragon that you don't know about."

   i. Tom: "Well, I suppose it *might be* some kind of lizard."

   j. His son: "I'll go look."

   k. Tom: "That's a good idea."

   l. His son comes back and says, "Guess what, Dad. It's a rat."

4. Make up your own dialogue:

SITUATION: You and your friend are at your home. You hear a noise. You discuss the noise: what *may/might/could/must/may not/couldn't/must not* be the cause. Then you finally find out what is going on.

2-15 DEGREES OF CERTAINTY: PAST TIME

PAST TIME: AFFIRMATIVE		In (a): The speaker is sure.
	--Why wasn't Mary in class?	In (b): The speaker is making a logical conclusion; e.g., "I saw Mary yesterday and found out that she was sick. I assume that is the reason why she was absent. I can't think of any other good reason."
(a)	**100%:** She *was* sick.	
(b)	**95%:** She *must have been* sick.	
(c) **less than 50%:**	$\begin{cases} \text{She } \textit{may have been} \text{ sick.} \\ \text{She } \textit{might have been} \text{ sick.} \\ \text{She } \textit{could have been} \text{ sick.} \end{cases}$	In (c): The speaker is mentioning one possibility.
PAST TIME: NEGATIVE		
(d)	**100%:** Sam *wasn't* hungry.	In (d): The speaker is sure.
(e)	**99%:** $\begin{cases} \text{Sam } \textit{couldn't have been} \text{ hungry.} \\ \text{Sam } \textit{can't have been} \text{ hungry.} \end{cases}$	In (e): The speaker believes that it is impossible for Sam to have been hungry.
(f)	**95%:** Sam *must not have been* hungry.	In (f): The speaker is making a logical conclusion.
(g) **less than 50%:**	$\begin{cases} \text{Sam } \textit{may not have been} \text{ hungry.} \\ \text{Sam } \textit{might not have been} \text{ hungry.} \end{cases}$	In (g): The speaker is mentioning one possibility.

□ **EXERCISE 30—ORAL (BOOKS CLOSED):** Respond first with *may have/might have/could have*. Then use *must have* after you get more information.

Example: Jack was absent yesterday afternoon. Where was he?

Possible response: *I don't know. He may have been at home. He might have gone to a movie. He could have decided to go to the zoo because the weather was so nice.*

Follow-up: What if you overhear him say, "My sister's plane was late yesterday afternoon. I had to wait almost three hours." Now what do you think?

Expected response: *He must have been at the airport to meet his sister's plane.*

1. Jack didn't stay home last night. Where did he go?
   --What if you overhear him say, "I usually go there to study in the evening because it's quiet, and if I need to use any reference books, they're right there."

2. How did Jack get to school today?
   --What if you see him pull some car keys out of his pocket?

3. Jack took a vacation in a warm sunny place. Where do you suppose he went?
   --What if you then overhear him say, "Honolulu is a nice city."

4. Jack visited a person in this class yesterday. Do you know who he visited?
   --What if I say this person (*supply a certain distinguishing characteristic*)?

5. Jack walked into class this morning with a broken arm. What happened?
   --Then you overhear him say, "After this I'm going to watch where I'm going when I'm riding my bicycle."

□ **EXERCISE 31—ORAL:** Discuss the speakers' meanings in the following. Supply possible reasons for each speaker's conclusion.

1. **SITUATION:** Bob didn't come to the meeting.
   Speaker A: He might not have known about it.
   Speaker B: He must not have known about it.
   Speaker C: He couldn't have known about it.
   Speaker D: He didn't know about it.

2. **SITUATION:** Last night in an old mansion, someone killed Mrs. Peacock with a revolver in the dining room.
   Speaker A: The killer might have been Colonel Mustard.
   Speaker B: But it may not have been Colonel Mustard. It could have been Mrs. White, you know.
   Speaker C: It couldn't have been Mrs. White. It can't have been Colonel Mustard either.
   Speaker D: I think it must have been Miss Scarlet.
   Speaker E: No, it wasn't Miss Scarlet, Colonel Mustard, or Mrs. White.

□ **EXERCISE 32:** Complete the dialogues. Use an appropriate form of *must* with the verbs in parentheses. Use the negative if necessary.

1. A: Paula fell asleep in class this morning.
   B: She (*stay up*) _____ *must have stayed up* _____ too late last night.

2. A: Jim is eating everything in the salad but the onions. He's pushed all of the onions over to the side of his plate with his fork.
   B: He (*like*) _____ onions.

3. A: George had to give a speech in front of 500 people.
   B: Whew! That's a big audience. He (*be*) _____
   nervous.
   A: He was, but nobody could tell.

4. A: What time is it?
   B: Well, we came at seven, and I'm sure we've been here for at least an hour. So it (*be*) _____ around eight o'clock.

5. A: My favorite magazine doesn't come in the mail anymore. I wonder why.

B: Did your subscription run out?

A: That's probably the problem. I (*forget*) _____ to renew it.

6. A: I met Marie's husband at the reception and we said hello to each other, but when I asked him a question in English, he just smiled and nodded.

B: He (*speak*) _____ much English.

7. A: Where's Dorothy? I've been looking all over for her.

B: I saw her about ten minutes ago in the living room. Have you looked there?

A: Yes, I've looked everywhere. She (*leave*) _____.

8. A: Listen. Do you hear a noise downstairs?

B: No, I don't hear a thing.

A: You don't? Then something (*be*) _____ wrong with your hearing.

9. A: You have a black eye! What happened?

B: I walked into a door.

A: Ouch! That (*hurt*) _____.

B: It did.

10. A: Who is your teacher?

B: I think his name is Mr. Rock, or something like that.

A: Mr. Rock? Oh, you (*mean*) _____ Mr. Stone.

11. A: I grew up in a small town.

B: That (*be*) _____ dull.

A: It wasn't at all. You can't imagine the fun we had.

12. A: Why are you here so early?

B: Sam told me that the party started at seven o'clock.

A: No, it doesn't start until eight o'clock. You (*misunderstand*) _____ _____.

2–16 DEGREES OF CERTAINTY: FUTURE TIME

100% sure: Kay *will do* well on the test. → *(The speaker feels sure.)*	
90% sure: { She *should do* well on the test. / She *ought to do* well on the test. } → *(The speaker is almost sure.)*	
less than 50% sure: { She *may do* well on the test. / She *might do* well on the test. / She *could do* well on the test. } → *(The speaker is guessing.)*	

(a) Kay has been studying hard. She *should do/ought to do* well on the test tomorrow.	*Should/ought to* can be used to express expectations about future events. In (a): The speaker is saying, "Kay will probably do well on the test. I expect her to do well. That is what I think will happen."
(b) I wonder why Sue hasn't written us. We *should have heard/ought to have heard* from her last week.	The past form of *should/ought to* is used to mean that the speaker expected something that did not occur.

☐ **EXERCISE 33:** Use *will, should/ought to,* or *must* in the following. In some, more than one of the modals is possible. Discuss the meanings that the modals convey.★

1. Look at all the people standing in line to get into that movie. It ___*must*___ be a good movie.

2. Let's go to the lecture tonight. It ___*should/ought to OR will*___ be interesting.

3. Look. Jack's car is in front of his house. He _____ be at home. Let's stop and visit him.

4. A: Hello. May I speak to Jack?

   B: He isn't here right now.

   A: What time do you expect him?

   B: He _____ be home around nine or so.

5. A: Who do you think is going to win the game tomorrow?

   B: Well, our team has better players, so we _____ win, but you never know. Anything can happen in sports.

★COMPARE: *Must* expresses a strong degree of certainty about a *present* situation. (See Chart 2-13.) *Should* and *ought to* express a fairly strong degree of certainty about a *future* situation. *Will* indicates that there is no doubt in the speaker's mind about a future event.

6. A: It's very important for you to be there on time.

   B: I _____ be there at seven o'clock. I promise!

7. A: What time are you going to arrive?

   B: Well, the trip takes about four hours. I think I'll leave sometime around noon, so I _____ get there around four.

8. A: Here are your tickets, Mr. Anton. Your flight _____ depart from Gate 15 on the Blue Concourse at 6:27.

   B: Thank you. Could you tell me where the Blue Concourse is?

9. A: Susie is yawning and rubbing her eyes.

   B: She _____ be sleepy. Let's put her to bed early tonight.

10. A: Martha has been working hard all day. She left for work before dawn this morning.

    B: She _____ be really tired when she gets home this evening.

11. A: Where can I find the address for the University of Chicago?

    B: I'm not sure, but you _____ be able to find that information at the library. The library carries catalogues of most of the universities in the United States.

12. A: When's dinner?

    B: We're almost ready to eat. The rice _____ be done in five minutes.

13. A: Where's your dictionary?

    B: Isn't it on my desk?

    A: No.

    B: Then it must be in the bookcase. You _____ find it on the second shelf. Is it there?

14. Hmmm. I wonder what's causing the delay. Ellen's plane _____ _____ have been here an hour ago.

15. I thought I had a dollar in my billfold, but I don't. I _____ _____ have spent it.

16. Ed has been acting strangely lately. He _____ be in love.

2–17 PROGRESSIVE FORMS OF MODALS

(a) Let's just knock on the door lightly. Tom **may be sleeping**. (*right now*) (b) All of the lights in Ann's room are turned off. She **must be sleeping**. (*right now*)	Progressive form, present time: *modal* **+ be + -ing**. Meaning: *in progress right now*.
(c) Sue wasn't at home last night when we went to visit her. She **might have been studying** at the library. (d) Al wasn't at home last night. He has a lot of exams coming up soon, and he is also working on a term paper. He **must have been studying** at the library.	Progressive form, past time: *modal* **+ have been + -ing**. Meaning: *in progress at a time in the past*.

☐ **EXERCISE 34:** Complete the sentences with the verbs in parentheses. Use *must*, *should*, or *may/might/could*. Use the appropriate progressive forms.

1. Look. Those people who are coming in the door are carrying wet

    umbrellas. It (*rain*) _____ *must be raining* _____.

2. A: Why is Margaret in her room?

    B: I don't know. She (*do*) _____ *may be doing* _____ her homework.

3. A: Do you smell smoke?

    B: I sure do. Something (*burn*) _____.

4. A: The line's been busy for over an hour. Who do you suppose Frank is

    talking to?

    B: I don't know. He (*talk*) _____ to his parents. Or

    he (*talk*) _____ to his sister in Chicago.

5. A: What's all that noise upstairs? It sounds like a herd of elephants.

    B: The children (*play*) _____ some kind of game.

    A: That's what it sounds like to me, too. I'll go see.

6. A: I need to call Howard. Do you know which hotel he's staying at in Boston?

   B: Well, he (*stay*) _____ at the Hilton, but I'm not sure. He (*stay*) _____ at the Holiday Inn.

7. A: What are you doing?

   B: I'm writing a letter to a friend, but I (*study*) _____ _____. I have a test tomorrow.

8. A: Did you know that Andy just quit school and started to hitchhike to Alaska?

   B: What? You (*kid*) _____.

9. A: Did Ed mean what he said about Andy yesterday?

   B: I don't know. He (*kid*) _____ when he said that, but who knows?

10. A: Did Ed really mean what he said yesterday?

    B: No, I don't think so. I think he (*kid*) _____.

2-18 USING *USED TO* (HABITUAL PAST) AND *BE USED TO*

(a) Jack **used to live** in Chicago.	In (a): At a time in the past, Jack lived in Chicago, but he does not live in Chicago now. **Used to** expresses a habit, activity, or situation that existed in the past but which no longer exists.
(b). Mary **is used to** cold weather. (c) Mary **is accustomed to** cold weather.	**Be used to** means **be accustomed to**. (b) and (c) have the same meaning: Living in a cold climate is usual and normal to Mary. Cold weather, snow, and ice do not seem strange to her.
COMPARE: (d) Jack **used to live** in Chicago. (e) Mary **is used to living** in a cold climate. She **is accustomed to living** there.	To express habitual past, **used** is followed by an infinitive, e.g., **to live** as in (d). **Be used to** and **be accustomed to** are followed by an **-ing** verb form (a gerund*), as in (e).
(f) Bob moved to Alaska. After a while he **got used to/got accustomed to** living in a cold climate.	In the expressions **get used to** and **get accustomed to**, **get** means **become**.

*See Chart 4-2, *Using Gerunds as the Objects of Prepositions*.

□ **EXERCISE 35:** Add an appropriate form of *be* if necessary. If no form of *be* is necessary, write Ø in the blank. (The symbol Ø means: "nothing is needed here.")

1. I have lived in Malaysia for a long time. I **_am_** used to consistently warm weather.

2. I **_Ø_** used to live in Finland, but now I live in France.

3. I _____ used to sitting at this desk. I sit here every day.

4. I _____ used to sit in the back of the classroom, but now I prefer to sit in the front row.

5. When I was a child, I _____ used to play games with my friends in a big field near my house after school every day.

6. It's hard for my children to stay inside on a cold, rainy day. They _____ used to playing outside in the big field near our house. They play there almost every day.

7. A teacher _____ used to answering questions. Students, especially good students, always have a lot of questions.

8. People _____ used to believe the world was flat.

9. Mrs. Hansen _____ used to do all of the laundry and cooking for her family. Now the children are older and Mrs. Hansen has gone back to teaching, so the whole family shares these household chores.

10. Trains _____ used to be the main means of cross-continental travel. Today, most people take airplanes for long-distance travel.

11. Ms. Stanton's job requires her to travel extensively throughout the world. She _____ used to traveling by plane.

12. You and I are from different cultures. You _____ used to having fish for breakfast. I _____ used to having cheese and bread for breakfast.

□ **EXERCISE 36—ORAL (BOOKS CLOSED):** Answer the questions in complete sentences.

I. *used to* (*habitual past*)

1. What did you use to do on summer days when you were a child?
2. . . . in class when you were in elementary school?

3. . . . for fun when you were younger?
4. . . . for exercise on weekends?
5. . . . after school was out when you were a teenager?
6. . . . with your family when you were growing up?
7. What was your daily routine when you were living (*in Bangkok*)?
8. How has your way of life changed in the last few years? What did you use to do that you don't do now?

II. *be used to/be accustomed to*

Example: You have to take a bus to school. Are you accustomed to that?
Response: No, I'm not accustomed to taking a bus to school. I'm accustomed to walking to school.

9. You have to get up at 6:30 every morning. Are you used to that? (*No . . . .*)
10. You have to eat your big meal at six o'clock. Are you accustomed to that?
11. Last night you went to bed at one A.M. Are you accustomed to that?
12. You are living (*in a dormitory*). Are you accustomed to that?
13. You have to speak English all the time. Are you used to that?
14. The weather is very cold. You have to wear heavy clothes. Are you used to that?
15. You borrowed your friend's car, so you have to drive a stick-shift car. Are you accustomed to that?
16. You have a roommate. You have to share your room with another person. Are you used to that?
17. Many people in the United States drink coffee with their meals. Are you accustomed to doing that?
18. You live in your own apartment now. You have to make your own breakfast. Are you used to that?

III. *get used to/get accustomed to*

19. What adjustments do young people have to make, what do they have to get used to or accustomed to when they move from their parents' houses into their own apartments?
20. . . . a person who moves from a warm to a cold climate?
21. . . . a student who moves into a dormitory?
22. . . . a woman when she gets married or a man when he gets married?
23. You are living in a new environment. You have had to make adjustments. What have you gotten used to? What haven't you gotten used to or can't you get used to?

2-19 USING *WOULD* TO EXPRESS A REPEATED ACTION IN THE PAST

(a) When I was a child, my father ***would read*** me a story at night before bed. (b) When I was a child, my father ***used to read*** me a story at night before bed.	***Would*** can be used to express *an action* that was repeated regularly in the past. When ***would*** is used to express this idea, it has the same meaning as ***used to*** (*habitual past*). (a) and (b) have the same meaning.
(c) I ***used to live*** in California. He ***used to be*** a Boy Scout. They ***used to have*** a Ford.	When ***used to*** expresses *a situation* that existed in the past, as in (c), ***would*** may not be used as an alternative. ***Would*** is used only for regularly repeated *actions* in the past.

☐ **EXERCISE 37:** In order to practice using ***would*** to express a repeated action in the past, use ***would*** whenever possible in the following sentences. Otherwise, use ***used to***.

1. I (*be*) _____*used to be*_____ very shy. Whenever a stranger came to our house, I (*hide*) _____*would hide*_____ in a closet.

2. I remember my Aunt Susan very well. Every time she came to our house, she (*give*) _____ me a big kiss and pinch my cheek.

3. Illiteracy is still a problem in my country, but it (*be*) _____ _____ much worse.

4. I (*be*) _____ afraid of flying. My heart (*start*) _____ pounding every time I stepped on a plane. But now I'm used to flying and enjoy it.

5. I (*be*) _____ an anthropology major. Once I was a member of an archaeological expedition. Every morning, we (*get*) _____ up before dawn. After breakfast, we (*spend*) _____ our entire day in the field. Sometimes one of us (*find*) _____ a particularly interesting item, perhaps an arrowhead or a piece of pottery. When that happened, other members of the group (*gather*) _____ around to see what had been unearthed.

6. I got a new bicycle when I was ten. My friends (*ask*) _____ _____ to ride it, but for years I (*let, never*) _____ _____ anyone else use it.

7. When my grandfather was a boy and had a cold, his mother (*make*) _____ him go to bed. Then she (*put*) _____ _____ goose fat on his chest.

8. When I was a child, I (*take*) _____ a flashlight to bed with me so that I could read comic books without my parents' knowing about it.

9. Last summer, my sister and I took a camping trip in the Rocky Mountains. It was a wonderful experience. Every morning, we (*wake*) _____ up to the sound of singing birds. During the day, we (*hike*) _____ through woods and along mountain streams. Often we (*see*) _____ deer. On one occasion we saw a bear and quickly ran in the opposite direction.

10. I can remember Mrs. Sawyer's fifth grade class well. When we arrived each morning, she (*sit*) _____ at her desk. She (*smile, always*) _____ and (*say*) _____ _____ hello to each student as he or she entered. When the bell rang, she (*stand*) _____ up and (*clear*) _____ her throat. That was our signal to be quiet. Class was about to begin.

2-20 EXPRESSING PREFERENCE: *WOULD RATHER*

(a) I **would rather go** to a movie tonight *than* **study** grammar. (b) **I'd rather study** history *than* (**study**) biology.	**Would rather** expresses preference. In (a): Notice that the simple form of a verb follows both **would rather** and **than**. In (b): If the verb is the same, it does not have to be repeated after **than**.
--How much do you weigh? (c) **I'd rather not tell** you.	Contraction: **I would = I'd.** Negative form: **would rather + not.**
(d) The movie was okay, but I **would rather have gone** to the concert last night.	The past form: **would rather have +** *past participle*. Usual pronunciation: "I'd rather-of."
(e) **I'd rather be lying** on a beach in Florida *than* (**be**) **sitting** in class right now.	Progressive form: **would rather + be + -ing.**

☐ **EXERCISE 38—ORAL:** Use **would rather** to complete the sentences.

1. A: Do you want to go to the concert tonight?
   B: Not really. I . . . .
2. A: Did you go to the concert last night?
   B: Yes, but I . . . .
3. A: What are you doing right now?
   B: I'm studying grammar, but I . . . .
4. A: Do you want to come with us to the museum tomorrow?
   B: Thanks, but I . . . .
5. A: I . . . than . . . .
   B: Not me. I . . . than . . . .

☐ **EXERCISE 39—ORAL (BOOKS CLOSED):** Answer in complete sentences.

1. You are in (*name of place*) right now. Where would you rather be?
2. What would you rather do than go to class?
3. What did you do last night? What would you have rather done?
4. What are you doing right now? What would you rather be doing?

Begin your answer with "No, I'd rather . . . ."

5. Do you want to go to a movie tonight? (to a concert?) (to the zoo tomorrow?)
6. Do you want to play tennis this afternoon? (go bowling?) (shoot pool?)
7. Do you want to eat at the cafeteria? (at a Chinese restaurant?)
8. Would you like to live in (*name of a city*)?

2–21 USING *CAN* AND *BE ABLE TO*

(a) Tom is strong. He **can lift** that heavy box. (b) I **can play** the piano. I've taken lessons for many years. (c) You **can see** fish at an aquarium. (d) That race car **can go** very fast.	**Can** usually expresses the idea that something is possible because certain characteristics or conditions exist. **Can** combines the ideas of *possibility* and *ability*. In (a): It is possible for Tom to lift that box because he is strong. In (b): It is possible for me to play the piano because I have acquired that ability. In (c): It is possible to see fish at an aquarium because an aquarium has fish. In (d): It is possible for that car to go fast because of its special characteristics.
(e) Dogs can bark, but they **cannot/can't talk**.	Negative form: **cannot** or **can't**. (Also possible, but not as common: **can not**, written as two words.)
COMPARE: (f) I **can walk** to school. It's not far. (g) I **may walk** to school. Or I may take the bus.	In (f): I can walk to school because certain conditions exist. In (g): I am less than 50% certain that I will walk to school.
COMPARE: (h) I'm not quite ready to go, but you **can leave** if you're in a hurry. I'll meet you later. (i) When you finish the test, you **may leave**.	**Can** is also used to give permission. In giving permission, **can** is usually used in informal situations, as in (h); **may** is usually used in formal situations, as in (i).
COMPARE: (j) Tom **can lift** that box. (k) *Uncommon*: Tom **is able to lift** that box. (l) Ann **will be able to lift** that box. Bob **may be able to lift** that box. Sue **should be able to lift** that box. Jim **used to be able to lift** that box.	The use of **be able to** in the simple present (*am/is/are able to*) is uncommon (but possible). **Be able to** is more commonly used in combination with other auxiliaries, as in (l).

☐ **EXERCISE 40:** *Can* is usually pronounced /kən/. *Can't* is usually pronounced /kænt/. Try to determine whether the teacher is saying *can* or *can't* in the following sentences.*

1. The secretary *can/can't* help you.
2. My mother *can/can't* speak English.
3. My friend *can/can't* meet you at the airport.
4. Mr. Smith *can/can't* answer your question.

_____

*Sometimes even native speakers have a little difficulty distinguishing between *can* and *can't*.

5. We *can/can't* come to the meeting.
6. *Can/can't* you come?
7. You *can/can't* take that course.
8. I *can/can't* cook.
9. Our son *can/can't* count to ten.
10. I *can/can't* drive a stick-shift car.

☐ **EXERCISE 41—ORAL:** Make sentences, answer questions, discuss meanings as suggested in the following.

1. Name a physical ability that you have and a physical ability you don't have.
2. Name an acquired ability that you have and an acquired ability you don't have.
3. There's no class tomorrow.
   a. What can you do tomorrow?
   b. What may (might) you do tomorrow?
   c. What are you going to do tomorrow?
4. a. What are the possible ways you can get to school?
   b. What are the possible ways you may get to school tomorrow?
5. What is the difference in use of **can** and **may** in the following?
   a. Sure! You can borrow five dollars from me. You *can pay* me back later.
   b. You *may pay* the bill either in person or by mail.
6. Compare the following, using **can** and **can't**:
   a. people and animals

      (*Example: Birds can fly, but people can't.*)

   b. adults and children
   c. women and men
7. Plan your next vacation and describe what you:
   a. may do on your vacation.
   b. can do on your vacation.
   c. will do on your vacation.
8. Make sentences that include the following verb phrases:
   a. might be able to
   b. will be able to
   c. should be able to
   d. may not be able to
   e. must not be able to
   f. should have been able to
   g. might not have been able to
   h. used to be able to

2-22 PAST ABILITY: *COULD*

(a) When I was younger, I **could run** fast. (*Probable meaning*: I used to be able to run fast, but now I can't run fast.)	In affirmative sentences about past ability, **could** usually means "used to be able to." The use of **could** usually indicates that the ability existed in the past but does not exist now.
(b) Tom has started an exercise program. He **was able to run** two miles yesterday without stopping or slowing down.	If the speaker is talking about an ability to perform an act at one particular time in the past, **was/were able to** can be used in affirmative sentences but not **could**. **Could** is not appropriate in (b).
--*Did you read the news about the mountain climbers?* (c) *INCORRECT:* They **could reach** the top of *Mt. Everest yesterday.* (d) CORRECT: They **were able to reach** the top yesterday. They **managed to reach** the top yesterday. They **reached** the top yesterday.	Note that (c) is incorrect. Instead of **could**, the speaker needs to use **were able to**, **managed to**, or *the simple past*.
(e) They *couldn't reach/weren't able to reach* the top yesterday. (f) Tom *couldn't run/wasn't able to run* five miles yesterday.	In negative sentences, there is no difference between using **could** and **was/were able to**.

☐ **EXERCISE 42—ORAL:** Substitute *could* for the italicized verbs if possible.

1. We had a good time yesterday. We *went* to the zoo. The children *enjoyed* themselves very much. They *saw* polar bears and elephants. (*No substitution of "could" is possible.*)

2. When I lived in St. Louis, I *went* to the zoo whenever I wanted to, but now I live in a small town and the nearest zoo is a long way away. ("*I could go*" *can be used instead of "I went" to give the idea of "used to be able to."*)

3. Usually I don't have time to watch TV, but last night I *watched* the news while I was eating dinner. I *heard* the news about the political situation in my country.

4. When I lived at home with my parents, I *watched* TV every day if I wanted to, but now while I'm going to school, I live in a small apartment and don't have a television set.

5. When I worked as a secretary, I *was able to type* 60 words a minute without making a mistake. My typing skills aren't nearly as good now.

6. Yesterday I *typed* these reports for my boss. I don't type very well, but I *was able to finish* the reports without making too many mistakes.

7. When I went to my favorite fishing hole last Sunday, I *caught* two fish. I *brought* them home and *fixed* them for dinner.

8. When I was a child, the river that flows through our town had plenty of fish. My mother used to go fishing two or three times a week. Usually she *caught* enough for our dinner within an hour or so.

9. Last night Mark and I had an argument about politics. Finally, I *managed to convince* him that I was right.

10. My grandfather was a merchant all his life. He knew how to make a sale by using psychology. He *was able to convince* anyone to buy anything, whether they needed it or not.

11. The game we went to yesterday was exciting. The other team *played* good defense, but my favorite player *managed to score* two goals.

12. At the sale yesterday, I *got* this new hat for half price. Quite a bargain, don't you think?

13. When I ran into Mrs. Forks yesterday, I *recognized* her even though I hadn't seen her for years.

14. The students are finished with this exercise. They *did* it without much trouble.

2–23 SUMMARY CHART OF MODALS AND SIMILAR EXPRESSIONS

AUXILIARY	USES	PRESENT/FUTURE	PAST
may	(1) polite request	*May* I *borrow* your pen?	
	(2) formal permission	You *may leave* the room.	
	(3) less than 50% certainty	--Where's John? He *may be* at the library.	He *may have been* at the library.
might	(1) less than 50% certainty	--Where's John? He *might be* at the library.	He *might have been* at the library.
	(2) polite request (*rare*)	*Might* I *borrow* your pen?	
should	(1) advisability	I *should study* tonight.	I *should have studied* last night
	(2) 90% certainty	She *should do* well on the test. (*future only, not present*)	She *should have done* well on the test.
ought to	(1) advisability	I *ought to study* tonight.	I *ought to have studied* last night.
	(2) 90% certainty	She *ought to do* well on the test. (*future only, not present*)	She *ought to have done* well on the test.

AUXILIARY	USES	PRESENT/FUTURE	PAST
had better	(1) advisability with threat of bad result	You **had better be** on time, or we will leave without you.	(*past form uncommon*)
be supposed to	(1) expectation	Class **is supposed to begin** at 10.	Class **was supposed to begin** at 10.
be to	(1) strong expectation	You **are to be** here at 9:00.	You **were to be** here at 9:00.
must	(1) strong necessity	I **must go** to class today.	I **had to go** to class yesterday.
	(2) prohibition (*negative*)	You **must not** open that door.	
	(3) 95% certainty	Mary isn't in class. She **must be** sick. (*present only*)	Mary **must have been** sick yesterday.
have to	(1) necessity	I **have to go** to class today.	I **had to go** to class yesterday.
	(2) lack of necessity (*negative*)	I **don't have to go** to class today.	I **didn't have to go** to class yesterday.
have got to	(1) necessity	I **have got to go** to class today.	I **had to go** to class yesterday.
will	(1) 100% certainty	He **will be** here at 6:00. (*future only*)	
	(2) willingness	--The phone's ringing. I**'ll get** it.	
	(3) polite request	**Will** you please **pass** the salt?	
be going to	(1) 100% certainty	He **is going to be** here at 6:00. (*future only*)	
	(2) definite plan	I**'m going to paint** my bedroom. (*future only*)	I **was going to paint** my room, but I didn't have time.
can	(1) ability/possibility	I **can run** fast.	I **could run** fast when I was a child, but now I can't.
	(2) informal permission	You **can use** my car tomorrow.	
	(3) informal polite request	**Can** I **borrow** your pen?	
	(4) impossibility (*negative only*)	That **can't be** true!	That **can't have been** true!

(*continued*)

AUXILIARY	USES	PRESENT/FUTURE	PAST
could	(1) past ability		I *could run* fast when I was a child.
	(2) polite request	*Could* I *borrow* your pen? *Could* you *help* me?	
	(3) suggestion	--I need help in math. You *could talk* to your teacher.	You *could have talked* to your teacher.
	(4) less than 50% certainty	--Where's John? He *could be* at home.	He *could have been* at home.
	(5) impossibility *(negative only)*	That *couldn't be* true!	That *couldn't have been* true!
be able to	(1) ability	I *am able to help* you. I *will be able to help* you.	I *was able to help* him.
would	(1) polite request	*Would* you please *pass* the salt? *Would* you *mind* if I left early?	
	(2) preference	I *would rather go* to the park than *stay* home.	I *would rather have gone* to the park.
	(3) repeated action in the past		When I was a child, I *would visit* my grandparents every weekend.
used to	(1) repeated action in the past		I *used to* visit my grandparents every weekend.
shall	(1) polite question to make a suggestion	*Shall* I *open* the window?	
	(2) future with "I" or "we" as subject	I *shall* arrive at nine. (*will* = *more common*)	

Note: Use of modals in reported speech is discussed in Chapter 7. Use of modals in conditional sentences is discussed in Chapter 10.

☐ **EXERCISE 43—ORAL:** Discuss the differences in meaning, if any, in the following groups of sentences.

    1. a. May I use your phone?
       b. Could I use your phone?
       c. Can I use your phone?

2. a. You should take an English course.
   b. You ought to take an English course.
   c. You're supposed to take an English course.
   d. You must take an English course.

3. a. You should see a doctor about that cut on your arm.
   b. You had better see a doctor about that cut on your arm.
   c. You have to see a doctor about that cut on your arm.

4. a. You must not use that door.
   b. You don't have to use that door.

5. a. I will be at your house by six o'clock.
   b. I should be at your house by six o'clock.

6. --*There is a knock at the door. Who do you suppose it is?*
   a. It might be Sally.
   b. It may be Sally.
   c. It could be Sally.
   d. It must be Sally.

7. --*There's a knock at the door. I think it's Mike.*
   a. It may not be Mike.
   b. It couldn't be Mike.
   c. It can't be Mike.

8. --*Where's Jack?*
   a. He might have gone home.
   b. He must have gone home.
   c. He had to go home.

9. a. Each student should have a health certificate.
   b. Each student is to have a health certificate.
   c. Each student must have a health certificate.

10. a. If you're having a problem, you could talk to Mrs. Anderson.
    b. If you're having a problem, you should talk to Mrs. Anderson.

11. a. I've got to go.
    b. I have to go.
    c. I should go.
    d. I'm supposed to go.
    e. I'd better go.
    f. I'd rather go.

12. --*I needed some help.*
    a. You should have asked Tom.
    b. You could have asked Tom.

13. a. When I was living at home, I would go to the beach every weekend with my friends.
    b. When I was living at home, I used to go the beach every weekend with my friends.

☐ **EXERCISE 44:** Use a modal or similar expression with each verb in parentheses. More than one auxiliary may be possible. Use the one that seems most appropriate to you.

1. It looks like rain. We (*shut*) _____ the windows.

2. Ann, (*hand, you*) _____ me that dish? Thanks.

3. I returned a book to the library yesterday. It was two weeks overdue, so I

   (*pay*) _____ a fine of $1.40. I (*return*) _____

   _____ the book when it was due.

4. Spring break starts on the thirteenth. We (*go, not*) _____

   _____ to classes again until the twenty-second.

5. (*Make, I*) _____ an appointment to see Dean

   Witherspoon?

6. Neither of us knows the way to their house. We (*take*) _____

   _____ a map with us or we'll probably get lost.

7. The baby is only a year old, but she (*say, already*) _____

   _____ a few words.

8. You (*tell, not*) _____ Jack about the party. It's a

   surprise birthday party for him.

9. Excuse me. I didn't understand. (*Repeat, you*) _____

   _____ what you said?

10. In the United States, elementary education is compulsory. All children

    (*attend*) _____ six years of elementary school.

11. When I was younger, I (*run*) _____ ten miles without stopping. But now I (*run, not*) _____ more than a mile or two.

12. There was a long line in front of the theater. We (*wait*) _____ _____ almost an hour to buy our tickets.

13. A: I'd like to go to a warm, sunny place next winter. Any suggestions?

    B: You (*go*) _____ to Hawaii or Mexico. Or how about Spain?

14. I don't feel like going to the library to study this afternoon. I (*go*) _____ to the shopping mall than to the library.

15. A: Mrs. Wilson got a traffic ticket. She didn't stop at a stop sign.

    B: That's surprising. Usually she's a very cautious driver and obeys all the traffic laws. She (*see, not*) _____ the sign.

16. Microwave ovens make cooking fast and easy. If you have a microwave, you (*cook*) _____ this frozen dinner in five minutes.

17. Annie, you (*clean*) _____ this mess before Dad gets home. He'll be mad if he sees all this stuff all over the living room floor.

18. A: This is Steve's tape recorder, isn't it?

    B: It (*be, not*) _____ his. He doesn't have a tape recorder, at least not that I know of. It (*belong*) _____ _____ to Lucy or to Linda. They sometimes bring their tape recorders to class.

19. I had a good time when I was a teenager. When my friends and I got together, we (*do*) _____ anything and everything that sounded like fun.

20. A: You're always too tense. It's not good for you. You (*learn*) _____ _____ to relax.

    B: How?

    A: Pay attention to your muscles. When they're tight, take a few long, deep breaths. Deep breaths (*be*) _____ very relaxing.

□ **EXERCISE 45:** Use a modal or similar expression with each verb in parentheses. More than one auxiliary may be possible. Use the one that seems most appropriate to you.

1. Don is putting on a little weight around his middle. He (*get*) _____ _____ more exercise.

2. I'm sleepy. I (*keep, not*) _____ my eyes open. I (*go*) _____ to bed before I fall asleep right here.

3. In my country, a girl and boy (*go, not*) _____ out on a date unless they are accompanied by a chaperone.

4. Jimmy was serious when he said he wanted to be a cowboy when he grew up. We (*laugh, not*) _____ at him. We hurt his feelings.

5. (*Cash, you*) _____ this check for me?

6. This is none of his business. He (*stick, not*) _____ his nose into other people's business.

7. My wife and ten children are coming to join me here. They (*live, not*) _____ in my dormitory room. I (*find*) _____ an apartment.

8. A: (*Speak, I*) _____ to Peggy?

    B: She (*come, not*) _____ to the phone right now. (*Take, I*) _____ message?

9. A: Where are you going?

    B: I (*go*) _____ to the library. I have to do some research for my term paper.

10. A: How are you planning to get to the airport?

    B: By taxi.

    A: You (*take*) _____ a shuttle bus instead. It's cheaper than a taxi. You (*get*) _____ one in front of the hotel. It picks up passengers there on a regular schedule.

11. A: Why didn't you come to the party last night?

    B: I (*study*) _____ .

A: You (*come*) _____. We had a good time.

12. A: Should I go to the University of Iowa or Iowa State University?

B: Think it over for a few days. You (*make, not*) _____
_____ up your mind right now. There's no
hurry.

13. A: The phone's ringing again. Let's not answer it. Just let it ring.

B: No, we (*answer*) _____ it. It (*be*) _____
_____ important.

14. Jane's looking at the test paper the teacher just returned. She's smiling.
She (*pass*) _____ the test.

15. It's not like Tony to be late. He (*be*) _____ here an
hour ago. I hope nothing bad happened.

16. A: This is a great open-air market. Look at all this wonderful fresh fish.
What kind of fish is this?

B: I'm not sure. It (*be*) _____ ocean perch. Let's ask.

17. The teacher called on Sam in class yesterday, but he kept looking out the
window and didn't respond. He (*daydream*) _____.

18. When I arrived home last night, I discovered that I had forgotten my key.
My roommate was asleep, but I (*wake*) _____ him
by knocking loudly on the door.

19. A: Did you enjoy the movie last night?

B: It was okay, but I (*stay*) _____ home and (*watch*)
_____ TV. There was a good program on that I
wanted to catch. I only went because my wife wanted to see the movie.

20. A: Somebody called you while you were out, but she didn't leave her
name.

B: Who did it sound like? Anybody you know?

A: Well, it (*be*) _____ Phyllis, but that's just a
guess. I (*ask*) _____ who was
calling, but I didn't.

B: That's okay.

☐ **EXERCISE 46—ERROR ANALYSIS:** Find and correct the errors in the following.

1. If you have a car, you can traveled around the United States.

2. During class the students must to sit quietly. When the students have questions, they must to raise their hands.

3. When you send for the brochure, you should included a self-addressed, stamped envelope.

4. A film director must has control over every aspect of a movie.

5. When I was a child, I can went to the roof of my house and saw all the other houses and streets.

6. While I was working in the fields, my son would brought me oranges or candy.

7. I used to break my leg in a soccer game three months ago.

8. May you please help me with this?

9. Many students would rather to study on their own than going to classes.

10. We supposed to bring our books to class every day.

☐ **EXERCISE 47—PREPOSITIONS:** Supply appropriate prepositions.

1. I am not familiar __*with*__ that author's works.

2. He doesn't approve _____ smoking.

3. I subscribe _____ several magazines.

4. Water consists _____ oxygen and hydrogen.

5. I became uncomfortable because she was staring _____ me.

6. She hid the candy _____ the children.

7. He never argues _____ his wife.

8. I arrived _____ this country two weeks ago.

9. We arrived _____ the airport ten minutes late.

10. Has Mary recovered _____ her illness?

11. I pray _____ peace.

12. I am envious _____ people who can speak three or four languages fluently.

13. Why are you angry _____ me? Did I do something wrong?

14. They are very patient _____ their children.

15. The students responded _____ the questions.

☐ **EXERCISE 48—PHRASAL VERBS:** Supply appropriate prepositions for the following two-word or three-word verbs.

1. A: Where did you grow ___*up*___?

   B: In Seattle, Washington.

2. A: I'm trying to find yesterday's newspaper. Have you seen it?

   B: I'm afraid I threw it *away/out*. I thought you had finished reading it.

3. A: Don't forget to turn the lights *out/off* before you go to bed.

   B: I won't.

4. A: I have a car, so I can drive us to the festival.

   B: Good.

   A: What time should I pick you ___*up*___?

   B: Any time after five would be fine.

5. A: We couldn't see the show at the outdoor theater last night.

   B: Why not?

   A: It was called ___*off*___ on account of rain.

   B: Did you get a raincheck?

6. A: Thomas looks sad.

   B: I think he misses his girlfriend. Let's try to cheer him ___*up*___.

7. A: I would like to check this book ___*out*___. What should I do?

   B: Take the book to the circulation desk and give the librarian your student I.D.

8. A: What brought ___*about*___ your decision to quit your present job?

   B: I was offered a better job.

9. A: How many people showed ___*up*___ for the meeting yesterday?

   B: About twenty.

10. A: How was your vacation?

    B: I had a great time.

    A: When did you get ___*back*___ home?

    B: A couple of days ago. I had planned to stay a little longer, but I ran ___*out*___ ___*of*___ money.

CHAPTER **3**

The Passive

3-1 FORMING THE PASSIVE

             S   **V**   **O**
ACTIVE: (a) Mary *helped* the boy.
 	
                S   **V**
PASSIVE: (b) The boy ***was helped*** by Mary.
	Form of the passive: ***be*** + *past participle*.

	In the passive, *the object* of an active verb *becomes the subject* of the passive verb: ''the boy'' in (a) becomes the subject of the passive verb in (b). (a) and (b) have the same meaning.
ACTIVE: (c) An accident ***happened***. PASSIVE: (d) *(none)*	Only transitive verbs (verbs that are followed by an object) are used in the passive. It is not possible to use verbs such as ***happen***, ***sleep***, ***come***, and ***seem*** (intransitive verbs) in the passive. (See Appendix 1, Chart A-1.)

	ACTIVE			PASSIVE	
simple present	Mary	*helps*	John.	John	*is helped* by Mary.
present progressive	Mary	*is helping*	John.	John	*is being helped* by Mary.
present perfect	Mary	*has helped*	John.	John	*has been helped* by Mary.
simple past	Mary	*helped*	John.	John	*was helped* by Mary.
past progressive	Mary	*was helping*	John.	John	*was being helped* by Mary.
past perfect	Mary	*had helped*	John.	John	*had been helped* by Mary.
simple future	Mary	*will help*	John.	John	*will be helped* by Mary.
be going to	Mary	*is going to help*	John.	John	*is going to be helped* by Mary.
future perfect*	Mary	*will have helped*	John.	John	*will have been helped* by Mary.

*The progressive forms of the present perfect, past perfect, future, and future perfect are very rarely used in the passive.

□ **EXERCISE 1:** Change the active to the passive by supplying the correct form of *be*.

1. Tom *opens* the door. → The door ____*is*____ *opened* by Tom.

2. Tom *is opening* the door. → The door _____ *opened* by Tom.

3. Tom *has opened* the door. → The door _____ *opened* by Tom.

4. Tom *opened* the door. → The door _____ *opened* by Tom.

5. Tom *was opening* the door. → The door _____ *opened* by Tom.

6. Tom *had opened* the door. → The door _____ *opened* by Tom.

7. Tom *will open* the door. → The door _____ *opened* by Tom.

8. Tom *is going to open* the door. → The door _____ *opened* by Tom.

9. Tom *will have opened* the door. → The door _____ *opened* by Tom.

□ **EXERCISE 2:** Change the active to the passive.

1. Shakespeare *wrote* that play. → *That play was written by Shakespeare.*

2. Bill *will invite* Ann to the party.

3. Alex *is preparing* that report.

4. Waitresses and waiters *serve* customers.

5. The teacher *is going to explain* the lesson.

6. Shirley *has suggested* a new idea.

7. Two horses *were pulling* the farmer's wagon.

8. Kathy *had returned* the book to the library.

9. By this time tomorrow, the president *will have made* the announcement.

10. I *didn't write* that note. Jim *wrote* it.

11. Alice *didn't make* that pie. *Did* Mrs. French *make* it?

12. *Does* Prof. Jackson *teach* that course? I know that Prof. Adams *doesn't teach* it.

13. Mrs. Andrews *hasn't signed* those papers yet. *Has* Mr. Andrews *signed* them yet?

14. *Is* Mr. Brown *painting* your house?

15. His tricks *won't fool* me.

□ **EXERCISE 3:** Change the active to passive if possible. Some verbs are intransitive and cannot be changed.

1. A strange thing happened yesterday. (*no change*)

2. Jackie scored the winning goal. → *The winning goal was scored by Jackie.*

3. My cat died.

4. I agree with Dr. Ikeda's theory.

5. Dr. Ikeda developed that theory.

6. Timmy dropped the cup.

7. The cup fell to the floor.

8. The assistant manager interviewed me.

9. It rained hard yesterday.

10. A hurricane destroyed the small fishing village.

11. Dinosaurs existed millions of years ago.

12. A large vase stands in the corner of our front hallway.

13. The children seemed happy when they went to the zoo.

14. After class, one of the students always erases the chalkboard.

15. The solution to my problem appeared to me in a dream.

3-2 USING THE PASSIVE

(a) Rice *is grown* in India. (b) Our house *was built* in 1890. (c) This olive oil *was imported* from Spain.	Usually the passive is used without a "*by* phrase." The passive is most frequently used when it is not known or not important to know exactly who performs an action. In (a): Rice is grown in India by people, by farmers, by someone. In sentence (a), it is not known or important to know exactly who grows rice in India. (a), (b), and (c) illustrate the most common use of the passive, i.e., without the "*by* phrase."
(d) *Life on the Mississippi was written* by Mark Twain.	The "*by* phrase" is included only if it is important to know who performs an action. In (d), *by Mark Twain* is important information.
(e) My aunt *made* this rug. (*active*) (f) This rug *was made* by my aunt. That rug *was made* by my mother.	If the speaker/writer knows who performs an action, usually the active is used, as in (e).
	The passive may be used with the "*by* phrase" instead of the active when the speaker/writer wants to focus attention on the subject of a sentence. In (f) the focus of attention is on two rugs.

☐ **EXERCISE 4:** Why is the use of the passive appropriate in the following sentences? What would be the active equivalents of the passive sentences?

1. My sweater was made in England.

2. The new highway will be completed sometime next month.

3. Language skills are taught in every school in the country.

4. Beethoven's Seventh Symphony was performed at the concert last night.

5. The World Cup soccer games are being televised all over the world.

6. This composition was written by Ali. That one was written by Yoko.

7. The Washington Monument is visited by hundreds of people every day.

8. The chief writing material of ancient times was papyrus. It was used in Egypt, Greece, and other Mediterranean lands.

9. Parchment, another writing material that was widely used in ancient times, was made from the skins of animals such as sheep and goats. After the hair had been removed, the skins were stretched and rubbed smooth.

10. Paper, the main writing material today, was invented by the Chinese.

□ **EXERCISE 5:** Change the following active sentences to passive sentences if possible. (Some of the verbs are intransitive and cannot be changed.) Keep the same tense. Include the "*by* phrase" only if necessary.

1. People grow corn in Iowa. → *Corn is grown in Iowa.*

2. Peter came here two months ago. (*no change*)

3. Someone made this antique table in 1734.

4. An accident happened at the corner of Fifth and Main.

5. Someone stole my purse.

6. Someone was making the coffee when I walked into the kitchen.

7. Translators have translated that book into many languages.

8. Jim's daughter drew that picture. My son drew this picture.

9. The judges will judge the applicants on the basis of their originality.

10. My sister's plane will arrive at 10:35.

11. Is Professor Rivers teaching that course this semester?

12. When did someone invent the radio?

13. The mail carrier had already delivered the mail by the time I left for school this morning.

14. When is someone going to announce the results of the contest?

15. After the concert was over, hundreds of fans mobbed the rock music star outside the theater.

16. Ever since I arrived here, I have been living in the dormitory because someone told me that it was cheaper to live there than in an apartment.

17. They* are going to build the new hospital next year. They have already built the new elementary school.

18. If you* expose a film to light while you are developing it, you will ruin the negatives.

---

*In #17, *they* is an impersonal pronoun; it refers to "some people" but to no people in particular. In #18, *you* is an impersonal pronoun; it refers to any person or people in general.

3-3 INDIRECT OBJECTS AS PASSIVE SUBJECTS

I.O. **D.O.** (a) Someone gave **Mrs. Lee** an award. (b) **Mrs. Lee** was given an award.	**I.O.** = indirect object. **D.O.** = direct object. Either an indirect object or a direct object may become the subject of a passive sentence.
(c) Someone gave **an award** to Mrs. Lee. (d) **An award** was given to Mrs. Lee.	(a), (b), (c), and (d) have the same meaning. Note in (d): When the direct object becomes the subject, **to** is usually used in front of the indirect object.*

*The omission of **to** is more common in British English than American English: *An award was given Mrs. Lee.*

☐ **EXERCISE 6:** Find the INDIRECT OBJECT in each sentence, and make it the focus of attention by using it as the subject of a passive sentence. Use the "**by** phrase" only if necessary.

1. Someone handed Ann a menu at the restaurant.
   (*indirect object = Ann*) → *Ann was handed a menu at the restaurant.*

2. Indiana University has awarded Peggy a scholarship.

3. Some company paid Fred three hundred dollars in consulting fees.

4. A local advertising company has offered Maria a good job.

5. They will send you a bill at the end of the month.

6. Someone will give the starving people a week's supply of rice as soon as the food supplies arrive in the famine-stricken area.

☐ **EXERCISE 7—ORAL (BOOKS CLOSED):** Change active to passive.

Example: Someone built that house ten years ago.
Response: That house was built ten years ago.

1. Someone invited you to a party.
2. Someone wrote that book in 1987.
3. (. . .) wrote that book in 1987.
4. People grow rice in many countries.
5. The secretary is typing the letter.
6. Someone is televising the game.
7. Teachers teach reading in the first grade.
8. Someone has offered (. . .) a good job.
9. Someone told you to be here at ten.
10. Someone published that book in 1985.
11. Someone has sent (. . .) an invitation to a wedding.
12. Someone made that hat in Mexico.

13. Someone will serve dinner at six.
14. Someone is going to serve dinner at six.
15. Someone will announce the news tomorrow.
16. Someone will give the exam next week.
17. Someone has paid the bill.
18. Someone has made a mistake.
19. Someone has watered the plants.
20. The teacher is giving a test in the next room right now.
21. The teacher is asking you to use the passive.

☐ **EXERCISE 8—ORAL (BOOKS CLOSED):** Use the passive in your response.

Example: Teacher to A: Someone stole your watch.
　　　　　　　　　A: My watch was stolen.
　　　　Teacher to B: What happened to (. . .)'s watch?
　　　　　　　　　B: It was stolen.
Example: Teacher to A: People speak Arabic in many countries.
　　　　　　　　　A: Arabic is spoken in many countries.
　　　　Teacher to B: Is Arabic a common language?
　　　　　　　　　B: Yes. It is spoken in many countries.

1. A: Someone stole your pen.
B: What happened to (. . .)'s pen?

2. A: People speak Spanish in many countries.
B: Is Spanish a common language?

3. A: People play soccer in many countries.
B: Is soccer a popular sport?

4. A: Mark Twain wrote that book.
B: Who is the author of that book?

5. A: You went to a movie last night, but it bored you.
B: Why did (. . .) leave the movie before it ended?

6. A: Someone returned your letter.
B: (. . .) sent a letter last week, but s/he put the wrong address on it. What happened to the letter?

7. A: Someone robbed the bank.
B: What happened to the bank?

8. A: The police caught the bank robber.
B: Did the bank robber get away?

9. A: A judge sent the bank robber to jail.
B: What happened to the bank robber?

10. A: The government requires each international student to have a visa.
B: Is it necessary for international students to have visas?

11. A: Someone established this school in 1900.
B: How long has this school been in existence?

12. A: There is a party tomorrow night. Someone has invited you to go to that party.

B: Is (. . .) going to the party?

13. A: Something confused you.

B: Why did (. . .) ask you a question?

14. A: Someone discovered gold in California in 1848.

B: What happened in California in 1848?

15. A: I read about a village in the newspaper. Terrorists attacked the village.

B: What happened to the village?

16. A: People used candles for light in the seventeenth century.

B: Was electricity used for light in the seventeenth century?

17. A: The pilot flew the hijacked plane to another country.

B: What happened to the hijacked plane?

18. A: When you had car trouble, a passing motorist helped you.

B: Yesterday (. . .) was driving down (*Highway 40*) when suddenly his/her car started to make a terrible noise. So s/he pulled over to the side of the road. Did anyone help him/her?

19. A: Someone had already made the coffee by the time you got up this morning.

B: Did (. . .) have to make the coffee when s/he got up?

20. A: Someone had already sold the chair by the time you returned to the store.

B: Did (. . .) buy the chair?

☐ **EXERCISE 9**: Use the words in the following list to complete the sentences. All of the sentences are passive. Use any appropriate tense.

build	frighten	report
cause	✔ invent	spell
confuse	kill	surprise
divide	offer	surround
expect	order	wear

1. The electric light bulb ____*was invented*____ by Thomas Edison.

2. An island _____ by water.

3. The *-ing* form of "sit" _____ with a double *t*.

4. Even though construction costs are high, a new dormitory _____
   _____ next year.

5. The class was too large, so it _____ into two sections.

6. A bracelet _____ around the wrist.

7. The Johnson's house burned down. According to the inspector, the fire _____ by lightning.

8. Al got a ticket for reckless driving. When he went to traffic court, he _____ to pay a fine of $100.

9. I read about a hunter who _____ by a wild animal.

10. The hunter's fatal accident _____ in the newspaper yesterday.

11. I didn't expect Lisa to come to the meeting last night, but she was there. I _____ to see her there.

12. Last week I _____ a job at a local bank, but I didn't accept.

13. The children _____ in the middle of the night when they heard strange noises in the house.

14. Could you try to explain this math problem to me again? Yesterday in class I _____ by the teacher's explanation.

15. A: Is the plane going to be late?
    B: No. It _____ to be on time.

☐ **EXERCISE 10:** Use active or passive, in any appropriate tense, for the verbs in parentheses.

1. The Amazon valley is extremely important to the ecology of the earth. Forty percent of the world's oxygen (*produce*) _____ there.

2. The game (*win, probably*) _____ by the other team tomorrow. They're a lot better than we are.

3. There was a terrible accident on a busy downtown street yesterday. Dozens of people (*see*) _____ it, including my friend, who (*interview*) _____ by the police.

4. In my country, certain prices (*control*) _____
   by the government, such as the prices of medical supplies. However, other
   prices (*determine*) _____ by how much
   people are willing to pay for a product.

5. Yesterday the wind (*blow*) _____ my hat off my head. I
   had to chase it down the street. I (*want, not*) _____
   to lose it because it's my favorite hat and it (*cost*) _____ a lot.

6. Right now Alex is in the hospital. He (*treat*) _____
   _____ for a bad burn on his hand and arm.

7. Yesterday a purse-snatcher (*catch*) _____ by a dog.
   While the thief (*chase*) _____ by the police, he
   (*jump*) _____ over a fence into someone's yard, where he
   encountered a ferocious dog. The dog (*keep*) _____ the
   thief from escaping.

8. Frostbite may occur when the skin (*expose*) _____ to
   extreme cold. It most frequently (*affect*) _____ the skin of
   the cheeks, chin, ears, fingers, nose, and toes.

9. The first fish (*appear*) _____ on the earth about 500 million
   years ago. Up to now, over 20,000 kinds of fish (*name*) _____
   and (*describe*) _____ by scientists. New species (*discover*)
   _____ every year, so the total increases continually.

10. Proper first aid can save a victim's life, especially if the victim is bleeding
    heavily, has stopped breathing, or (*poison*) _____.

11. The government used to support the school. Today it (*support*) _____
    _____ by private funds as well as by the tuition the
    students pay.

12. Richard Anderson is a former astronaut. Several years ago, at age 52,
    Anderson (*inform*) _____ by his superior at the aircraft
    corporation that he could no longer be a test pilot. He (*tell*) _____
    _____ that he was being relieved of his duties because of
    his age. Claiming age discrimination, he took the corporation to court.

13. In the early 80s, photographs of Mars (*send*) _____ back to earth by unmanned space probes. From these photographs, scientists have been able to make detailed maps of the surface of Mars.

14. A network of lines (*discover*) _____ on Mars' surface by an Italian astronomer around the turn of the century. The astronomer (*call*) _____ these lines "channels," but when the Italian word (*translate*) _____ into English, it became "canals." As a result, some people thought the lines were waterways that (*build*) _____ by some unknown living creatures. We now know that the lines are not really canals. Canals (*exist, not*) _____ on Mars.

3-4 THE PASSIVE FORM OF MODALS AND SIMILAR EXPRESSIONS*

THE PASSIVE FORM: *modal* + ***be*** + *past participle*			
(a) Tom	*will*	*be invited*	to the picnic.
(b) The window	*can't*	*be opened.*	
(c) Children	*should*	*be taught*	to respect their elders.
(d)	*May I*	*be excused*	from class?
(e) This book	*had better*	*be returned*	to the library before Friday.
(f) This letter	*ought to*	*be sent*	before June 1st.
(g) Mary	*has to*	*be told*	about our change in plans.
(h) Fred	*is supposed to*	*be told*	about the meeting.
THE PAST-PASSIVE FORM: *modal* + ***have been*** + *past participle*			
(i) The letter	*should*	*have been sent*	last week.
(j) This house	*must*	*have been built*	over 200 years ago.
(k) Jack	*ought to*	*have been invited*	to the party.

*See Chapter 2 for a discussion of the form, meaning, and use of modals and similar expressions.

□ **EXERCISE 11:** Complete the sentences with the given words, active or passive.

1. James _____*should be told*_____ the news as soon as possible.

   (*should* + *tell*)

2. Someone _____ *should tell* _____ James the news immediately.

 (*should + tell*)

3. James _____ *should have been told* _____ the news a long time ago.

 (*should + tell*)

4. Meat _____ in a refrigerator or it will spoil.

 (*must + keep*)

5. You _____ meat in a refrigerator or it will spoil.

 (*must + keep*)

6. We tried, but the window _____. It was painted shut.

 (*couldn't + open*)

7. I tried, but I _____ the window.

 (*couldn't + open*)

8. Good news! I _____ a job soon. I had an interview at an engineering firm yesterday.

 (*may + offer*)

9. Chris has good news. The engineering firm where she had an interview yesterday _____ her a job soon.

 (*may + offer*)

10. I hope Chris accepts our job offer, but I know she's been having interviews with several companies. She _____

 _____ a job by a competing firm before we made our offer.

 (*may + already + offer**)

11. A competing firm _____ Chris a job before we made our offer.

 (*may + already + offer**)

---

*A midsentence adverb such as **already** may be placed after the first auxiliary (e.g., *might already have come*) or after the second auxiliary (e.g., *might have already come*).

12. The class for next semester is too large. It _____

_____ in half, but there's not enough money in

the budget to hire another teacher.

(*ought to + divide*)

13. Last semester's class was too large. It _____

_____ in half.

(*ought to + divide*)

14. These books _____ to the library

by tomorrow.

(*have to + return*)

15. Polly _____ these books by next Friday.

(*have to + return*)

16. A: Andy, your chores _____

by the time I get home, including taking out the garbage.

B: Don't worry, Mom. I'll do everything you told me to do.

(*had better + finish*)

17. A: Andy, you _____ your chores before

Mom gets home.

B: I know. I'll do them in a minute. I'm busy right now.

(*had better + finish*)

18. This application _____ to the

personnel department soon.

(*be supposed to + send*)

19. Ann's birthday was on the 5th, and now it's already the 8th. Her birthday

card _____ a week ago. Maybe we'd

better give her a call to wish her a belated happy birthday.

(*should + send*)

20. A: Ann didn't expect to see her boss at the labor union meeting.

B: She _____ when she saw him.

A: She was.

(*must + surprise*)

☐ **EXERCISE 12:** Use the verb in parentheses with any appropriate modal or similar expression. All of the sentences are passive. In many sentences, more than one modal is possible. Use the modal that sounds best to you.

1. The entire valley (*see*) _____*can be seen*_____ from their mountain home.

2. He is wearing a gold band on his fourth finger. He (*marry*) _____ _____.

3. According to our teacher, all of our compositions (*write*) _____ _____ in ink. He won't accept papers written in pencil.

4. I found this book on my desk when I came to class. It (*leave*) _____ _____ by one of the students in the earlier class.

5. Five of the committee members will be unable to attend the next meeting. In my opinion, the meeting (*postpone*) _____ _____.

6. A child (*give, not*) _____ everything he or she wants.

7. Your daughter has a good voice. Her interest in singing (*encourage*) _____.

8. Try to speak slowly when you give your speech. If you don't, some of your words (*misunderstand*) _____.

9. Some UFO sightings (*explain, not*) _____ easily. No one is able to explain them easily.

10. What? You tripped over a chair at the party and dropped your plate of food into a woman's lap? You (*embarrass*) _____ _____!

11. She is very lazy. If you want her to do anything, she (*push*) _____ _____.

12. The hospital in that small town is very old and can no longer serve the needs of the community. A new hospital (*built*) _____ _____ years ago.

13. Whales (*save*) _____ from extinction.

14. We can't wait any longer! Something (*do*) _____ immediately!

15. In my opinion, she (*elect*) _____ because she is honest, knowledgeable, and competent.

☐ **EXERCISE 13—ORAL/WRITTEN:** Create sentences from the given subjects and verbs. Use the passive if possible, with or without a "*by* phrase." Use the active only if the verb is intransitive. Make the subject singular or plural as you wish. Use modals as you wish.

Example: tape recorder/make

Possible responses: This tape recorder was made in Korea.
My tape recorder was made in Japan.
The tape recorders we use in lab class were made in the United States.

Example: automobile accident/happen

Possible responses: An automobile accident happened near my apartment building a few days ago.
The automobile accident I read about in the newspaper happened on Highway 5 during rush hour.
The automobile accident Tom told me about must have happened not far from my uncle's house.

1. (*name of a language*)/speak
2. (*kind of game*)/play
3. earthquake/occur
4. news/report
5. steel/produce
6. food/serve
7. dark cloud/appear
8. jeans/wear
9. gold/mine
10. bill/pay

11. (*name of a thing*)/invent
12. (*name of a place/thing*)/discover
13. (*kind of car*)/manufacture
14. computer/cost
15. newspaper/sell
16. I/bite
17. (*name of a person*)/respect
18. friend/agree
19. bride/kiss
20. I/influence
21. movie/show
22. rice/cook
23. rule/obey
24. damage/cause

3-5 STATIVE PASSIVE

(a) The door *is old*. (b) The door *is green*. (c) The door *is locked*.	In (a) and (b): *old* and *green* are adjectives. They describe the door. In (c): *locked* is a past participle. It is used as an adjective. It describes the door.
(d) I locked the door five minutes ago. (e) The door was locked by me five minutes ago. (f) Now the door *is locked*.	The passive form may be used to describe an existing situation or state, as in (f) and (i). No action is taking place. The action happened before. There is no "*by* phrase." The past participle functions as an adjective.
(g) Ann broke the window. (h) The window was broken by Ann. (i) Now the window *is broken*.	When the passive form expresses an existing state rather than an action, it is called the "stative passive."
(j) I *am interested in* Chinese art. (k) He *is satisfied with* his job. (l) Ann *is married to* Alex.	Often stative passive verbs are followed by a preposition other than *by*. (See Appendix 2.)
(m) I don't know where I am. I *am lost*. (n) I can't find my purse. It *is gone*. (o) I *am finished with* my work. (p) I *am done with* my work.	(m) through (p) are examples of idiomatic usage of the passive form. These sentences have no equivalent active sentences.

□ **EXERCISE 14:** Supply the stative passive of the given verbs. Use the SIMPLE PRESENT or the SIMPLE PAST.

1. It is hot in this room because the window (*close*) _____*is closed*_____.

2. Yesterday it was hot in this room because the window (*close*) _____

_____.

3. Sarah is wearing a blouse. It (*make*) _____ of cotton.

4. The door to this room (*shut*) _____ .

5. Jim is sitting quietly. His elbows (*bend*) _____ and his hands (*fold*) _____ in front of him.

6. We can leave now because class (*finish*) _____ .

7. The lights in this room (*turn*) _____ on.

8. This room (*crowd, not*) _____ .

9. We can't go any farther. The car (*stick*) _____ in the mud.

10. We couldn't go any farther. The car (*stick*) _____ in the mud.

11. My room is very neat right now. The bed (*make*) _____ , the floor (*sweep*) _____ , and the dishes (*wash*) _____ .

12. We are ready to sit down and eat dinner. The table (*set*) _____ , the meat and rice (*do*) _____ , and the candles (*light*) _____ .

13. Where's my wallet? It (*go*) _____ ! Did you take it?

14. Hmmm. My dress (*tear*) _____ . I wonder how that happened.

15. Don't look in the hall closet. Your birthday present (*hide*) _____ there.

☐ **EXERCISE 15:** Use an appropriate form of the words in the following list to complete the sentences.

*bear (born)**	*exhaust*	*plug in*
block	*go*	*qualify*
confuse	*insure*	*schedule*
crowd	*locate*	*spoil*
divorce	✔ *lose*	*stick*
do	*marry*	*turn off*

_____

*In the passive, **born** is used as the past participle of **bear** to express "given birth to."

1. Excuse me, sir. Could you give me some directions? I _____ *am lost* _____.

2. Let's find another restaurant. This one _____ too _____. We would have to wait at least an hour for a table.

3. The meeting _____ for tomorrow at nine.

4. That's hard work! I _____. I need to rest for a while.

5. You told me one thing and John told me another. I don't know what to think. I _____.

6. Louise is probably sleeping. The lights in her room _____.

7. Mrs. Wentworth's jewelry _____ for $50,000.

8. I can't open the window. It _____.

9. Carolyn and Joe were married to each other for five years, but now they

_____.

10. I thought I had left my book on this desk, but it isn't here. It _____. I wonder where it is.

11. I'm sorry. You _____ not _____ for the job. We need someone with a degree in electrical engineering.

12. I love my wife. I _____ to a wonderful woman.

13. We can't eat this fruit. It _____. We'll have to throw it away.

14. We'd better call a plumber. The water won't go down the drain. The drain _____.

15. Vietnam _____ in Southeast Asia.

16. A: How old is Jack?

    B: He _____ in 1970.

17. A: The TV set doesn't work.

    B: Are you sure? _____ it _____?

18. A: Is dinner ready?

    B: Not yet. The potatoes _____ not _____. They need another

    ten minutes.

□ **EXERCISE 16:** Supply the correct form of the verb in parentheses and an appropriate preposition. Use the SIMPLE PRESENT.

1. (*interest*)   Carol _____*is interested in*_____ ancient history.

2. (*compose*)   Water _____ hydrogen and

    oxygen.

3. (*accustom*)   I _____ living here.

4. (*terrify*)   Our son _____ dogs.

5. (*finish*)   Pat _____ her composition.

6. (*oppose*)   I _____ that suggestion.

7. (*cover*)   It's winter, and the ground _____

    snow.

8. (*satisfy*)   I _____ the

    progress I have made.

9. (*marry*)   Jack _____ Ruth.

10. (*divorce*)   Elaine _____ Ed.

11. (*acquaint*)   I _____ not _____

    that author's work.

12. (*tire*)   I _____ sitting here.

13. (*relate*)   Your name is Mary Smith. _____ you

    _____ John Smith?

14. (*dedicate*)   Mrs. Robinson works in an orphanage. She _____

    _____ her work.

15. (*disappoint*) Jim got a bad grade because he didn't study. He _____

_____ himself.

16. (*scare*) Bobby is not very brave. He _____

_____ his own shadow.

17. (*commit*) The administration _____

improving the quality of education at our school.

18. (*devote*) Mr. and Mrs. Miller _____

each other.

19. (*dress*) Walter _____ his best suit for his

wedding today.

20. (*do*) We _____ this exercise.

3–6 THE PASSIVE WITH *GET*

(a) **I'm getting hungry**. Let's eat soon. (b) You shouldn't eat so much. You**'ll get fat**. (c) I stopped working because I **got sleepy**.	**Get** may be followed by certain adjectives.*
(d) I stopped working because I **got tired**. (e) They **are getting married** next month. (f) I **got worried** because he was two hours late.	**Get** may also be followed by a past participle. The past participle functions as an adjective; it describes the subject. The passive with **get** is common in spoken English but is often not appropriate in formal writing.

*Some of the common adjectives that follow **get** are: *angry, anxious, bald, better, big, busy, chilly, cold, dark, dizzy, empty, fat, full, good, heavy, hot, hungry, late, light, mad, nervous, old, rich, sick, sleepy, tall, thirsty, warm, well, wet, worse.*

☐ **EXERCISE 17:** Use any appropriate tense of **get** and an adjective from the following list to complete the sentences.

better	hot	nervous
busy	✔ hungry	sleepy
dark	late	well
full	light	wet

1. What time are we going to eat? I _____*am getting hungry*_____.

2. A: I _____.

   B: Why don't you take a nap? A couple of hours of sleep will do you good.

3. A: What time is it?

   B: Almost ten.

   A: I'd better leave soon. It _____. I have to be at the airport by eleven.

4. I didn't have an umbrella, so I _____ while I was waiting for the bus yesterday.

5. Let's turn on the air conditioner. It _____ in here.

6. Every time I have to give a speech, I _____.

7. Would you mind turning on the light? It _____ in here.

8. A: It's a long drive from Denver to here. I'm glad you finally arrived. What time did you leave this morning?

   B: At sunrise. We left as soon as it _____ outside.

9. A: Won't you have another helping?

   B: All of the food is delicious, but I really can't eat much more. I

   _____.

10. Maria's English is improving. It _____.

11. Shake a leg! We don't have all day to finish this work! Get moving! Let's step on it! _____ and finish your work. There's no time to waste.

12. My friend was sick, so I sent him a card. It said, "_____ soon."

□ **EXERCISE 18:** Complete the sentences by using an appropriate form of *get* and the given verbs.

    1. (*tire*)   I think I'll stop working. I ___*am getting tired*___.

    2. (*hurt*)   There was an accident, but nobody _____.

    3. (*lose*)   We didn't have a map, so we _____.

4. (*dress*)   We can leave as soon as you _____.

5. (*marry*)   When _____ you _____?

6. (*accustom*)   How long did it take you to _____ to living here?

7. (*worry*)   Sam was supposed to be home an hour ago, but he still isn't here. I _____.

8. (*upset*)   Just try to take it easy. Don't _____.

9. (*confuse*)   I _____ because everybody gave me different advice.

10. (*do*)   We can leave as soon as I _____ with this work.

11. (*depress*)   Chris _____ when she lost her job, so I tried to cheer her up.

12. (*invite*)   _____ you _____ to the party?

13. (*bore*)   I _____, so I didn't stay for the end of the movie.

14. (*pack*)   I'll be ready to leave as soon as I _____.

15. (*pay*)   I _____ on Fridays. I'll give you the money I owe you next Friday. Okay?

16. (*hire*)   After Ed graduated, he _____ by an engineering firm.

17. (*fire*)   But later he _____ because he didn't do his work.

18. (*finish, not*)   Last night I _____ with my homework until after midnight.

19. (*disgust*)   I _____ and left because the things they were saying at the meeting were ridiculous.

20. (*engage*)   First, they _____.

   (*marry*)   Then, they _____.

   (*divorce*)   Later, they _____.

(*remarry*)   Finally, they _____. Today they
                are very happy.

☐ **EXERCISE 19—ORAL (BOOKS CLOSED):** Create sentences with *get* and the given
   words.

   Example: dizzy
   Possible response: I went on a really neat ride at the carnival last summer. It
                        was a lot of fun even though I got dizzy.

   1. sleepy   13. finished
   2. confused   14. lost
   3. married   15. hurt
   4. wet   16. cheated
   5. done   17. bored
   6. full   18. elected
   7. mad   19. older
   8. nervous   20. worried
   9. excited   21. worse
   10. scared   22. prepared
   11. dressed   23. wrinkled
   12. rich   24. better and better

☐ **EXERCISE 20:** Use active or passive, in any appropriate tense, for the verbs in
   parentheses.

   1. It's noon. The mail should be here soon. It (*deliver, usually*) _____

      _____ sometime between noon and one o'clock.

   2. Only five of us (*work*) _____ in the laboratory

      yesterday when the explosion (*occur*) _____.

      Luckily, no one (*hurt*) _____.

   3. I was supposed to take a test yesterday, but I (*admit, not*) _____

      _____ into the testing room because the

      examination (*begin, already*) _____.

   4. According to a recent survey, out of every dollar an American spends on

      food, thirty-six cents (*spend*) _____ at restaurants.

5. I'm sorry I'm late. I (*hold up*) _____ by the rush hour traffic. It (*take*) _____ thirty minutes for me to get here instead of fifteen.

6. Before she graduated last May, Susan (*offer, already*) _____ _____ a position with a law firm.

7. According to many scientists, solar energy (*use*) _____ _____ extensively in the twenty-first century.

8. I (*study*) _____ English here for the last two months. My English (*get*) _____ better, but I still find it difficult to understand lectures.

9. Right now a student trip to the planetarium (*organize*) _____ _____ by Mrs. Hunt. You can sign up for it at her office.

10. He is a man whose name will go down in history. He (*forget, never*) _____ _____.

11. When you (*arrive*) _____ at the airport tomorrow, you (*meet*) _____ by a friend of mine. He (*wear*) _____ a red shirt and blue jeans. He (*be*) _____ fairly tall and (*have*) _____ dark hair. He (*stand*) _____ _____ near the main entrance. I'm sure you will be able to find him.

12. A: Yesterday (*be*) _____ a terrible day.

    B: What (*happen*) _____?

    A: First, I (*flunk*) _____ a test, or at least I think I did. Then I (*drop*) _____ my books while I (*walk*) _____ across campus and they (*fall*) _____ into a mud puddle. And finally, my bicycle (*steal*) _____ _____.

    B: You should have stayed in bed.

3-7 PARTICIPIAL ADJECTIVES

--The problem confuses the students. (a) It is a **confusing** problem.	The present participle conveys an active meaning. The noun it modifies does something. In (a): The noun "problem" does something; it "confuses." Thus, it is described as a "confusing problem."
--The students are confused by the problem. (b) They are **confused** students.	The past participle conveys a passive meaning. In (b): The students are confused by something. Thus, they are described as "confused students."
--The story amuses the children. (c) It is an **amusing** story.	In (c): The noun "story" performs the action.
--The children are amused by the story. (d) They are **amused** children.	In (d): The noun "children" receives the action.

☐ **EXERCISE 21:** Complete the sentences with the present or past participle of the verbs in italics.

1. The class *bores* the students. It is a _____ *boring* _____ class.

2. The students *are bored by* the class. They are _____ *bored* _____ students.

3. The game *excites* the people. It is an _____ game.

4. The people *are excited by* the game. They are _____ people.

5. The news *surprised* the man. It was _____ news.

6. The man *was surprised by* the news. He was a _____ man.

7. The child *was frightened by* the strange noise. The _____ child sought comfort from her father.

8. The strange noise *frightened* the child. It was a _____ sound.

9. The work *exhausted* the men. It was _____ work.

10. The men *were exhausted*. The _____ men sat down to rest under the shade of a tree.

☐ **EXERCISE 22—ORAL (BOOKS CLOSED):** Respond with a present or past participle.

Example: If a book confuses you, how would you describe the book?
Response: confusing

Example: If a book confuses you, how would you describe yourself?
Response: confused

1. If a story amazes you, how would you describe the story?
   How would you describe yourself?
2. If a story depresses you, how would you describe the story?
   How would you describe yourself?
3. If some work tires you, how would you describe yourself?
   How would you describe the work?
4. If a movie bores you, how would you describe the movie?
   How would you describe yourself?
5. If a painting interests you, how would you describe yourself?
   How would you describe the painting?
6. If a situation embarrasses you . . . .
7. If a book disappoints you . . . .
8. If a person fascinates you . . . .
9. If a situation frustrates you . . . .
10. If a noise annoys you . . . .
11. If an event shocks you . . . .
12. If an experience thrills you . . . .

☐ **EXERCISE 23:** Complete the sentences with the present or past participle of the verbs in parentheses.

1. The (*steal*) _____*stolen*_____ jewelry was recovered.

2. Success in one's work is a (*satisfy*) _____ experience.

3. The dragon was a (*terrify*) _____ sight for the villagers.

4. The (*terrify*) _____ villagers ran for their lives.

5. I found myself in an (*embarrass*) _____ situation last night.

6. A kid accidentally threw a ball at one of the school windows. Someone
   needs to repair the (*break*) _____ window.

7. A (*damage*) _____ earthquake occurred recently.

8. People are still in the process of repairing the many (*damage*)
   _____ buildings and streets.

9. I elbowed my way through the (*crowd*) _____ room.

10. The value endures. A gift given in love has (*endure*) _____
    value.

11. No one lives in that (*desert*) _____ house except a few ghosts.

12. The thief tried to pry open the (*lock*) _____ cabinet.

13. Parents have a (*last*) _____ effect on their children.

14. The (*injure*) _____ woman was put into an ambulance.

15. I bought some (*freeze*) _____ vegetables at the supermarket.

☐ **EXERCISE 24:** Complete the sentences with the present or past participle of the verbs in parentheses.

1. I like to talk with her. I think she is an (*interest*) ___*interesting*___ person.

2. That (*annoy*) _____ buzz is coming from the fluorescent light.

3. Use the (*give*) _____ words in the (*follow*) _____ _____ sentences.

4. The teacher gave us a (*challenge*) _____ assignment, but we all enjoyed doing it.

5. The (*expect*) _____ event did not occur.

6. A (*grow*) _____ child needs a (*balance*) _____ _____ diet.

7. There is an old saying: Let (*sleep*) _____ dogs lie.

8. No one appreciates a (*spoil*) _____ child.

9. At present, the (*lead*) _____ candidate in the senatorial race is Henry Moore.

10. It is sad. She led a (*waste*) _____ life.

11. We had a (*thrill*) _____ but hair-raising experience on our back-packing trip into the wilderness.

12. Last night while we were walking home, we saw an unidentified (*fly*) _____ object.

13. The (*abandon*) _____ car was towed away by a tow truck.

14. Any (*think*) _____ person knows that smoking is a destructive habit.

15. I still have five more (*require*) _____ courses to take.

16. The streets bustled with activity. We made our way through the (*bustle*) _____ streets.

□ **EXERCISE 25—ERROR ANALYSIS:** Find and correct the errors in the following.

Example: I dressed my clothes.
Correction: I got dressed.

1. I am interesting in his ideas.

2. How many peoples have you been invited to the party?

3. When I returned home, everything is quite. I walk to my room, get undress, and going to bed.

4. I didn't go to dinner with them because I had already been eaten.

5. In class yesterday, I was confusing. I didn't understand the lesson.

6. I couldn't move. I was very frighten.

7. When we were children, we are very afraid of caterpillars. Whenever we saw one of these monsters, we run to our house before the caterpillars could attack us. I am still scare when I saw a caterpillar close to me.

8. One day, while the old man was cutting down a big tree near the stream, his axe was fallen into the water. He sat down and begin to cry because he does not have enough money to buy another axe.

☐ **EXERCISE 26—WRITTEN:** Write a brief biography of someone you know well and admire—perhaps a parent, spouse, brother or sister, friend, colleague, or neighbor.

☐ **EXERCISE 27—PHRASAL VERBS:** Supply appropriate prepositions. All of the following contain two-word or three-word verbs.

1. A: When do we have to turn _____ our assignments?

   B: They're due next Tuesday.

2. A: How does this tape recorder work?

   B: Push this button to turn it _____ and push that button to shut it _____ .

3. A: May I borrow your dictionary?

   B: Sure. But please be sure to put it _____ on the shelf when you're finished.

4. A: I'm going to be in your neighborhood tomorrow.

   B: Oh? If you have time, why don't you drop _____ to see us?

   A: Thanks. That sounds like a good idea. Should I call first?

5. A: Look _____ ! A car is coming!

6. A: I got very irritated at one of my dinner guests last night.

   B: Why?

   A: There was an ashtray on the table, but she put her cigarette _____ on one of my good plates!

7. A: I need to talk to Karen.

   B: Why don't you call her _____ ? She's probably at home now.

8. A: Oh-oh. I made a mistake on the check I just wrote.

   B: Don't try to correct the mistake. Just tear _____ the check and throw it _____ .

9. A: Are you here to apply for a job?

   B: Yes.

   A: Here is an application form. Fill it _____ and then give it _____ to me when you are finished.

10. A: Look. There's Mike.

    B: Where?

    A: At the other end of the block, walking toward the administration building. If we run, we can catch _____ with him.

11. A: Is your roommate here?

    B: Yes. She decided to come to the party after all. Have you ever met her?

    A: No, but I'd like to.

    B: She's the one standing over there by the far window. She has a blue dress _____. Come on. I'll introduce you.

12. A: Do you have a date for Saturday night?

    B: Yes. Jim Brock asked me _____. We're going bowling.

CHAPTER *4*

Gerunds and Infinitives

A gerund = *the -ing form of a verb* (e.g., talking, playing, understanding).

An infinitive = *to + the simple form of a verb* (e.g., to talk, to play, to understand).

4–1 GERUNDS: INTRODUCTION

S   **V**
(a) **Playing** tennis is fun.
     S   **V**   **O**
(b) We enjoy **playing** tennis.
               PREP   **O**
(c) He's excited about **playing** tennis.
	A gerund is the **-ing** form of a verb used as a noun.* A gerund is used in the same ways as a noun, i.e., as a subject or an object.
	In (a): **playing** is a gerund. It is used as the subject of the sentence. **Playing tennis** is a gerund phrase.
	In (b): **playing** is used as the object of the verb *enjoy*.
	In (c): **playing** is used as the object of the preposition *about*.

*COMPARE the uses of the **-ing** form of verbs:
    (1) **Walking** is good exercise. → **walking** = a gerund, used as the subject of the sentence.
    (2) Bob and Ann are **playing** tennis. → **playing** = a present participle, used in the present progressive tense.
    (3) I heard some **surprising** news. → **surprising** = a present participle, used as an adjective.

4–2   USING GERUNDS AS THE OBJECTS OF PREPOSITIONS

(a) We talked **about going** to Canada for our vacation. (b) Sue is in charge **of organizing** the meeting. (c) I'm interested **in learning** more about your work.	A gerund is frequently used as the object of a preposition.
(d) I'**m used to sleeping** with the window open. (e) I'**m accustomed to sleeping*** with the window open. (f) I **look forward to going** home next month. (g) They **object to changing** their plans at this late date.	In (d) through (g): **to** is a preposition, not part of an infinitive form, so a gerund follows.
(h) We **talked about not going** to the meeting, but finally decided we should go.	Negative form: **not** precedes a gerund.

*Possible in British English: I'**m accustomed to sleep** with the window open.

☐ **EXERCISE 1:** Supply an appropriate preposition and verb form.

1. Alice isn't interested _____*in*_____ (look) _____*looking*_____ for a new job.

2. Henry is excited _*about*_ (leave) _____ for India.

3. You are capable __*of*__ (do) _____ better work.

4. I have no excuse _*for*_ (be) _____ late.

5. I'm accustomed __*to*__ (have) _____ a big breakfast.

6. The rain prevented us _*from*_ (complete) _____ the work.

7. Fred is always complaining _*about*_ (have) _____ a headache.

8. Instead _*of*_ (study) _____, Margaret went to a ball game with some of her friends.

9. Thank you _*for*_ (help) _____ me carry the packages to the post office.

10. Mrs. Grant insisted _*on*_ (know) _____ the whole truth.

11. He showed us how to get to his house _*by*_ (draw) _____ a map.

12. You should take advantage _*of*_ (live) _____ here.

13. Laura had a good reason _*for*_ (go, not) _____ to class yesterday.

14. Everyone in the neighborhood participated _*in*_ (*search*) _____
_____ for the lost child.

15. I apologized to Diane _*for*_ (*make*) _____ her wait for
me.

16. The weather is terrible tonight. I don't blame you _*for*_ (*want, not*)
_____ to go to the meeting.

17. Who is responsible _*for*_ (*wash*) _____ and (*dry*) _____
_____ the dishes after dinner?

18. In addition _*to*_ (*go*) _____ to school full-time, Sam has
a part-time job.

19. The angry look on his face stopped me _*from*_ (*speak*) _____
_____ my mind.

20. Where should we go for dinner tonight? Would you object _*to*_ (*go*)
_____ to an Italian restaurant?

21. The mayor made another public statement for the purpose _*of*_
(*clarify*) _____ the new tax proposal.

22. The thief was accused _*of*_ (*steal*) _____ a woman's
purse.

23. The jury found Mr. Adams guilty _*of*_ (*take*) _____
money from the company he worked for and (*keep*) _____ it for
himself.

24. Bill isn't used _*to*_ (*wear*) _____ a suit and tie every day.

25. I'm going to visit my family during the school vacation. I'm looking
forward _*to*_ (*eat*) _____ my mother's cooking and
(*sleep*) _____ in my own bed.

☐ **EXERCISE 2—ORAL (BOOKS CLOSED):** To practice using gerunds following
prepositions, answer the questions in complete sentences. Answer either yes or
no.

Example: Your friend was late. Did she apologize?
Response: Yes, she apologized/No, she didn't apologize *for being* late.

1. You were late for class yesterday. Did you have a good excuse?

2. You are going to (*Baltimore*) to visit your friends this weekend. Are you looking forward to that?

3. (. . .) picked up your pen when you dropped it. Did you thank him/her?

4. You're living in a cold/warm climate. Are you accustomed to that?

5. You're going to (*Hawaii*) for a vacation. Are you excited?

6. You interrupted (. . .) while s/he was speaking. Did you apologize?

7. The students in the class did pantomimes. Did all of them participate?

8. Someone broke the window. Do you know who is responsible?

9. Americans usually have their biggest meal in the evening. Are you used to doing that?

10. The weather is hot/cold. What does that prevent you from doing?

11. (. . .) has to do a lot of homework. Does s/he complain?

12. (. . .) was sick last week, so s/he stayed home in bed. Do you blame him/her?

13. (. . .) didn't study last night. What did s/he do instead?

14. You studied grammar last night. What did you do in addition?

☐ **EXERCISE 3:** Using the words in parentheses and any other necessary words, complete the sentences.

1. Ken went to bed instead _____*of finishing his work.*_____ (*finish*)

2. I thanked her _____ (*lend*)

3. I'm excited _____ (*go*)

4. I'm not accustomed _____ (*live*)

5. He didn't feel good. He complained _____ (*have*)

6. I don't blame you _____ (*want, not*)

7. I have a good reason _____ (*be*)

8. It's getting late. I'm worried _____ (*miss*)

9. I'm interested _____ (*find out about*)

10. I'm thinking _____ (*go*)

11. I apologized to my friend _____ (*be*)

12. I am/am not used _____ (*drive*)

13. Nothing can stop me _____ (*go*)

14. In that office, who is responsible _____
(*take care of*)

□ **EXERCISE 4:** *By* + *a gerund or gerund phrase* is used to express how something is done. Complete the following by using *by* + *a gerund or gerund phrase.*

1. Pat turned off the tape recorder _____ *by pushing the stop button.*

2. We show people we are happy _____ *by smiling.*

3. We decided who should get the last piece of pie _____ *by flipping a coin.*

4. We satisfy our hunger _____

5. We quench our thirst _____

6. I found out what "quench" means _____

7. Tony improved his listening comprehension _____

8. Alex caught my attention _____

9. They got rid of the rats in the building _____

10. My dog shows me she is happy _____

11. He accidentally electrocuted himself _____

12. Sometimes teenagers get into trouble with their parents _____

4–3 COMMON VERBS FOLLOWED BY GERUNDS

VERB + GERUND (a) I *enjoy* *playing* tennis.	Gerunds are used as the objects of certain verbs. In (a), *enjoy* is followed by a gerund (*playing*). *Enjoy* is not followed by an infinitive. *INCORRECT: I enjoy to play tennis.* Common verbs that are followed by gerunds are given in the list below.
(b) Joe *quit smoking*. (c) Joe *gave up smoking*.	(b) and (c) have the same meaning. Some two-word verbs, e.g., *give up*, are followed by gerunds. These two-word verbs are given in parentheses in the list below.

VERB + GERUND

enjoy	*quit (give up)*	*avoid*	*consider (think about)*
appreciate	*finish (get through)*	*postpone (put off)*	*discuss (talk about)*
mind	*stop**	*delay*	*mention*
		keep (keep on)	*suggest*

*Stop can also be followed immediately by an infinitive of purpose (*in order to*). See Chart 4-11.
COMPARE the following:
   (1) *stop* + *gerund*: When the professor entered the room, the students *stopped talking*. The room became quiet.
   (2) *stop* + *infinitive of purpose*: While I was walking down the street, I ran into an old friend. I *stopped to talk* to him. (I stopped walking *in order to talk* to him.)

Make sentences from the given words. Use any tense. Use any subject.

Example: enjoy + read the newspaper
Possible response: I enjoy reading the newspaper every morning while I'm
                      having my first cup of coffee.

1. enjoy + watch TV
2. mind + open the window
3. quit + eat desserts
4. give up + eat desserts
5. finish + eat dinner
6. get through + eat dinner
7. stop + rain
8. avoid + answer my question
9. postpone + do my work
10. put off + do my work

11. delay + leave on vacation
12. keep + work
13. keep on + work
14. consider + get a job
15. think about + get a job
16. discuss + go to a movie
17. talk about + go to a movie
18. mention + go to a concert
19. suggest + go on a picnic★
20. enjoy + listen to music

□ **EXERCISE 6:** By using a gerund, supply any appropriate completion for each of the following.

1. When Beth got tired, she stopped ___*working/studying*___ .

2. Would you mind _____ the door? Thanks.

3. The weather will get better soon. We can leave as soon as it quits _____

    _____ .

4. The police officer told him to stop, but the thief kept _____ .

5. I enjoy _____ a long walk every morning.

6. I have a lot of homework tonight, but I'd still like to go with you later on.

    I'll call you when I get through _____ .

7. I would like to have some friends over. I'm thinking about _____

    _____ a dinner party.

8. He told a really funny joke. We couldn't stop _____ !

9. Jack almost had an automobile accident. He barely avoided _____

    _____ another car at the intersection of 4th and Elm.

_____
★For other ways of expressing ideas with *suggest*, see Chart 7-8.

10. Where are you considering _____ for vacation?

11. Sometimes I put off _____ my homework.

12. You have to decide where you want to go to school next year. You can't postpone _____ that decision much longer.

13. I wanted to go to Mexico. Sally suggested _____ to Hawaii.

14. Tony mentioned _____ the bus to school instead of walking.

15. I appreciate _____ able to study in peace and quiet.

4-4 *GO* + GERUND

(a) Did you **go shopping**? (b) We **went fishing** yesterday.	**Go** is followed by a gerund in certain idiomatic expressions to express, for the most part, recreational activities.

GO + GERUND		
go birdwatching	*go hiking*	*go sightseeing*
go boating	*go hunting*	*go skating*
go bowling	*go jogging*	*go skiing*
go camping	*go mountain climbing*	*go sledding*
go canoeing	*go running*	*go swimming*
go dancing	*go sailing*	*go tobogganing*
go fishing	*go shopping*	*go window shopping*

□ **EXERCISE 7—ORAL (BOOKS CLOSED):** Make up sentences using the given words. Use any subject. Use any tense.

Example: enjoy + go
Possible responses: I enjoy going to the zoo./My friend and I enjoyed going to a rock concert last weekend./Where do you enjoy going in (*this city*) when you have some free time?

1. finish + study
2. go + dance
3. keep + work
4. go + bowl
5. think about + wear
6. enjoy + play
7. go + fish
8. talk about + go + swim
9. stop + fight

10. postpone + go + camp
11. quit + rain
12. avoid + go + shop
13. give up + ask
14. discuss + go + birdwatch
15. appreciate + hear
16. mind + wait
17. think about + not go
18. suggest + go + window shop

4-5 COMMON VERBS FOLLOWED BY INFINITIVES

VERB + INFINITIVE (a) I *hope to see* you again soon. (b) He *promised to be* here by ten. (c) He *promised not to be* late.	Some verbs are followed immediately by an infinitive, as in (a) and (b). See Group A below. Negative form: *not* precedes the infinitive.
VERB + (PRO)NOUN + INFINITIVE (d) Mr. Lee *told me to be* here at ten o'clock. (e) The police *ordered the driver to stop*.	Some verbs are followed by a (pro)noun and then an infinitive, as in (d) and (e). See Group B below.
(f) I *was told to be* here at ten o'clock. (g) The driver *was ordered to stop*.	These verbs are followed immediately by an infinitive when they are used in the passive, as in (f) and (g).
(h) I *expect to pass* the test. (i) I *expect Mary to pass* the test.	*Ask, expect, would like, want,* and *need* may or may not be followed by a (pro)noun object. COMPARE: In (h): I think I will pass the test. In (i): I think Mary will pass the test.

GROUP A: VERB + INFINITIVE

hope to	*promise* to	*seem* to	*ask* to
plan to	*agree* to	*appear* to	*expect* to
intend to*	*offer* to	*pretend* to	*would like* to
decide to	*refuse* to		*want* to
			need to

GROUP B: VERB + (PRO)NOUN + INFINITIVE

tell someone to	*invite* someone to	*require* someone to	*ask* someone to
advise someone to**	*permit* someone to	*order* someone to	*expect* someone to
encourage someone to	*allow* someone to	*force* someone to	*would like* someone to
remind someone to	*warn* someone to		*want* someone to
			need someone to

*__Intend__ is usually followed by an infinitive (*I intend to go* to the meeting) but sometimes may be followed by a gerund (*I intend going* to the meeting) with no change in meaning.
A gerund is used after **advise (active) if there is no (pro)noun object. COMPARE:
    (1) He *advised buying* a Fiat.
    (2) He *advised me to buy* a Fiat. I *was advised to buy* a Fiat.

☐ **EXERCISE 8:** Supply any appropriate completion for each sentence. Use either a gerund or an infinitive.

1. We're going out for dinner. Would you like _____*to join*_____ us?

2. Jack avoided _____*looking at*_____ me.

3. Fred didn't have any money, so he decided _____ a job.

4. The teacher reminded the students _____ their assignments.

5. Do you enjoy _____ soccer?

6. I was broke, so Jenny offered _____ me a little money.

7. Mrs. Allen promised _____ tomorrow.

8. My boss expects me _____ this work ASAP.*

9. Jane had to go out again because she had forgotten _____ some bread at the market.

10. Even though I asked the people in front of me at the movie _____ _____ quiet, they kept _____.

11. Joan and David were considering _____ married in June, but they finally decided _____ until August.

12. Our teacher encourages us _____ a dictionary whenever we are uncertain of the spelling of a word.

13. Before I left home to go away to college, my mother reminded me _____ _____ her a letter at least once a week.

14. Mrs. Jackson warned her young son _____ the hot stove. She was afraid he would burn his fingers.

15. I don't mind _____ alone.

16. The teacher seems _____ in a good mood today, don't you think?

17. Lucy pretended _____ the answer to my question.

18. Dick intends _____ his friend a letter.

---

*ASAP = as soon as possible.

19. Residents are not allowed _____ pets in my apartment building.

20. All applicants are required _____ an entrance examination.

21. Someone asked me _____ this package.

22. I was asked _____ this package.

23. Jack advised me _____ a new apartment.

24. I was advised _____ a new apartment.

25. Jack advised _____ a new apartment.

26. Jack suggested _____ a new apartment.

27. Ann advised her sister _____ the plane instead of driving to Oregon.

28. Ann advised _____ the plane instead of driving to Oregon.

☐ **EXERCISE 9:** Using the given ideas and the verb in parentheses, make sentences, both active and passive, by using an infinitive phrase. (Omit the "*by* phrase" in the passive sentences.)

1. The teacher said to me, "You may leave early."

   (*permit*)   *The teacher permitted me to leave early.*   (active)

   _____*I was permitted to leave early.*_____   (passive)

2. The secretary said to me, "Please give this note to Sue."

   (*ask*)   _____   (active)

   _____   (passive)

3. My advisor said to me, "You should take Biology 109."

   (*advise*)   _____

   _____

4. When I went to traffic court, the judge said to me, "You must pay a thirty-dollar fine."

   (*order*)   _____

   _____

5. During the test, the teacher said to Greg, "Keep your eyes on your own paper."

    (*warn*) _____

    _____

6. During the test, the teacher said to Greg, "Don't look at your neighbor's paper."

    (*warn*) _____

    _____

7. At the meeting, the head of the department said to the faculty, "Don't forget to turn in your grade reports by the 15th."

    (*remind*) _____

    _____

8. Mr. Lee said to the children, "Be quiet."

    (*tell*) _____

    _____

9. The hijacker said to the pilot, "You must land the plane."

    (*force*) _____

    _____

10. When I was growing up, my parents said to me, "You may stay up late on Saturday night."

    (*allow*) _____

    _____

11. The teacher said to the students, "Speak slowly and clearly."

    (*encourage*) _____

    _____

12. The teacher always says to the students, "You are supposed to come to class on time."

    (*expect*) _____

    _____

□ **EXERCISE 10—ORAL:** In each of the following, report what someone said by using one of the verbs in the given list to introduce an infinitive phrase.

advise	*expect*	*remind*
allow	*force*	*require*
ask	*order*	*tell*
encourage	*permit*	*warn*

1. The professor said to Alan, "You may leave early."
   → *The professor allowed Alan to leave early.*
   Alan was allowed to leave early.
2. The general said to the soldiers, "Surround the enemy!"
3. Nancy said to me, "Would you please open the window?"
4. Bob said to me, "Don't forget to take your book back to the library."
5. Paul thinks I have a good voice, so he said to me, "You should take singing lessons."
6. Mrs. Anderson was very stern and a little angry. She shook her finger at the children and said to them, "Don't play with matches!"
7. I am very relieved because the Dean of Admissions said to me, "You may register for school late."
8. The law says, "Every driver must have a valid driver's license."
9. My friend said to me, "You should get some automobile insurance."
10. The robber had a gun. He said to me, "Give me all of your money."
11. Before the examination began, the teacher said to the students, "Work quickly."
12. My boss said to me, "Come to the meeting ten minutes early."

□ **EXERCISE 11—ORAL (BOOKS CLOSED): STUDENT A:** Make an active sentence from the given verbs. **STUDENT B:** Change the sentence to the passive; omit the "*by* phrase."

Example: allow me + leave
Student A: The teacher allowed me to leave class early last Friday because I had an appointment with my doctor.
Student B: (. . .) was allowed to leave class early last Friday because s/he had an appointment with his/her doctor.

1. remind me + finish
2. ask me + go
3. permit me + have
4. expect me + be
5. allow me + leave

6. warn me + not go
7. advise me + take
8. tell me + open
9. encourage me + visit
10. require us + take

4-6 COMMON VERBS FOLLOWED BY EITHER INFINITIVES OR GERUNDS

Some verbs can be followed by either an infinitive or a gerund, sometimes with no difference in meaning, as in Group A below, and sometimes with a difference in meaning, as in Group B below.		

GROUP A: VERB + INFINITIVE OR GERUND (WITH NO DIFFERENCE IN MEANING)

begin *start* *continue*	*like* *love* *prefer**	*hate* *can't stand* *can't bear*	The verbs in Group A may be followed by either an infinitive or a gerund with little or no difference in meaning.
(a) It **began to rain**. / It **began raining**. (b) I **started to work**. / I **started working**. (c) It **was beginning to rain**.			In (a): There is no difference between "began to rain" and "began raining." If the main verb is progressive, an infinitive (not a gerund) is usually used.

GROUP B: VERB + INFINITIVE OR GERUND (WITH A DIFFERENCE IN MEANING)

remember *forget*	*regret* *try*	The verbs in Group B may be followed by either an infinitive or a gerund, but the meaning is different.
(d) Judy always **remembers to lock** the door.		**Remember** + *infinitive* = remember to perform responsibility, duty, or task, as in (d).
(e) Sam often **forgets to lock** the door.		**Forget** + *infinitive* = forget to perform a responsibility, duty, or task, as in (e).
(f) I **remember seeing** the Alps for the first time. The sight was impressive.		**Remember** + *gerund* = remember (recall) something that happened in the past, as in (f).
(g) I'**ll never forget seeing** the Alps for the first time.		**Forget** + *gerund* = forget something that happened in the past, as in (g).**
(h) I **regret to tell** you that you failed the test.		**Regret** + *infinitive* = regret to say, to tell someone, to inform someone of some bad news, as in (h).
(i) I **regret lending** him some money. He never paid me back.		**Regret** + *gerund* = regret something that happened in the past, as in (i).
(j) I'**m trying to learn** English.		**Try** + *infinitive* = make an effort, as in (j).
(k) The room was hot. I **tried opening** the window, but that didn't help. So I **tried turning** on the fan, but I was still hot. Finally, I turned on the air conditioner.		**Try** + *gerund* = experiment with a new or different approach to see if it works, as in (k).

*Notice the patterns with **prefer**:
  prefer + *gerund:* I **prefer staying** home **to going** to the concert.
  prefer + *infinitive:* I **prefer to stay** home **than (to) go** to the concert.

****Forget** followed by a gerund usually occurs in a negative sentence or a question: e.g., *I'll never forget, I can't forget, Have you ever forgotten,* and *Can you ever forget* can be followed by a gerund phrase.

□ **EXERCISE 12:** Complete the sentences with the correct form(s) of the verbs in parentheses.

1. I like (*go*) _____*to go/going*_____ to the zoo.

2. The play wasn't very good. The audience started (*leave*) _____ _____ before it was over.

3. After a brief interruption, the professor continued (*lecture*) _____ _____.

4. The children love (*swim*) _____ in the ocean.

5. I hate (*see*) _____ any living being suffer. I can't bear it.

6. I'm afraid of flying. When a plane begins (*move*) _____ down the runway, my heart starts (*race*) _____. Oh-oh! The plane is beginning (*move*) _____ and my heart is starting (*race*) _____.

7. When I travel, I prefer (*drive*) _____ to (*take*) _____ a plane.

8. I prefer (*drive*) _____ rather than (*take*) _____ a plane.

9. I always remember (*turn*) _____ off all the lights before I leave my house.

10. I can remember (*be*) _____ very proud and happy when I graduated.

11. Did you remember (*give*) _____ Jake my message?

12. I remember (*play*) _____ with dolls when I was a child.

13. What do you remember (*do*) _____ when you were a child?

14. What do you remember (*do*) _____ before you leave for class every day?

15. What did you forget (*do*) _____ before you left for class this morning?

16. I'll never forget (*carry*) _____ my wife over the threshold when we moved into our first home.

17. I can't ever forget (*watch*) _____ our team score the winning goal in the last seconds of the game to capture the national championship.

18. Don't forget (*do*) _____ your homework tonight!

19. I regret (*inform*)_____ you that your loan application has not been approved.

20. I regret (*listen, not*) _____ to my father's advice. He was right.

21. When a student asks a question, the teacher always tries (*explain*) _____ _____ the problem as clearly as possible.

22. I tried everything, but the baby still wouldn't stop crying. I tried (*hold*) _____ him. I tried (*feed*) _____ him. I tried (*burp*) _____ him. I tried (*change*) _____ _____ his diapers. Nothing worked.

☐ **EXERCISE 13:** Supply an appropriate form, gerund or infinitive, of the verbs in parentheses.

1. Mary reminded me (*be, not*) _____ *not to be* _____ late for the meeting.

2. We went for a walk after we finished (*clean*) _____ up the kitchen.

3. I forgot (*take*) _____ a book back to the library, so I had to pay a fine.

4. When do you expect (*leave*) _____ on your trip?

5. The baby started (*talk*) _____ when she was about eighteen months old.

6. I don't mind (*wait*) _____ for you. Go ahead and finish (*do*) _____ your work.

7. I've decided (*stay*) _____ here over vacation and (*paint*) _____ my room.

8. We discussed (*quit*) _____ our jobs and (*open*) _____ _____ our own business.

9. I'm getting tired. I need (*take*) _____ a break.

10. Sometimes students avoid (*look*) _____ at the teacher if they don't want (*answer*) _____ a question.

11. The club members discussed (*postpone*) _____ the next meeting until March.

12. Most children prefer (*watch*) _____ television to (*listen*) _____ to the radio.

13. My grandfather prefers (*read*) _____.

14. Did Carol agree (*go*) _____ (*camp*) _____ with you?

15. As the storm approached, the birds quit (*sing*) _____.

16. The taxi driver refused (*take*) _____ a check. He wanted the passenger (*pay*) _____ in cash.

17. The soldiers were ordered (*stand*) _____ at attention.

18. The travel agent advised us (*wait, not*) _____ until August.

□ **EXERCISE 14—ORAL (BOOKS CLOSED):** Make sentences from the following verb combinations. Use "I" or the name of another person in the room. Use any appropriate tense or modal.

Example: like + go
Possible response: I like to go (OR: going) to the park.

Example: ask + open
Possible response: (. . .) asked me to open the window.

1. enjoy + listen
2. offer + lend
3. start + laugh
4. remind + take
5. postpone + go
6. look forward to + see
7. forget + bring
8. remember + go
9. prefer + live
10. finish + do
11. encourage + go
12. can't stand + have to wait
13. continue + walk
14. stop + walk
15. be interested in + learn
16. be used to + speak
17. consider + not go
18. suggest + go

19. advise + go
20. be allowed + have
21. order + stay
22. regret + take
23. want + go + shop
24. like + go + swim
25. keep + put off + do
26. decide + ask + come

□ **EXERCISE 15:** Supply an appropriate form, gerund or infinitive, of the verbs in parentheses.

1. Keep (*talk*) _____. I'm listening to you.

2. The children promised (*play*) _____ more quietly. They promised (*make, not*) _____ so much noise.

3. Linda offered (*look after*) _____ my cat while I was out of town.

4. You shouldn't put off (*pay*) _____ your bills.

5. Alex's dog loves (*chase*) _____ sticks.

6. Mark mentioned (*go*) _____ to the market later today. I wonder if he's still planning (*go*) _____.

7. Fred suggested (*go*) _____ (*ski*) _____ in the mountains this weekend. How does that sound to you?

8. The doctor ordered Mr. Gray (*smoke, not*) _____.

9. Don't tell me his secret. I prefer (*know, not*) _____.

10. Could you please stop (*whistle*) _____? I'm trying (*concentrate*) _____ on my work.

11. She finally decided (*quit*) _____ her present job and (*look for*) _____ another one.

12. Did you remember (*turn off*) _____ the stove?

13. Jack was allowed (*renew*) _____ his student visa.

14. Pat told us (*wait, not*) _____ for her.

15. Mr. Buck warned his daughter (*play, not*) _____ with matches.

16. Would you please remind me (*call*) _____ Alice tomorrow?

17. Liz encouraged me (*throw away*) _____ my old running shoes and (*buy*) _____ a new pair without holes in the toes.

18. I'm considering (*drop out of*) _____ school, (*hitchhike*) _____ to New York, and (*try*) _____ (*find*) _____ a job.

19. Don't forget (*tell*) _____ Jane (*call*) _____ me about (*go*) _____ (*swim*) _____ tomorrow.

20. Sally reminded me (*ask*) _____ you (*tell*) _____ Bob (*remember*) _____ (*bring*) _____ his soccer ball to the picnic.

4–7 REFERENCE LIST OF VERBS FOLLOWED BY GERUNDS

1.	*admit*	He **admitted stealing** the money. *przyznać się*
2.	*advise*	She **advised waiting** until tomorrow.
3.	*anticipate*	I **anticipate having** a good time on vacation. *przewidywać*
4.	*appreciate*	I **appreciated hearing** from them.
5.	*avoid*	He **avoided answering** my question. *unikać, stronić*
6.	*complete*	I finally **completed writing** my term paper.
7.	*consider*	I **will consider going** with you. *rozważać, brać pod uwagę*
8.	*delay*	He **delayed leaving** for school. *zwlekać, opóźniać*
9.	*deny*	She **denied committing** the crime. *zaprzeczać*
10.	*discuss*	They **discussed opening** a new business.
11.	*dislike*	I **dislike driving** long distances.
12.	*enjoy*	We **enjoyed visiting** them.
13.	*finish*	She **finished studying** about ten.
14.	*forget*	I'**ll never forget visiting** Napoleon's tomb.
15.	*can't help*	I **can't help worrying** about it.
16.	*keep*	I **keep hoping** he will come.
17.	*mention*	She **mentioned going** to a movie. *wspomnieć, nadmienić*
18.	*mind*	**Would** you **mind helping** me with this?
19.	*miss*	I **miss being** with my family.
20.	*postpone*	Let's **postpone leaving** until tomorrow. *odwlekać*
21.	*practice*	The athlete **practiced throwing** the ball.
22.	*quit*	He **quit trying** to solve the problem.
23.	*recall*	I **don't recall meeting** him before.
24.	*recollect*	I **don't recollect meeting** him before. *przypominać sobie*
25.	*recommend*	She **recommended seeing** the show.
26.	*regret*	I **regret telling** him my secret. *żałować*
27.	*remember*	I **can remember meeting** him when I was a child.
28.	*resent*	I **resent her interfering** in my business. *czuć się urażonym*
29.	*resist*	I **couldn't resist eating** the dessert. *powstrzymywać się*
30.	*risk*	She **risks losing** all of her money. *ryzykować*
31.	*stop*	She **stopped going** to classes when she got sick.
32.	*suggest*	She **suggested going** to a movie.
33.	*tolerate*	She **won't tolerate cheating** during an examination.
34.	*understand*	I **don't understand his leaving** school.

4–8 REFERENCE LIST OF VERBS FOLLOWED BY INFINITIVES

A. VERBS FOLLOWED IMMEDIATELY BY AN INFINITIVE

1.	*afford*	I **can't afford to buy** it.
2.	*agree*	They **agreed to help** us.
3.	*appear*	She **appears to be** tired.
4.	*arrange*	I'll **arrange to meet** you at the airport.
5.	*ask*	He **asked to come** with us.
6.	*beg*	He **begged to come** with us.
7.	*care*	I **don't care to see** that show.
8.	*claim*	She **claims to know** a famous movie star.
9.	*consent*	She finally **consented to marry** him.

(continued)

10.	*decide*	I **have decided to leave** on Monday.
11.	*demand*	I **demand to know** who is responsible.
12.	*deserve*	She **deserves to win** the prize.
13.	*expect*	I **expect to enter** graduate school in the fall.
14.	*fail*	She **failed to return** the book to the library on time.
15.	*forget*	I **forgot to mail** the letter.
16.	*hesitate*	**Don't hesitate to ask** for my help.
17.	*hope*	Jack **hopes to arrive** next week.
18.	*learn*	He **learned to play** the piano.
19.	*manage*	She **managed to finish** her work early.
20.	*mean*	I **didn't mean to hurt** your feelings.
21.	*need*	I **need to have** your opinion.
22.	*offer*	They **offered to help** us.
23.	*plan*	I **am planning to have** a party.
24.	*prepare*	We **prepared to welcome** them.
25.	*pretend*	He **pretends not to understand**.
26.	*promise*	I **promise not to be** late.
27.	*refuse*	I **refuse to believe** his story.
28.	*regret*	I **regret to tell** you that you failed.
29.	*remember*	I **remembered to lock** the door.
30.	*seem*	That cat **seems to be** friendly.
31.	*struggle*	I **struggled to stay** awake.
32.	*swear*	She **swore to tell** the truth.
33.	*threaten*	She **threatened to tell** my parents.
34.	*volunteer*	He **volunteered to help** us.
35.	*wait*	I **will wait to hear** from you.
36.	*want*	I **want to tell** you something.
37.	*wish*	She **wishes to come** with us.

Handwritten note next to 33: Qretn ... zaopozic, zaqroza l

B. VERBS FOLLOWED BY A (PRO)NOUN + AN INFINITIVE

38.	*advise*	She **advised me to wait** until tomorrow.
39.	*allow*	She **allowed me to use** her car.
40.	*ask*	I **asked John to help** us.
41.	*beg*	They **begged us to come**.
42.	*cause*	Her laziness **caused her to fail**.
43.	*challenge*	She **challenged me to race** her to the corner.
44.	*convince*	I couldn't **convince him to accept** our help.
45.	*dare*	He **dared me to do** better than he had done.
46.	*encourage*	He **encouraged me to try** again.
47.	*expect*	I **expect you to be** on time.
48.	*forbid*	I **forbid you to tell** him.
49.	*force*	They **forced him to tell** the truth.
50.	*hire*	She **hired a boy to mow** the lawn.
51.	*instruct*	He **instructed them to be careful**.
52.	*invite*	Harry **invited the Johnsons to come** to his party.
53.	*need*	We **needed Chris to help** us figure out the solution.
54.	*order*	The judge **ordered me to pay** a fine.
55.	*permit*	He **permitted the children to stay** up late.
56.	*persuade*	I **persuaded him to come** for a visit.
57.	*remind*	She **reminded me to lock** the door.
58.	*require*	Our teacher **requires us to be** on time.
59.	*teach*	My brother **taught me to swim**.
60.	*tell*	The doctor **told me to take** these pills.
61.	*urge*	I **urged her to apply** for the job.
62.	*want*	I **want you to be** happy.
63.	*warn*	I **warned you not to drive** too fast.

☐ **EXERCISE 16—ORAL (BOOKS CLOSED):** Complete the sentence with *doing it* or *to do it*.

Example: I promise . . . .
Response: . . . to do it.

1. I enjoyed . . . .
2. I can't afford . . . .
3. She didn't allow me . . . .
4. We plan . . . .
5. Please remind me . . . .
6. I am considering . . . .
7. They postponed . . . .
8. He persuaded me . . . .
9. I don't mind . . . .
10. He avoided . . . .
11. I refused . . . .
12. I hope . . . .
13. She convinced me . . . .
14. He mentioned . . . .
15. I expect . . . .
16. I encouraged him . . .
17. I warned him not . . . .
18. We prepared . . . .
19. I don't recall . . . .
20. We decided . . . .
21. They offered . . . .
22. When will you finish . . . .
23. Did you practice . . . .
24. She agreed . . . .
25. Keep . . . .
26. Stop . . . .
27. I didn't force him . . . .
28. I couldn't resist . . . .
29. How did he manage . . . .
30. He admitted . . . .
31. He denied . . . .
32. I didn't mean . . . .
33. She swore . . . .
34. I volunteered . . . .
35. He suggested . . . .
36. He advised me . . . .
37. He struggled . . . .
38. I don't want to risk . . . .
39. He recommended . . . .
40. I miss . . . .

(To the teacher: Repeat the exercise by having the students complete the sentences with their own words.)

☐ **EXERCISE 17:** Complete the sentences with the correct form, gerund or infinitive, of the words in parentheses.

1. Margaret challenged me (*race*) _____ her across the pool.

2. David volunteered (*bring*) _____ some food to the reception.

3. The students practiced (*pronounce*) _____ the "th" sound in the phrase "these thirty-three dirty trees."

4. In the fairy tale, the wolf threatened (*eat*) _____ a girl named Little Red Riding Hood.

5. Susie! How many times do I have to remind you (*hang up*) _____

   _____ your coat when you get home from school?

6. The horses struggled (*pull*) _____ the wagon out of the mud.

7. Janice demanded (*know*) _____ why she had been fired.

8. My skin can't tolerate (*be*) _____ in the sun all day long. I

   get sunburned easily.

9. I avoided (*tell*) _____ Mary the truth because I knew she

   would be angry.

10. Fred Washington claims (*be*) _____ a descendant of

    George Washington.

11. Alex broke the antique vase. I'm sure he didn't mean (*do*) _____

    it.

12. I urged Al (*return*) _____ to school and (*finish*) _____

    _____ his education.

13. Mrs. Freeman can't help (*worry*) _____ about her

    children.

14. Children, I forbid you (*play*) _____ in the street. There's

    too much traffic.

15. My little cousin is a blabbermouth! He can't resist (*tell*) _____

    everyone my secrets!

16. I appreciate your (*take*) _____ the time to help me.

17. I can't afford (*buy*) _____ a new car.

18. Ted managed (*change*) _____ my mind.

19. I think Sam deserves (*have*) _____ another chance.

20. Julie finally admitted (*be*) _____ responsible for the

    problem.

21. I don't recall ever (*hear*) _____ you mention his name

    before.

22. She keeps (*promise*) _____ (*visit*) _____

    us, but she never does.

23. He keeps (hope) _____ and (pray) _____

that things will get better.

24. I finally managed (persuade) _____ Jane (stay)

_____ in school and (finish) _____ her

degree.

4–9 USING GERUNDS AS SUBJECTS; USING *IT* + INFINITIVE

(a) **Riding** *with a drunk driver* is dangerous.	A gerund is frequently used as the subject of a sentence, as in (a).
(b) **To ride** *with a drunk driver* is dangerous. (c) **It** is dangerous **to ride** *with a drunk driver.*	Sometimes an infinitive is used as the subject of a sentence, as in (b). However, an infinitive is more commonly used with *it*, as in (c). The word *it* refers to and has the same meaning as the infinitive phrase at the end of the sentence.*

*Sometimes a gerund is used with *it* when the speaker is talking about a particular situation and wants to give the idea of "while": *Tom was drunk. It was dangerous **riding** with him.* = *We were in danger while we were riding with him.*

☐ **EXERCISE 18—ORAL:** Complete the sentences. Use gerund phrases as subjects.

1. . . . isn't easy. → *Climbing to the top of a mountain isn't easy.*
2. . . . is hard.
3. . . . is usually a lot of fun.
4. . . . is boring.
5. . . . can be interesting.
6. . . . was a good experience.
7. Does . . . sound like fun to you?
8. . . . is considered impolite in my country.

☐ **EXERCISE 19—ORAL:** Restate the sentences by changing a sentence with a gerund as the subject to a sentence with *it* + *an infinitive phrase*, and vice-versa.

1. Teasing animals is cruel. → *It is cruel to tease animals.*
2. It wasn't difficult to find their house. → *Finding their house wasn't difficult.*
3. Voting in every election is important.
4. It was exciting to meet the king and queen.
5. Hearing the other side of the story would be interesting.
6. It is unusual to see Joan awake early in the morning.
7. If you know how, it is easy to float in water for a long time.

8. Mastering a second language takes time and patience.
9. Driving to Atlanta will take us ten hours.
10. It takes courage to dive into the sea from a high cliff.

☐ **EXERCISE 20—ORAL:** **STUDENT A:** Complete the sentence with an infinitive phrase. **STUDENT B:** Give a sentence with the same meaning by using a gerund phrase as the subject.

1. It is fun . . . .
   A: *. . . to ride a horse.*
   B: *Riding a horse is fun.*
2. It's dangerous . . . .
3. It's easy . . . .
4. It's impolite . . . .
5. It is important . . . .
6. It is wrong . . . .
7. It takes a lot of time . . . .
8. It's a good idea . . . .
9. Is it difficult . . . ?

☐ **EXERCISE 21—ORAL:** The phrase "*for (someone)*" may precede an infinitive to identify exactly who the speaker is talking about. Add "*for (someone)*" to the following sentences and any other words to give a more specific meaning.

1. It's important to take advanced math courses. → *It's important for science students to take advanced math courses.*
2. It isn't possible to be on time. → *It isn't possible for me to be on time to class if the bus drivers are on strike and I have to walk to class in a rainstorm.*
3. It's easy to speak Spanish.
4. It's important to learn English.
5. It's unusual to be late.
6. It is essential to get a visa.
7. It is dangerous to play with matches.
8. It's difficult to communicate.
9. It was impossible to come to class.
10. It is a good idea to study gerunds and infinitives.

4–10 INFINITIVE OF PURPOSE: *IN ORDER TO*

(a) He came here *in order to study* English. (b) He came here *to study* English.	*In order to* is used to express *purpose*. It answers the question "Why?" *In order* is often omitted, as in (b).
(c) *INCORRECT: He came here for studying English.* (d) *INCORRECT: He came here for to study English.* (e) *INCORRECT: He came here for study English.*	To express purpose, use (*in order*) *to* not *for*, with a verb.*
(f) I went to the store *for* some bread. (g) I went to the store *to buy* some bread.	*For* is sometimes used to express purpose, but it is a preposition and is followed by a noun object, as in (f).

*Exception: The phrase *be used for* expresses the typical or general purpose of a thing. In this case, the preposition *for* is followed by a gerund: *A saw is used for cutting wood.* Also possible: *A saw is used to cut wood.*

However, to talk about a particular thing and a particular situation, *be used* + *an infinitive* is used: *A chain saw was used to cut down the old oak tree.* (INCORRECT: *A chain saw was used for cutting down the old oak tree.*)

☐ **EXERCISE 22—ERROR ANALYSIS:** Correct the errors in the following.

1. Helen borrowed my dictionary for look up the spelling of "occurrence."

2. I went to the library for to study last night.

3. The teacher opened the window for getting some fresh air in the room.

4. I came to this school for learn English.

5. I need to get a part-time job for to earn some money for my school expenses.

☐ **EXERCISE 23:** Make up completions to the following. Express the *purpose* of the action.

1. I went to Chicago to ___*visit my relatives.*___

2. Tom went to Chicago for ___*a business conference.*___

3. I went to the market to _____

4. Mary went to the market for _____

5. I went to the doctor to _____

6. My son went to the doctor for _____

7. I swim every day to _____

8. My friend swims every day for _____

9. I drove into the service station to _____

10. They stopped at the service station for _____

4–11 ADJECTIVES FOLLOWED BY INFINITIVES

(a) We **were sorry to hear** the bad news. (b) I **was surprised to see** Tim at the meeting.	Certain adjectives can be immediately followed by infinitives, as in (a) and (b). In general, these adjectives describe a person (or persons), not a thing. Many of these adjectives describe a person's feelings or attitudes.

SOME COMMON ADJECTIVES FOLLOWED BY INFINITIVES

glad to	*sorry to*★	*ready to*	*careful to*	*surprised to*★
happy to	*sad to*★	*prepared to*	*hesitant to*	*amazed to*★
pleased to	*upset to*★	*anxious to*	*reluctant to*	*astonished to*★
delighted to	*disappointed to*★	*eager to*	*afraid to*	*shocked to*★
content to		*willing to*		*stunned to*★
relieved to	*proud to*	*motivated to*		
lucky to	*ashamed to*	*determined to*		
fortunate to				

★The expressions with asterisks are usually followed by infinitive phrases with verbs such as **see, learn, discover, find out, hear**.

☐ **EXERCISE 24:** Complete the sentences with infinitives.

1. I was glad _____*to get*_____ a letter from you.

2. I was relieved _____*to find out*_____ that I had passed the exam.

3. Sue is lucky _____ alive after the accident.

4. The soldiers were prepared _____.

5. The children are anxious _____ to the circus.

6. Dick didn't feel like going anywhere. He was content _____

   home and _____ a book.

7. The teacher is always willing _____ us.

8. The students are motivated _____ English.

9. Be careful not _____ on the icy sidewalks!

10. Tom was hesitant _____ home alone on the dark street.

11. Sally is afraid _____ home alone.

12. Ann is proud _____ the top student in her class.

13. I was surprised _____ Mr. Yamamoto at the meeting.

14. We were sorry _____ the bad news.

☐ **EXERCISE 25—ORAL (BOOKS CLOSED):** Answer "yes" to the question. Use an infinitive phrase in your response.

Example: You saw your friend at the airport. Were you happy?

Response: Yes, I was happy to see my friend at the airport.

1. (. . .) has a lot of good friends. Is s/he fortunate?
2. You're leaving on vacation next week. Are you eager?
3. You met (. . .)'s wife/husband. Were you delighted?
4. You went to (*name of a faraway place in the world*) last summer. You saw (. . .) there. Were you surprised?
5. You're going to take a test tomorrow. Are you prepared?
6. You're thinking about asking (. . .) a personal question. Are you hesitant?
7. Your friend was ill. Finally you found out that she was okay. Were you relieved?
8. You heard about (. . .)'s accident. Were you sorry?

Answer the following questions in complete sentences.

9. What are you careful to do before you cross a busy street?
10. What are children sometimes afraid to do?
11. When you're tired in the evening, what are you content to do?
12. If one of your friends has a problem, what are you willing to do?
13. Sometimes when people don't know English very well, what are they reluctant to do?
14. If I announce there is a test tomorrow, what will you be motivated to do tonight?
15. What are you determined to do before you are 60 years old?
16. What are some things people should be ashamed to do?

17. Can you tell me something you were shocked to find out?/astonished to learn?

18. Can you tell me something you were disappointed to discover?/sad to hear?

4–12 USING INFINITIVES WITH *TOO* AND *ENOUGH*

(a) That box is *too heavy* for Bob *to lift*. COMPARE: (b) That box is *very heavy*, but Bob can lift it.	In the speaker's mind, the use of *too* implies a negative result. In (a): *too heavy* = It is *impossible* for Bob to lift that box. In (b): *very heavy* = It is *possible but difficult* for Bob to lift that box.
(c) I am *strong enough to lift* that box. I can lift it.	*Enough* follows an adjective, as in (c).
(d) I have *enough strength to lift* that box. (e) I have *strength enough to lift* that box.	*Enough* may precede a noun, as in (d), or follow a noun, as in (e).

□ **EXERCISE 26:** Think of a negative result, and then complete the sentence with an infinitive phrase.

1. That ring is too expensive. → *Negative result: I can't buy it. That ring is too expensive for me to buy.*

2. I'm too tired. → *Negative result: I can't/don't want to go to the meeting. I'm too tired to go to the meeting.*

3. It's too late. → *Negative result:* . . .

4. It's too cold.

5. Nuclear physics is too difficult.

6. I'm too busy.

7. My son is too young.

8. The mountain cliff is too steep.

Now think of a positive result, and complete the sentence with an infinitive phrase.

9. That ring is very expensive, but it isn't too expensive. → *Positive result: I can buy it. That ring isn't too expensive for me to buy.*

10. I'm very tired, but I'm not too tired. → *Positive result:* . . .

11. My suitcase is very heavy, but it's not too heavy.

12. I'm very busy, but I'm not too busy.

1. What is a child too young to do but an adult old enough to do?
2. (. . .)'s daughter is 18 months old. Is she too young or very young?
3. Who had a good dinner last night? Was it too good or very good?
4. Is it very difficult or too difficult to learn English?
5. After you wash your clothes, are they too clean or very clean?
6. Who stayed up late last night? Did you stay up too late or very late?
7. What is my pocket big enough to hold? What is it too small to hold?
8. Compare a mouse with an elephant. Is a mouse too small or very small?
9. What is the highest mountain in (*this country/the world*)? Is it too high or very high?
10. What did you have enough time/time enough to do before class today?

4–13 PASSIVE AND PAST FORMS OF INFINITIVES AND GERUNDS

PASSIVE INFINITIVE: **to be** + *past participle* (a) I didn't expect **to be invited** to his party.	In (a): **to be invited** is passive. The understood "**by** phrase" is "by him": *I didn't expect to be invited by him.*
PASSIVE GERUND: **being** + *past participle* (b) I appreciated **being invited** to your home.	In (b): **being invited** is passive. The understood "**by** phrase" is "by you": *I appreciated being invited by you.*
PAST INFINITIVE: **to have** + *past participle* (c) The rain seems **to have stopped**.	The event expressed by a past infinitive or past gerund happened before the time of the main verb. In (c): *The rain seems now to have stopped a few minutes ago.* *
PAST GERUND: **having** + *past participle* (d) I appreciate **having had** the opportunity to meet the king.	In (d): I met the king yesterday. *I appreciate now having had the opportunity to meet the king yesterday.* *
PAST-PASSIVE INFINITIVE: **to have been** + *past participle* (e) Jane is fortunate **to have been given** a scholarship.	In (e): Jane was given a scholarship last month by her government. She is fortunate. *Jane is fortunate now to have been given a scholarship last month by her government.*
PAST-PASSIVE GERUND: **having been** + *past participle* (f) I appreciate **having been told** the news.	In (f): I was told the news yesterday by someone. I appreciate that. *I appreciate now having been told the news yesterday by someone.*

*If the main verb is past, the action of the past infinitive or gerund happened before a time in the past:
   *The rain **seemed to have stopped**.* = The rain seemed at six P.M. to have stopped before six P.M.
   *I **appreciated having had** the opportunity to meet the king.* = I met the king in 1985. I appreciated in 1987 having had the opportunity to meet the king in 1985.

□ **EXERCISE 28:** Supply an appropriate form for each verb in parentheses.

1. I don't enjoy (*laugh*) _being laughed_ at by other people.

2. I'm angry at him for (*tell, not*) _not telling / not having told*_ me the truth.

3. It is easy (*fool*) _to be fooled_ by his lies.

4. Jack had a narrow escape. He was almost hit by a car. He barely avoided (*hit*) _____ by the speeding automobile.

5. Sharon wants us to tell her the news as soon as we hear anything. If we find out anything about the problem, she wants (*tell*) _____ about it immediately.

6. Yesterday Anna wrote a check for fifty dollars, but when she wrote it she knew she didn't have enough money in the bank to cover it. Today she is very worried about (*write*) _____ that check. She has to find a way to put some money in her account right away.

7. A: What's the difference between "burn up" and "burn down"?
   B: Hmmm. That's an interesting question. I don't recall ever (*ask*) _____ that question before.

8. Living in a foreign country has been a good experience for me. I am glad that my company sent me to another country to study. I am very pleased (*give*) _____ the opportunity to learn about another culture.

9. You must tell me the truth. I insist on (*tell*) _____ the truth.

10. Don't all of us want (*love*) _____ and (*need*) _____ _____ by other people?

11. I enjoy (*watch*) _____ television in the evenings.

12. Dear Jim: I feel guilty about (*write, not*) _____ to you sooner, but I've been swamped with work lately.

---

*The past gerund is used to emphasize that the action of the gerund took place *before* that of the main verb. However, often there is little difference in meaning between a simple gerund and a past gerund.

☐ **EXERCISE 29:** Supply an appropriate form for each verb in parentheses.

1. Martha doesn't like to have her picture taken. She avoids (*photograph*)

    _____.

2. Tim was in the army during the war. He was caught by the enemy but he managed to escape. He is lucky (*escape*) _____ with his life.

3. A: It's been nice talking to you. I really have enjoyed our conversation, but I have to leave now. I'm very happy (*have*) _____ this opportunity to meet you and talk with you. Let's try to get together again soon.

    B: I'd like that.

4. A: Is Ted a transfer student?

    B: Yes.

    A: Where did he go to school before he came here?

    B: I'm not sure, but I think he mentioned something about (*go*) _____ to UCLA or USC.

5. A: You know Jim Frankenstein, don't you?

    B: Jim Frankenstein? I don't think so. I don't recall ever (*meet*) _____ _____ him.

6. A: This letter needs (*send*) _____ immediately. Will you take care of it?

    B: Right away.

7. Sally is very quick. You have to tell her how to do something only once. She doesn't need (*tell*) _____ twice.

8. A: I thought Sam was sick.

    B: So did I. But he seems (*recover*) _____ very quickly. He certainly doesn't seem (*be*) _____ sick now.

9. Last year I studied abroad. I appreciate (*have*) _____ the opportunity to live and study in a foreign country.

10. This year I am studying abroad. I appreciate (*have*) _____ this opportunity to live and study in a foreign country.

11. Ms. Walters complained about (*tell, not*) _____ about the meeting. In the future, she expects (*inform*) _____ _____ of any and all meetings.

4–14 USING GERUNDS OR PASSIVE INFINITIVES FOLLOWING *NEED*

(a) I **need to borrow** some money. (b) John **needs to be told** the truth.	Usually an infinitive follows **need**, as in (a) and (b).
(c) The house **needs painting**. (d) The house **needs to be painted**.	In certain situations, a gerund may follow **need**. In this case, the gerund carries a passive meaning. Usually the situations involve fixing or improving something. (c) and (d) have the same meaning.

☐ **EXERCISE 30:** Supply an appropriate form for the verbs in parentheses.

1. The chair is broken. I need (*fix*) _____ it. The chair needs (*fix*) _____.

2. What a mess! This room needs (*clean*) _____ up. We need (*clean*) _____ it up before the company arrives.

3. The baby's diaper needs (*change*) _____. It's wet.

4. My shirt is wrinkled. It needs (*iron*) _____.

5. There is a hole in our roof. The roof needs (*repair*) _____.

6. I have books and papers all over my desk. I need (*take*) _____ some time to straighten up my desk. It needs (*straighten*) _____ _____ up.

7. The apples on the tree are ripe. They need (*pick*) _____.

8. The dog needs (*wash*) _____. He's been digging in the mud.

4-15 USING A POSSESSIVE TO MODIFY A GERUND

We came to class late. Mr. Lee complained about that fact.	
(a) FORMAL: Mr. Lee complained about **our coming** to class late.*	In formal English, a possessive pronoun (e.g., **our**) is used to modify a gerund, as in (a).
(b) INFORMAL: Mr. Lee complained about **us coming** to class late.	In informal English, the object form (e.g., **us**) is frequently used, as in (b).
(c) FORMAL: Mr. Lee complained about **Mary's coming** to class late.	In very formal English, a possessive noun (e.g., **Mary's**) is used to modify a gerund.
(d) INFORMAL: Mr. Lee complained about **Mary coming** to class late.	The possessive form is often not used in informal English, as in (d).

*"Coming to class late" occurred before "Mr. Lee complained," so a past gerund is also possible: *Mr. Lee complained about* **our having come** *to class late*.

☐ **EXERCISE 31:** Combine the following. Change *"that fact"* to a gerund phrase. Use formal English. Discuss informal usage.

1. Mary won a scholarship. We are excited about *that fact.* → *We are excited about Mary's winning a scholarship.*
2. He didn't want to go. I couldn't understand *that fact.* → *I couldn't understand his not wanting to go.*
3. You took the time to help us. We greatly appreciate *that fact.*
4. We talked about him behind his back. The boy resented *that fact.*
5. They ran away to get married. *That fact* shocked everyone.
6. You don't want to do it. I don't understand *that fact.*
7. Ann borrowed Sally's clothes without asking her first. Sally complained about *that fact.*
8. Helen is here to answer our questions about the company's new insurance plan. We should take advantage of *that fact.*

☐ **EXERCISE 32:** Supply an appropriate form for each verb in parentheses.

1. Alice didn't expect (*ask*) _____ to Bill's party.

2. I'm not accustomed to (*drink*) _____ coffee with my meals.

3. I'll help you with your homework as soon as I finish (*wash*) _____ _____ the dishes.

4. She took a deep breath (*relax*) _____ herself before she got up to give her speech.

5. I'm prepared (*answer*) _____ any question that might be asked during my job interview tomorrow.

6. Matthew left without (*tell*) _____ anyone.

7. It's useless. Give up. Enough's enough. Don't keep (*beat*) _____ _____ your head against a brick wall.

8. His (*be, not*) _____ able to come is disappointing.

9. I hope (*award*) _____ a scholarship for the coming semester.

10. We are very pleased (*accept*) _____ your invitation.

11. I have considered (*get*) _____ a part-time job (*help*) _____ pay for my school expenses.

12. It is exciting (*travel*) _____ to faraway places and (*leave*) _____ one's daily routine behind.

13. (*Help*) _____ the disadvantaged children learn how to read was a rewarding experience.

14. He wants (*like*) _____ and (*trust*) _____ by everyone.

15. I can't help (*wonder*) _____ why Larry did such a foolish thing.

16. Mr. Carson is very lucky (*choose*) _____ by the committee as their representative to the meeting in Paris.

17. (*Live*) _____ in a city has certain advantages.

18. Keep on (*do*) _____ whatever you were doing. I didn't mean (*interrupt*) _____ you.

19. It is very kind of you (*take*) _____ care of that problem for me.

20. She opened the window (*let*) _____ in some fresh air.

21. They agreed (*cooperate*) _____ with us to the fullest extent.

22. Did you remember (*turn*) _____ in your assignment?

23. I don't remember ever (*hear*) _____ that story before.

24. Does your son regret (*leave*) _____ home and (*go*) _____ to a foreign country (*study*) _____?

25. I appreciate your (*ask*) _____ my opinion on the matter.

26. You should stop (*drive*) _____ if you get sleepy. It's dangerous (*drive*) _____ when you're not alert.

27. After driving for three hours, we stopped (*get*) _____ something to eat.

28. Please forgive me for (*be, not*) _____ here to help you yesterday.

4–16 USING VERBS OF PERCEPTION

(a) I **saw** my friend **run** down the street. (b) I **saw** my friend **running** down the street. (c) I **heard** the rain **fall** on the roof. (d) I **heard** the rain **falling** on the roof.	Certain verbs of perception are followed by either *the simple form** or *the -ing form*** of a verb. There is usually little difference in meaning between the two forms except that the **-ing** form usually gives the idea of "while." In (b): I saw my friend while she was running down the street.
(e) I **heard** a famous opera star **sing** at the concert last night. (f) When I walked into the apartment, I **heard** my roommate **singing** in the shower.	Sometimes (not always) there is a clear difference between using the simple form or the **-ing** form. In (e): I heard the singing from beginning to end. In (f): The singing was in progress when I heard it.

VERBS OF PERCEPTION FOLLOWED BY THE SIMPLE FORM OR THE *-ING* FORM			
see *notice* *watch* *look at* *observe*	*hear* *listen to*	*feel*	*smell*

*The simple form of a verb = the infinitive form without "to." INCORRECT: *I saw my friend to run down the street.*
The **-ing form refers to the present participle.

☐ **EXERCISE 33:** Complete the sentences with the words in the list. Use both possible forms.

✔ chase   land   shake
    come   look at   sing
    knock   ring   take off

1. When I was downtown yesterday, I saw the police ___*chase/chasing*___ a thief.

2. There was an earthquake in my hometown last year. It was just a small one, but I could feel the ground _____.

3. Polly was working in her garden, so she didn't hear the phone _____ _____.

4. I like to listen to the birds _____ when I get up early in the morning.

5. The guard observed a suspicious-looking person _____ into the bank.

6. I was almost asleep last night when I suddenly heard someone _____ _____ on the door.

7. Did you notice Max _____ another student's paper during the exam?

8. While I was waiting for my plane, I watched other planes _____ _____ and _____.

In the following, choose the more appropriate form (either simple or -ing) of the verbs in parentheses.

9. Last weekend I went to my daughter's soccer game. I enjoyed watching the children ___*play*___ soccer. (*play*)

10. When I walked past the park, I saw some children ___*playing*___ baseball. (*play*)

11. Do you see Mary _____ up the street? Isn't that her, the woman in the red dress? (*walk*)

12. I remember it distinctly. At 5:30 yesterday afternoon, I saw Jim _____ _____ to his car, _____ the door, and _____ _____. (*walk, open, get in*)

13. When I glanced out the window, I saw Jack _____ toward my house. (*walk*)

14. Do you hear someone _____ for help in the distance? I do. (*call*)

15. When I heard the principal of the school _____ my name at the graduation ceremony, I walked to the front of the auditorium to receive my diploma. (*call*)

16. Last night while I was trying to fall asleep, I could hear the people in the next apartment _____ and _____. (*sing, laugh*)

17. Do you smell something _____? (*burn*)

18. As soon as I saw the fly _____ on the table, I swatted it with a rolled up newspaper. (*land*)

4–17 USING THE SIMPLE FORM AFTER *LET* AND *HELP*

(a) My father *let* me *drive* his car. (b) I *let* my friend *borrow* my bicycle.	*Let* is always followed by the simple form of a verb, not an infinitive. (*INCORRECT: My father let me to drive his car.*)
(c) My brother *helped* me *wash* my car. (d) My brother *helped* me *to wash* my car.	*Help* is often followed by the simple form of a verb, as in (c). An infinitive is also possible, as in (d). Both (c) and (d) are correct.

☐ **EXERCISE 34:** Complete the sentences with verb phrases.

1. Don't let me _*forget to take my keys to the house with me.*_____

2. The teacher usually lets us _____

3. Why did you let your roommate _____

4. You shouldn't let other people _____

5. A stranger helped the lost child _____

6. It was very kind of my friend to help me _____

7. Keep working. Don't let me _____

8. Could you help me _____

4–18 USING CAUSATIVE VERBS: *MAKE, HAVE, GET*

(a) I *made* my brother *carry* my suitcase. (b) I *had* my brother *carry* my suitcase. (c) I *got* my brother *to carry* my suitcase. FORM: X *makes* Y *do* something. (simple form) X *has* Y *do* something. (simple form) X *gets* Y *to do* something. (infinitive)	*Make*, *have*, and *get* can be used to express the idea that "X" causes "Y" to do something. When they are used as causative verbs, their meanings are similar but not identical. In (a): My brother had no choice. I insisted that he carry my suitcase. In (b): My brother carried my suitcase simply because I asked him to. In (c): I managed to persuade my brother to carry my suitcase.
(d) Mrs. Lee *made* her son *clean* his room. (e) Sad movies *make* me *cry*.	Causative *make* is followed by the simple form of a verb, not an infinitive. (*INCORRECT: She made him to clean his room.*) *Make* gives the idea that "X" forces "Y" to do something. In (d): Mrs. Lee's son had no choice.
(f) I *had* the plumber *repair* the leak. (g) Jane *had* the waiter *bring* her some tea.	Causative *have* is followed by the simple form of a verb, not an infinitive. (*INCORRECT: I had him to repair the leak.*) *Have* gives the idea that "X" requests "Y" to do something. In (f): The plumber repaired the leak because I asked him to.
(h) The students *got* the teacher *to dismiss* class early. (i) Jack *got* his friends *to play* soccer with him after school.	Causative *get* is followed by an infinitive. *Get* gives the idea that "X" persuades "Y" to do something. In (h): The students managed to persuade the teacher to let them leave early.
(j) I *had* my watch *repaired* (by someone). (k) I *got* my watch *repaired* (by someone).	The past participle is used after *have* and *get* to give a passive meaning. In this case, there is usually little or no difference in meaning between *have* and *get*. In (j) and (k): I caused my watch to be repaired by someone.

☐ **EXERCISE 35:** Complete the sentences with the words in parentheses.

1. The doctor made the patient _____*stay*_____ in bed. (*stay*)

2. Mrs. Crane had her house _____*painted*_____. (*paint*)

3. The teacher had the class _____ a 2000-word research paper. (*write*)

4. I made my son _____ the windows before he could go outside to play. (*wash*)

5. Don got some kids in the neighborhood _____ out his garage. (*clean*)

6. I went to the bank to have a check _____. (*cash*)

7. Tom had a bad headache yesterday, so he got his twin brother Tim _____ to class for him. The teacher didn't know the difference. (*go*)

8. When Scott went shopping, he found a jacket that he really liked. After he had the sleeves _____, it fit him perfectly. (*shorten*)

9. My boss made me _____ my report because he wasn't satisfied with it. (*redo*)

10. Alice stopped at the service station to have the tank _____. (*fill*)

11. I got Mary _____ me some money so I could go to a movie last night. (*lend*)

12. Mr. Fields went to a doctor to have the wart on his nose _____ _____. (*remove*)

13. Peeling onions always makes me _____. (*cry*)

14. Tom Sawyer was supposed to paint the fence, but he didn't want to do it. He was a very clever boy. Somehow he got his friends _____ it for him. (*do*)

15. We had a professional photographer _____ pictures of everyone who participated in our wedding. (*take*)

▶ 16. I spilled some tomato sauce on my suit coat. Now I need to get my suit _____. (*clean*)

☐ **EXERCISE 36**: Complete the sentences with verb phrases.

1. I got my friend _____ *to translate a letter for me.*

2. Sometimes parents make their children _____

3. When I'm at a restaurant, I sometimes have the waiter _____

4. Many people take their cars to service stations to get the oil _____

5. Teachers sometimes have their students _____

6. I'm more than willing to help you _____

7. Before I left on my trip, I had the travel agent _____

8. My cousin's jokes always make me _____

9. When I was a child, my parents wouldn't let me _____

10. We finally got our landlady _____

4–19 SPECIAL EXPRESSIONS FOLLOWED BY THE -*ING* FORM OF A VERB

(a) We *had fun* We *had a good time* } *playing* volleyball.	*have fun* + -*ing* *have a good time* + -*ing*

(b) I *had trouble*
    I *had difficulty*
    I *had a hard time*
    I *had a difficult time* } *finding* his house.
	have trouble + -*ing*
	have difficulty + -*ing*
	have a hard time + -*ing*
	have a difficult time + -*ing*

(c) Sam *spends most of his time* *studying*. (d) I *waste a lot of time* *watching* TV.	*spend* + *expression of time or money* + -*ing* *waste* + *expression of time or money* + -*ing*
(e) She *sat at her desk* *writing* a letter. (f) I *stood there* *wondering* what to do next. (g) He *is lying in bed* *reading* a novel.	*sit* + *expression of place* + -*ing* *stand* + *expression of place* + -*ing* *lie* + *expression of place* + -*ing*
(h) When I walked into my office, I *found George using* my telephone. (i) When I walked into my office, I *caught a thief looking* through my desk drawers.	*find* + (*pro*)*noun* + -*ing* *catch* + (*pro*)*noun* + -*ing* In (h) and (i): Both *find* and *catch* mean *discover*. *Catch* expresses anger or displeasure.

☐ **EXERCISE 37:** Complete the following.

1. We had a lot of fun _____*playing*_____ games at the picnic.

2. I have trouble _____ Mrs. Maxwell when she speaks. She talks too fast.

3. I spent five hours _____ my homework last night.

4. Martha is standing at the corner _____ for the bus.

5. Michael is sitting in class _____ notes.

6. Ms. Anderson is a commuter. Every work day, she spends almost two hours _____ to and from work.

7. It was a beautiful spring day. Dorothy was lying under a tree _____ _____ to the birds sing.

8. We wasted our money _____ to that movie. It was very boring.

9. Joe spent all day _____ ready to leave on vacation.

10. Ted is an indecisive person. He has a hard time _____ up his mind about anything.

11. I wondered what the children were doing while I was gone. When I got home, I found them _____ TV.

12. When Mr. Brown walked into the kitchen, he caught the children _____ some candy even though he'd told them not to spoil their dinners.

13. A: My friend is going to Germany next month, but he doesn't speak German. What do you suppose he will have difficulty _____?

    B: Well, he might have trouble _____.

14. A: Did you enjoy your trip to New York City?

    B: Very much. We had a good time _____.

15. A: This is your first semester at this school. Have you had any problems?

    B: Not really, but sometimes I have a hard time _____.

16. A: What did you do yesterday?

    B: I spent almost all day _____.

☐ **EXERCISE 38:** Supply an appropriate form for each verb in parentheses.

1. Edward stood on the beach (*look*) _____ out over the ocean.

2. Why don't you let him (*make*) _____ up his own mind?

3. Jean sat on a park bench (*watch*) _____ the ducks (*swim*) _____ in the pond.

4. They refused (*pay*) _____ their taxes, so they were sent to jail.

5. It is foolish (*ignore*) _____ physical ailments.

6. Sara is going to spend next year (*study*) _____ at a university in Japan.

7. The sad expression on his face made me (*feel*) _____ sorry for him.

8. I didn't know how to get to Harry's house, so I had him (*draw*) _____ a map for me.

9. Barbara has a wonderful sense of humor. She can always make me (*laugh*) _____.

10. The little boy had a lot of trouble (*convince*) _____ anyone that he had seen a mermaid.

11. The teacher had the class (*open*) _____ their books to page 185.

12. It was a hot day and the work was hard. I could feel sweat (*trickle*) _____ down my back.

13. I went to the pharmacy to have my prescription (*fill*) _____.

14. Mr. Flynn is good at (*tell*) _____ the difference between diamonds and cut glass.

15. Many people think Mr. Peel will win the election. He has a good chance of (*elect*) _____.

16. I found a penny (*lie*) _____ on the sidewalk.

17. My cousins helped me (*move*) _____ into my new apartment.

18. I was tired, so I just watched them (*play*) _____ volleyball instead of (*join*) _____ them.

19. You can lead a horse to water, but you can't make him (*drink*) _____.

20. You shouldn't let children (*play*) _____ with matches.

21. I finally told him (*be*) _____ quiet for a minute and (*listen*) _____ to what I had to say.

22. Irene was lying in bed (*think*) _____ about what a wonderful time she'd had.

23. When Shelley needed a passport photo, she had her picture (*take*) _____ by a professional photographer.

24. If you hear any news, I want (*tell*) _____ immediately.

25. Let's (*have*) _____ Ron and Maureen (*join*) _____ us for dinner tonight, okay?

26. There's a great difference between (*be*) _____ a freshman and (*be*) _____ a senior.

27. My English is pretty good, but sometimes I have trouble (*understand*) _____ lectures at school.

28. The illogic of his statements made me (*tear*) _____ my hair out.

29. Recently Jo has been spending most of her time (*do*) _____ research for a book on pioneer women.

30. I was getting sleepy, so I had my friend (*drive*) _____ the car.

□ **EXERCISE 39:** Supply an appropriate form for each verb in parentheses.

1. Jason wouldn't let them (*take*) _____ his picture.

2. I couldn't understand what the passage said, so I had my friend (*translate*) _____ it for me.

3. No, that's not what I meant (*say*) _____. How can I make you (*understand*) _____?

4. I have finally assembled enough information (*begin*) _____ writing my thesis.

5. It's a serious problem. Something needs (*do*) _____ about it soon.

6. I was terribly disappointed (*discover*) _____ that he had lied to me.

7. I had the operator (*put*) _____ the call through for me.

8. No one could make Ted (*feel*) _____ afraid. He refused (*intimidate*) _____ by anyone.

9. I don't see how she can possibly avoid (*fail*) _____ the course.

10. Do something! Don't just sit there (*twiddle*) _____ your thumbs.

11. Emily stopped her car (*let*) _____ a black cat (*run*) _____ across the street.

12. He's a terrific soccer player! Did you see him (*make*) _____ that last goal?

13. We spent the entire class period (*talk*) _____ about the revolution.

14. Karen got along very well in France despite not (*be*) _____ able to speak French.

15. Mary Beth suggested (*go*) _____ on a picnic.

► 16. I don't like (*force*) _____ (*leave*) _____ the room (*study*) _____ whenever my roommate feels like (*have*) _____ a party.

17. He's at an awkward age. He's old enough (*have*) _____ adult problems but too young (*know*) _____ how (*handle*) _____ them.

18. (*Look*) _____ at the car after the accident made him (*realize*) _____ that he was indeed lucky (*be*) _____ alive.

19. We sat in his kitchen (*sip*) _____ very hot, strong tea and (*eat*) _____ chunks of hard cheese.

20. I admit (*be*) _____ a little nervous about the job interview. I don't know what (*expect*) _____.

21. I'm tired. I wouldn't mind just (*stay*) _____ home tonight and (*get*) _____ to bed early.

22. It is the ancient task of the best artists among us (*force*) _____ _____ us (*use*) _____ our ability (*feel*) _____ _____ and (*share*) _____ emotions.

23. Please speak softly. My roommate is in the other room (*sleep*) _____ _____ .

24. I don't anticipate (*have*) _____ any difficulties (*adjust*) _____ to a different culture when I go abroad.

25. Isabel expected (*admit*) _____ to the university, but she wasn't.

26. When Franco went to the barber shop (*get*) _____ his hair (*cut*) _____ , he had his beard (*trim*) _____ , too.

☐ **EXERCISE 40—ERROR ANALYSIS:** Find and correct the errors in the following.

Example: I am considering to go to a show tonight.
Correction: I am considering **going** to a show tonight.

1. My parents made me to promise to write them once a week.
2. I don't mind to have a roommate.
3. Most students want return home as soon as possible.
4. When I went to shopping last Saturday, I saw a man to drive his car onto the sidewalk.
5. I asked my roommate to let me to use his shoe polish.
6. To learn about another country it is very interesting.
7. I don't enjoy to play card games.
8. I heard a car door to open and closing.
9. I had my friend to lend me his car.
10. I tried very hard to don't make any mistakes.
11. You should visit my country. It is too beautiful.
12. The music director tapped his baton for beginning the rehearsal.
13. Some people prefer save there money to spend it.

14. The task of find a person who could help us wasn't difficult.

15. All of us needed to went to the cashier's window.

16. I am looking forward to go to swim in the ocean.

17. When your planting a garden, it's important to be known about soils.

18. My mother always make me to be slow down if she think I am driving to fast.

19. One of our fights ended up with me having to sent to the hospital for getting stitches.

□ **EXERCISE 41—WRITTEN:** Following are composition topics.

1. Write about your first day or week here (in this city/at this school/etc.). Did you have any unusual, funny, or difficult experiences? What were your first impressions and reactions? Whom did you meet?

2. Write about your childhood. What are some of the pleasant memories you have of your childhood? Do you have any unpleasant memories?

3. Whom do you like to spend some of your free time with? What do you enjoy doing together? Include an interesting experience the two of you have had.

□ **EXERCISE 42—PHRASAL VERBS:** Supply appropriate prepositions. All of the sentences contain two-word verbs.

1. A: I think we should increase the membership dues from one dollar to two.

   B: That might solve some of our financial problems. Why don't you bring that _____ at the next meeting?

2. A: Did you hand _____ your composition?

   B: No. I didn't like it, so I decided to do it _____.

3. A: What time did you get _____ this morning?

   B: I slept late. I didn't drag myself out of bed until after nine.

4. A: What's the baby's name?

   B: Helen. She was named _____ her paternal grandmother.

5. A: I need to get more exercise.

   B: Why don't you take _____ tennis?

6. A: You can't go in there.

   B: Why not?

   A: Look at that sign. It says, "Keep _____. No trespassing."

7. A: I can't reach Fred. There's a busy signal.

   B: Then hang _____ and try again later.

8. A: The radio is too loud. Would you mind if I turned it _____ a little?

   B: No.

9. A: I can't hear the radio. Could you turn it _____ a little?

   B: Sure.

10. A: What are you doing Saturday night, Bob?

    B: I'm taking Virginia _____ for dinner and a show.

CHAPTER *5*

Singular and Plural

☐ **EXERCISE 1**: In the following sentences, add final *-s/-es* where necessary. Discuss why you need to add *-s/-es*. Do not change or omit any other words in the sentences. All of the sentences are SIMPLE PRESENT.

1. I have two **pens**. (***pens** = a plural noun*)

2. Tom work hard every day.

3. Our solar system consist of nine planet.

4. The earth rotate around the sun.

5. All animal need water.

6. A dog need fresh water every day.

7. Student take test.

8. Hawaii has beautiful sunset.

9. A library contain a lot of book.

10. Encyclopedia contain information about many thing.

11. Butterfly are beautiful.

12. Martha watch TV every evening.

13. Alex almost never change his mind.

5-1 FINAL -S/-ES

(a) NOUN + **-S**: **Friends** are important. NOUN + **-ES**: I like my **classes**.	A final **-s** or **-es** is added to a noun to make a noun plural. **friend** = *a singular noun* **friends** = *a plural noun*
(b) VERB + **-S**: John **works** at the bank. VERB + **-ES**: She **watches** birds.	A final **-s** or **-es** is added to a simple present verb when the subject is a singular noun or third person singular pronoun.* **John works** = *singular* **The students work** = *plural* **He works** = *singular* **They work** = *plural*
SPELLING: FINAL -S vs. -ES (c) sing → *sings* song → *songs*	For most words (whether a verb or a noun), simply a final **-s** is added to spell the word correctly.

(d) wash → *washes*
     watch → *watches*
     class → *classes*
     buzz → *buzzes*
     box   → *boxes*
	Final **-es** is added to words that end in **-sh**, **-ch**, **-s**, **-z**, and **-x**.

(e) toy   → *toys*
     buy   → *buys*
(f) baby → *babies*
     cry   → *cries*
	For words that end in **-y**:
	In (e): If **-y** is preceded by a vowel, only **-s** is added.
	In (f): If **-y** is preceded by a consonant, the **-y** is changed to **-i** and **-es** is added.

*A singular noun = *Mary, my father, the machine.*
A third person singular subject pronoun = *she, he, it.*

☐ **EXERCISE 2:** Add **-s** or **-es** to the following words to spell them correctly.

1. passenger ___*s*___   14. mix _____
2. tax ___*es*___   15. try _____
3. talk _____   16. tray _____
4. blush _____   17. ferry _____
5. discover _____   18. guy _____
6. develop _____   19. enemy _____
7. season _____   20. pry _____
8. flash _____   21. pray _____
9. hall _____
10. touch _____
11. sketch _____
12. press _____
13. method _____

☐ **EXERCISE 3—ORAL:** Practice pronouncing the following words. Say the final *-s/-es* sounds loudly and clearly.

> **GROUP A:** Final *-s* is pronounced /s/ after voiceless sounds.
>
> *Examples:* seats = seat + /**s**/
> ropes = rope + /**s**/
> backs = back + /**s**/

1. hats
2. hates
3. sleeps
4. trips
5. books

6. unlocks
7. sniffs
8. laughs
9. asks

> **GROUP B:** Final *-s* is pronounced /z/ after voiced sounds.
>
> *Examples:* seeds = seed + /**z**/
> robes = robe + /**z**/
> bags = bag + /**z**/
> sees = see + /**z**/

10. feeds
11. lids
12. robs
13. grabs
14. homes
15. occurs

16. fills
17. miles
18. rugs
19. days
20. pies
21. agrees

> **GROUP C:** Final *-es* and *-s* are pronounced /əz/ after *-sh*, *-ch*, *-s*, *-z*, and *-ge/dge* sounds.
>
> *Examples:* dishes = dish + /əz/   mixes = mix + /əz/
> catches = catch + /əz/   prizes = prize + /əz/
> kisses = kiss + /əz/   edges = edge + /əz/

22. wishes
23. ashes
24. matches
25. sandwiches
26. guesses
27. courses
28. faces
29. fixes

30. relaxes
31. quizzes
32. sizes
33. rises
34. pages
35. judges
36. arranges

□ **EXERCISE 4—ORAL:** Practice the pronunciation of final -*s*/-*es* by reading the following sentences aloud.

1. The teacher encourages the students to speak freely.
2. Chickens, ducks, and turkeys lay eggs.
3. He possesses many fine qualities.
4. My wages are low, but my taxes are high.
5. The cafeteria serves good sandwiches.
6. He coughs, sneezes, and wheezes.
7. People come in many shapes and sizes.
8. She scratches her chin when it itches.
9. He practices pronunciation by reading sentences aloud.
10. She bought some shirts, shoes, socks, dresses, slacks, blouses, earrings, and necklaces.

□ **EXERCISE 5—ORAL (BOOKS CLOSED):** What do the following people or things do? Follow the pattern in the example. Say final -*s*/-*es* sounds loudly and clearly.

Example: bird watcher
Response: A bird watcher watches birds.

1. stamp collector	7. ticket taker
2. animal trainer	8. fire extinguisher
3. bank robber	9. mind reader
4. dog catcher	10. bullfighter
5. book publisher	11. wage earner
6. tax collector	12. storyteller

□ **EXERCISE 6—ORAL (BOOKS CLOSED):** What do the following people, animals, and things do? Respond in complete sentences. Say the final -*s*/-*es* sounds loudly and clearly.

Example: bird
Response: A bird flies (sings, builds nests, etc.).

1. baby	9. cat
2. telephone	10. door
3. star	11. clock
4. dog	12. airplane
5. duck	13. doctor
6. ball	14. teacher
7. heart	15. psychologist
8. river	

5-2 IRREGULAR PLURAL NOUNS

The nouns in (a) have irregular plural forms:

(a) man–**men**   child–**children**   mouse–**mice**   foot–**feet**
    woman–**women**   ox–**oxen**   louse–**lice**   goose–**geese**
                                                                     tooth–**teeth**

Some nouns that end in **-o** add **-es** to form the plural:

(b) **echoes**   **heroes**   **potatoes**   **tomatoes**

Some nouns that end in **-o** add only **-s** to form the plural:

(c) **autos**   **photos**   **solos**   **tatoos**
    kilos   **pianos**   **sopranos**   **videos**
    memos   **radios**   **studios**   **zoos**

Some nouns that end in **-o** add either **-es** or **-s** to form the plural:

(d) **mosquitoes/mosquitos**   **volcanoes/volcanos**
    tornadoes/tornados   **zeroes/zeros**

Some nouns that end in **-f** or **-fe** are changed to **-ves** in the plural:

(e) calf–**calves**   leaf–**leaves**   self–**selves**   wolf–**wolves**
    half–**halves**   life–**lives**   shelf–**shelves**   scarf–**scarves/scarfs**
    knife–**knives**   loaf–**loaves**   thief–**thieves**

Some nouns that end in **-f** simply add **-s** to form the plural:

(f) belief–**beliefs**   chief–**chiefs**   cliff–**cliffs**   roof–**roofs**

Some nouns have the same singular and plural form: (e.g., One deer is . . . . Two deer are . . . .)

(g) **deer**   **fish**   **means**   **series**   **sheep**   **species**

Some nouns that English has borrowed from other languages have foreign plurals:

(h) criterion–**criteria**   (k) analysis–**analyses**   (m) bacterium–**bacteria**
    phenomenon–**phenomena**   basis–**bases**   curriculum–**curricula**
                            crisis–**crises**   datum–**data**
(i) cactus–**cacti/cactuses**   hypothesis–**hypotheses**   medium–**media**
    stimulus–**stimuli**   oasis–**oases**   memorandum–**memoranda**
    syllabus–**syllabi/syllabuses**   parenthesis–**parentheses**
                            thesis–**theses**

(j) formula–**formulae/formulas** (l) appendix–**appendices/appendixes**
    vertebra–**vertebrae**   index–**indices/indexes**

☐ **EXERCISE 7:** Write the plural form of the following nouns.

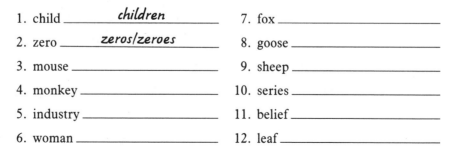

1. child _____*children*_____   7. fox _____

2. zero _____*zeros/zeroes*_____   8. goose _____

3. mouse _____   9. sheep _____

4. monkey _____ 10. series _____

5. industry _____ 11. belief _____

6. woman _____ 12. leaf _____

13. self _____	17. hypothesis _____
14. echo _____	18. curriculum _____
15. photo _____	19. phenomenon _____
16. analysis _____	20. stimulus _____

5–3 POSSESSIVE NOUNS

(a) **SINGULAR NOUN** **POSSESSIVE FORM**	To show possession, add an apostrophe (') and -s to a singular noun: *The **girl's** book is on the table.*
the girl ***the girl's*** Tom ***Tom's*** my wife ***my wife's*** a lady ***a lady's*** Thomas ***Thomas's/Thomas'***	If a singular noun ends in -s, there are two possible forms: (1) Add an apostrophe and -s: ***Thomas's** book.* (2) Add only an apostrophe: ***Thomas'** book.*
(b) **PLURAL NOUN** **POSSESSIVE FORM** the girls ***the girls'*** their wives ***their wives'*** the ladies ***the ladies'***	Add only an apostrophe to a plural noun that ends in -s: *The **girls'** books are on the table.*
the men ***the men's*** my children ***my children's***	Add an apostrophe and -s to plural nouns that do not end in -s: *The **men's** books are on the table.*

☐ **EXERCISE 8:** Complete the sentences with the possessive form of the nouns in parentheses.

1. (*Mrs. Smith*) ___Mrs. Smith's___ husband often gives her flowers.

2. (*boy*) The _____ hat is red.

3. (*boys*) The _____ hats are red.

4. (*children*) The _____ toys are all over the floor.

5. (*child*) I fixed the _____ bicycle.

6. (*baby*) The _____ toys are in her crib.

7. (*babies*) The _____ toys are in their cribs.

8. (*wives*) Tom and Bob are married. Their _____ names are Cindy and Jane, respectively.

9. (*wife*) That is my _____ coat.

10. (*Sally*) _____ last name is White.

11. (*Phyllis*) _____ last name is Young.

12. (*boss*)   That's my _____ office.

13. (*bosses*)   Those are my _____ offices.

14. (*woman*)   This is a _____ purse.

15. (*women*)   That store sells _____ clothes.

16. (*sister*)   Do you know my _____ husband?

17. (*sisters*)   Do you know my _____ husbands?

18. (*yesterday*)   Did you read _____ newspaper?

19. (*today*)   There are many problems in _____ world.

20. (*month*)   It would cost me a _____ salary
                    to buy that refrigerator.

5–4   USING NOUNS AS MODIFIERS

(a) The soup has vegetables in it. It is ***vegetable soup***. (b) The building has offices in it. It is an ***office building***.	Notice: When a noun is used as a modifier, it is in its singular form.
(c) The test lasted two hours. It was a ***two-hour test***. (d) Her son is five years old. She has a ***five-year-old son***.	When a noun used as a modifier is combined with a number expression, the noun is singular and a hyphen (-) is used.

☐ **EXERCISE 9:** Use the italicized noun or noun phrase in the first sentence as a modifier in the second sentence.

1. My garden has *flowers* in it. It is _____ *a flower garden.* _____

2. That handbook is for *students*. It is _____

3. Their baby is *ten months old*. They have _____

4. Our trip lasted for *three days*. We took _____

5. She is a psychologist for *children*. She is _____

6. I wrote a check for *fifty dollars*. I wrote _____

7. I will get *three credits* for that course. It is _____

8. Their house has *nine rooms*. It is _____

9. That food is for *dogs*. It is _____

10. That room is for *guests*. It is _____

11. The professor asked us to write a paper of *five pages*. She asked us to

    write _____

12. I have a sister who is *ten years old* and a brother who is *twelve years old*. I

    have _____

5–5 COUNT AND NONCOUNT NOUNS

(a) I bought **a chair**. Sam bought **three chairs**. (b) We bought **some furniture**. INCORRECT: *We bought a furniture.* INCORRECT: *We bought some furnitures.*	**Chair** is a count noun; chairs are items that can be counted. **Furniture** is a noncount noun. In grammar, furniture cannot be counted.

	SINGULAR	**PLURAL**	
COUNT NOUN	a chair one chair	chairs two chairs some chairs a lot of chairs many chairs*	A count noun: (1) may be preceded by **a/an** in the singular; (2) takes a final **-s/-es** in the plural.
NONCOUNT NOUN	furniture some furniture a lot of furniture much furniture*		A noncount noun: (1) is not immediately preceded by **a/an**; (2) has no plural form; does not take a final **-s/-es**.

*See Chart 5-8 for other expressions of quantity that are used with count and noncount nouns.

□ **EXERCISE 10:** Look at the italicized nouns in the following sentences. Write ''**C**'' above the count nouns and ''**NC**'' above the noncount nouns.

1. I bought some *chairs*, *tables*, and *desks*. In other words, I bought some

   furniture.

2. I have some *pennies*, *nickels*, and *dimes* in my pocket. In other words, I

   have some *money* in my pocket.

3. Ann likes to wear *jewelry*. Today she is wearing four *rings*, six *bracelets*,

   and a *necklace*.

4. We saw beautiful *mountains*, *fields*, and *lakes* on our trip. In other words,

   we saw beautiful *scenery*.

5. Would you like some *food*? How about a *sandwich* and an *apple*?

6. We had *meat, rice, bread, butter, cheese, fruit, vegetables*, and *tea* for dinner.

7. *Gold* and *iron* are metals.

8. I used an *iron* to press my shirt because it was wrinkled.

9. I wish you *happiness, health*, and *luck* in your life.

10. Tom is studying *chemistry, history*, and *English*.

11. In the United States, *baseball* is called the national pastime. To play it, you need a *baseball* and a bat.

12. My hometown has *rain, thunder, fog, sleet*, and *snow* in the winter months. In other words, it has bad *weather*.

13. Ed has black *hair* and brown *eyes*.

5–6 NONCOUNT NOUNS

Notice in the following: Most noncount nouns refer to a "whole" that is made up of different parts.	
(a) I bought some chairs, tables, and desks. In other words, I bought some *furniture*.	In (a): *furniture* represents a whole group of things that is made up of similar but separate items.
(b) I put some *sugar* in my *coffee*.	In (b): *sugar* and *coffee* represent whole masses made up of individual particles or elements.*
(c) I wish you *luck*.	In (c): *luck* is an abstract concept, an abstract "whole." It has no physical form; you can't touch it. You can't count it.
(d) *Sunshine* is warm and cheerful.	In (d): Phenomena of nature, such as *sunshine*, are frequently used as noncount nouns.
(e) NONCOUNT: Ann has brown *hair*. COUNT: Tom has *a hair* on his jacket.	Many nouns can be used as either noncount or count nouns, but the meaning is different; e.g., *hair* in (e) and *light* in (f).
(f) NONCOUNT: I opened the curtains to let in some *light*. COUNT: Don't forget to turn off the *lights* before you go to bed.	(Dictionaries written especially for learners of English as a second language are a good source of information on count/noncount usages of nouns.)

*To express a particular quantity, some noncount nouns may be preceded by unit expressions: e.g., *a spoonful of sugar, a glass of water, a cup of coffee, a quart of milk, a loaf of bread, a grain of rice, a bowl of soup, a bag of flour, a pound of meat, a piece of furniture, a piece of paper, a piece of jewelry.*

5–7 SOME COMMON NONCOUNT NOUNS

<table>
<tr><td colspan="2">The following are typical of nouns that are commonly used as noncount nouns. Many other nouns can be used as noncount nouns. This list serves only as a sample.</td></tr>
<tr><td>(a)</td><td>WHOLE GROUPS MADE UP OF SIMILAR ITEMS: baggage, clothing, equipment, food, fruit, furniture, garbage, hardware, jewelry, junk, luggage, machinery, mail, makeup, money/cash/change, postage, scenery, traffic</td></tr>
<tr><td>(b)</td><td>FLUIDS: water, coffee, tea, milk, oil, soup, gasoline, blood, etc.</td></tr>
<tr><td>(c)</td><td>SOLIDS: ice, bread, butter, cheese, meat, gold, iron, silver, glass, paper, wood, cotton, wool, etc.</td></tr>
<tr><td>(d)</td><td>GASES: steam, air, oxygen, nitrogen, smoke, smog, pollution, etc.</td></tr>
<tr><td>(e)</td><td>PARTICLES: rice, chalk, corn, dirt, dust, flour, grass, hair, pepper, salt, sand, sugar, wheat, etc.</td></tr>
<tr><td>(f)</td><td>ABSTRACTIONS:
—beauty, confidence, courage, education, enjoyment, fun, happiness, health, help, honesty, hospitality, importance, intelligence, justice, knowledge, laughter, luck, music, patience, peace, pride, progress, recreation, significance, sleep, truth, violence, wealth, etc.
—advice, information, news, evidence, proof
—time, space, energy
—homework, work
—grammar, slang, vocabulary</td></tr>
<tr><td>(g)</td><td>LANGUAGES: Arabic, Chinese, English, Spanish, etc.</td></tr>
<tr><td>(h)</td><td>FIELDS OF STUDY: chemistry, engineering, history, literature, mathematics, psychology, etc.</td></tr>
<tr><td>(i)</td><td>RECREATION: baseball, soccer, tennis, chess, bridge, poker, etc.</td></tr>
<tr><td>(j)</td><td>GENERAL ACTIVITIES: driving, studying, swimming, traveling, walking (and other gerunds)</td></tr>
<tr><td>(k)</td><td>NATURAL PHENOMENA: weather, dew, fog, hail, heat, humidity, lightning, rain, sleet, snow, thunder, wind, darkness, light, sunshine, electricity, fire, gravity</td></tr>
</table>

☐ **EXERCISE 11:** Complete the sentences with the given nouns. Add final *-s/-es* if necessary. Use each noun only one time.

advice	information	screwdriver
✔ change	junk	stuff
city	luggage/baggage	thunder
garbage	music	traffic
hardware	progress	traveling
homework	✔ river	trip

1. I have some coins in my pocket. In other words, I have some

   _____*change*_____ in my pocket.

2. The Mississippi, the Amazon, and the Nile are well-known

   _____*rivers*_____ in the world.

3. I like to listen to operas, symphonies, and folk songs. I enjoy

   _____ .

4. Since I came to the United States, I have visited Chicago, New York, and Miami. I want to visit other _____ before I return to my country.

5. The street is full of cars, trucks, and buses. This street always has heavy _____, especially during rush hour.

6. In the last couple of years, I've gone to France, India, and the Soviet Union. I like to take _____. In other words, _____ _____ is one of my favorite activities.

7. I put some banana peels, rotten food, and broken bottles in the waste can. The can is full of _____.

8. They have a rusty car without an engine, broken chairs, and an old refrigerator in their front yard. Their yard is full of _____.

9. Paul has books, pens, papers, notebooks, a clock, scissors, a tape recorder, and some other things on his desk. He has a lot of _____ on his desk.*

10. The children got scared when they heard _____ during the storm.

11. Tools that are used to fasten screws into wood are called _____ _____.

12. I went to the store to get some nails, hammers, and screws. In other words, I bought some _____.

13. Tonight I have to read 20 pages in my history book, do 30 problems in algebra, and write a composition for my English teacher. In other words, I have a lot of _____ to do tonight.

14. Ann took three suitcases, a shoulder bag, and a cosmetics case. In other words, she took a lot of _____ on her trip.

---

*As a noncount noun, **stuff** usually means "a group of various things." It is an inexact term used primarily in very informal spoken English. (*Junk* sometimes has the same meaning.)
Examples: I keep a lot of stuff in my desk drawers.
        Look at all the stuff in this room.

15. Toronto is 356 ft./109 m above sea level. The average annual precipitation in Toronto is 32 in./81 cm. The population of the metropolitan area is over 3,000,000. I found (*this*, *these*) _____ in the encyclopedia.

16. I didn't feel good. Ann said, ''You should see a doctor.''

    Tom said, ''You should go home and go to bed.''

    Martha said, ''You should drink fruit juice and rest.''

    I got _____ from three people.

17. My English is slowly getting better. My vocabulary is increasing. It's getting easier for me to write and I make fewer mistakes. I can often understand people even when they talk fast. I'm satisfied with the _____ I have made in learning English.

□ **EXERCISE 12:** Add final *-s/-es* to the nouns in italics if necessary. Do not add or change any other words.

1. I had *chicken* and *rice* for dinner last night. (*no changes*)

2. Mary always has fresh *egg* available because she raises *chicken* in her yard.
   > **eggs** ... **chickens**

3. Outside my window, I can see a lot of *tree, bush, grass, dirt,* and *flower*.

4. Tom gave me some good *advice*. Milly also gave me some good *suggestion*.

5. Yoko learned several new *word* today. She increased her *vocabulary* today.

6. I drank two *glass* of *water*.

7. *Window* are made of *glass*.

8. Jack wears *glass* because he has poor *eyesight*.

9. It took me a lot of *time* to finish my *homework*. I had a lot of *assignment*.

10. I have been in Mexico three *time*. I've spent a lot of *time* there.

11. There are *typewriter, copier, telephone,* and *stapler* in a typical business office. A business office needs a lot of *equipment*.

12. The *air* is full of *smoke, dust,* carbon *monoxide,* and many other harmful *substance*. We must seek to reduce air *pollution*.

13. I like to read good *literature*. I especially like to read *novel, poetry,* and *essay*. My favorite *poet* are Longfellow and Wordsworth. I have always liked their *poem*.

14. You can find a lot of time-saving *machine* in a modern *factory*. Modern *factory* need modern *machinery*.

15. There are more *star* in the universe than there are *grain* of *sand* on all the beaches on earth.

☐ **EXERCISE 13—PRETEST:** Before you look at Chart 5-8, try this exercise. Draw a line through the expressions that *cannot* be used to complete the sentence correctly.

Example: I bought _____ furniture.
    a. some
    ~~b. a couple of~~
    ~~c. several~~
    d. too much
    ~~e. too many~~

1. I received _____ letters.
    a. two
    b. a couple of
    c. both
    d. several
    e. some
    f. a lot of
    g. plenty of
    h. too many
    i. too much
    j. a few
    k. a little
    l. a number of
    m. a great deal of
    n. hardly any
    o. no

2. I received _____ mail.
    a. two
    b. a couple of
    c. both
    d. several
    e. some
    f. a lot of
    g. plenty of
    h. too many
    i. too much
    j. a few
    k. a little
    l. a number of
    m. a great deal of
    n. hardly any
    o. no

5-8 EXPRESSIONS OF QUANTITY

An expression of quantity (e.g., **one**, **several**, **many**, **much**) may precede a noun. *Notice below*: Some expressions of quantity are used only with count nouns; some only with noncount nouns; some with either count or noncount nouns.

EXPRESSIONS OF QUANTITY	USED WITH COUNT NOUNS	USED WITH NONCOUNT NOUNS
one each every	*one apple* *each apple* *every apple*	Ø* Ø Ø
two both a couple of three, etc. a few several many a number of	*two apples* *both apples* *a couple of apples* *three apples* *a few apples* *several apples* *many apples* *a number of apples*	Ø Ø Ø Ø Ø Ø Ø Ø
a little much a great deal of	Ø Ø Ø	*a little rice* *much rice* *a great deal of rice*
not any/no some a lot of lots of plenty of most all	*not any/no apples* *some apples* *a lot of apples* *lots of apples* *plenty of apples* *most apples* *all apples*	*not any/no rice* *some rice* *a lot of rice* *lots of rice* *plenty of rice* *most rice* *all rice*

*Ø = "not used." For example, you can say "*I ate one apple*" but NOT "*I ate one rice.*"

☐ **EXERCISE 14:** Draw a line through the expressions that *cannot* be used to complete the sentence correctly.

1. Isabel has _____ assignments.
   a. three
   b. several
   c. some
   d. a lot of
   e. too much
   f. too many
   g. a few
   h. a little
   i. a number of
   j. a great deal of
   k. hardly any
   l. no

2. Jake has _____ homework.
   a. three
   b. several
   c. some
   d. a lot of
   e. too much
   f. too many
   g. a few
   h. a little
   i. a number of
   j. a great deal of
   k. hardly any
   l. no

3. Ann is wearing _____ rings.
   a. four
   b. several
   c. some
   d. lots of
   e. too many
   f. too much
   g. a few
   h. a little
   i. hardly any
   j. no

4. Sue is wearing _____ jewelry.
   a. four
   b. several
   c. some
   d. lots of
   e. too many
   f. too much
   g. a few
   h. a little
   i. hardly any
   j. no

☐ **EXERCISE 15—ORAL (BOOKS CLOSED):** Use *many* or *much** with the following words, changing the words to plural if necessary. Pronounce final *-s/-es* loudly and clearly.

Examples: sentence → *many sentences*
water → *much water*
thief → *many thieves*

1. furniture
2. desk
3. branch
4. equipment
5. machinery
6. machine
7. woman
8. piece
9. mouse
10. advice
11. sheep
12. homework
13. prize
14. goose
15. music
16. progress
17. race
18. knowledge
19. marriage
20. information
21. luck
22. hypothesis
23. mail
24. office
25. slang
26. roof
27. phenomenon
28. human being
29. shelf
30. tooth

---

*You may want to practice using some of these words in sentences. **Much** is usually not used in affirmative sentences; instead, **a lot of** or **a great deal of** is frequently used. **Much** is used primarily in negative sentences and questions.

5–9 USING *A FEW* AND *FEW*; *A LITTLE* AND *LITTLE*

a few	(a) She has been here only two weeks, but she has already made ***a few friends***. *(Positive idea: She has made some friends.)*	***A few*** and ***a little*** give a positive idea; they indicate that something exists, is present, as in (a) and (b).
a little	(b) I'm very pleased. I've been able to save ***a little money*** this month. *(Positive idea: I have saved some money instead of spending all of it.)*	
few	(c) I feel sorry for her. She has ***(very) few friends***. *(Negative idea: She does not have many friends; she has almost no friends.)*	***Few*** and ***little*** (without ***a***) give a negative idea; they indicate that something is largely absent.
little	(d) I have ***(very) little money***. I don't even have enough money to buy food for dinner. *(Negative idea: I do not have much money; I have almost no money.)*	***Very*** (+ ***few/little***) makes the negative idea stronger, the number/amount smaller.

***A few** and **few** are used with plural count nouns. **A little** and **little** are used with noncount nouns.

☐ **EXERCISE 16:** Complete the sentences with *a few, (very) few, a little*, or *(very) little*.

1. Do you have _____*a few*_____ minutes? I'd like to ask you _____*a few*_____ questions. I need _____*a little*_____ more information.

2. Ann's previous employer gave her a good recommendation because she makes _____*(very) few*_____ mistakes in her work.

3. After Rodney tasted the soup, he added _____ salt to it.

4. I don't like a lot of salt on my food. I add _____ salt to my food.

5. The professor lectured very clearly. As a result, _____ students had questions at the end of the class period.

6. I like music. I like to listen to _____ music after dinner before I begin studying.

7. Jim is having a lot of trouble adjusting to eighth grade. He seems to be unpopular. Unfortunately, he has _____ friends.

8. I have to go to the post office because I have _____ letters to mail.

9. Every day Max goes to his mailbox, but it is usually empty. He gets _____ mail.

10. We're looking forward to our vacation. We're planning to spend _____ days with my folks and then _____ days with my husband's folks. After that, we're going to go to a fishing resort in Canada.

11. Driving downtown to the stadium for the baseball game was easy. We got there quickly because there was _____ traffic.

12. My friend arrived in the United States _____ months ago.

13. I think you could use some help. Let me give you _____ advice.

14. Because the family is very poor, the children have _____ clothes.

15. A: Are you finished?
    B: Not yet. I need _____ more minutes.

16. A: Are you finished?
    B: Not yet. I need _____ more time.

17. _____ days ago I met a very interesting person.

18. Into each life, _____ rain must fall. (*a saying*)

19. I was hungry, so I ate _____ nuts.

20. Margaret likes sweet tea. She usually adds _____ honey to her tea. Sometimes she adds _____ milk, too.

21. Has anyone ever called you on the phone and tried to sell you something you didn't want? I have _____ patience with people who interrupt my dinner to try to sell me a magazine.

22. He's a lucky little boy. Because his parents have taken good care of him, he has had _____ problems in his young life.

5–10 USING *OF* IN EXPRESSIONS OF QUANTITY

MOST* + NONSPECIFIC NOUN** (a) ***Most books are interesting.	In (a): The speaker is not referring to specific books. The speaker is not referring to "those books" or "your books" or "the books written by Mark Twain." The noun "books" is nonspecific.
(b) *INCORRECT: Most of books are interesting.*	In (b): The word *of* is not added to an expression of quantity (e.g., ***most***) if the noun it modifies is nonspecific.
MOST* + *OF* + SPECIFIC NOUN** (c) *Most* ***of those books are mine. (d) *Most* ***of my*** books are in English. (e) *Most* ***of the*** books on that table are mine.	A noun is specific when it is preceded by: —***this, that, these, those***, as in (c); OR —***my, John's, their*** (any possessive) as in (d); OR —***the***, as in (e). When a noun is specific, *of* is used with an expression of quantity.*

EXPRESSIONS OF QUANTITY FOLLOWED BY *OF* + A SPECIFIC NOUN
all, most, some/any + *of* + specific plural *count* noun or *noncount* noun, as in (f) ***many, (a) few, several, both, two, one*** + *of* + specific plural *count* noun, as in (g) ***much, (a) little*** + *of* + specific *noncount* noun, as in (h)

(f) *count:* ***Most of those chairs*** are uncomfortable. *noncount:* ***Most of that furniture*** is uncomfortable. (g) *count:* ***Many of those chairs*** are uncomfortable. (h) *noncount:* ***Much of that furniture*** is uncomfortable.

*NOTE: *of* is always a part of the following expressions of quantity, whether the noun is nonspecific or specific: ***a lot of, lots of, a couple of, plenty of, a number of, a great deal of***.
　　NONSPECIFIC: I've read *a lot* ***of books***.　　SPECIFIC: I've read *a lot* ***of those books***.

☐ **EXERCISE 17:** Add *of* if necessary. Write Ø if *of* is not necessary.

1. I know several __*of*__ Jack's friends.

2. I've made several __Ø__ friends lately.

3. Some _____ students are lazy, and some _____ students are hard-working.

4. Some _____ the students in Mrs. Gray's class are a little lazy.

5. Most _____ books have an index.

6. Most _____ Ali's books are written in Arabic.

7. I bought a few _____ books yesterday.

8. I've read a few _____ those books.

9. I'm new here. I don't know many _____ people yet.

10. I've just moved into a new apartment. I don't know many _____ my neighbors yet.

11. Have you taken any _____trips lately?

12. Sam hasn't met any _____ the students in the other class.

13. I usually get a lot _____ mail.

14. A lot _____ the mail I get is junk mail.

15. Our class has 30 students. Mr. Freeman's class has 25 students. Ms. North's class has 20 students. Of the three classes, our class has the most _____ students.*

16. Most _____ the students in our class are very smart.*

17. Out of all the students, Ali usually asks the most _____ questions during class. Most _____ his questions are about grammar.

18. Most _____ people need six to eight hours of sleep every night.

19. Most _____ the people in this class always hand in their assignments on time.

20. China has the most _____ people of any country in the world.

□ **EXERCISE 18:** Study the examples.

(a) CORRECT: **_All of the students_** in my class are here. (b) CORRECT: **_All the students_** in my class are here.	When a noun is specific (*e.g.*, *the students*), using **_of_** after **_all_** is optional.
(c) CORRECT: **_All students_** must have an I.D. card. (d) INCORRECT: *All of students must have an I.D. card.*	When a noun is nonspecific, **_of_** does NOT follow **_all_**.
(e) I know **_both (of) those men._**	Similarly, using **_of_** after **_both_** is optional when the noun is specific.

_____

*COMPARE:

    (1) **_The most_** = superlative. The superlative is used to compare three or more persons or things. **_The most_** is never immediately followed by *of. Example: Out of all the boys, Tom ate **the most food**.*

    (2) **_Most_** (not preceded by **_the_**) = an expression of quantity whose meaning ranges from "over fifty percent" to "almost all." *Example: **Most of the food** at that restaurant is good, but not all of it.*

Notice that of is not necessary in any of the following sentences. However, if it is possible to use of, write (of) in the blank. If of is not possible because the noun is nonspecific, write Ø.

1. All ____(of)____ the children listened to the story.

2. Almost all ____Ø____ children like fairy tales.

3. Both _____ those books are mine.

4. I bought two books. Both _____ books were expensive.

5. Almost all _____ students study hard for exams.

6. All _____ the students in my class are studying English.

7. I have two brothers. Both _____ my brothers are in school.

8. Do you know all _____ the people in your biology class?

9. Not all _____ people are friendly, but most _____ people have kind hearts.

10. All _____ birds have wings, but not all _____ birds can fly.

5-11 SINGULAR EXPRESSIONS OF QUANTITY: *ONE, EACH, EVERY*

(a) *One student* was late to class. (b) *Each student* has a schedule. (c) *Every student* has a schedule.	*One*, *each*, and *every* are followed immediately by *singular count nouns* (never plural nouns, never noncount nouns).
(d) *One of the students* was late to class. (e) *Each (one) of the students* has a schedule. (f) *Every one of the students* has a schedule.	*One of*, *each of*, and *every one of** are followed by *specific plural count nouns* (never singular nouns, never noncount nouns).

*COMPARE:
    Every one (spelled as two words) is an expression of quantity; e.g., *I have read **every one** of those books.*
    Everyone (spelled as one word) is an indefinite pronoun; it has the same meaning as *everybody*; e.g.,
    Everyone/Everybody has a schedule.
NOTE: *Each* and *every* have essentially the same meaning.
    Each is used when the speaker is thinking of one person/thing at a time: *Each student has a schedule.* = *Mary has a schedule. John has a schedule. Hiroshi has a schedule. Carlos has a schedule. Sabrina has a schedule. (etc.)*
    Every is used when the speaker means "all." *Every student has a schedule.* = *All of the students have schedules.*

☐ **EXERCISE 19:** Complete the sentences with the correct form, singular or plural, of the noun in parentheses.

1. There is only one ____girl____ on the sixth-grade soccer team. (*girl*)

2. Only one of the _____ in the sixth grade is on the soccer team. (*girl*)

3. Mrs. Hoover gave a present to each _____. (*child*)

4. Each of the _____ got a present. (*child*)

5. We invited every _____ of the club. (*member*)

6. Every one of the _____ came. (*member*)

☐ **EXERCISE 20—ERROR ANALYSIS:** Some (but not all) of the following sentences contain errors. Find and correct the errors.

                        student

1. It's important for every students to have a book.

2. Each of the students in my class has a book.

3. Spain is one of the country I want to visit.

4. The teacher gave each of students a test paper.

5. Every student in the class did well on the test.

6. Every furniture in that room is made of wood.

7. One of the equipment in our office is broken.

8. I gave a present to each of the woman in the room.

9. One of my favorite place in the world is an island in the Caribbean Sea.

10. Each one of your suitcases will be checked when you go through customs.

11. It's impossible for one human being to know every languages in the world.

12. I found each of the error in this exercise.

☐ **EXERCISE 21—PRETEST:** Choose the correct answer in parentheses.

1. The weather in the southern states (*gets, get*) very hot during the summer.

2. The results of Dr. Noll's experiment (*was, were*) published in a scientific journal.

3. Bob and his friend (*is, are*) coming to the anniversary party tomorrow night.

4. Every man, woman, and child (*is, are*) protected under the law.

5. Washing the dishes (*is, are*) the children's job.

6. A lot of the students (*is, are*) already here.

7. Some of the furniture in our apartment (*is, are*) secondhand.

8. Some of the desks in the classroom (*is, are*) broken.

9. At least three-quarters of that book on famous Americans (*is, are*) about people who lived in the nineteenth century.

10. One of the countries I would like to visit (*is, are*) Italy.

11. Some of the cities I would like to visit (*is, are*) Rome and Venice.

12. Each student in the class (*has, have*) to have a book.

13. Each of the students (*has, have*) a notebook.

14. None of the students (*was, were*) late today.

15. The number of students in this room right now (*is, are*) twenty.

16. A number of students in the class (*speaks, speak*) English very well.

17. There (*is, are*) some interesting pictures in today's paper.

18. There (*is, are*) an incorrect statement in that newspaper article.

19. The United States (*is, are*) located in North America.

20. Economics (*is, are*) Don's favorite subject.

21. Ten minutes (*is, are*) more than enough time to complete this exercise.

22. Most people (*likes, like*) to go to the zoo.

23. The police (*is, are*) coming. I've already called them.

24. Japanese (*is, are*) very difficult for English speakers to learn.

25. The Japanese (*has, have*) a long and interesting history.

26. The old in my country (*is, are*) cared for by their children and grandchildren.

27. This exercise on singular–plural agreement of subjects and verbs (*is, are*) easy.

5–12 BASIC SUBJECT–VERB AGREEMENT

SINGULAR VERB	PLURAL VERB	
(a) My *friend* **lives** in Boston.	(b) My *friends* **live** in Boston.	*verb* + *-s/-es* = third person singular in the simple present tense *noun* + *-s/-es* = plural
(c) That *book* on political parties **is** interesting.	(d) The *ideas* in that book **are** interesting.	A prepositional phrase that comes between a subject and a verb does not affect the verb.
	(e) My *brother and sister* **live** in Boston.	Two (or more) subjects connected by **and** take a plural verb.
(f) *Every man, woman, and child* **needs** love. (g) *Each book and magazine* **is** listed in the card catalog.		EXCEPTION: **Every** and **each** are always followed immediately by singular nouns. In this case, even when there are two (or more) nouns connected by **and**, the verb is singular.
(h) *Growing* flowers **is** her hobby.		A gerund used as the subject of a sentence takes a singular verb.

☐ **EXERCISE 22:** Choose the correct answer in parentheses.

1. The extent of Jane's knowledge on various complex subjects (*astounds, astound*) me.
2. The subjects you will be studying in this course (*is, are*) listed in the syllabus.
3. Massachusetts and Connecticut (*is, are*) located in New England.
4. Only the black widow spider, of all the spiders in the United States, (*has, have*) caused death among human beings.
5. Oranges, tomatoes, fresh strawberries, cabbage, and green lettuce (*is, are*) rich in vitamin C.
6. The professor and the student (*agrees, agree*) on that point.
7. Almost every professor and student at the university (*approves, approve*) of the choice of Dr. Brown as the new president.
8. Each girl and boy in the sixth-grade class (*has, have*) to do a science project.
9. Making pies and cakes (*is, are*) Mrs. Reed's specialty.
10. Getting to know students from all over the world (*is, are*) one of the best parts of my job.
11. Annie had a hard time when she was coming home from the store because the bag of groceries (*was, were*) too heavy for her to carry.

12. Where (*does, do*) your parents live?
13. Why (*was, were*) Susan and Alex late for the meeting?
14. (*Is, Are*) having the responsibility for taking care of pets good for young children?

5-13 SUBJECT–VERB AGREEMENT: USING EXPRESSIONS OF QUANTITY

SINGULAR VERB	PLURAL VERB	

(a) *Some of the book is* good.
 (c) *A lot of the equipment is* new.
 (e) *Two-thirds of the money is* mine.
	(b) *Some of the books are* good.
	 (d) *A lot of my friends are* here.
	 (f) *Two-thirds of the pennies are* mine.
		The verb is determined by the noun (or pronoun) that follows *of* in most expressions of quantity. Notice in (a) and (b):
		    some of + singular noun + singular verb
		    some of + plural noun + plural verb

(g) *One of my friends is* here.
 (h) *Each of my friends is* here.
 (i) *Every one of my friends is* here.
		EXCEPTIONS: *One of, each of,* and *every one of* take singular verbs.
		    one of
		    each of } *+ plural noun + singular verb*
		    every one of

(j) *None of the boys is* here.	(k) *None of the boys are* here. *(informal)*	Subjects with *none of* are considered singular in very formal English, but plural verbs are often used in informal speech and writing.
(l) *The number of students* in the class *is* fifteen.	(m) *A number of students were* late for class.	COMPARE: In (l): *The number* is the subject. In (m): *A number of* is an expression of quantity meaning "a lot of." It is followed by a plural noun and a plural verb.

☐ **EXERCISE 23:** Choose the correct answer in parentheses.

1. Some of the fruit in this bowl (*is, are*) rotten.
2. Some of the apples in that bowl (*is, are*) rotten.
3. Half of the students in the class (*is, are*) from Arabic-speaking countries.
4. Half of this money (*belongs, belong*) to you.
5. A lot of the students in the class (*is, are*) from Southeast Asia.
6. A lot of clothing in those stores (*is, are*) on sale this week.
7. One of my best friends (*is, are*) coming to visit me next month.
8. Each boy in the class (*has, have*) his own notebook.
9. Each of the boys in the class (*has, have*) his own notebook.
10. Every one of the students (*is, are*) required to take the final test.
11. None of the animals at the zoo (*is, are*) free. All of them (*is, are*) in enclosures.
12. A number of students (*is, are*) absent today.

13. The number of students at that university (*is, are*) approximately 10,000.
14. One of the chief materials in bones and teeth (*is, are*) calcium.
15. (*Does, Do*) all of the children have their books?
16. (*Does, Do*) all of this homework have to be finished by tomorrow?
17. Why (*was, were*) some of the students excused from the examination?
18. Why (*was, were*) one of the students excused from the examination?
19. What percentage of the earth's surface (*is, are*) covered by water?
20. What percentage of the people in the world (*is, are*) illiterate?
21. (*Does, Do*) any of you know the answer to that question?

5–14 SUBJECT–VERB AGREEMENT: USING *THERE + BE*

SINGULAR VERB   **PLURAL VERB**

(a) There ***is*** *a book* on the shelf.	(b) There ***are*** *some books* on the shelf.	The subject follows ***be*** when ***there*** is used.* In (a): The subject is *book*. In (b): The subject is *books*.

*In the structure ***there*** + ***be***, ***there*** is called an *expletive*.

□ **EXERCISE 24:** Choose the correct answer in parentheses.

1. There (*isn't, aren't*) any letters in the mail for you today.
2. There (*isn't, aren't*) any mail for you today.
3. There (*is, are*) a lot of problems in the world.
4. There (*is, are*) a fly in this room. Where's the flyswatter?
5. There (*is, are*) over 600,000 kinds of insects in the world.
6. How many kinds of birds (*is, are*) there in the world?
7. Why (*isn't, aren't*) there a hospital close to those villages?
8. There (*is, are*) a green pen on Tim's desk.
9. There (*is, are*) a blue pen and a yellow notebook on Sue's desk.★
10. There (*is, are*) some pens and notebooks on Jack's desk.

★Sometimes in informal English, a singular verb is used after ***there*** when the first of two subjects connected by ***and*** is singular. For example:
    Formal: There ***are a book and a pen*** on the desk.
    Informal: There ***is a book and a pen*** on the desk.

5–15 SUBJECT–VERB AGREEMENT: SOME IRREGULARITIES

SINGULAR VERB

(a) *The news **is** interesting.* (b) *The United States **is** big.* (c) *The Philippines **consists** of more than 7,000 islands.* (d) *The United Nations **has** its headquarters in New York City.* (e) *Sears **is** a department store.* (f) *Mathematics **is** easy for her. Physics **is** easy for her, too.*	Sometimes a noun that ends in **-s** is singular. Notice the examples: If the noun is changed to a pronoun, the singular pronoun **it** is used (not the plural pronoun **they**) because the noun is singular. In (a): **news = it** (not **they**). In (b): **the United States = it** (not **they**). Note: Fields of study, as in (f), that end in **-ics** take singular verbs.
(g) *Eight hours of sleep **is** enough.* (h) *Ten dollars **is** too much to pay.* (i) *Five thousand miles **is** too far to travel.*	Expressions of *time, money,* and *distance* usually take a singular verb.

PLURAL VERB

(j) *Those people **are** from Canada.* (k) *The police **have** been called.*	**People*** and **police** do not end in **-s** but are plural nouns and take plural verbs.

SINGULAR VERB	**PLURAL VERB**	
(l) *English **is** spoken in many countries.* (n) *Chinese **is** his native language.*	(m) *The English **drink** tea.* (o) *The Chinese **have** an interesting history.*	In (l): **English** = language. In (m): **the English** = people from England. Some nouns of nationality that end in **-sh**, **-ese**, and **-ch** can mean either language or people; e.g., *English, Spanish, Chinese, Japanese, Vietnamese, Portuguese, French.*
	(p) *The poor **have** many problems.* (q) *The rich **get** richer.*	A few adjectives can be preceded by **the** and used as a plural noun (without final **-s**) to refer to people who have this quality. Other examples: *the young, the old, the living, the dead, the blind, the deaf, the handicapped.*

*The word **people** has a final **-s** (*peoples*) only when it is used to refer to nations or ethnic groups: *All the peoples of the world desire peace.*

□ **EXERCISE 25:** Choose the correct answer in parentheses.

1. The United States (*has, have*) a population of around 250 million.

2. The news about Mr. Hogan (*is, are*) surprising.

3. Massachusetts (*is, are*) a state in the northeastern part of the United States.

4. Physics (*seeks, seek*) to understand the mysteries of the physical world.

5. Statistics (*is, are*) a branch of mathematics.

6. The statistics in that report on oil production (*is, are*) incorrect.*

7. Fifty minutes (*is, are*) the maximum length of time allowed for the exam.

8. Twenty dollars (*is, are*) an unreasonable price for the necklace.

9. Many people in the world (*does, do*) not have enough to eat.

10. The police (*is, are*) prepared in case there is a riot.

11. The English (*is, are*) proud, independent people.

12. English (*is, are*) not my native language.

13. Many Japanese (*commutes, commute*) to their places of work.

14. Portuguese (*is, are*) somewhat similar to Spanish, (*isn't, aren't*) it?

15. The poor (*is, are*) helped by government programs.

16. The effect of a honeybee's sting on a human being (*depends, depend*) on that person's susceptibility to the bee's venom. Most people (*is, are*) not in danger if they are stung, but there (*has, have*) been instances of allergic deaths from a single honeybee sting.

☐ **EXERCISE 26—ORAL (BOOKS CLOSED):** Respond with *is* or *are*.

> *Examples:* Some of my classmates....   Some of that information....
> *Response:* ...are   ...is

1. His idea....
2. His ideas....
3. People....
4. Each of the students....
5. Most of the fruit....
6. Most of the students....
7. The United States....
8. The news in this morning's paper....
9. One of the girls....
10. French....
11. The Vietnamese....
12. Two-thirds of the food....
13. The number of students....
14. Some of the people....
15. Ninety-three million miles....
16. The story about his adventures....
17. A lot of the chairs....
18. A lot of the furniture....
19. Everyone in the English classes....
20. The clothes in that store....
21. Most of the information in those books....
22. The news from home....
23. Fifty percent of the people in the world....

---

*Statistics is singular when it refers to a field of study: e.g., *Statistics is an interesting field of study.* When it refers to particular numbers, it is used as a count noun: *singular = one statistic (no final -s); plural = two statistics.* For example: *This statistic is* correct. *Those statistics are* incorrect.

24. Fifty percent of the world's population....

25. The clothing in those stores....

26. Her husband's relatives....

27. Over half of the books by that author....

28. A million dollars....

29. The rich....

30. His method of doing things....

31. A number of people....

32. Most of the stores in this city....

33. Mathematics....

34. The police....

35. Everybody in the whole world....

☐ **EXERCISE 27:** Write the correct form of the given verb. Use only the SIMPLE PRESENT.

1. My alarm clock _____ *rings* _____ at seven every morning. (*ring*)

2. There _____ *are* _____ a lot of sheep in the field. (*be*)

3. One of my friends _____ a goldfish bowl on her kitchen table. (*keep*)

4. Sensitivity to other people's feelings _____ him a kind and understanding person. (*make*)

5. Each penny, nickel, dime, and quarter _____ counted carefully by the bank teller. (*be*)

6. My driver's license _____ in my wallet. (*be*)

7. _____ John's uncle live in the suburbs? (*do*)

8. _____ most of the students live in the dormitories? (*do*)

9. An orange and black bird _____ sitting in that tree. (*be*)

10. An orange bird and a black bird _____ sitting in that tree. (*be*)

11. The insurance rates on our car _____ high because we live in a city. (*be*)

12. _____ January and February the coldest months of the year? (*be*)

13. Almost two-thirds of the land in the southwestern areas of the country _____ unsuitable for farming. (*be*)

14. The economic and cultural center of the United States _____ New York City. (*be*)

15. Two hours of skiing _____ plenty of exercise. (*provide*)

16. In many respects, this magazine article on wild animals in North America _____ the very real danger of extinction that many species face. (*oversimplify*)

17. A car with poor brakes and no brake lights _____ dangerous. (*be*)

18. A number of people from the company _____ to attend the conference. (*plan*)

19. Most of the news on the front pages of both daily newspapers _____ the progress of the peace conference. (*concern*)

20. The northernmost town in the forty-eight contiguous states _____ Angle Inlet, Minnesota. (*be*)

21. The number of human skeletons found at the archaeological site _____ seven. (*be*)

22. Almost all the information in those texts on the Aztec Indians and their civilization _____ to be well researched. (*appear*)

23. Every day there _____ more than a dozen traffic accidents in the city. (*be*)

24. No news _____ good news. (*be*)

25. Every member of this class _____ English very well. (*speak*)

□ **EXERCISE 28—WRITTEN/ORAL:** Complete the following sentences with your own words. Use only present tenses.

Examples: One of my . . . *teachers knows Chinese.*
Some of my . . . *friends are coming to visit me.*

1. All of the rooms in . . . .
2. In my country, there . . . .
3. A lot of . . . .
4. The people in my country . . . .
5. The number of students . . . .
6. A number of students . . . .
7. Each of . . . .
8. The United States . . . .
9. The English language . . . .
10. The English . . . .
11. English . . . .
12. One of my . . . .
13. Most of the food . . . .
14. Most of my classmates . . . .
15. Linguistics . . . .
16. Linguists . . . .

5-16 PERSONAL PRONOUNS: AGREEMENT WITH NOUNS

(a) **A student** walked into the room. **She** was looking for the teacher.	A singular pronoun is used to refer to a singular noun, as in (a) and (b).
(b) **A student** walked into the room. **He** was looking for the teacher.	
(c) **Some students** walked into the room. **They** were looking for the teacher.	A plural pronoun is used to refer to a plural noun, as in (c).
(d) **A student** should always do **his** assignments.	With a "generic noun"* (e.g, in (d): **a student** = *anyone who is a student*) a singular masculine pronoun has been used traditionally, but many English speakers now use both masculine and feminine pronouns, as in (e).
(e) **A student** should always do **his/her** assignments. **A student** should always do **his or her** assignments.	

*A generic noun does not refer to any person or thing in particular; rather, it represents a whole group. (See Appendix 1, Chart D-1, *Basic Article Usage*.)

5-17 PERSONAL PRONOUNS: AGREEMENT WITH INDEFINITE PRONOUNS

The following are indefinite pronouns:			
everyone	*someone*	*anyone*	*no one*
everybody	*somebody*	*anybody*	*nobody*
everything	*something*	*anything*	*nothing*

(f) **Somebody** left **his** book on the desk.	A singular personal pronoun is used in formal English to refer to an indefinite pronoun, as in (f) and (g).
(g) **Everyone** has **his or her** own ideas.	
(h) INFORMAL: **Somebody** left **their** book on the desk. **Everyone** has **their** own ideas.	In everyday informal English, a plural personal pronoun is often used to refer to an indefinite pronoun, as in (h).

☐ **EXERCISE 29:** Complete the sentences with pronouns. In some of the blanks there is more than one possibility. Choose the appropriate singular or plural verb in parentheses where necessary.

1. When a student wants to study, _s/he; he or she; he_ should try to find a quiet place.*

---

*Notice in 1 through 4: The problem of masculine/feminine pronouns can be avoided if a plural instead of singular generic noun is used.

2. A citizen has two primary responsibilities. _____ should vote in every election, and _____ should willingly serve on a jury.

3. Each student in Biology 101 has to spend three hours per week in the laboratory, where _____ (*does, do*) various experiments by following the directions in _____ lab manual.

4. A pharmacist fills prescriptions, but _____ (*is, are*) not allowed to prescribe medicine. By law, only a doctor can prescribe medicine.

5. Anyone can learn how to dance if _____ (*wants, want*) to.

6. Hmmm. Someone forgot _____ umbrella. I wonder whose it is.

7. Everyone who came to the picnic brought _____ own food.

8. A: Is that your notebook?

   B: No. It belongs to one of the other students.

   A: Look on the inside cover. Did _____ write _____ name there?

9. A dog makes a good pet if _____ (*is, are*) properly trained.

10. Tom's cat is named Maybelle Alice. _____ is very independent. _____ obeys Tom only if _____ feels like it.*

5–18 PERSONAL PRONOUNS: AGREEMENT WITH COLLECTIVE NOUNS

<table>
<tr><td colspan="2">The following are examples of collective nouns:

    audience   *couple*   *family*   *public*
    class   *crowd*   *government*   *staff*
    committee *faculty*   *group*   *team*</td></tr>
<tr><td>(a) My family is large. It is composed of nine members.</td><td>When a collective noun refers to a single impersonal unit, a singular pronoun (it, its) is used, as in (a).</td></tr>
<tr><td>(b) My family is loving and supportive. They are always ready to help me.</td><td>When a collective noun refers to a collection of various individuals, a plural pronoun (they, them, their) is used, as in (b).*</td></tr>
</table>

*NOTE: When the collective noun refers to a collection of individuals, the verb may be either singular or plural: *My family is* OR *are loving and supportive.* A singular verb is generally preferred in American English. A plural verb is used more frequently in British English, especially with the words *government* and *public.* (American: **The government is** *planning many changes.* British: **The government are** *planning many changes.*)

---

*If the sex of a particular animal is known, usually **she** or **he** is used instead of **it**.

□ **EXERCISE 30:** Complete the sentences with pronouns. In some of the sentences, there is more than one possibility. Choose the appropriate singular or plural verb in parentheses where necessary.

1. I have a wonderful family. I love _____*them*_____ very much, and
   _____*they love*_____ (*loves, love*) me.

2. I looked up some information about the average American family. I
   found out that _____ (*consists, consist*) of 2.3 children.

3. The soccer team felt unhappy because _____ had lost in the
   closing moments of the game.

4. A basketball team is relatively small. _____ (*doesn't, don't*)
   have as many members as a baseball team.

5. The audience clapped enthusiastically. Obviously _____
   had enjoyed the concert.

6. The audience filled the room to overflowing. _____ (*was,
   were*) larger than I had expected.

7. The crowd became more and more excited as the premier's motorcade
   approached. _____ began to shout and wave flags in the air.

8. The crowd at the soccer game was huge. _____ exceeded 100,000
   people.

9. The office staff gave _____ boss a gold watch when she retired.

10. The office staff isn't large. _____ (*consists, consist*) of a
    secretary, a file clerk, and a receptionist.

11. The young couple finally saved enough money to make a downpayment
    on _____ own house.

12. The class is planning a party for the last day of school. _____
    (*is, are*) going to bring many different kinds of food and invite some of
    _____ friends to celebrate with _____.

13. The class is too small. _____ (*is, are*) going to be cancelled.

5-19 USING REFLEXIVE PRONOUNS

The following are reflexive pronouns:	
myself *ourselves* *yourself* *yourselves* *himself, herself, itself* *themselves*	
(a) *He* looked at *himself* in the mirror.	A reflexive pronoun usually refers to the subject of a sentence. In (a): *he* and *himself* refer to the same person.
(b) *He himself* answered the phone, not his secretary. (c) *He* answered the phone *himself*.	Sometimes reflexive pronouns are used for emphasis, as in (b) and (c).
(d) She lives *by herself*.	The expression *by* + *a reflexive pronoun* usually means "alone," as in (d).

□ **EXERCISE 31:** Complete the following by using appropriate reflexive pronouns.

1. I can't help you, Bob. You'll have to solve your problem by *yourself*.

2. Jane did not join the rest of us. She sat in the back of the room by

   _____.

3. You may think Stan is telling the truth, but I _____ don't

   believe him.

4. It is important for all of us to be honest with _____.

5. Now that their children are grown, Mr. and Mrs. Grayson live by

   _____.

6. You _____ have to make that decision, Ann. No one can

   make it for you.

7. I don't know what to tell you, Sue and Jack. You will have to take care of

   that problem _____.

8. When everybody else forgot his birthday, Ralph decided to give

   _____ a birthday present. He bought a new shirt for

   _____.

☐ **EXERCISE 32:** Complete the sentences by using a word or expression from the given list and an appropriate reflexive pronoun.

angry at	*introduced*	*promised*
enjoy	*killed*	*proud of*
entertained	*laugh at*	*talking to*
feeling sorry for	*pat*	✔ *taught*

1. Karen Williams never took lessons. She ___*taught herself*___ how to play the piano.

2. Did Hank have a good time at the party? Did he _____?

3. All of you did a good job. You should be _____.

4. You did a good job, Barbara. You should _____ on the back.

5. A man down the street committed suicide. We were all shocked by the news that he had _____.

6. The children played very well without adult supervision. They _____ by playing school.

7. I had always wanted to meet Mr. Anderson. When I saw him at a party last night, I walked over and _____ to him.

8. Yesterday Fred's car ran out of gas. Fred had to walk two miles to a gas station. He is still _____ for forgetting to fill the tank.

9. Nothing good ever comes from self-pity. You should stop _____, George, and start doing something to solve your problems.

10. Carol made several careless mistakes at work last week, and her boss is getting impatient with her. Carol has _____ to do better work in the future.

11. People might think you're a little crazy, but _____ _____ is one way to practice using English.

12. Humor can ease the trials and tribulations of life. Sometimes we have to be able to _____.

5–20 USING *YOU* AND *ONE* AS IMPERSONAL PRONOUNS

(a) ***One*** should always be polite. (b) How does ***one*** get to 5th Avenue from here?	In (a) and (b): ***one*** means "any person, people in general."
(c) ***You*** should always be polite. (d) How do ***you*** get to 5th Avenue from here?	In (c) and (d): ***you*** means "any person, people in general." ***One*** is more formal than ***you***. Impersonal ***you***, rather than ***one***, is used more frequently in everyday English.

(e) ***One*** should take care of ***one's*** health.
    One should take care of ***his*** health.
    One should take care of ***his or her*** health.
	In (e): Notice the pronouns that may be used in the same sentence to refer back to ***one***.

□ **EXERCISE 33—ERROR ANALYSIS:** All the following have errors. Make the pronoun usage in the following consistent and correct.

1. One should always try to be friendly to your neighbors.
   *One should always try to be friendly to **one's** neighbors* (OR ***his or her** neighbors*).
   ***You** should always try to be friendly to **your** neighbors.*
   ***People** should always try to be friendly to **their** neighbors.*
   ***A person** should always try to be friendly to **his or her** neighbors.*

2. One can't know what he can actually do until you try.

3. It is important for a person to listen to your conscience.

4. You can get to the airport by taxi or by bus. People can catch the airport bus at the hotel.

5. Self-esteem is important to one's mental health. It is important for you to like yourself.

6. It is important for one to take care of their health. For example, you should not smoke. Smoking has been shown to cause various life-threatening diseases. One should also be careful to get plenty of exercise. Adequate rest is important, too. People can't be their best if one is tired all the time. We also need to eat a wide variety of food to make sure you get all the nutrients your body needs.

5-21 FORMS OF *OTHER*

	ADJECTIVE	PRONOUN	
singular:	**another book** (is)	**another** (is)	Forms of *other* are used as either adjectives or pronouns.
plural:	**other books** (are)	**others** (are)	
singular:	**the other book** (is)	**the other** (is)	Notice: A final *-s* is used only for a plural pronoun (*others*).
plural:	**the other books** (are)	**the others** (are)	

(a) The students in the class come from many countries. One of the students is from Mexico. *Another student is* from Iraq. *Another is* from Japan. *Other students are* from Brazil. *Others are* from Algeria.	The meaning of *another*: *one more in addition to the one(s) already mentioned.* The meaning of *other/others* (without *the*): *several more in addition to the one(s) already mentioned.*
(b) I have three books. Two are mine. *The other book* is yours. (*The other* is yours.) (c) I have three books. One is mine. *The other books* are yours. (*The others* are yours.)	The meaning of *the other(s)*: *all that remains from a given number; the rest of a specific group.*
(d) We write to *each other* every week. (e) We write to *one another* every week.	*Each other* and *one another* indicate a reciprocal relationship. In (d) and (e): I write to him every week, and he writes to me every week.
(f) Please write on *every other* line. (g) I see her *every other* week.	*Every other* can give the idea of "alternate." In (f): Write on the first line. Do not write on the second line. Write on the third line. Do not write on the fourth line. (etc.)
(h) I will be here for *another three years*. (i) I need *another five dollars*. (j) We drove *another ten miles*.	*Another* is used with expressions of time, money, and distance, even if these expressions contain plural nouns.

☐ **EXERCISE 34:** Supply a form of *other* in the following.

1. I got three letters. One was from my father. ___*Another*___ one was from my sister. ___*The other*___ letter was from my girlfriend.

2. Look at your hand. There is a total of five fingers. One is your thumb. _____ is your index finger. _____ one is your middle finger. _____ finger is your ring finger. And _____ finger (the last of the five) is your little finger.

3. Look at your hands. One is your right hand. _____ is your left hand.

4. I invited five people to my party. Out of those five people, only John and Mary can come. _____ can't come.

5. I invited five people to my party. Out of those five people, only John and Mary can come. _____ people can't come.

6. I would like some more books on this subject. Do you have any _____ that you could lend me?

7. I would like to read more about this subject. Do you have any _____ books that you could lend me?

8. There are many means of transportation. The airplane is one means of transportation. The train is _____.

9. There are many means of transportation. The airplane is one. _____ are the train, the automobile, and the horse.

10. There are two women standing on the corner. One is Helen Jansen and _____ is Pat Hendricks.

11. Alice reads *The New York Times* every day. She doesn't read any _____ newspapers.

12. Some people prefer classical music, but _____ prefer rock music.

13. Mr. and Mrs. Jay are a happily married couple. They love _____. They support _____. They like _____.

14. He will graduate in _____ two years.

15. I'm almost finished. I just need _____ five minutes.

□ **EXERCISE 35:** Supply a form of *other* in the following.

1. One common preposition is *from*. _____ common one is *in*. _____ are *by, for,* and *of.* The most frequently used prepositions in English are *at, by, for, from, in, of, to,* and *with.* What are some _____ prepositions?

2. Two countries border on the United States. One is Canada. _____ is Mexico.

3. One of the countries I would like to visit is Sweden. _____ is Mexico. Of course, besides these two countries, there are many _____ places I would like to see.

4. They have three children. One has graduated from college and has a job. _____ is in school at the University of Arkansas. _____ _____ is still living at home.

5. Thank you for inviting me to go on the picnic. I'd like to go with you, but I've already made _____ plans.

6. Most of the guests have already arrived, and I'm sure that all of _____ _____ will be here soon.

7. Some people are tall; _____ are short. Some people are fat; _____ are thin. Some people are nearsighted; _____ people are farsighted.

8. That country has two basic problems. One is inflation, and _____ is the instability of their government.

9. I have been in only three cities since I came to the United States. One is New York, and _____ are Washington, D.C., and Chicago.

10. When his alarm went off this morning, he shut it off, rolled over, and slept for _____ twenty minutes.

11. Louis and I have been friends for a long time. We've known _____ _____ since we were children.

12. Individual differences in children must be recognized. Whereas one child might have a strong interest in mathematics and science, _____ child might tend toward more artistic endeavors.

13. It's a long trip. I'm getting tired of riding in the car, but we still have _____ two hundred miles to go.

14. In just _____ three weeks, he will be a married man.

15. Prices continually rise. Next year a new car will cost _____ three or four hundred dollars.

□ **EXERCISE 36—ORAL (BOOKS CLOSED):** Complete the sentences, using an appropriate form of *other*.

Example: There are two books on the desk. One is . . . .
Response: (One is . . .) mine, and the other is yours.
          (One is . . .) red. The other is blue.

1. I speak two languages. One is . . . .
2. I speak three languages. One is . . . .
3. I lost my textbook, so I had to buy . . . .
4. Some people have straight hair, but . . . .
5. I'm still thirsty. I'd like . . . .
6. George Washington is one American hero. Abraham Lincoln . . . .
7. I have two books. One is . . . .
8. Some TV programs are excellent, but . . . .
9. Some people need at least eight hours of sleep each night, but . . . .
10. Only two of the students failed the quiz. All of . . . .
11. Mary and John are in love. They love . . . .
12. There are three colors that I especially like. One is . . . .
13. I have two candy bars. I want only one of them. Would you like . . . .
14. I'm still hungry. I'd like . . . .
15. There are three places in particular that I would like to visit while I am in (*the United States*). One is . . . .

☐ **EXERCISE 37—ERROR ANALYSIS:** The following sentences are adapted from student writing and contain typical errors. Test your skill by finding and correcting these errors.

1. That book contain many different kind of story and article.

2. There is a lot of differences between United States and my country.

3. The English is one of the most important language in the world.

4. She is always willing to help her friends in every possible ways.

5. I don't have enough time to make all of my homeworks.

6. He succeeded in creating one of the best army in the world.

7. There are many equipments in the research laboratory, but undergraduates are not allowed to use them.

8. All of the guest enjoyed themself at the reception.

9. I have a five years old daughter and a three years old son.

10. I am not accustomed to a cold weather.

11. Each states in the country have a different language.

12. Most of people in my apartment building is friendly.

13. A political leader should have the ability to adapt themselves to a changing world.

14. In my opinion, a foreign student should live in a dormitory because they will meet many people and can practice their English every day. Also, if you live in a dormitory, your food is provided for you.

15. When I lost my passport, I had to apply for the another one.

16. When I got to class, all of the others students were already in their seats.

☐ **EXERCISE 38—PREPOSITIONS:** Supply an appropriate preposition for each of the following.

1. Do you believe _____ ghosts?

2. Anthony is engaged _____ my cousin.

3. Ms. Ballas substituted _____ our regular teacher yesterday.

4. I can't distinguish one twin _____ the other.

5. Did you forgive him _____ lying to you?

6. Children rely _____ their parents for food and shelter.

7. Tim wore sunglasses to protect his eyes _____ the sun.

8. Chris excels _____ sports.

9. Andrea contributed her ideas _____ the discussion.

10. I hope you succeed _____ your new job.

11. I'm very fond _____ their children.

12. The firefighters rescued many people _____ the burning building.

13. I don't care _____ spaghetti. I'd rather eat something else.

14. Charles doesn't seem to care _____ his bad grades.

15. Sometimes Bobby seems to be jealous _____ his brother.

☐ **EXERCISE 39—PHRASAL VERBS:** Supply appropriate prepositions for the following two-word or three-word verbs.

1. A: Omar, would you please pass these papers _____ to the rest of the class?

   B: I'd be happy to.

2. A: When are we expected to be at the hotel?

   B: According to our reservation, we are supposed to check _____ the hotel before 6 P.M. Monday and check _____ before noon Tuesday.

3. A: How do you get _____ with your roommate?

   B: Fine. He's a nice guy.

4. A: Thanks for the ride. I appreciate it.

   B: Where should I drop you _____?

   A: The next corner would be fine.

5. A: I'm going to be out of town for a couple of days. Would you mind looking _____ my cat?

   B: Not at all. I'd be happy to. Just tell me what I'm supposed to do.

6. A: I think I'm going to turn _____ now. Good night.

   B: 'Night. See you in the morning. Sleep well.

7. A: Don't you think it's hot in here?

   B: Not especially. If you're hot, why don't you take your sweater _____?

8. A: How do you spell "occasionally"?

   B: I'm not sure. You'd better look it _____ in your dictionary.

9. A: How much lettuce should we get?

   B: I think we could use two heads. Pick _____ two that feel fresh and firm.

10. A: Why are you sniffling?

    B: I had a cold last week, and I can't seem to get _____ it.

CHAPTER **6**
Adjective Clauses

6–1 ADJECTIVE CLAUSES: INTRODUCTION

Terms:	**clause:**	*A clause* is a group of words containing a subject and a verb.
	independent clause:	*An independent clause* is a complete sentence. It contains the main subject and verb of a sentence. (It is also called *a main clause*.)
	dependent clause:	*A dependent clause* is not a complete sentence. It must be connected to an independent clause.
	adjective clause:	*An adjective clause* is a dependent clause that modifies a noun. It describes, identifies, or gives further information about a noun. (An adjective clause is also called *a relative clause*.)

6–2 USING SUBJECT PRONOUNS: *WHO, WHICH, THAT*

	I thanked the woman. **She** helped me. ↓ (a) I thanked the woman **who** *helped me.* (b) I thanked the woman **that** *helped me.*	In (a): *I thanked the woman* = an independent clause *who helped me* = an adjective clause The adjective clause modifies the noun *woman*.
		In (a): **who** is the subject of the adjective clause. In (b): **that** is the subject of the adjective clause. Note: (a) and (b) have the same meaning.
	The book is mine. **It** is on the table. ↓ (c) The book **which** *is on the table* is mine. (d) The book **that** *is on the table* is mine.	**who** = used for people **which** = used for things **that** = used for both people and things

☐ **EXERCISE 1—ORAL:** Combine the two sentences. Use the second sentence as an adjective clause.

1. I saw the man. He closed the door. →

   I saw the man $\left\{\begin{matrix} who \\ that \end{matrix}\right\}$ *closed the door.*

2. The girl is happy. She won the race.
3. The student is from China. He sits next to me.
4. The students are from China. They sit in the front row.
5. We are studying sentences. They contain adjective clauses.
6. I am using a sentence. It contains an adjective clause.
7. Algebra problems contain letters. They stand for unknown numbers.
8. The taxi driver was friendly. He took me to the airport.

6–3 USING OBJECT PRONOUNS: *WHO(M), WHICH, THAT*

1. PRONOUN USED AS THE OBJECT OF A VERB The man was Mr. Jones. I saw *him*. (e) The man *who(m)* *I saw* was Mr. Jones. (f) The man *that* *I saw* was Mr. Jones. (g) The man Ø *I saw* was Mr. Jones. The movie wasn't very good. We saw *it* last night. (h) The movie *which* *we saw last night* wasn't very good. (i) The movie *that* *we saw last night* wasn't very good. (j) The movie Ø *we saw last night* wasn't very good.	Notice in the examples: The adjective clause pronouns are placed at the *beginning* of the clause. (General guideline: Place an adjective clause pronoun as close as possible to the noun it modifies.)
	In (e): *who* is usually used instead of *whom*, especially in speaking. *Whom* is generally used only in very formal English.
	In (g) and (j): An object pronoun is often omitted from an adjective clause. (A subject pronoun, however, may not be omitted.)
	who(m) = used for people *which* = used for things *that* = used for both people and things

☐ **EXERCISE 2—ORAL:** Combine the sentences, using the second sentence as an adjective clause. Give all the possible patterns.

1. The book was good. I read it.
2. I liked the woman. I met her at the party last night.
3. I liked the composition. You wrote it.
4. The people were very nice. We visited them yesterday.

2. PRONOUN USED AS THE OBJECT OF A PREPOSITION						In very formal English, the preposition comes at the beginning of the adjective clause, as in (k) and (o). Usually, however, in everyday usage, the preposition comes after the subject and verb of the adjective clause, as in the other examples.
		She is the woman.				
		I told you *about her*.				
(k)	She is the woman	*about whom*	I told you.			
(l)	She is the woman		*who(m)*	I told you *about*.		
(m)	She is the woman		*that*	I told you *about*.		
(n)	She is the woman		Ø	I told you *about*.		
		The music was good.				Note: If the preposition comes at the beginning of the adjective clause, only *whom* or *which* may be used. A preposition is never immediately followed by *that* or *who*.
		We listened *to it* last night.				
(o)	The music	*to which*	we listened	last night	was good.	
(p)	The music	*which*	we listened *to*	last night	was good.	
(q)	The music	*that*	we listened *to*	last night	was good.	
(r)	The music	Ø	we listened *to*	last night	was good.	

□ **EXERCISE 3—ORAL:** Combine the sentences, using the second sentence as an adjective clause. Give all the possible patterns.

1. The meeting was interesting. I went to it.
2. The man was very kind. I talked to him yesterday.
3. I must thank the people. I got a present from them.
4. The picture was beautiful. She was looking at it.
5. The man is standing over there. I was telling you about him.

6–4 USING *WHOSE*

I know the man. *His bicycle* was stolen. (s) I know the man *whose bicycle was stolen*. The student writes well. I read *her composition*. (t) The student *whose composition I read* writes well.	*Whose* is used to show possession. It carries the same meaning as other possessive pronouns used as adjectives: *his, her, its,* and *their*. Like *his, her, its,* and *their*, *whose* is connected to a noun: *his bicycle → whose bicycle* *her composition → whose composition* Both *whose* and the noun it is connected to are placed at the beginning of the adjective clause. *Whose* cannot be omitted.
Mr. Catt has a painting. *Its value* is inestimable. (u) Mr. Catt has a painting *whose value is inestimable*.	*Whose* usually modifies "people," but it may also be used to modify "things," as in (u).

□ **EXERCISE 4—ORAL:** Combine the two sentences, using the second sentence as an adjective clause.

1. I apologized to the woman. I spilled her coffee.
2. The man called the police. His wallet was stolen.
3. I met the woman. Her husband is the president of the corporation.
4. The professor is excellent. I am taking her course.
5. Mr. North teaches a class for students. Their native language is not English.
6. I come from a country. Its history goes back thousands of years.
7. The people were nice. We visited their house.
8. I live in a dormitory. Its residents come from many countries.
9. I have to call the man. I accidentally picked up his umbrella after the meeting.
10. The man poured a glass of water on his face. His beard caught on fire when he lit a cigarette.

□ **EXERCISE 5:** Identify the adjective clause in each sentence. Then give the other possible patterns, if any.

1. The dress which she is wearing is new. →
   Adjective clause: *which she is wearing*
   Other possible patterns: *The dress* $\begin{Bmatrix} that \\ \varnothing \end{Bmatrix}$ *she is wearing is new.*
2. The doctor who examined the sick child was very gentle.
3. The people I was waiting for were late.
4. The term paper David is writing must be finished by Friday.
5. The man whose opinions I respect most is my father.
6. Did I tell you about the woman I met last night?

7. Did you hear about the earthquake that occurred in California?

8. The woman I was dancing with stepped on my toe.

☐ **EXERCISE 6:** Combine the following sentences. Use sentence (b) as an adjective clause. Give all the possible adjective clause patterns.*

1. (a) The scientist is well-known for her research. (b) We met her yesterday. →

    The scientist $\begin{Bmatrix} \varnothing \\ who(m) \\ that \end{Bmatrix}$ *we met yesterday is well-known for her research.*

2. (a) She lectured on a topic. (b) I know very little about it.

3. (a) The students missed the assignment. (b) They were absent from class.

4. (a) Yesterday I ran into an old friend. (b) I hadn't seen him for years.

5. (a) I explained my absence to the teacher. (b) I had missed his class.

6. (a) The young women are all from Japan. (b) We met them at the meeting last night.

7. (a) I am reading a book. (b) It was written by Jane Austen.

8. (a) The man gave me good advice. (b) I spoke to him.

9. (a) The instructor gives difficult tests. (b) I failed her course.

10. (a) I returned the money. (b) I had borrowed it from my roommate.

11. (a) The dogcatcher caught the dog. (b) It bit my neighbor's daughter.

12. (a) The people are very kind. (b) I am staying at their house.

---

*In everyday usage, often one pattern is used more commonly than another:
  (1) As a subject pronoun, **who** is more common than **that**.
  (2) As a subject pronoun, **that** is more common than **which**.
  (3) Object pronouns are usually omitted.

6-5 USING *WHERE*

	The building is very old. He lives *there* (*in that building*).			*Where* is used in an adjective clause to modify a place (*city, country, room, house, etc.*).
(a)	The building	*where*	*he lives*	is very old.
(b)	The building	*in which*	*he lives*	is very old.
	The building	*which*	*he lives in*	is very old.
	The building	*that*	*he lives in*	is very old.
	The building	Ø	*he lives in*	is very old.

Where is used in an adjective clause to modify a place (*city, country, room, house, etc.*). If *where* is used, a preposition is not included in the adjective clause. If *where* is not used, the preposition must be included.

☐ **EXERCISE 7—ORAL:** Combine the sentences, using the second sentence as an adjective clause.

1. The city was beautiful. We spent our vacation there (in that city).
2. That is the restaurant. I will meet you there (at that restaurant).
3. The town is small. I grew up there (in that town).
4. That is the drawer. I keep my jewelry there (in that drawer).

6-6 USING *WHEN*

	I'll never forget the day. I met you *then* (*on that day*).			*When* is used in an adjective clause to modify a noun of time (*year, day, time, century, etc.*)
(c)	I'll never forget the day	*when*	*I met you.*	
(d)	I'll never forget the day	*on which*	*I met you.*	
(e)	I'll never forget the day	*that*	*I met you.*	
(f)	I'll never forget the day	Ø	*I met you.*	

When is used in an adjective clause to modify a noun of time (*year, day, time, century, etc.*)
The use of a preposition in an adjective clause that modifies a noun of time is somewhat different from that in other adjective clauses: A preposition is used preceding *which*, as in (d). Otherwise, the preposition is omitted.

☐ **EXERCISE 8—ORAL:** Combine the sentences, using the second sentence as an adjective clause.

1. Monday is the day. We will come then (on that day).
2. 7:05 is the time. My plane arrives then (at that time).
3. 1960 is the year. The revolution took place then (in that year).
4. July is the month. The weather is usually the hottest then (in that month).

☐ **EXERCISE 9—ORAL (BOOKS CLOSED):** Begin your response with "That is . . . ." Use *where* in an adjective clause.

Example: You were born in *that* city.
Response: That is *the* city where I was born.

1. We have class in that room.
2. We ate dinner at that restaurant.
3. He works in that building.
4. He lives on that street.
5. You eat lunch at that cafeteria.
6. You keep your money at that bank.
7. You do your grocery shopping at that store.
8. You spent your vacation on that island.
9. You went swimming in that lake.
10. You grew up in that town.
11. The examination will be given in that room.
12. The earthquake occurred in that country.
13. Your sister went to graduate school at that university.
14. We are going to have a picnic at that park.
15. You lived in that city until you were ten years old.

☐ **EXERCISE 10—ORAL (BOOKS CLOSED):** Begin your response with "Did she tell you about . . . ?" (*To the teacher: Write "Did she tell you about . . . ?" on the board.*)

Example: She wrote *a* letter.
Response: Did she tell you about *the* letter she wrote?

1. She wrote a report.
2. She got a letter.
3. She went to a party.
4. She met some people.
5. She took a trip.
6. She went to a movie.
7. She saw a program on TV.
8. She took a test.
9. She read a book.
10. She bought some furniture.
11. She saw an accident.
12. She met a man.
13. She talked to a woman.
14. She had a problem.
15. She took a physics course.

☐ **EXERCISE 11—ORAL (BOOKS CLOSED):** Begin your response with "She told me about . . . ."

Example: Did she write *a* letter to her parents yesterday?
Response: Yes. She told me about *the* letter she wrote to her parents yesterday.

1. Did she write a letter to the President of the United States?
2. Did she get a letter from her brother yesterday?
3. Did she go to a party yesterday?
4. Did she meet some people at that party?

5. Did she take a trip to Mexico last summer?

6. Did she have some experiences in Mexico?

7. Did she use to live in a small town?

8. Did she get some presents for her birthday?

9. Did she do an experiment in chemistry lab yesterday?

10. Did she have to write a term paper for her English course?

11. Did she take an American history course last semester?

12. Is she reading a science fiction book?

☐ EXERCISE 12—ORAL (BOOKS CLOSED):

Example: You read *a* book. Was it interesting?
Response: Yes, *the* book I read was interesting.

Example: You drank *some* tea. Did it taste good?
Response: Yes, *the* tea I drank tasted good.

1. You are sitting in a chair. Is it comfortable?

2. You saw a man. Was he wearing a brown suit?

3. You talked to a woman. Did she answer your question?

4. You had some meat for dinner last night. Was it good?

5. You bought a coat. Does it keep you warm?

6. You went to a soccer game. Was it exciting?

7. You watched a TV program last night. Was it good?

8. You are wearing boots/tennis shoes/loafers. Are they comfortable?

9. You stayed at a hotel. Was it in the middle of the city?

10. You eat at a cafeteria. Does it have good food?

11. You got a package in the mail. Was it from your parents?

12. You are doing an exercise. Is it easy?

☐ EXERCISE 13—ORAL (BOOKS CLOSED):

Example: A stranger gave you directions to the post office. Did she speak too fast?
Response: Yes, the stranger who gave me directions to the post office spoke too fast.

1. A waiter served you at a restaurant. Was he polite?

2. A barber cut your hair. Did he do a good job?

3. A clerk cashed your check. Did he ask for identification?

4. A man stopped you on the street. Did he ask you for directions?

5. A student stopped you in the hall. Did she ask you for the correct time?

6. A woman stepped on your toe. Did she apologize?

7. A car drove through a red light. Did it hit another car?

8. Some students took a test. Did most of them pass?

9. Some students are sitting in this room. Can all of them speak English?

10. A woman shouted at you. Was she angry?

11. A police officer helped you. Did you thank her? (*Yes, I thanked . . . .*)

12. A person is sitting next to you. Do you know him/her?

13. A professor teaches Chemistry 101. Do you like him?

14. A taxi driver took you to the bus station. Did you have a conversation with her?

15. A woman came into the room. Did you recognize her?

16. A man opened the door for you. Did you thank him?

17. A student is wearing a (*blue shirt/blouse*). Are you sitting next to him/her?

18. Some students were sitting on the grass outside the classroom building. Did you join them?

19. You were reading a book. Did you finish it?

20. You went to a party last night. Did you enjoy it?

21. You were looking for a book. Did you find it?

22. (. . .) told a story. Did you believe it?

23. (. . .) gave you a present. Did you open it?

24. You borrowed a pen from (. . .). Did you return it?

25. (. . .) told a joke. Did you laugh at it?

☐ **EXERCISE 14—ORAL (BOOKS CLOSED):** Follow the pattern and supply your own completion.

Example: You spoke to a woman.
Response: The woman I spoke to . . . (was Mrs. Jones/was very kind/etc.).

1. You are looking at a person.

2. You are sitting at a desk.

3. This book belongs to a student.

4. You are interested in a field of study.

5. (. . .) and you listened to some music.

6. (. . .) went to a movie last night.

7. (. . .) was talking about a movie.

8. The police are looking for a man.

9. (. . .) is married to a man/woman.

10. You are living in a city/town.

11. You waited for a person.

12. You are studying at a school.

13. You got a letter from a person.

14. You grew up in a city/town.

15. I am pointing at a person.

16. (. . .) spoke to some people.

17. You are living with some people.

18. You went to a doctor to get some medicine.

□ **EXERCISE 15—ORAL (BOOKS CLOSED):** You are in a room full of people. You are speaking to a friend. You are identifying various people in the room for your friend. Begin your response with "There is . . . ."

Example: That man's wife is your teacher.
Response: There is the man whose wife is my teacher.

1. That woman's husband is a football player.
2. That boy's father is a doctor.
3. That girl's mother is a dentist.
4. That person's picture was in the newspaper.
5. That man's dog bit you.
6. That man's daughter won a gold medal at the Olympic Games.
7. That woman's car was stolen.
8. You borrowed that student's lecture notes.
9. You found that woman's keys.
10. You are in that teacher's class.
11. You read that author's book.
12. We met that man's wife.

□ **EXERCISE 16—ORAL (BOOKS CLOSED):** Use *whose* in the response.

Example: Dr. Jones is a professor. You are taking his course.
Response: Dr. Jones is the professor whose course I am taking.

1. (. . .) is a student. You found his/her book.
2. (. . .) is a student. You borrowed his/her dictionary.
3. Mark Twain is an author. You like his books best.
4. You used a woman's phone. You thanked her.
5. You broke a child's toy. He started to cry.
6. You stayed at a family's house. They were very kind.
7. A woman's purse was stolen. She called the police.
8. (*Name of a famous singer*) is a singer. You like his/her music best.
9. A girl's leg is in a cast. She has trouble climbing stairs.
10. Everyone tried to help a family. Their house had burned down.

□ **EXERCISE 17—ORAL (BOOKS CLOSED):** Begin your response with either "I'll never forget . . ." or "I'll always remember . . . ."

Example: trip
Response: I'll never forget the trip . . . (I took to France).

1. trip
2. experiences
3. day
4. first day
5. time
6. first time
7. person
8. people
9. woman
10. man
11. house
12. story
13. accident
14. wonderful food
15. room
16. friends

☐ EXERCISE 18—ORAL (BOOKS CLOSED):

(To the teacher: Use the questions to elicit information from someone in the class. Then ask another student to summarize this information in one sentence beginning with "The . . . .")

Example:	Who got a letter yesterday?
Response:	I did.
	Who was it from?
Response:	My brother.
(to another student):	Can you summarize this information? Begin with "the."
Response:	The letter (*Ali*) got yesterday was from his brother.

1. Who got a letter last week?
   Where was it from?

2. Who is wearing earrings?
   What are they made of?

3. Who lives in an apartment?
   Is it close to school?

4. Pick up something that doesn't belong to you.
   Whose is it?

5. Who grew up in a small town?
   In what part of the country is it located?

6. Who has bought something recently?
   What did you buy?
   Was it expensive?

7. Hold up a book.
   What is the title?

8. Who went to a bar/restaurant last night?
   Was it crowded?

9. What did you have for dinner last night?
   Was it good?

10. Who watched a TV program last night?
    What was it about?

11. Who has borrowed something recently?
    What did you borrow?
    Who does it belong to?

12. Who shops for groceries?
    What is the name of the store?

13. Who eats lunch away from home?
    Where do you usually eat?
    Does it have good food?

14. Who took the bus to class today?
    Was it late or on time?

15. Who read a newspaper yesterday?
    Which newspaper?

16. Point at a person.
    Who is s/he pointing at?

6–7 USING ADJECTIVE CLAUSES TO MODIFY PRONOUNS

(a) There is **someone** *(whom) I want you to meet.* (b) **Everything** *he said* was pure nonsense. (c) **Anybody** *who wants to come* is welcome.	Adjective clauses can modify indefinite pronouns (e.g., *someone, everybody*). Object pronouns (e.g., *whom, which*) are usually omitted in the adjective clause.
(d) Paula was **the only one** *I knew at the party.* (e) Scholarships are available for **those** *who need financial assistance.*	Adjective clauses can modify **the one(s)** and **those.***
(f) It is **I** *who am responsible.* (g) **He** *who laughs last* laughs best.	Adjective clauses rarely modify personal pronouns. (f) is very formal and uncommon. (g) is a well-known saying in which "he" is used as an indefinite pronoun (meaning "anyone," "any person").

*An adjective clause with **which** can also be used to modify the pronoun **that**. For example:
We sometimes fear **that which** *we do not understand.*
The bread my mother makes is much better than **that which** *you can buy at a store.*

□ **EXERCISE 19:** Complete the sentences with adjective clauses.

1. Ask Jack. He's the only one ___*who knows the answer.*___

2. I have a question. There is something _____

3. He can't trust anyone. There's no one _____

4. I'm powerless to help her. There's nothing _____

5. I know someone _____

6. Susan makes a good first impression. She charms everyone _____

7. What was Mrs. Wood talking about? I didn't understand anything _____
_____

8. I listen to everything _____

9. You can believe him. Everything _____

10. All of the students are seated. The teacher is the only one _____

11. The test we took yesterday was easier than the one _____

12. The courses I'm taking this term are more difficult than the ones _____
_____

13. The concert had already begun. Those _____
had to wait until intermission to be seated.

14. The class was divided in half. Those _____

were assigned to Section A. Those _____

were assigned to Section B.

6-8 PUNCTUATION OF ADJECTIVE CLAUSES

<table>
<tr>
<td colspan="2">General guidelines for the punctuation of adjective clauses:
(1) DO NOT USE COMMAS IF the adjective clause is necessary to identify the noun it modifies.*
(2) USE COMMAS IF the adjective clause simply gives additional information and is not necessary to identify the noun it modifies.**</td>
</tr>
<tr>
<td>(a) The professor who teaches Chemistry 101 is an excellent lecturer.
(b) Professor Wilson_☉ who teaches Chemistry 101_☉ is an excellent lecturer.</td>
<td>In (a): No commas are used. The adjective clause is necessary to identify which professor is meant.
In (b): Commas are used. The adjective clause is not necessary to identify who Professor Wilson is. We already know who he is: he has a name. The adjective clause simply gives additional information.</td>
</tr>
<tr>
<td>(c) Hawaii_☉ which consists of eight principal islands_☉ is a favorite vacation spot.
(d) Mrs. Smith_☉ who is a retired teacher_☉ does volunteer work at the hospital.</td>
<td>Guideline: Use commas, as in (b), (c), and (d), if an adjective clause modifies a proper noun. (A proper noun begins with a capital letter, not a small letter.)
Note: A comma reflects a pause in speech.</td>
</tr>
<tr>
<td>(e) The man   who(m)
           that   I met teaches chemistry.
           Ø

(f) Mr. Lee_☉ whom I met yesterday_☉ teaches chemistry.</td>
<td>In (e): If no commas are used, any possible pronoun may be used in the adjective clause. Object pronouns may be omitted.
In (f): When commas are necessary, the pronoun that may not be used (only who, whom, which, whose, where, and when may be used), and object pronouns cannot be omitted.</td>
</tr>
<tr>
<td>COMPARE THE MEANING
(g) We took some children on a picnic. The children_☉ who wanted to play soccer_☉ ran to an open field as soon as we arrived at the park.

(h) We took some children on a picnic. The children who wanted to play soccer ran to an open field as soon as we arrived at the park. The others played a different game.</td>
<td>In (g): The use of commas means that all of the children wanted to play soccer and all of the children ran to an open field. The adjective clause is used only to give additional information about the children.
In (h): The lack of commas means that only some of the children wanted to play soccer. The adjective clause is used to identify which children ran to the open field.</td>
</tr>
</table>

*Adjective clauses that do not require commas are called "essential" or "restrictive" or "identifying."
**Adjective clauses that require commas are called "nonessential" or "nonrestrictive" or "nonidentifying."
Note: Nonessential adjective clauses are more common in writing than in speaking.

☐ **EXERCISE 20:** Add commas where necessary. Change the adjective clause pronoun to *that* if possible.

1. Alan and Jackie , who did not come to class yesterday , explained their absence to the teacher. (*Commas necessary; "who" cannot be changed to "that."*)

2. The students who did not come to class yesterday explained their absence to the teacher. (*No commas; "who" can be changed to "that."*)

3. The geologist who lectured at Browning Hall last night predicted another earthquake.

4. Dr. Fields who lectured at Browning Hall last night predicted another earthquake.

5. Only people who speak Russian should apply for the job.

6. Matthew who speaks Russian applied for the job.

7. The rice which we had for dinner last night was very good.

8. Rice which is grown in many countries is a staple food throughout much of the world.

9. I have fond memories of my hometown which is situated in a valley.

10. I live in a town which is situated in a valley.

11. The Mississippi River which flows south from Minnesota to the Gulf of Mexico is the major commercial river in the United States.

12. A river which is polluted is not safe for swimming.

13. Mr. Brown whose son won the spelling contest is very proud of his son's achievement. The man whose daughter won the science contest is also very pleased and proud.

14. Goats which were first tamed more than 9,000 years ago in Asia have provided people with milk, meat, and wool since prehistoric times.

15. Mrs. Clark has two goats. She's furious at the goat which got on the wrong side of the fence and is eating her flowers.

☐ **EXERCISE 21:** Circle the correct explanation (a. or b.) of the meaning of each sentence.

1. The teacher thanked the students, who had given her some flowers.

   a. The flowers were from *only some* of the students.

   b. The flowers were from *all* of the students.

2. The teacher thanked the students who had given her some flowers.

   a. The flowers were from *only some* of the students.

   b. The flowers were from *all* of the students.

3. There was a terrible flood. The villagers who had received a warning of the impending flood escaped to safety.

   a. *Only some* of the villagers had been warned; only some escaped.

   b. *All* of the villagers had been warned; all escaped.

4. There was a terrible flood. The villagers, who had received a warning of the impending flood, escaped to safety.

   a. *Only some* of the villagers had been warned; *only some* escaped.

   b. *All* of the villagers had been warned; *all* escaped.

5. Tom stood under the oak tree which was near the house.

   a. There was *only one* oak tree in the yard.

   b. There were *more than one* oak trees in the yard.

6. Tom stood under the oak tree, which was near the house.

   a. There was *only one* oak tree in the yard.

   b. There were *more than one* oak trees in the yard.

Discuss the differences in meaning in the following pairs of sentences.

7. He reached in the basket and threw away the apples that were rotten.
8. He reached in the basket and threw away the apples, which were rotten.
9. The students who had done well on the test were excused from class early.
10. The students, who had done well on the test, were excused from class early.
11. Cindy was delighted when she opened the present, which was from her grandmother.
12. Cindy was delighted when she opened the present that was from her grandmother.
13. The teacher pointed to the maps that were hanging on the rear wall of the classroom.
14. The teacher pointed to the maps, which were hanging on the rear wall of the classroom.

□ **EXERCISE 22**: Add commas where necessary.

1. We enjoyed the city where we spent our vacation.
2. We enjoyed Mexico City where we spent our vacation.
3. An elephant which is the earth's largest land mammal has few natural enemies other than human beings.
4. One of the elephants which we saw at the zoo had only one tusk.
5. At the botanical gardens, you can see a Venus's-Flytrap which is an insectivorous plant.
6. In Venezuela, there are plants which eat insects with their roots.
7. One of the most useful materials in the world is glass which is made chiefly from sand, soda, and lime.
8. Glaciers which are huge masses of ice that flow slowly over land form in the cold polar regions and in high mountains.
9. A rebel is a person who resists or fights against authority.
10. Petroleum which some people refer to as black gold is one of the most valuable resources in the world today.
11. You don't need to take heavy clothes when you go to Bangkok which has one of the highest average temperatures of any city in the world.
12. A political party is an organized group of people who control or seek to control a government.
13. Child labor was a social problem in late eighteenth-century England where employment in factories became virtual slavery for children.
14. We had to use a telephone, so we went to the nearest house. The woman who answered our knock listened cautiously to our request.
15. According to a newspaper article which I read, the police arrested the man who had robbed the First National Bank. The man who was wearing a plaid shirt and blue jeans was caught shortly after he had left the bank.
16. I watched a scientist conduct an experiment on bees. The research scientist who was well protected before she stepped into the special chamber holding the bees was not stung. A person who was unprotected by the special clothing could have gotten 300–400 bee stings within a minute.

6-9 USING EXPRESSIONS OF QUANTITY IN ADJECTIVE CLAUSES

In my class there are 20 students. *Most of **them*** are from the Far East. (a) In my class there are 20 students, *most of **whom*** are from the Far East.	An adjective clause may contain an expression of quantity with ***of***: *some of, many of, most of, none of, two of, half of, both of, neither of, each of, all of, both of, several of, a few of, little of, a number of,* etc.
He gave several reasons. *Only a few of **them*** were valid. (b) He gave several reasons, *only a few of **which*** were valid.	The expression of quantity precedes the pronoun. Only ***whom, which,*** and ***whose*** are used in this pattern.
The teachers discussed Jim. *One of **his** problems* was poor study habits. (c) The teachers discussed Jim, *one of **whose** problems* was poor study habits.	Adjective clauses that begin with an expression of quantity are more common in writing than speaking. Commas are used.

☐ **EXERCISE 23:** Combine the two sentences. Use (b) as an adjective clause.

1. (a) The city has sixteen schools. (b) Two of them are junior colleges.
   → *The city has sixteen schools, two of which are junior colleges.*
2. (a) Last night the orchestra played three symphonies. (b) One of them was Beethoven's Seventh.
3. (a) I tried on six pairs of shoes. (b) I liked none of them.
4. (a) The village has around 200 people. (b) The majority of them are farmers.
5. (a) That company currently has five employees. (b) All of them are computer experts.
6. (a) After the riot, over one hundred people were taken to the hospital. (b) Many of them had been innocent bystanders.

☐ **EXERCISE 24:** Complete the following sentences.

1. Al introduced me to his roommates, both of *whom are from California.*
2. The Paulsons own four automobiles, one of _____
3. I have three brothers, all of _____
4. I am taking four courses, one of _____
5. I have two roommates, neither of _____
6. This semester I had to buy fifteen books, most of _____
7. The company hired ten new employees, some of _____
8. In my apartment building, there are twenty apartments, several of _____

6–10 USING *NOUN + OF WHICH*

We have an antique table. *The top of it* has jade inlay. (a) We have an antique table, ***the top of which*** has jade inlay.	An adjective clause may include *a noun + of which* (e.g., *the top of which*). This pattern carries the meaning of ***whose*** (e.g., We have *an antique table whose top has jade inlay.*). This pattern is used in an adjective clause that modifies a "thing" and occurs primarily in formal written English. Commas are used.

☐ **EXERCISE 25:** Combine the sentences. Use (b) as an adjective clause.

1. (a) We toured a 300-year-old house. (b) The exterior of the house consisted of logs cemented with clay.
   → *We toured a 300-year-old house, the exterior of which consisted of logs cemented with clay.*

2. (a) They own an original Picasso painting. (b) The value of the painting is over a million dollars.

3. (a) I bought a magazine. (b) The title of the magazine is *Contemporary Architectural Styles*.

4. (a) My country is dependent upon its income from coffee. (b) The price of coffee varies according to fluctuations in the world market.

5. (a) The genetic engineers are engaged in significant experiments. (b) The results of the experiments will be published in the *Journal of Science*.

6. (a) The professor has assigned the students a research paper. (b) The purpose of the research paper is to acquaint them with methods of scholarly inquiry.

6–11 USING *WHICH* TO MODIFY A WHOLE SENTENCE

(a) Tom was late. (b) ***That*** surprised me. (c) Tom was late, ***which*** surprised me.	The pronouns ***that*** and ***this*** can refer to the idea of a whole sentence which comes before. In (b): The word ***that*** refers to the whole sentence "Tom was late."
(d) The elevator is out of order. (e) ***This*** is too bad. (f) The elevator is out of order, ***which*** is too bad.	Similarly, an adjective clause with ***which*** may modify the idea of a whole sentence. In (c): The word ***which*** refers to the whole sentence "Tom was late."*

*Using ***which*** to modify a whole sentence is informal and occurs most frequently in spoken English. This structure is generally not appropriate in formal writing. Whenever it is written, however, it is preceded by a comma to reflect a pause in speech.

□ **EXERCISE 26:** Use the second sentence as an adjective clause.

1. Max isn't home yet. That worries me.
   → *Max isn't home yet, which worries me.*
2. Jack was fired from his job. That surprised all of his co-workers.
3. My roommate never picks up after herself. This irritates me.
4. Mrs. Anderson responded to my letter right away. I appreciated that very much.
5. There was an accident on Highway 5. That means I'll be late to work this morning.
6. I shut the car door on my necktie. That was really stupid of me.

□ **EXERCISE 27:** Make up a sentence to precede the given sentence. Then combine the two sentences, using the second sentence as an adjective clause.

1. *The student next to me kept cracking his knuckles*. That bothered me a lot. →

   The student next to me kept cracking his knuckles, which bothered me a lot.

2. _____ That disappointed me.
3. _____ That made me nervous.
4. _____ That shocked all of us.
5. _____ That means he's probably in trouble.
6. _____ That was a pleasant surprise.
7. _____ That made her very unhappy.
8. _____ I appreciated that very much.
9. _____ That made it difficult for me to concentrate.
10. _____ That bothered me so much that I couldn't get to sleep.

6-12 REDUCTION OF ADJECTIVE CLAUSES TO ADJECTIVE PHRASES: INTRODUCTION

Terms: **clause:** *A clause* is a group of related words that contains a subject and a verb. **phrase:** *A phrase* is a group of related words that does not contain a subject and a verb.	

(a) ADJECTIVE CLAUSE:
    The girl ***who is sitting next to me*** is Mary.
(b) ADJECTIVE PHRASE:
    The girl ***sitting next to me*** is Mary.
	An adjective phrase is a reduction of an adjective clause. It modifies a noun. It does not contain a subject and a verb. The adjective clause in (a) can be reduced to the adjective phrase in (b). (a) and (b) have the same meaning.

(c) CLAUSE: The boy ***who is playing the piano*** is Ben. (d) PHRASE: The boy ***playing the piano*** is Ben. (e) CLAUSE: The boy ***(whom) I saw*** was Tom. (f) PHRASE: *(none)*	Only adjective clauses that have a subject pronoun—***who***, ***which***, or ***that***—are reduced to modifying adjective phrases. The adjective clause in (e) cannot be reduced to an adjective phrase.

6-13 CHANGING AN ADJECTIVE CLAUSE TO AN ADJECTIVE PHRASE

There are two ways in which an adjective clause is changed to an adjective phrase:

(1) The subject pronoun is omitted AND the ***be*** form of the verb is omitted.
    (a) CLAUSE: The ***man who is talking*** to John is from Korea.
        PHRASE: The ***man   Ø   Ø talking*** to John is from Korea.
    (b) CLAUSE: The ***ideas which are presented*** in that book are interesting.
        PHRASE: The ***ideas   Ø   Ø presented*** in that book are interesting.
    (c) CLAUSE: Ann is the ***woman who is responsible*** for preparing the budget.
        PHRASE: Ann is the ***woman   Ø   Ø responsible*** for preparing the budget.
    (d) CLAUSE: The ***books that are on that shelf*** are mine.
        PHRASE: The ***books   Ø   Ø on that shelf*** are mine.

(2) If there is no ***be*** form of a verb in the adjective clause, it is sometimes possible to omit the subject pronoun and change the verb to its ***-ing*** form.
    (e) CLAUSE: English has an ***alphabet   that   consists*** of 26 letters.
        PHRASE: English has an ***alphabet   Ø   consisting*** of 26 letters.
    (f) CLAUSE: ***Anyone who wants*** to come with us is welcome.
        PHRASE: ***Anyone   Ø   wanting*** to come with us is welcome.

(g) *George Washington,⊙ who was the first president of the United States,⊙* was a wealthy colonist and a general in the army. (h) *George Washington,⊙ the first president of the United States,⊙* was a wealthy colonist and a general in the army.	If the adjective clause requires commas, as in (g), the adjective phrase also requires commas, as in (h).

☐ **EXERCISE 28:** Change the adjective clauses to adjective phrases.

1. Do you know the woman who is coming toward us?
   → *Do you know the woman coming toward us?*
2. The people who are waiting for the bus in the rain are getting wet.
3. I come from a city that is located in the southern part of the country.
4. The children who attend that school receive a good education.
5. The scientists who are researching the causes of cancer are making progress.
6. The fence which surrounds our house is made of wood.
7. They live in a house that was built in 1890.
8. We have an apartment which overlooks the park.

☐ **EXERCISE 29:** Change the adjective clauses to adjective phrases.

1. Dr. Stanton, who is the president of the university, will give a speech at the commencement ceremonies.
2. Did you get the message which concerned the special meeting?
3. Be sure to follow the instructions that are given at the top of the page.
4. The conclusion which is presented in that book states that most of the automobiles which are produced by American industry have some defect.
5. The rules that allow public access to wilderness areas need to be reconsidered.
6. The photographs which were published in the newspaper were extraordinary.
7. There is almost no end to the problems that face a head of state.
8. Nero, who was Emperor of Rome from 54 to 68 A.D., is believed to have murdered both his mother and his wife.
9. The psychologists who study the nature of sleep have made important discoveries.
10. The experiment which was conducted at the University of Chicago was successful.
11. Pictures that showed the brutality of war entered the living rooms of millions of Americans on the nightly news.
12. Kuala Lumpur, which is the capital city of Malaysia, is a major trade center in Southeast Asia.
13. The Indians who lived in Peru before the discovery of the New World by Europeans belonged to the Incan culture.
14. Many of the students who hope to enter the university will be disappointed because only one-tenth of those who apply for admission will be accepted.
15. There must exist in a modern community a sufficient number of persons who possess the technical skill that is required to maintain the numerous devices upon which our physical comforts depend.

☐ **EXERCISE 30:** Change the adjective phrases to adjective clauses.

1. David Keller, a young poet known for his sensitive interpretations of human relationships, has just published another volume of poems.
   → *David Keller,* ***who is*** *a young poet* ***who is*** *known for his sensitive interpretations of human relationships, has just published another volume of poems.*

2. Corn was one of the agricultural products introduced to the European settlers by the Indians. Some of the other products introduced by the Indians were potatoes, peanuts, and tobacco.

3. He read *The Old Man and the Sea*, a novel written by Ernest Hemingway.

4. The sunlight coming through the window wakes me up early every morning.

5. Mercury, the nearest planet to the sun, is also the smallest of the nine planets orbiting the sun.

6. The pyramids, the monumental tombs of ancient Egyptian pharaohs, were constructed from 3000 to 1800 B.C.

7. The sloth, a slow-moving animal found in the tropical forests of Central and South America, feeds entirely on leaves and fruit.

8. Two-thirds of those arrested for car theft are under twenty years of age.

9. St. Louis, Missouri, known as "The Gateway to the West," traces its history to 1793, when Pierre Laclede, a French fur trader, selected this site on the Mississippi River as a fur-trading post.

10. Any student not wanting to go on the trip should inform the office.

☐ **EXERCISE 31:** Combine the sentences. Use the second sentence as an adjective phrase.

1. Louisville was founded in 1778. It is the largest city in Kentucky.

   Louisville, the largest city in Kentucky, was founded in 1778.

2. John Quincy Adams was born on July 11, 1767. He was the sixth president of the United States.

   _____

   _____

3. Two languages, Finnish and Swedish, are used in Helsinki. It is the capital of Finland.

   _____

   _____

4. The Washington National Monument is a famous landmark in the nation's capital. It is a towering obelisk made of white marble.

   _____

   _____

5. Honolulu has consistently pleasant weather. It is best known to the traveler for Waikiki Beach.

_____

_____

6. Libya is a leading producer of oil. It is a country in North Africa.

_____

_____

☐ **EXERCISE 32—ERROR ANALYSIS:** All of the following sentences adapted from student compositions contain errors. Test your skill by seeing how many of the errors you can find and correct.

1. It is important to be polite to people who lives in the same building.

2. She lives in a hotel is restricted to senior citizens.

3. My sister has two childrens, who their names are Ali and Talal.

4. He comes from Venezuela that is a Spanish-speaking country.

5. There are ten universities in Thailand, seven of them locate in Bangkok is the capital city.

6. I would like to write about several problems which I have faced them since I come to United State.

7. There is a small wooden screen separates the bed from the rest of the room.

8. At the airport, I was waiting for some relatives which I had never met them before.

9. It is almost impossible to find two person who their opinions are the same.

10. On the wall, there is a colorful poster which it consists of a group of young people who dancing.

☐ **EXERCISE 33—PREPOSITIONS:** Supply appropriate prepositions.

1. Max is known _____ his honesty.

2. Mr. and Mrs. Jones have always been faithful _____ each other.

3. Do you promise to come? I'm counting _____ you to be there.

4. Trucks are prohibited _____ using residential streets.

5. The little girl is afraid _____ an imaginary bear that lives in her closet.

6. Do you take good care _____ your health?

7. I'm worried _____ this problem.

8. I don't agree _____ you.

9. We decided _____ eight o'clock as the time we should meet.

10. Who did you vote _____ in the last election?

11. How many students were absent _____ class yesterday?

12. It is important to be polite _____ other people.

13. The farmers are hoping _____ rain.

14. Jason was late because he wasn't aware _____ the time.

15. We will fight _____ our rights.

□ **EXERCISE 34—PHRASAL VERBS:** Supply appropriate prepositions for the following two-word or three-word verbs.

1. A: Are you ready to leave?

   B: Almost. I'll be ready to go just as soon as I get _____ putting the clean dishes away.

2. A: I'm going crazy! I've been trying to solve this math problem for the last hour and I still can't get it.

   B: Why don't you give _____ for a while? Take a break and then go back to it.

3. A: I hear you had a frightening experience yesterday. What happened?

   B: Ed suddenly got dizzy and then passed _____. I tried to revive him, but he was out cold. Luckily there was a doctor in the building.

4. A: What happened when the pilot of the plane passed out during the flight?

   B: The co-pilot took _____.

5. A: Cindy is only three. She likes to play with the older kids, but when they're running and playing, she can't keep _____ with them.

   B: Does she mind?

   A: She doesn't seem to.

6. A: I made a mistake in my composition. What should I do?

   B: Since it's an in-class composition, just cross it _____.

7. A: I need my dictionary, but I lent it to Jose.

   B: Why don't you get it _____ from him?

8. A: I wish the teacher wouldn't call _____ me in class.

   B: Why not?

   A: I get nervous.

   B: Why?

   A: I don't know.

9. I took a plane from Atlanta to Miami. I got _____ the plane in Atlanta. I got _____ the plane in Miami.

10. It was a snowy winter day, but I still had to drive to work. First I got _____ the car to start the engine. Then I got _____ of the car to scrape the snow and ice from the windows.

11. Last year I took a train trip. I got _____ the train in Chicago. I got _____ the train in Des Moines.

12. Phyllis takes the bus to work. She gets _____ the bus at Lindbergh Boulevard and gets _____ the bus about two blocks from her office on Tower Street.

CHAPTER *7*

Noun Clauses

7–1   NOUN CLAUSES: INTRODUCTION

A noun is used as a subject or an object. *A noun clause* is used as a subject or an object. In other words, a noun clause is used in the same ways as a noun.	
(a) ***His story*** was interesting. (b) ***What he said*** was interesting.	In (a): ***story*** is a noun. It is used as the subject of the sentence. In (b): ***what he said*** is a noun clause. It is used as the subject of the sentence. The noun clause has its own subject (*he*) and verb (*said*).
(c) I heard ***his story***. (d) I heard ***what he said***.	In (c): ***story*** is a noun. It is used as the object of the verb ***heard***. In (d): ***what he said*** is a noun clause. It is used as the object of the verb ***heard***.

WORDS USED TO INTRODUCE NOUN CLAUSES

(1) *question words:**   (2) ***whether***   (3) ***that***
    when   ***who***   ***if***
    where ***whom***
    why   ***what***
    how   ***which***
               whose

*See Appendix 1, Unit B, for more information about question words and question forms.

7-2 NOUN CLAUSES WHICH BEGIN WITH A QUESTION WORD

QUESTION	NOUN CLAUSE	
Where does she live?	(a) I don't know *where she lives*.	In (a): *where she lives* is the object of the verb *know*. Do not use question word order in a noun clause. In a noun clause, the subject precedes the verb.
What did he say?	(b) I couldn't hear *what he said*.	
When do they arrive?	(c) Do you know *when they arrive*?	Notice: *does*, *did*, and *do* are used in questions but not in noun clauses.
S V Who lives there?	S V (d) I don't know *who lives there*.	In (d): The word order is the same in both the question and the noun clause because *who* is the subject in both.
What happened?	(e) Please tell me *what happened*.	
Who is at the door?	(f) I wonder *who is at the door*.	
V S Who is she?	S V (g) I don't know *who she is*.	In (g): *she* is the subject of the question, so it is placed in front of the verb *be* in the noun clause.*
Who are those men?	(h) I don't know *who those men are*.	
Whose house is that?	(i) I wonder *whose house that is*.	
What did she say?	(j) *What she said* surprised me.	In (j): *what she said* is the subject of the sentence. Notice in (k): A noun clause subject takes a singular verb (e.g., *is*).
What should they do?	(k) *What they should do* is obvious.	

*COMPARE: *Who is at the door?* = *who* is the subject of the question.
             Who are those men? = *those men* is the subject of the question, so *be* is plural.

☐ **EXERCISE 1:** Change the question in parentheses to a noun clause.

1. (*How old is he?*) I don't know ___how old he is___.

2. (*What was he talking about?*) ___What he was talking about___
   was interesting.

3. (*Where do you live?*) Please tell me _____.

4. (*What did she say?*) _____ wasn't true.

5. (*When are they coming?*) Do you know _____?

6. (*How much does it cost?*) I can't remember _____.

7. (*Which one does he want?*) Let's ask him _____.

8. (*Who is coming to the party?*) I don't know _____.

9. (*Who are those people?*) I don't know _____.

10. (*Whose pen is this?*) Do you know _____?

11. (*Why did they leave the country?*) _____ is a secret.

12. (*What are we doing in class?*) _____ is easy.

13. (*Where did she go?*) _____ is none of your business.

14. (*How many letters are there in the English alphabet?*) I don't remember

_____.

15. (*Who is the mayor of New York City?*) I don't know _____.

16. (*How old does a person have to be to get a driver's license.*) I need to find

out _____.

☐ **EXERCISE 2—ORAL (BOOKS CLOSED):** Begin your response with "I don't know . . . ."

Example: What time is it?

Response: I don't know what time it is.

1. Where does (. . .) live?
2. What country is (. . .) from?
3. How long has (. . .) been living here?
4. What is (. . .)'s telephone number?
5. Where is the post office?
6. How far is it to (*Kansas City*)?
7. Why is (. . .) absent?
8. Where is my book?
9. What kind of watch does (. . .) have?
10. Why was (. . .) absent yesterday?
11. Where did (. . .) go yesterday?
12. What is (. . .)'s favorite color?
13. How long has (. . .) been married?
14. How did (. . .) meet his wife/her husband?
15. What is the capital of (*Texas*)?
16. What is the population of (*Texas*)?
17. Why was (. . .) late to class?
18. Why are we doing this exercise?
19. What kind of government does (*Italy*) have?
20. Where is (. . .) going to eat lunch/dinner?
21. When does (the semester) end?
22. When does (*Thanksgiving*) vacation start?
23. Where did (. . .) go after class yesterday?
24. Why is (. . .) smiling?
25. How many questions have I asked in this exercise?
26. How often does (. . .) go to the library?
27. Whose book is that?
28. How much did that book cost?

☐ **EXERCISE 3:** Make a question from the given sentence. The words in parentheses should be the answer to the question you make. Use a question word (**who, what, how,** etc.). Then change the question to a noun clause.

1. That man is (*Mr. Robertson*).

   QUESTION: *Who is that man?*

   NOUN CLAUSE: I want to know *who that man is.*

2. George lives (*in Los Angeles*).

   QUESTION: _____

   NOUN CLAUSE: I want to know_____

3. Ann bought (*a new dictionary*).

   QUESTION: _____

   NOUN CLAUSE: Do you know_____

4. It is (*350 miles*) to Denver from here.

   QUESTION: _____

   NOUN CLAUSE: I need to know_____

5. Jack was late to class (*because he missed the bus.*)

   QUESTION: _____

   NOUN CLAUSE: The teacher wants to know_____

6. That is (*Ann's*) pen.

   QUESTION: _____

   NOUN CLAUSE: Tom wants to know_____

7. Alex saw (*Ms. Frost*) at the meeting.

   QUESTION: _____

   NOUN CLAUSE: I don't know_____

8. (*Jack*) saw Ms. Frost at the meeting.

   QUESTION: _____

   NOUN CLAUSE: I don't know_____

9. Alice likes (*this*) book best, (*not that one*).

   QUESTION: _____

   NOUN CLAUSE: I want to know_____

10. The plane is supposed to land (*at 7:14 P.M.*).

    QUESTION: _____

    NOUN CLAUSE: Could you tell me_____

☐ **EXERCISE 4—ORAL:** Make questions and noun clauses.

Student A: Make a question from the given sentence. The words in parentheses should be the answer to your question.

Student B: Keep your book closed. Change Student A's question into a noun clause. Begin your sentence with "(Name of Student A) wants to know . . . ."

1. Fred* lives (*in an apartment*).
   Student A: Where does Fred live?
   Student B: (Yoko) wants to know where Fred lives.
2. It's (*ten o'clock*).
   Student A: What time is it?
   Student B: (Roberto) wants to know what time it is.
3. Tom wants (*a watch*) for his birthday.
4. Jane gets to school (*by bus*).
5. Vacation starts (*on June 3rd*).
6. Sue left class early (*because she didn't feel well*).
7. The movie is going to last (*two hours and ten minutes*).
8. Mary called (*Jim*).
9. (*Mary*) called Jim.
10. Alice talked to the teacher about (*the test*).
11. Alice talked to (*the teacher*) about the test.
12. (*Alice*) talked to the teacher about the test.
13. Sue's plane will arrive (*at 8:05*).
14. (*Two*) students will be absent from class tomorrow.
15. There are (*over 10,000*) lakes in Minnesota.
16. It's (*twenty-five miles*) to Springfield from here.
17. Jane (*studied*) last night.
18. We're supposed to buy (*this*) book, (*not that book*).
19. Ann likes (*chocolate*) ice cream the best.
20. A robin's egg is (*turquoise blue*).
21. That woman is (*Mrs. Anderson*).
22. (*Mr. Anderson*) is talking on the telephone.
23. That's (*Sam's*) notebook.
24. (*Jessica's*) car was stolen.

---

*To Student A: Use the name of a class member instead of the name in the exercise if you wish. For example: *Where does Ali live?* (instead of *Where does Fred live?*).

7-3 NOUN CLAUSES WHICH BEGIN WITH WHETHER OR IF

YES/NO QUESTION	NOUN CLAUSE	
Will she come?	(a) I don't know **whether she will come.** I don't know **if she will come.**	When a yes/no question is changed to a noun clause, **whether** or **if** is used to introduce the clause.
Does he need help?	(b) I wonder **whether he needs help.** I wonder **if he needs help.**	(Note: **whether** is more acceptable in formal English, but **if** is quite commonly used, especially in speaking.)
	(c) I wonder **whether or not** she will come. (d) I wonder **whether** she will come **or not.** (e) I wonder **if** she will come **or not.**	In (c), (d), and (e): Notice the patterns when **or not** is used.
	(f) **Whether she comes or not** is unimportant to me.	In (f): Notice that the noun clause is in the subject position.

☐ **EXERCISE 5—ORAL (BOOKS CLOSED):** Begin your response with "I wonder . . . ."

Example: Does (. . .) need any help?
Response: I wonder whether/if (. . .) needs any help.

Example: Where is (. . .)?
Response: I wonder where (. . .) is.

1. Where is your friend?
2. Should we wait for him?
3. Should you call him?
4. Where is your dictionary?
5. Who took your dictionary?
6. Did (. . .) borrow your dictionary?
7. Did you leave your dictionary at the library?
8. Who is that woman?
9. Does she need any help?
10. Who is that man?
11. What is he doing?
12. Is he having trouble?
13. Should you offer to help him?
14. How far is it to (Florida)?
15. Do we have enough time to go to (Florida) over vacation?
16. Whose book is this?
17. Does it belong to (. . .)?
18. Why is the sky blue?
19. How long does a butterfly live?
20. What causes earthquakes?
21. When was the first book written?
22. Why did dinosaurs become extinct?
23. Is there life on other planets?
24. How did life begin?
25. Will people live on the moon someday?

□ **EXERCISE 6—ORAL (BOOKS CLOSED):** Begin your response with "Could you please tell me . . . ."

> *Example:* What is this?
> *Response:* Could you please tell me what this is?

1. Where is the library? The nearest phone? The rest room?
2. How much does this book cost?
3. When is Flight 62 expected to arrive?
4. Does this bus go downtown?
5. Is this word spelled correctly?
6. What time is it?
7. Is this information correct?
8. How much does it cost to fly from (*Chicago*) to (*New York*)?
9. Where is the bus station?
10. Whose pen is this?

7-4 QUESTION WORDS FOLLOWED BY INFINITIVES

(a) I don't know *what I should do.* (b) I don't know **what to do.** (c) Pam can't decide *whether she should go or stay home.* (d) Pam can't decide **whether to go or (to) stay home.** (e) Please tell me *how I can get to the bus station.* (f) Please tell me **how to get to the bus station.** (g) Jim told us *where we could find it.* (h) Jim told us **where to find it.**	Question words (***when, where, how, who, whom, whose, what, which***) and ***whether*** may be followed by an infinitive. Each pair of sentences in the examples has the same meaning. Notice that the meaning expressed by the infinitive is either ***should*** or ***can/could***.

□ **EXERCISE 7:** Give sentences with the same meaning by using infinitives.

1. He told me when I should come. → *He told me when to come.*
2. The plumber told me how I could fix the leak in the sink.
3. Please tell me where I should meet you.
4. Don had an elaborate excuse for being late for their date, but Sandy didn't know whether she should believe him or not.
5. Jim found two shirts he liked, but he had trouble deciding which one he should buy.
6. I've done everything I can think of to help Andy get his life straightened out. I don't know what else I can do.

Complete the following; use infinitives in your completions.

7. I was tongue-tied. I didn't know what _____.

8. A: I can't decide _____ to the reception.

   B: How about your green suit?

9. A: Where are you going to live when you go to the university?

   B: I'm not sure. I can't decide whether _____.

10. A: Do you know how _____?

    B: No, but I'd like to learn.

11. A: I don't know what _____ for her birthday. Got any

    suggestions?

    B: How about a book?

12. My cousin has a dilemma. He can't decide whether _____

    or _____. What do you think he should do?

13. Before you leave on your trip, read this tour book. It tells you where

    _____ and how _____.

7–5 NOUN CLAUSES WHICH BEGIN WITH *THAT*

STATEMENT *(Expression of an idea or fact)*	NOUN CLAUSE	
He is a good actor. The world is round.	(a) I think *that he is a good actor.* (b) I think *he is a good actor.* (c) We know *(that) the world is round.*	In (a): *that he is a good actor* is a noun clause. It is used as the object of the verb *think.* The word *that*, when it introduces a noun clause, has no meaning in itself. It simply marks the beginning of the clause. Frequently it is omitted, as in (b), especially in speaking. (If used in speaking, it is unstressed.)
She doesn't understand spoken English. The world is round.	(d) *That she doesn't understand spoken English* is obvious. (e) *It* is obvious *(that)* she doesn't understand spoken English. (f) *That the world is round* is a fact. (g) *It* is a fact *that the world is round.*	In (d): The noun clause (*That she doesn't understand spoken English*) is used as the subject of the sentence. The word *that* is not omitted when it introduces a noun clause used as the subject of a sentence, as in (d) and (f). More commonly, the word *it* functions as the subject, and the noun clause is placed at the end of the sentence, as in (e) and (g).

☐ EXERCISE 8—ORAL:

Student A: Change the given sentence into a noun clause. Use *it* + any appropriate expression from the list.

Student B: Give the equivalent sentence by using a "*that* clause" as the subject.

a fact	*surprising*	*obvious*	*too bad*	*a shame*
a well-known fact	*strange*	*apparent*	*unfortunate*	*a pity*
true	*unfair*			

1. The world is round.

   Student A: It is a fact that the world is round.

   Student B: That the world is round is a fact.

2. Drug abuse can ruin one's health.

3. Tim hasn't been able to make any friends.

4. Some women do not earn equal pay for equal work.

5. The earth revolves around the sun.

6. Irene failed her entrance examination.

7. Smoking can cause cancer.

8. English is the principal language of the business community throughout much of the world.

☐ EXERCISE 9—ORAL:

Student A: Make an original sentence by using *it* and the given expression.

Student B: Give the equivalent sentence by using a "*that* clause" as the subject.

1. true

   Student A: It is true that plants need water in order to grow.

   Student B: That plants need water in order to grow is true.

2. a fact
3. surprising
4. obvious
5. too bad
6. a well-known fact

7. unfortunate
8. true
9. strange
10. unlikely

☐ EXERCISE 10—ORAL/WRITTEN: Complete the following.

1. It is my belief that . . . *the war between those two countries will end soon.*

2. It seems to me that . . . .
3. It is my impression that . . . .
4. It is my belief that . . . .
5. It is my theory that . . . .

6. It is widely believed that . . . .
7. It is thought that . . . .
8. It has been said that . . . .
9. It is a miracle that . . . .

☐ **EXERCISE 11—ORAL:** "***That* clauses**" may follow *be + certain adjectives* that express feelings or attitudes. Complete the following.

1. I'm sorry (that) . . . *I was late for class.*
2. I'm glad (that) . . . .
3. I'm disappointed (that) . . . .
4. I'm pleased (that) . . . .
5. I'm surprised (that) . . . .
6. I'm sure (that) . . . .
7. I'm amazed (that) . . . .
8. I'm happy (that) . . . .
9. Yesterday I was annoyed (that) . . . .
10. I'm afraid (that)* . . . .

☐ **EXERCISE 12:** A "***that* clause**" may follow *be* directly. Complete the sentences with your own ideas by using "***that* clauses**."

1. He says he is twenty-one, but the truth is . . . *that he is only eighteen.*
2. There are two reasons why I do not want to go out tonight.
   The first reason is . . . *that I have to study.*
   The second reason is . . . *that I do not have enough money.***
3. There are several reasons why I am studying English.
   One reason is . . . .
   Another reason is . . . .
   A third reason is . . . .
4. I have had three problems since I came here.
   One problem is that . . . .
   Another problem is that . . . .
   The third problem I have had is that . . . .
5. One advantage of owning your own car is . . . .
   Another advantage is . . . .
   One disadvantage, however, of owning your own car is . . . .

☐ **EXERCISE 13:** A "***that* clause**" is frequently used with ***the fact***. Combine the sentences using "the fact that" to introduce a noun clause.

1. Ann was late. *That* didn't surprise me.
   → *The fact that Ann was late didn't surprise me.*
2. Mary didn't come. *That* made me angry.
3. I'm a little tired. I feel fine except for *that*.

*****To be afraid** has two possible meanings:
    (1) It can express fear: *I'm afraid of dogs. I'm afraid that his dog will bite me.*
    (2) In informal English, it often expresses a meaning similar to "to be sorry": *I'm afraid that I can't accept your invitation. I'm afraid you have the wrong number.*
******Notice: *That* is used, not *because*, to introduce the clause. (*Because* might occur only in very informal spoken English: *The first reason is because I have to study.*)

4. She didn't pass the entrance examination. She was not admitted to the university due to *that*.

5. Many people in the world live in intolerable poverty. *That* must concern all of us.

6. He is frequently absent from class. *That* indicates his lack of interest in school.

7. I was supposed to bring my passport to the examination for identification. I was not aware of *that*. As a result, I was not allowed to take the test.

8. The people of the town were given no warning of the approaching tornado. Due to *that*, there were many casualties.

7–6 QUOTED SPEECH*

Quoted speech refers to reproducing words exactly as they were originally spoken. Quotation marks ("...") are used.**	
QUOTING ONE SENTENCE (a) She said, "My brother is a student."	In (a): Use a comma after **she said**. Capitalize the first word of the quoted sentence. Put the final quotation marks outside of the period at the end of the sentence.
(b) "My brother is a student," she said.	In (b): Use a comma, not a period, at the end of the quoted sentence when it precedes **she said**.
(c) "My brother," she said, "is a student."	In (c): If the quoted sentence is divided by **she said**, use a comma after the first part of the quote. Do not capitalize the first word of the second half of the quoted sentence.
QUOTING MORE THAN ONE SENTENCE (d) "My brother is a student. He is attending a university," she said.	In (d): Quotation marks are placed at the beginning and end of the complete quote. Notice: There are no quotation marks after **student**.
QUOTING A QUESTION OR AN EXCLAMATION (e) She asked, "When will you be here?"	In (e): The question mark is inside the quotation marks.
(f) "When will you be here?" she asked.	In (f): If a question mark is used, no comma is used before **she asked**.
(g) She said, "Watch out!"	In (g): The exclamation point is inside the quotation marks.

Quoted speech is also called *direct speech*. Reported speech (discussed in Chart 7–7) is also called *indirect speech*.
**In British English, quotation marks are called *inverted commas*.

□ **EXERCISE 14:** Add the necessary punctuation and capitalization to the following.

1. Henry said   there is a phone call for you
2. There is a phone call for you   he said
3. There is   said Henry   a phone call for you   ∗
4. There is a phone call for you   it's your sister   said Henry
5. There is a phone call for you   he said   it's your sister
6. I asked him   where is the phone
7. Where is the phone   she asked
8.   When the police officer came over to my car, he said   let me see your driver's license, please

What's wrong, Officer   I asked   was I speeding

No, you weren't speeding   he replied   you went through a red light at the corner of Fifth Avenue and Main Street   you almost caused an accident

Did I really do that   I said   I didn't see the red light   ∗∗

□ **EXERCISE 15:** Choose two of your classmates to have a brief conversation in front of the class, and decide upon a topic for them (what they did last night, what they are doing right now, sports, music, books, etc.). Give them a few minutes to practice their conversation. Then, while they are speaking, take notes so that you can write their conversation. Use quoted speech in your written report. Be sure to start a new paragraph each time the speaker changes.

———————

∗Notice in sentences 3 and 4: The noun subject (Henry) follows **said**. A noun subject often follows the verb when the subject and verb come in the middle or at the end of a sentence. A pronoun subject almost always precedes the verb.

∗∗Notice: A new paragraph begins each time the speaker changes.

7-7 REPORTED SPEECH AND THE FORMAL SEQUENCE OF TENSES IN NOUN CLAUSES

Reported speech refers to using a noun clause to report what someone has said. No quotation marks are used. Notice the changes in the verb forms from quoted speech to reported speech in the following examples.

QUOTED SPEECH	REPORTED SPEECH
(a) She said, "I *watch* TV every day."	→ She said (that) she *watched* TV every day.
(b) She said, "I *am watching* TV."	→ She said she *was watching* TV.
(c) She said, "I *have watched* TV."	→ She said she *had watched* TV.
(d) She said, "I *watched* TV."	→ She said she *had watched* TV.
(e) She said, "I *will watch* TV."	→ She said she *would watch* TV.
(f) She said, "I *am going to watch* TV."	→ She said she *was going to watch* TV.
(g) She said, "I *can watch* TV."	→ She said she *could watch* TV.
(h) She said, "I *may watch* TV."	→ She said she *might watch* TV.
(i) She said, "I *might watch* TV."	→ She said she *might watch* TV.
(j) She said, "I *must watch* TV."	→ She said she *had to watch* TV.
(k) She said, "I *have to watch* TV."	→ She said she *had to watch* TV.
(l) She said, "I *should watch* TV."	→ She said she *should watch* TV.
(m) She said, "I *ought to watch* TV."	→ She said she *ought to watch* TV.
(n) She said, "*Watch* TV."	→ She *told me to watch* TV.*
(o) She said, "*Do* you *watch* TV?"	→ She *asked (me) if* I *watched* TV.

GENERAL GUIDELINES ON TENSE USAGE IN A NOUN CLAUSE

(1) If the reporting verb (the main verb of the sentence, e.g., *said*) is in the past, the verb in the noun clause will usually also be in a past form.

(2) This formal sequence of tenses in noun clauses is used in both speaking and writing. However, sometimes in spoken English, no change is made in the noun clause verb, especially if the speaker is reporting something immediately or soon after it was said.

Immediate reporting: *A: What did the teacher just say? I didn't hear him.*
                                 *B: He said he **wants** us to read Chapter Six.*

Later reporting: *A: I didn't go to class yesterday. Did Mr. Jones make any assignments?*
                                 *B: Yes. He said he **wanted** us to read Chapter Six.*

(3) Also, sometimes the present tense is retained even in formal English when the reported sentence deals with a general truth: *She said that the world **is** round.*

(4) When the reporting verb is simple present, present perfect, or future, the noun clause verb is not changed.

She *says*, "I *watch* TV every day."	→ She *says* she *watches* TV every day.
She *has said*, "I *watch* TV every day."	→ She *has said* that she *watches* TV every day.
She *will say*, "I *watch* TV every day."	→ She *will say* that she *watches* TV every day.

*In reported speech, an imperative sentence is changed to an infinitive. *Tell* is used instead of *say* as the reporting verb. (See Chart 4-5 for other verbs followed by an infinitive that are used to report speech.) Also note that *tell* is immediately followed by a (pro)noun object, but *say* is not:

    *He told **me** he would be late. He said he would be late. Also possible: He said **to me** he would be late.*

□ **EXERCISE 16:** Complete the sentences by reporting the speaker's words in a noun clause. Use formal sequence of tenses where appropriate.

1. Bob said, "I will help you."

   Bob said ___(that) he would help me.___

2. "Do you need a pen?" Annie asked.

   Annie asked me ___if I needed a pen.___

3. Jennifer asked, "What do you want?"

   Jennifer asked me ___what I wanted.___

4. Sid asked, "Are you hungry?"

   Sid wanted to know _____

5. "I want a sandwich," Jennifer said.

   Jennifer said _____

6. "I'm going to move to Ohio," said Bruce.

   Bruce informed me _____

7. "Did you enjoy your trip?" asked Connie.

   Connie asked me _____

8. Dick asked, "What are you talking about?"

   Dick asked me _____

9. Nancy asked, "Have you seen my grammar book?"

   Nancy wanted to know _____

10. Susan said, "I don't want to go."

    Susan said _____

11. Sam asked, "Where is Amanda?"

    Sam wanted to know _____

12. "Can you come to my party?" asked David.

    David asked me _____

13. "I may be late," said Mike.

    Mike told me _____

14. Felix said, "You should study harder."

    Felix told me _____

15. Barbara said, "I have to go downtown."

    Barbara said _____

16. "Why is the sky blue?" my young daughter often asks.

My young daughter often asks me _____

17. My mother asked, "Why are you tired?"

My mother wondered _____

18. "I will come to the meeting," said Juan.

Juan told me _____

19. Ms. Adams just asked, "Will you be in class tomorrow?"

Ms. Adams wants to know _____

20. "The sun rises in the east," said Mr. Clark.

Mr. Clark, an elementary school teacher, explained to his students _____

_____

□ **EXERCISE 17:** Complete the sentences by changing the quoted speech to reported speech. Use formal sequence of tenses.

1. "Have you ever met Ms. Powell?"

Mr. Peterson asked me _*if I had ever met Ms. Powell.*_

2. "I'm going to postpone the examination."

Professor Williams announced _____

3. "Someday we'll be in contact with beings from outer space."

The scientist predicted _____

4. "I think I'll go to the library to study."

Joe said _____

5. "Is there anything I can do to help?"

Sally wanted to know _____

6. "Does Jim know what he's doing?"

I wondered _____

7. "Is what I've heard true?"

I wondered _____

8. "Is what I wrote correct?"

Maria wanted to know _____

9. "I need to go to the market before it closes."

Janet suddenly remembered _____

10. "Sentences with noun clauses are a little complicated."

Elsa thinks _____

☐ **EXERCISE 18:** Change the quoted speech to reported speech. Study the example carefully and use the same pattern: *said that . . . and that* OR *said that . . . but that.*

1. "My father is a businessman. My mother is an engineer."

He said that ___*his father was a businessman and that his mother*___
was an engineer. _____

2. "I'm excited about my new job. I've found a nice apartment."

I got a letter from my sister yesterday. She said _____

_____

3. "Your Uncle Harry is in the hospital. Your Aunt Sally is very worried about him."

The last time my mother wrote to me, she said _____

_____

4. "I expect you to be in class every day. Unexcused absences may affect your grades."

Our sociology professor said _____

_____

5. "Highway 66 will be closed for two months. Commuters should seek alternate routes."

The newspaper said _____

_____

6. "I'm getting good grades, but I have difficulty understanding lectures."

My brother is a junior at the state university. In his last letter, he wrote

_____

7. "I'll come to the meeting, but I can't stay for more than an hour."

Julia told me _____

_____

8. "Every obstacle is a steppingstone to success. You should view problems in your life as opportunities to prove yourself."

My father often told me _____

_____

☐ **EXERCISE 19—WRITTEN:** Think of a letter written in English that you have received recently. In a short paragraph, summarize some of the news or information in this letter. (If you have not received a letter written in English recently, invent one.) Include at least one or two sentences that use the pattern you practiced in the preceding exercise: *said that . . . and that/said that . . . but that.*

☐ **EXERCISE 20—ORAL (BOOKS CLOSED):** Begin your response with "He (She) asked me . . . ."

(To the teacher: Suggest to the students that they practice using the formal sequence of tenses.)

Example: Where is your friend?
Response: He (She) asked me where my friend was.

1. What time is it?
2. What is your name?
3. Can you speak Arabic?
4. Have you met my brother?
5. Where are you living?
6. Will you be here tomorrow?
7. What kind of camera do you have?
8. How tall are you?
9. What courses are you taking?
10. Do you feel okay?
11. Have you read any good books lately?
12. How do you like living here?
13. Did you finish your assignment?
14. What are you doing?
15. Whose briefcase is that?
16. May I borrow your dictionary?
17. Where will you be tomorrow around three o'clock?
18. Did you go to class yesterday?
19. What are you going to do during vacation?
20. What is the capital city of your country?
21. Did you go to a party last night?
22. How many people have you met in the last couple of months?
23. Can I use your pen?
24. Where should I meet you after class?
25. Do you understand what I am saying?
26. What country are you from?
27. Is what you said really true?
28. How do you know that it is true?
29. Who do you think will win the game?
30. Is what you want to talk to me about important?

☐ **EXERCISE 21:** Using the information in the conversation, complete the sentences in the reported conversation.

CONVERSATION:

"Where are you from?" asked the passenger sitting next to me on the plane.
"Chicago," I said.
"That's nice. I'm from Mapleton. It's a small town in northern Michigan."

"Oh yes. I've heard of it," I said. "Michigan is a beautiful state. I've been there on vacation many times."

"Were you in Michigan on vacation this year?"

"No. I went far away from home this year. I went to India," I replied.

"Oh, that's nice. Is it a long drive from Chicago to India?" she asked me. My mouth fell open. I didn't know how to respond. Some people certainly need to study geography.

REPORTED CONVERSATION:

(1)   The passenger sitting next to me on the plane _____*asked*_____ me

(2) where I _____*was*_____ from. I _____ her I _____

(3) from Chicago. She _____ that she _____ from

(4) Mapleton, a small town in northern Michigan. She wondered if I _____

(5) _____ of it, and I told her that I _____. I went on to

(6) say that I thought Michigan _____ a beautiful state and

(7) explained that I _____ there on vacations many times. She

(8) _____ me if I _____ in Michigan on vacation

(9) this year. I replied that I _____ and _____ her

(10) that I _____ far away, to India. Then she asked me if it

(11) _____ a long drive from Chicago to India! My mouth fell open. I didn't know how to respond. Some people certainly need to study geography.

☐ **EXERCISE 22—WRITTEN:** Complete the following. Use formal sequence of tenses if appropriate.

1. I cannot understand why . . . .
2. One of the students remarked that . . . .
3. I was not sure whose . . . .
4. What . . . surprised.
5. That she . . . surprised me.
6. One of the students stated that . . . .
7. I could not . . . due to the fact that . . . .
8. What he said was that . . . .
9. No one knows who . . . .
10. The instructor announced that . . . .
11. What I want to know is why . . . .
12. What . . . is not important.
13. We discussed the fact that . . . .
14. I wonder whether . . . .

□ **EXERCISE 23—ORAL:**

Student A: Ask a question on the given topic—whatever comes into your mind. Use a question word (***when, how, where, what, why,*** *etc.*).

Student B: Answer the question in a complete sentence.

Student C: Report what Student A and Student B said.

Example: tonight   ROSA: What are you going to do tonight?

ALI: I'm going to study.

YUNG: Rosa asked Ali what he was going to do tonight, and Ali replied that he was going to study.

1. tonight
2. music
3. courses
4. tomorrow
5. book
6. this city
7. population
8. last year
9. television
10. dinner
11. next year
12. vacation

□ **EXERCISE 24—ORAL/WRITTEN:** Give a one-minute impromptu speech. Your classmates will take notes, and then in a short paragraph, or orally, they will report what you said. Choose any topic that comes to mind (pollution, insects, soccer, dogs, etc.), or have your classmates help select a topic.

□ **EXERCISE 25—ERROR ANALYSIS:** All of the following sentences contain errors. These sentences are from student compositions. Test your skill by seeing how many of the errors you can find and correct.

1. Tell the taxi driver where do you want to go.

2. My roommate came into the room and asked me why aren't you in class? I said I am waiting for a telephone call from my family.

3. It was my first day at the university, and I am on my way to my first class. I wondered who else will be in the class. What the teacher would be like?

4. He asked me that what did I intend to do after I graduate?

5. Many of the people in the United States doesn't know much about geography. For example, people will ask you where is Japan located.

6. What does a patient tell a doctor it is confidential.

7. The reason I decided to come here, because this university has a good meteorology department.

8. We looked back to see where are we and how far are we from camp. We don't know, so we decided to turn back. We are afraid that we wander too far.

9. After the accident, I opened my eyes slowly and realize that I am still alive.

10. My country is prospering due to it is a fact that it has become a leading producer of oil.

11. Is true that one must to know english in order to study at an american university.

12. My mother told me what it was the purpose of our visit.

7–8 USING THE SUBJUNCTIVE IN NOUN CLAUSES

(a) The teacher **demands** that we **be** on time. (b) I **insisted** that he **pay** me the money. (c) I **recommended** that she **not go** to the concert. (d) **It is important** that they **be told** the truth.	In (a): **be** is a subjunctive verb. The subjunctive is used in a noun clause that follows certain verbs and expressions. The sentences generally *stress importance*. In these sentences, the subjunctive verb is used only in its simple form. It does not have present, past, or future form; it is neither singular nor plural. Negative: **not** + *simple form*, as in (c). Passive: simple form of **be** + *past participle*, as in (d).
(e) I **suggested** that she **see** a doctor. (f) I **suggested** that she **should see** a doctor.	**Should** is also possible after **suggest** and **recommend**.*

COMMON VERBS AND EXPRESSIONS FOLLOWED BY THE SUBJUNCTIVE IN A NOUN CLAUSE

demand *(that)*	suggest *(that)*	it is important *(that)*
insist *(that)*	recommend *(that)*	it is necessary *(that)*
request *(that)*	advise *(that)*	it is essential *(that)*
ask *(that)*	propose *(that)*	it is vital *(that)*
		it is imperative *(that)*

*The subjunctive is more common in American English than British English. In British English, **should** + *simple form* is more usual than the subjunctive: e.g., *The teacher **insists** that we **should be** on time.*

☐ **EXERCISE 26:** Complete the following. In many of the sentences there is more than one possible completion.

1. Mr. Adams insists that we _____*be*_____ careful in our writing.

2. They requested that we not _____ after midnight.

3. She demanded that I _____ her the truth.

4. I recommended that Jane _____ to the head of the department.

5. I suggest that everyone _____ a letter to the governor.

6. It is essential that I _____ you tomorrow.

7. It is important that he _____ the director of the English program.

8. It is necessary that everyone _____ here on time.

☐ **EXERCISE 27:** Give the correct form of the verb in parentheses. Some of the verbs are passive.

1. Her advisor recommended that she (*take*) _____ five courses.

2. He insisted that the new baby (*name*) _____ after his grandfather.

3. The doctor recommended that she (*stay*) _____ in bed for a few days.

4. The students requested that the test (*postpone*) _____, but the instructor decided against a postponement.

5. I requested that I (*permit*) _____ to change my class.

6. It is essential that pollution (*control*) _____ and eventually (*eliminate*) _____.

7. It was such a beautiful day that one of the students suggested we (*have*) _____ class outside.

8. The movie director insisted that everything about his productions (*be*) _____ authentic.

9. It is vital that no one else (*know*) _____ about the secret government operation.

10. She asked that we (*be*) _____ sure to lock the door behind us.

11. It is essential that no one (*admit*) _____ to the room without proper identification.

12. It is important that you (*be, not*) _____ late.

13. It is imperative that he (*return*) _____ home immediately.

14. The governor proposed that a new highway (*build*) _____.

15. She specifically asked that I (*tell, not*) _____ anyone else

about it. She said it was important that no one else (*tell*) _____

_____ about it.

7–9 USING *-EVER* WORDS

The following *-ever* words give the idea of "any." Each pair of sentences in the examples has the same meaning.		
whoever	(a)	**Whoever** wants to come is welcome. *Anyone who* wants to come is welcome.
who(m)ever	(b)	He makes friends easily with **who(m)ever** he meets.* He makes friends easily with *anyone who(m)* he meets.
whatever	(c)	He always says **whatever** comes into his mind. He always says *anything that* comes into his mind.
whichever	(d)	There are four good programs on TV at eight o'clock. We can watch **whichever program (whichever one)** you prefer. We can watch *any of the four programs that* you prefer.
whenever	(e)	You may leave **whenever** you wish. You may leave *at any time that* you wish.
wherever	(f)	She can go **wherever** she wants to go. She can go *anyplace that* she wants to go.
however	(g)	The students may dress **however** they please. The students may dress *in any way that* they please.

*In (b): **whomever** is the object of the verb **meets**. In American English, **whomever** is rare and very formal. In British English, **whoever** (not **whomever**) is used as the object form: *He makes friends easily with whoever he meets.*

☐ **EXERCISE 28:** Complete the following by using *-ever* words.

1. He is free to go anyplace he wishes. He can go ___*wherever*___ he

wants.

2. He is free to go anytime he wishes. He can go _____ he

wants.

3. I don't know what you should do about that problem. Do

_____ seems best to you.

4. There are five flights going to Chicago every day. I don't care which one we take. We can take _____ one fits in best with your schedule.

5. I want you to be honest. I hope you feel free to say _____ is on your mind.

6. _____ leads a life full of love and happiness is rich.

7. No one can tell him what to do. He does _____ he wants.

8. If you want to rearrange the furniture, go ahead. You can rearrange it _____ you want. I don't care one way or the other.

9. Those children are wild. I feel sorry for _____ has to be their babysitter.

10. I have a car. I can take you _____ you want to go.

11. He likes to tell people about his problems. He will talk to _____ will listen to him. But he bores _____ he talks to.

12. I know you're failing all of your courses, but there is nothing I can do about it. It is up to you to do _____ is necessary to improve your grades.

13. I have four. Take _____ one pleases you most.

14. Irene does _____ she wants to do, goes _____ she wants to go, gets up _____ she wants to get up, makes friends with _____ she meets, and dresses _____ she pleases.

☐ **EXERCISE 29—PHRASAL VERBS:** Supply appropriate prepositions for the following two-word or three-word verbs.

1. A: Why don't we try to call _____ the O'Briens sometime this weekend? We haven't seen them for a long time.

   B: Sounds like a good idea. I'd like to see them again.

2. A: Did you go _____ your paper carefully before you handed it _____?

   B: Yes. I looked it _____ carefully.

3. A: Do you believe his story about being late because he had a flat tire?

   B: No. I think he made it _____.

4. A: Could you pick _____ a newspaper on your way home from work tonight?

   B: Sure.

5. A: Did you hear the bad news?

   B: About what?

   A: Gary's grandmother passed _____. Gary went home to be with his family and attend the funeral.

6. A: I like your new shoes.

   B: Thanks. I had to try _____ almost a dozen pairs before I decided to get these.

7. A: Have you decided to accept that new job?

   B: Not yet. I'm still thinking it _____.

8. A: I'm tired. I wish I could get _____ of going to the meeting tonight.

   B: Do you have to go?

9. A: Why hasn't Mary been in class for the last two weeks?

   B: She dropped _____ _____ school.

10. A: What time does your plane take _____?

    B: 10:40.

    A: How long does the flight take?

    B: I think we get _____ around 12:30.

11. A: Do you like living in the dorm?

    B: It's okay. I've learned to put _____ with all the noise.

12. A: What brought _____ your decision to quit your job?

    B: I couldn't get _____ _____ my boss.

CHAPTER **8**

Showing Relationships Between Ideas—Part I

8–1 PARALLEL STRUCTURE

One use of a conjunction is to connect words or phrases that have the same grammatical function in a sentence. This use of conjunctions is called *parallel structure.* The conjunctions used in this pattern are: *and, but, or, nor.**

(a) *Steve and* his *friend* are coming to dinner.	In (a): *noun + and + noun*
(b) Susan *raised* her hand *and snapped* her fingers.	In (b): *verb + and + verb*
(c) He *is waving* his arms *and (is) shouting* at us.	In (c): *verb + and + verb* (The second auxiliary may be omitted if it is the same as the first auxiliary.)
(d) These shoes are *old but comfortable.*	In (d): *adjective + but + adjective*
(e) He wants *to watch* TV *or (to) listen* to some music.	In (e): *infinitive + or + infinitive* (The second *to* may be omitted.)
(f) *Steve, Joe, and Alice* are coming to dinner.	A parallel structure may contain more than two parts. In a series, commas are used to separate each unit. The final comma that precedes the conjunction is optional but is customarily used. (*No* commas are used if there are only two parts to a parallel structure.)
(g) Susan *raised* her hand, *snapped* her fingers, *and asked* a question.	
(h) The colors in that fabric are *red, gold, black, and green.*	

*More specifically, *and, but, or, nor* are called *coordinating conjunctions.*

☐ **EXERCISE 1:** Underline the parallel structure in each sentence, and give the pattern that is used, as in the examples.

1. The old man is extremely <u>kind</u> and <u>generous</u>.   _adjective_ + and + _adjective_

2. He received a pocket <u>calculator</u> and a wool <u>sweater</u> for his birthday.   _noun_ + and + _noun_

3. She spoke angrily and bitterly about the war.

_____ + and + _____

4. I looked for my book but couldn't find it.

_____ + but + _____

5. I hope to go to that university and study under Dr. Liu.

_____ + and + _____

6. In my spare time, I enjoy reading novels or watching television.

_____ + or + _____

7. He will leave at eight and arrive at nine.

_____ + and + _____

8. He should have broken his engagement to Beth and married Sue instead.

_____ + and + _____

☐ **EXERCISE 2:** Parallel structure makes repeating the same words unnecessary.* Combine the given sentences into one concise sentence that contains parallel structure. Punctuate carefully.

1. Mary opened the door. Mary greeted her guests.
   → *Mary opened the door and greeted her guests.*
2. Mary is opening the door. Mary is greeting her guests.
3. Mary will open the door. Mary will greet her guests.
4. Alice is kind. Alice is generous. Alice is trustworthy.
5. Please try to speak more loudly. Please try to speak more clearly.
6. He gave her flowers on Sunday. He gave her candy on Monday. He gave her a ring on Tuesday.

---

*This form of parallel structure, in which unnecessary words are omitted but are understood, is termed *ellipsis.*

7. While we were in New York, we attended an opera. While we were in New York, we ate at marvelous restaurants. While we were in New York, we visited some old friends.

8. He decided to quit school. He decided to go to California. He decided to find a job.

9. I am looking forward to going to Italy. I am looking forward to eating wonderful pasta every day.

10. I should have finished my homework. I should have cleaned up my room.

11. The boy was old enough to work. The boy was old enough to earn some money.

12. He preferred to play baseball. Or he preferred to spend his time in the streets with other boys.

13. I like coffee. I do not like tea.
I like coffee but not tea.*

14. I have met his mother. I have not met his father.

15. Jake would like to live in Puerto Rico. He would not like to live in Iceland.

☐ **EXERCISE 3:** In each group, complete the unfinished sentence. Then combine the sentences into one concise sentence that contains parallel structure. Punctuate carefully.

1. The country lane was narrow.

The country lane was steep.

The country lane was _____ *muddy.* _____
_____ *The country lane was narrow, steep, and muddy.* _____

2. I like to become acquainted with the people of other countries.

I like to become acquainted with the customs of other countries.

I like to become acquainted with _____ of other countries.

_____ _____

3. I dislike living in a city because of the air pollution.

I dislike living in a city because of the crime.

I dislike living in a city because of _____

_____

---

*Sometimes a comma precedes ***but not***: *I like coffee, but not tea.*

4. We discussed some of the social problems of the United States.

   We discussed some of the political problems of the United States.

   We discussed some of the _____ problems of the United

   States.

   _____

5. Hawaii has _____

   Hawaii has many interesting tropical trees.

   Hawaii has many interesting tropical flowers.

   Hawaii has beautiful beaches.

   _____

6. Mary Hart would make a good president because she _____

   Mary Hart would make a good president because she works effectively

   with others.

   Mary Hart would make a good president because she has a reputation for

   integrity.

   Mary Hart would make a good president because she has a reputation for

   independent thinking.

   _____

☐ **EXERCISE 4:** Choose the letter of the phrase from the list that best completes each
sentence. Use each phrase in the list only once.

A. affordable health care	G. provide quality education
B. by leaders who are committed to public service and hard work	H. to reduce health care costs
	I. responsible
C. efficiently	J. seeking practical solutions
D. excellence in	K. tolerant of those who are weak
✔ E. in agriculture	L. who finds a way to get the
F. integrity	important jobs done

1. Mr. Turner has had wide experience. He has worked in business, in the
   news media, and ___*E*___ .

2. Judge Holmes served the people of this country with impartiality, ability,
   and ____.

3. The people want safe homes, good schools, and ____.

4. As a taxpayer, I want my money used wisely and _____.

5. Mr. Adams is respected for researching issues and _____.

6. Ms. Hunter has established a record of effective and _____ leadership in government.

7. The challenges that face us today will not be met by politicians who focus on partisan bickering and political expediency but _____.

8. Resolve to be tender with the young, compassionate with the aged, understanding of those who are wrong, and _____. Sometime in life, you will have been all of these.

9. Carol is a hard-working personnel manager who welcomes challenges and _____.

10. I will continue to fight for adequate funding of and _____ education.

11. She has worked hard to control excess government spending, protect our environment, and _____.

12. I see the need to eliminate unfair taxes, to improve the business climate, and _____.

8-2 USING PAIRED CONJUNCTIONS:
*BOTH . . . AND; NOT ONLY . . . BUT ALSO; EITHER . . . OR; NEITHER . . . NOR**

(a) **Both my mother and my sister *are*** here. (b) **Not only my mother but also my sister *is*** here. (c) **Not only my sister but also my parents *are*** here. (d) **Neither my mother nor my sister *is*** here. (e) **Neither my sister nor my parents *are*** here.	Two subjects connected by ***both . . . and*** take a plural verb. When two subjects are connected by ***not only . . . but also, either . . . or***, or ***neither . . . nor***, the subject that is closer to the verb determines whether the verb is singular or plural.
(f) The research project will take ***both*** *time **and** money*. (g) Yesterday it ***not only*** *rained **but (also)** snowed*. (h) I'll take ***either*** *chemistry **or** physics* next quarter. (i) That book is ***neither*** *interesting **nor** accurate*.	Notice the parallel structure in the examples. The *same* grammatical form should follow each word of the pair. In (f): ***both*** + *noun* + ***and*** + *noun* In (g): ***not only*** + *verb* + ***but also*** + *verb* In (h): ***either*** + *noun* + ***or*** + *noun* In (i): ***neither*** + *adjective* + ***nor*** + *adjective*

*Paired conjunctions are also called *correlative conjunctions*.

□ **EXERCISE 5:** Supply *is* or *are* in the following.

1. Both the teacher and the student _____ here.

2. Neither the teacher nor the student _____ here.

3. Not only the teacher but also the student _____ here.

4. Not only the teacher but also the students _____ here.

5. Either the students or the teacher _____ planning to come.

6. Either the teacher or the students _____ planning to come.

□ **EXERCISE 6—ERROR ANALYSIS:** What is wrong with the following sentences?

1. Either John will call Mary or Bob.

2. Not only Sue saw the mouse but also the cat.

3. Both my mother talked to the teacher and my father.

□ **EXERCISE 7—ORAL:** Answer the questions. Use paired conjunctions.

Use both . . . and.

1. You have met his father. Have you met his mother?
   → *Yes, I have met both his father and his mother.*

2. The driver was injured in the accident. Was the passenger injured in the accident?

3. Wheat is grown in Kansas. Is corn grown in Kansas?

4. He buys used cars. Does he sell used cars?

5. You had lunch with your friends. Did you have dinner with them?

6. The city suffers from air pollution. Does it suffer from water pollution?

Use not only . . . but also.

7. I know you are studying math. Are you studying chemistry too?
   → *Yes, I'm studying not only math but also chemistry.*

8. I know his cousin is living with him. Is his mother-in-law living with him too?

9. I know your country has good universities. Does the United States have good universities too?

10. I know you lost your wallet. Did you lose your keys too?

11. I know she goes to school. Does she have a full-time job too?

12. I know he bought a coat. Did he buy a new pair of shoes too?

Use either . . . or.

13. John has your book, or Mary has your book. Is that right?
    → *Yes, either John or Mary has my book.*

14. You're going to give your friend a book for her birthday, or you're going to give her a pen. Is that right?
15. Your sister will meet you at the airport, or your brother will meet you there. Right?
16. They can go swimming, or they can play tennis. Is that right?
17. You're going to vote for Mr. Smith, or you're going to vote for Mr. Jones. Right?
18. You'll go to New Orleans for your vacation, or you'll go to Miami. Right?

*Use **neither . . . nor.***

19. He doesn't like coffee. Does he like tea?
    → *No, he likes neither coffee nor tea.*
20. Her husband doesn't speak English. Do her children speak English?
21. The students aren't wide awake today. Is the teacher wide awake today?
22. They don't have a refrigerator for their new apartment. Do they have a stove?
23. She doesn't enjoy hunting. Does she enjoy fishing?
24. The result wasn't good. Was the result bad?

☐ **EXERCISE 8:** Combine the following into sentences that contain parallel structure. Use appropriate paired conjunctions: *both . . . and; not only . . . but also; either . . . or; neither . . . nor.*

1. He does not have a pen. He does not have paper.
   → *He has neither a pen nor paper.*
2. Ron enjoys horseback riding. Bob enjoys horseback riding.
3. You can have tea, or you can have coffee.
4. Arthur is not in class today. Ricardo is not in class today.
5. Arthur is absent. Ricardo is absent.
6. We can fix dinner for them here, or we can take them to a restaurant.
7. She wants to buy a Chevrolet, or she wants to buy a Toyota.
8. The leopard faces extinction. The tiger faces extinction.
9. The library does not have the book I need. The bookstore does not have the book I need.
10. We could fly, or we could take the train.
11. The President's assistant will not confirm the story. The President's assistant will not deny the story.
12. Coal is an irreplaceable natural resource. Oil is an irreplaceable natural resource.
13. Small pox is a dangerous disease. Malaria is a dangerous disease.
14. Her roommates don't know where she is. Her brother doesn't know where she is.
15. According to the news report, it will snow tonight, or it will rain tonight.

□ **EXERCISE 9—ERROR ANALYSIS:** Find and correct the errors in parallel structure in the following sentences.

1. By obeying the speed limit, we can save energy, lives, and it costs us less.

2. My home offers me a feeling of security, warm, and love.

3. The pioneers labored to clear away the forest and planting crops.

4. When I refused to help her, she became very angry and shout at me.

5. In my spare time, I enjoy taking care of my aquarium and to work on my stamp collection.

6. Either Mr. Anderson or Ms. Wiggins are going to teach our class today.

7. I enjoy not only reading novels but also magazines.

8. Oxygen is plentiful. Both air contains oxygen and water.

8–3 COMBINING INDEPENDENT CLAUSES WITH CONJUNCTIONS

(a) It was raining hard. There was a strong wind. (b) *INCORRECT PUNCTUATION:* It was raining hard, there was a strong wind.	Example (a) contains two independent clauses (i.e., two complete sentences). Notice the punctuation. A period,* NOT A COMMA, is used to separate two independent clauses. The punctuation in (b) is not correct; the error in (b) is called *a run-on sentence*.
(c) It was raining hard, *and* there was a strong wind. (d) It was raining hard *and* there was a strong wind. (e) It was raining hard. *And* there was a strong wind.	A conjunction may be used to connect two independent clauses. *Punctuation:* In (c): Usually a comma immediately precedes the conjunction. In (d): Sometimes in short sentences the comma is omitted. In (e): Sometimes in informal writing a conjunction may begin a sentence.
(f) He was tired, *so* he went to bed. (g) The child hid behind his mother's skirt, *for* he was afraid of the dog. (h) He did not study, *yet* he passed the exam.	In addition to *and*, *but*, *or*, and *nor*, other conjunctions are used to connect two independent clauses: *so* (meaning *therefore, as a result*) *for* (meaning *because*) *yet* (meaning *but, nevertheless*) A comma almost always precedes *so*, *for*, and *yet* when they are used as conjunctions.**

*In British English, *a period* is called *a full stop*.
**So, for*, and *yet* have other meanings in other structures: e.g., *He is not so tall as his brother.* (*so* = *as*) *We waited for the bus.* (*for* = a preposition) *She hasn't arrived yet.* (*yet* = an adverb meaning *up to this time*).

☐ **EXERCISE 10:** Punctuate the following sentences by adding commas or periods as necessary. Do not add any words. Capitalize letters where necessary.

1. The boys walked the girls ran. → *The boys walked. The girls ran.*

2. The teacher lectured the students took notes.

3. The teacher lectured and the students took notes.

4. Jessica came to the meeting but Ron stayed home.

5. Jessica came to the meeting her brother stayed home.

6. Her academic record was outstanding yet she was not accepted by the university.

7. I have not finished writing my term paper yet I will not be finished until sometime next week.

8. We had to go to the grocery store for some milk and bread.

9. We had to go to the grocery store for there was nothing in the house to fix for dinner.

10. Frank did not have enough money to buy an airplane ticket so he couldn't fly home for the holiday.

☐ **EXERCISE 11:** Punctuate the following sentences by adding commas or periods as necessary. Do not add any words. Capitalize letters where necessary.

1. A thermometer is used to measure temperature a barometer measures air pressure.

2. Daniel made many promises but he had no intention of keeping them.

3. I always enjoyed studying mathematics in high school so I decided to major in it in college.

4. The ancient Egyptians had good dentists archaeologists have found mummies that had gold fillings in their teeth.

5. Both John and I had many errands to do yesterday John had to go to the post office and the bookstore I had to go to the drugstore the travel agency and the bank.

6. Anna is in serious legal trouble for she had no car insurance at the time of the accident.

7. Last night Martha had to study for a test so she went to the library.

8. I did not like the leading actor yet the movie was quite good on the whole.

9. The team of researchers has not finished compiling the statistics yet their work will not be made public until later.

10. We have nothing to fear for our country is strong and united.

11. He slapped his desk in disgust he had failed another examination and had ruined his chances for a passing grade in the course.

12. I struggled to keep my head above water I tried to yell for help but no sound came from my mouth.

13. The earthquake was devastating tall buildings crumbled and fell to the earth.

14. It was a wonderful picnic the children waded in the stream collected rocks and insects and flew kites the teenagers played an enthusiastic game of baseball the adults busied themselves preparing the food supervising the children and playing a game or two of volleyball.

15. The butterfly is a marvel it begins as an ugly caterpillar and turns into a work of art.

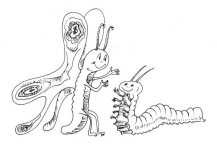

16. Caterpillars eat plants and cause damage to some crops but adult butterflies feed principally on nectar from flowers and do not cause any harm.

17. Some people collect butterflies for a hobby these collectors capture them with a net and put them in a jar that has poison in it the dead butterflies are then mounted on a board.

18. The sight of a butterfly floating from flower to flower on a warm sunny day brightens anyone's heart a butterfly is a charming and gentle creature.

19. When cold weather comes some butterflies travel great distances to reach tropical climates.

20. Butterflies are admired throughout the world because they are beautiful they can be found on every continent except Antarctica.

8–4 ADVERB CLAUSES: INTRODUCTION

(a) ***When we were in New York***, we saw several plays. (b) We saw several plays ***when we were in New York***.	***When we were in New York*** is an adverb clause. It is a dependent clause. It cannot stand alone as a sentence. It must be connected to an independent clause. *Punctuation:* When an adverb clause precedes an independent clause, as in (a), a comma is used to separate the clauses. When the adverb clause follows, as in (b), usually no comma is used.
(c) ***Because he was sleepy***, he went to bed. (d) He went to bed ***because he was sleepy***.	Like ***when, because*** introduces an adverb clause. ***Because he was sleepy*** is an adverb clause.

SUMMARY LIST OF WORDS USED TO INTRODUCE ADVERB CLAUSES*			
TIME	CAUSE AND EFFECT	OPPOSITION	CONDITION
after	*because*	*even though*	*if*
before	*since*	*although*	*unless*
when	*now that*	*though*	*only if*
while	*as*		*whether or not*
as	*as/so long as*		*even if*
by the time (that)	*inasmuch as*	*whereas*	*providing (that)*
since		*while*	*provided (that)*
until			*in case (that)*
as soon as	*so (that)*		*in the event (that)*
once	*in order that*		
as/so long as			
whenever			
every time (that)			
the first time (that)			
the last time (that)			
the next time (that)			

*Words that introduce adverb clauses are called *subordinating conjunctions*.

8–5 USING ADVERB CLAUSES TO SHOW TIME RELATIONSHIPS

after	(a) ***After** she graduates*, she will get a job. (b) ***After** she (had) graduated*, she got a job.	A present tense, *not* a future tense, is used in an adverb clause of time. Notice examples (b) and (d). (See Chart 1-21 for tense usage in future time clauses.)
before	(c) I will leave ***before** he comes*. (d) I (had) left ***before** he came*.	
when	(e) ***When** I arrived*, he was talking on the phone. (f) ***When** I got there*, he had already left. (g) ***When** it began to rain*, I stood under a tree. (h) ***When** I was in Chicago*, I visited the museums. (i) ***When** I see him tomorrow*, I will ask him.	***when** = at that time* (Notice the different time relationships expressed by the tenses.
while *as*	(j) ***While** I was walking home*, it began to rain. (k) ***As** I was walking home*, it began to rain.	***while**, **as** = during that time*
by the time	(l) ***By the time** he arrived*, we had already left. (m) ***By the time** he comes*, we will already have left.	***by the time** = one event is completed before another event* (Notice the use of the past perfect and future perfect in the main clause.)
since	(n) I haven't seen him ***since** he left this morning*.	***since** = from that time to the present* (Notice: The present perfect tense is used in the main clause.
until *till*	(o) We stayed there ***until** we finished our work*. (p) We stayed there ***till** we finished our work*.	***until**, **till** = to that time and then no longer* (***Till** is used primarily in speaking rather than writing.)
as soon as *once*	(q) ***As soon as** it stops raining*, we will leave. (r) ***Once** it stops raining*, we will leave.	***as soon as**, **once** = when one event happens, another event happens soon afterwards*
as long as *so long as*	(s) I will never speak to him again ***as long as** I live*. (t) I will never speak to him again ***so long as** I live*.	***as long as**, **so long as** = during all that time, from beginning to end*
whenever *every time*	(u) ***Whenever** I see her*, I say hello. (v) ***Every time** I see her*, I say hello.	***whenever** = every time*
the first time *the last time* *the next time*	(w) ***The first time** I went to New York*, I went to an opera. (x) I saw two plays ***the last time** I went to New York*. (y) ***The next time** I go to New York*, I'm going to see a ballet.	Adverb clauses can be introduced by the following: *the* $\left\{ \begin{array}{l} \textbf{first} \\ \textbf{second} \\ \textbf{third} \\ \textbf{last} \\ \textbf{next} \end{array} \right\}$ *time*

□ **EXERCISE 12:** Complete the following. Pay special attention to verb tenses.

1. Last night I went to bed after I _____ my homework.

2. Tonight I will go to bed after I _____ my homework.

3. Ever since I was a child, I _____ afraid of dogs.

4. Jane's contact lens popped out while she _____ basketball.

5. Be sure to reread your composition for errors before you _____ _____ it in to the teacher tomorrow.

6. By the time I left my apartment this morning, the mail carrier _____ _____ the mail.

7. I have known Jim Bates since he _____ ten years old.

8. A black cat ran across the road as I _____ my car to work this morning.

9. By the time I leave this city, I _____ here for four months.

10. Whenever Mark _____ angry, his nose gets red.

11. I _____ to the beach whenever the weather was nice, but now I don't have time to do that because I have to study.

12. We will have a big party when _____ .

13. The next time I _____ to Hawaii, I'm going to visit Mauna Loa, the world's largest volcano.

14. I had fried chicken the last time I _____ at that restaurant.

□ **EXERCISE 13:** Make sentences with *until* from the given situations.

1. I can't pay my bills. I haven't gotten my paycheck yet.

   ___*I can't pay my bills*___ until ___*my paycheck comes*___.

2. We can't leave yet. We have to wait for Nancy.

   _____ until _____.

3. Tell me the truth, or I am not going to leave this room.

   _____ until _____.

4. Finally, Donald arrived. Before that, it had been a dull party.

   _____ until _____.

5. Dinner won't be ready for a while. I think we should just sit here by the fire.

   Let's _____ until _____.

6. When I go to bed at night, I like to read. After a while, I get sleepy.

   _____ until _____.

□ **EXERCISE 14:** Combine the ideas by using either *as soon as* or *once*. (*As soon as* and *once* basically have the same meaning, but *as soon as* is more immediate. Often, *just* is used with *as soon as* to emphasize the idea of "immediately": *I'll call him just as soon as I get home.*)

1. The taxi will get here in five minutes or so. Then we can leave for the airport.

   As soon as the taxi gets here, we can leave for the airport.

2. The rice will be done in about ten minutes. Immediately after that, we can eat.

   _____

3. First, I have to graduate. Then I can return home.

   _____

4. Spring will come and the weather will be nice again. Then we can start playing tennis every morning before class.

   _____

5. My roommate walked into the room. Immediately, I knew that something was wrong.

   _____

6. Your English will get better. Then you will begin to feel more comfortable living in the United States.

_____

7. Immediately after the singer finished her song, the audience burst into applause.

_____

8. I'm watching a baseball game on TV, but it will be over in a few minutes. Then I'll take out the garbage.

_____

☐ **EXERCISE 15:** Using the given information, make a sentence in which you use *just after*, *just before*, or *just as*. Notice that *just* adds the idea of "immediately."

1. I got to the airport at 8:15. My plane left ten minutes later.
   I got to the airport just before my plane left.

2. You shouldn't eat a heavy meal and then go to bed immediately afterwards.

_____

3. I went to bed at 11:00. The phone rang at 11:05.

_____

4. We were sitting down to eat. At that moment, someone knocked on the door.

_____

5. I was getting on the bus. At that moment, I remembered that I had left my briefcase at home.

_____

6. I got up to give my speech. Immediately before that, I got butterflies in my stomach.

_____

7. The guests will come at 7:00. At 6:55, I'll light the candles.

_____

8. I was bending over to pick up my pencil. My pants split.

_____

□ **EXERCISE 16:** Compare *after* and *afterwards.*

(a) *After I ate dinner*, I took a walk. I took a walk *after I ate dinner.* (b) I ate dinner. *Afterwards*, I took a walk. I ate dinner. *I took a walk afterwards.*	*After* can be used to introduce an adverb clause. *Afterwards** is an adverb meaning *"later, after that."*

**Afterwards* can also be spelled without *-s: afterward.*

> *Combine the sentences by using **after** and **afterwards**, as in the previous examples.*
> *Punctuate carefully.*

1. *First:* I studied.
   Then: I went to bed.
2. *First:* We went to the museum.
   Then: We had some lunch.
3. *First:* He was in an automobile accident.
   Then: He had to walk on crutches for two months.

□ **EXERCISE 17—WRITTEN:** Complete the following. Punctuate carefully. Pay special attention to verb tense usage.

1. Since I came to . . . .
2. Just as I was falling asleep last night . . . .
3. I'll help you with your homework as soon as I . . . .
4. I was late. By the time I got to the airport . . . .
5. One of my friends gets nervous every time . . . .
6. I will be here until I . . . .
7. . . . as long as I live.
8. I heard . . . while I . . . .
9. Once summer/winter comes . . . .
10. Just before I . . . .
11. I have been in . . . for . . . . By the time I leave, I . . . .
12. The last time I . . . .
13. The next time you . . . .
14. I . . . after I . . . .
15. I . . . . Afterwards I . . . .
16. I had already . . . when . . . .
17. Whenever . . . .
18. Ever since . . . .

8–6 USING ADVERB CLAUSES TO SHOW CAUSE AND EFFECT RELATIONSHIPS

because	(a) **Because** he was sleepy, he went to bed. (b) He went to bed **because** he was sleepy.	An adverb clause may precede or follow the independent clause. Notice the punctuation in (a) and (b).
since	(c) **Since** he's not interested in classical music, he decided not to go to the concert.	In (c): **since** means because.
now that	(d) **Now that** the semester is finished, I'm going to rest a few days and then take a trip.	In (d): **now that** means because now. **Now that** is used for present and future situations.
as	(e) **As** she had nothing in particular to do, she called up a friend and asked her if she wanted to take in a movie.	In (e): **as** means because.
as/so long as	(f) **As long as (So long as)** you're not busy, could you help me with this work?	In (f): **as long as** means because.
inasmuch as	(g) **Inasmuch as** the two government leaders could not reach an agreement, the possibilities for peace are still remote.	In (g): **inasmuch as** means because. **Inasmuch as** is usually found only in formal writing and speech.

☐ **EXERCISE 18:** Using the given information, make sentences using *now that*.

1. Peggy used to take the bus to school, but last week she bought a car. Now she can drive to school.

   Now that Peggy has a car, she can drive to school.

2. You just had your sixteenth birthday. Now you can get a driver's license.

   Now that you are

3. We have to wear warm clothes. It's winter now.

   _____

4. Bob used to live in the dorm, but a couple of weeks ago he moved into an apartment. Now he can cook his own food.

   _____

5. Whew! I've finally finished painting the house. Now I can go fishing.

   _____

6. I can get a job as a bilingual secretary. I know English now.

    _____

7. My brother got married last month. He's a married man now, so he has more responsibilities.

    _____

8. Do you want to go for a walk? The rain has stopped.

    _____

9. It's been a long, hard week, but final exams are finally over. We can relax.

    _____

10. The civil war has ended. A new government is being formed.

    _____

□ **EXERCISE 19:** Complete the following.

1. As long as it's such a nice day, why don't _____

2. As long as the movie is free, let's _____

3. As long as it's raining, I think I'll _____

4. As long as the coffee is already made, I guess I'll _____

5. As long as you're here, why don't _____

6. As long as you're up, would you mind _____

□ **EXERCISE 20:** Combine the given ideas by using *since*. Also, decide which sentences might be found in somewhat formal writing and use *inasmuch as*.

1. Monday is Bob's birthday. Let's give him a party.

    _____

2. Monday is a national holiday. All government offices will be closed.

    _____

3. The guys I live with don't know any Arabic. I have to speak English with them.

    _____

4. Oil is an irreplaceable natural resource. We must do whatever we can in order to conserve it.

_____

5. Mary, maybe you could help me with this calculus problem. You're a math major.

_____

6. Many young people move to the cities in search of employment. There are few jobs available in the rural areas.

_____

☐ **EXERCISE 21—WRITTEN:** Complete the following. Punctuate carefully.

1. Now that I . . . .
2. The teacher didn't . . . because . . . .
3. Since heavy fog is predicted for tonight . . . .
4. He was not admitted to the university inasmuch as . . . .
5. Jack can't stay out all night with his friends now that . . . .
6. Since we don't have class tomorrow . . . .
7. Inasmuch as her application arrived after the deadline . . . .

8–7 USING PREPOSITIONS TO SHOW CAUSE AND EFFECT: *BECAUSE OF* AND *DUE TO*

(a) *Because the weather was cold*, we stayed home.	*Because* introduces an adverb clause; it is followed by a subject and verb.
(b) *Because of the cold weather*, we stayed home. (c) *Due to the cold weather*, we stayed home.	*Because of* and *due to* are prepositions; they are followed by a noun object.
(d) *Due to the fact that the weather was cold*, we stayed home.	Sometimes, usually in more formal writing, *due to* is followed by a noun clause introduced by *the fact that*.
(e) We stayed home *because of the cold weather*. We stayed home *due to the cold weather*. We stayed home *due to the fact that the weather was cold*.	Like adverb clauses, these phrases can also follow the main clause, as in (e).

☐ **EXERCISE 22:** Using the ideas given in parentheses, complete the sentences.

1. (*My parents are generous.*) Because of ___*my parents' generosity*___,

   all of the children in our family have received the best of everything.

2. (*The traffic was heavy.*) We were late to the meeting due to _____

   _____.

3. (*Bill's wife is ill.*) Bill has to do all of the cooking and cleaning because of

   _____.

4. (*Dr. Robinson has done excellent research on wolves.*) Due to _____

   _____,

   we know much more today about that endangered species than we did

   even five years ago.

5. (*It was noisy in the next apartment.*) I couldn't get to sleep last night

   because of _____.

6. (*Circumstances are beyond my control.*) Due to _____

   _____, I regret to say that I cannot be

   present at your daughter's wedding.

8–8 USING TRANSITIONS TO SHOW CAUSE AND EFFECT: *THEREFORE* AND *CONSEQUENTLY*

(a) Al failed the test because he didn't study. (b) Al didn't study. ***Therefore***, he failed the test. (c) Al didn't study. ***Consequently***, he failed the test.	(a), (b), and (c) have the same meaning. ***Therefore*** and ***consequently*** mean "as a result." In grammar, they are called *transitions* (or *conjunctive adverbs*). Transitions connect the ideas between two sentences.
(d) Al didn't study. ***Therefore***, he failed the test. (e) Al didn't study. He, ***therefore***, failed the test. (f) Al didn't study. He failed the test, ***therefore***. **POSITIONS OF A TRANSITION:** **transition + S + V** (+ rest of sentence) **S + transition + V** (+ rest of sentence) **S + V** (+ rest of sentence) **+ transition**	A transition occurs in the second of two related sentences. Notice the patterns and punctuation in the examples. A period (NOT a comma) is used at the end of the first sentence. The transition has several possible positions in the second sentence. The transition is set off from the rest of the sentence by commas.
(g) Al didn't study, *so* he failed the test.	COMPARE: A transition (e.g., ***therefore***) has different possible positions within the second sentence of a pair. A conjunction (e.g., *so*) has only one possible position: between the two sentences. (See Chart 8-3.) *So* cannot move around in the second sentence as ***therefore*** can.

□ **EXERCISE 23:** Restate the sentences using the given transitions. Use three alternative positions for the transitions, as shown in Chart 8-8. Punctuate carefully.

1. The children stayed home because a storm was approaching. (Use ***therefore***.)

_____

_____

_____

2. I didn't have my umbrella, so I got wet. (Use ***consequently***.)

_____

_____

_____

□ **EXERCISE 24:** Punctuate the following sentences. Add capital letters if necessary.

1. *adverb clause:*   Because it was cold she wore a coat.

2. *adverb clause:*   She wore a coat because it was cold.

3. *prepositional phrase:*   Because of the cold weather she wore a coat.

4. *prepositional phrase:*   She wore a coat because of the cold weather.

5. *transition:*   The weather was cold therefore she wore a coat.

6. *transition:*   The weather was cold she therefore wore a coat.

7. *transition:*   The weather was cold she wore a coat therefore.

8. *conjunction:*   The weather was cold so she wore a coat.

□ **EXERCISE 25:** Punctuate the following sentences. Add capital letters if necessary.

1. Pat always enjoyed studying sciences in high school therefore she decided to major in biology in college.
2. Due to recent improvements in the economy fewer people are unemployed.
3. Last night's storm damaged the power lines consequently the town was without electricity for several hours.
4. Because of the snowstorm only five students came to class the teacher therefore cancelled the class.
5. Anna always makes numerous spelling mistakes in her compositions because she does not use a dictionary when she writes.

8–9 SUMMARY OF PATTERNS AND PUNCTUATION

ADVERB CLAUSE	(a) ***Because** it was hot*, we went swimming. (b) We went swimming ***because** it was hot.*	An adverb clause may precede or follow an independent clause. *Punctuation:* A comma is used if the adverb clause comes first.
PREPOSITION	(c) ***Because of** the hot weather*, we went swimming. (d) We went swimming ***because of** the hot weather.*	A preposition is followed by a noun object, not by a subject and verb. *Punctuation:* A comma is usually used if the prepositional phrase precedes the subject and verb of the independent clause.
TRANSITION	(e) It was hot. ***Therefore**, we went swimming.* (f) It was hot. *We, **therefore**, went swimming.* (g) It was hot. *We went swimming, **therefore**.*	A transition is used with the second sentence of a pair. It shows the relationship of the second idea to the first idea. A transition is movable within the second sentence. *Punctuation:* A period is used between the two independent clauses.* A comma may NOT be used to separate the clauses. Commas are usually used to set the transition off from the rest of the sentence.
CONJUNCTION	(h) It was hot, *so we went swimming.*	A conjunction comes between two independent clauses. *Punctuation:* Usually a comma is used immediately in front of a conjunction.

*A semicolon (;) may be used instead of a period between the two independent clauses.

> *It was hot; therefore, we went swimming.*
> *It was hot; we, therefore, went swimming.*
> *It was hot; we went swimming, therefore.*

In general, a semicolon can be used instead of a period between any two sentences that are closely related in meaning. Example: *Peanuts are not nuts; they are beans.* Notice that a small letter, not a capital letter, immediately follows a semicolon.

☐ **EXERCISE 26:** Using the given words, combine the following two ideas.

We postponed our trip. The weather was bad.

1. because → *We postponed our trip because the weather was bad.*

    → *Because the weather was bad, we postponed our trip.*

2. therefore	4. so	6. consequently
3. since	5. because of	7. due to (the fact that)

□ **EXERCISE 27:** Using the given words, combine the following two ideas.

She missed class. She was ill.

1. because of
2. because
3. consequently
4. so
5. due to (the fact that)
6. therefore

8–10 OTHER WAYS OF EXPRESSING CAUSE AND EFFECT: *SUCH . . . THAT* AND *SO . . . THAT*

(a) Because the weather was nice, we went to the zoo. (b) It was *such nice weather that* we went to the zoo. (c) The weather was *so nice that* we went to the zoo.	Examples (a), (b), and (c) have the same meaning.
(d) It was *such good coffee that* I had another cup. (e) It was *such a foggy day that* we couldn't see the road.	*Such . . . that* encloses a modified noun: *such + adjective + noun + that*
(f) The coffee is *so hot that* I can't drink it. (g) I'm *so hungry that* I could eat a horse. (h) She speaks *so fast that* I can't understand her. (i) He walked *so quickly that* I couldn't keep up with him.	*So . . . that* encloses an adjective or adverb: $so + \begin{Bmatrix} adjective \\ or \\ adverb \end{Bmatrix} + that$
(j) She made *so many mistakes that* she failed the exam. (k) He has *so few friends that* he is always lonely. (l) She has *so much money that* she can buy whatever she wants. (m) He had *so little trouble* with the test *that* he left twenty minutes early.	*So . . . that* is used with *many*, *few*, *much*, and *little*.
(n) It was *such a good book* (that) I couldn't put it down. (o) I was *so hungry* (that) I didn't wait for dinner to eat something.	Sometimes, primarily in speaking, *that* is omitted.

□ **EXERCISE 28:** Combine the following sentences by using *so . . . that* or *such . . . that*.

1. This tea is good. I think I'll have another cup.

   → *This tea is so good that I think I'll have another cup.*

2. This is good tea. I think I'll have another cup.

   → *This is such good tea that I think I'll have another cup.*

3. The car was expensive. We couldn't afford to buy it.

4. It was an expensive car. We couldn't afford to buy it.

5. I had to wear my wool coat. It was a cold day.

6. The weather was hot. You could fry an egg on the sidewalk.

7. I don't feel like going to class. We're having beautiful weather.

8. Grandpa held me tightly when he hugged me. I couldn't breathe for a moment.

9. I couldn't understand her. She talked too fast.

10. The audience booed the actors. It was a bad performance.

11. I've met too many people in the last few days. I can't possibly remember all of their names.

12. It took us only ten minutes to get there. There was little traffic.

13. There were few people at the meeting. It was cancelled.

14. The wastepaper basket overflowed. Sally used too much paper when she was writing her report.

☐ **EXERCISE 29:** Combine the sentences by using *so . . . that* or *such . . . that*.

1. The classroom has comfortable chairs. The students find it easy to fall asleep.
2. Ted couldn't get to sleep last night. He was worried about the exam.
3. Jerry got angry. He put his fist through the wall.

4. I have many problems. I can use all the help you can give me.
5. The tornado struck with great force. It lifted automobiles off the ground.
6. During the summer, we had hot and humid weather. It was uncomfortable just sitting in a chair doing nothing.
7. I can't figure out what this sentence says. His handwriting is illegible.
8. David has too many girlfriends. He can't remember all of their names.
9. Too many people came to the meeting. There were not enough seats for everyone.
10. In some countries, few students are accepted by the universities. As a result, admission is virtually a guarantee of a good job upon graduation.

☐ **EXERCISE 30—ORAL (BOOKS CLOSED):** Use *so . . . that* or *such . . . that.*

Example: You are sleepy.
Response: I am so sleepy that . . . (I could fall asleep in five minutes).

Example: ''Book'' is a common word.
Response: ''Book'' is such a common word that . . . (everyone knows what it means).

1. The weather is hot/cold/nice today.
2. Mary is a good student.
3. John speaks too softly.
4. You are tired.
5. On your way to class this morning/afternoon/evening, the traffic was heavy.
6. The teacher in one of your classes speaks too fast.
7. Your instructor assigned too much homework.
8. You and your husband/wife have a baby. The baby had a high temperature last night.
9. You took a test last week. It was an easy test.
10. You were home alone last night. You heard a noise. You were frightened.
11. You went to a movie last night. It was a good movie.
12. Your roommate makes too much noise at night.
13. Yesterday, there were too many students absent due to the flu.
14. You waited too long to mail your application to the university.
15. Think of a time you were nervous. How nervous were you?
16. Think of a time you were angry. How angry were you?
17. Think of a time you were happy. How happy were you?
18. Think of a time you were exhausted. How exhausted were you?
19. Think of a time you were surprised. How surprised were you?
20. Think of a time you were unhappy/embarrassed/glad/disappointed/sick.

□ **EXERCISE 31:** Complete the following.

1. This box is so heavy _that I can't lift it._

2. This box is too heavy _(for me) to lift._

3. That car is too expensive _____

4. That car is so expensive _____

5. The coffee was too hot _____

6. The coffee was so hot _____

7. It is so dark in here _____

8. It is too dark in here _____

8-11 EXPRESSING PURPOSE: USING *SO THAT*

(a) I turned off the TV *in order to enable my roommate to study in peace and quiet.*	***In order to*** expresses *purpose.* (See Chart 4-10.) In (a): I turned off the TV for a purpose. The purpose was to make it possible for my roommate to study in peace and quiet.
(b) I turned off the TV *so (that) my roommate could study in peace and quiet.*	***So that*** also expresses *purpose.** It expresses the same meaning as ***in order to***. The word "that" is often omitted, especially in speaking.
SO THAT* + *CAN* or *COULD (c) I'm going to cash a check *so that I can buy my textbooks.* (d) I cashed a check *so that I could buy my textbooks.*	***So that*** is often used instead of ***in order to*** when the idea of ability is being expressed. ***Can*** is used in the adverb clause for a present/future meaning. In (c): *so that I can buy = in order to be able to buy.* ***Could*** is used after ***so that*** in past sentences.**
SO THAT* + *WILL*/SIMPLE PRESENT or *WOULD (e) I'll take my umbrella *so that I won't get wet.* (f) I'll take my umbrella *so that I don't get wet.* (g) Yesterday I took my umbrella *so that I wouldn't get wet.*	In (e): *so that I won't get wet = in order to make sure that I won't get wet.* In (f): It is sometimes possible to use the simple present after ***so that*** in place of ***will***; the simple present expresses a future meaning. ***Would*** is used in past sentences.

*NOTE: ***In order that*** has the same meaning as ***so that*** but is less commonly used.

Example: *I turned off the TV **(in order) that** my roommate could study in peace and quiet.*

Both ***so that*** and ***in order that*** introduce adverb clauses. It is unusual, but possible, to put these adverb clauses at the beginning of a sentence: *So that my roommate could study in peace and quiet, I turned off the TV.*

Also possible but less common: the use of ***may* or ***might*** in place of ***can*** or ***could***: e.g., *I cashed a check **so that I might** buy my textbooks.*

☐ **EXERCISE 32:** Combine the ideas by using *so (that)*.

1. Please turn down the radio. I want to be able to get to sleep.
   → *Please turn down the radio so (that) I can get to sleep.*

2. My wife turned down the radio. I wanted to be able to get to sleep.
   → *My wife turned down the radio so (that) I could get to sleep.*

3. Put the milk in the refrigerator. We want to make sure it won't (OR doesn't) spoil.
   → *Put the milk in the refrigerator so (that) it won't (OR doesn't) spoil.*

4. I put the milk in the refrigerator. I wanted to make sure it didn't spoil.
   → *I put the milk in the refrigerator so (that) it wouldn't spoil.*

5. Please be quiet. I want to be able to hear what Sharon is saying.

6. I asked the children to be quiet. I wanted to be able to hear what Sharon was saying.

7. I'm going to cash a check. I want to make sure that I will have (OR have) enough money to go to the market.

8. I cashed a check yesterday. I wanted to make sure that I had enough money to go to the market.

9. Ann and Larry have a six-year-old child. Tonight they're going to hire a babysitter. They want to be able to go out with some friends.

10. Last week Ann and Larry hired a babysitter. They wanted to be able to go to a dinner party at the home of Larry's boss.

11. Be sure to put the meat in the oven at 5:00. You want to be sure that it will be (OR is) ready to eat by 6:30.

12. Yesterday I put the meat in the oven at 5:00. I wanted it to be ready to eat by 6:30.

☐ **EXERCISE 33:** Combine the ideas by using *so (that)*.

1. I'm going to leave the party early. I want to be able to get a good night's sleep tonight.

2. When it started to rain, Harry opened his umbrella. He wanted to be sure he didn't get wet.

3. It's a good idea for you to learn how to type. You'll be able to type your own papers when you go to the university.

4. Lynn tied a string around her finger. She wanted to make sure that she didn't forget to take her book back to the library.

5. Ed took some change from his pocket. He wanted to buy a newspaper.

6. The little boy pretended to be sick. He wanted to stay home from school.

7. A lot of people were standing in front of me. I stood on my tiptoes. I wanted to see the parade better.

8. I turned on the TV. I wanted to listen to the news while I was making dinner.

9. I unplugged the phone. I didn't want to be interrupted while I was working.
10. Yesterday Linda was driving on the highway when her car started making strange noises. After she pulled over to the side of the road, she raised the hood of her car in order to make sure that other drivers knew that she had car trouble.

□ **EXERCISE 34:** Complete the following.

1. I'm going to take my camera to the zoo so (that) . . . .
2. I stayed home last night so (that) . . . .
3. Tommy, keep your pennies in your pocket so (that) . . . .
4. Please be quiet so (that) . . . .
5. You'd better put the food in the refrigerator so (that) . . . .
6. I'd better call Jane so (that) . . . .
7. I'm going on a diet so (that) . . . .
8. I'll give you my phone number so (that) . . . .
9. She sang a lullaby so (that) the baby . . . .
10. It's winter. Yesterday I put on two pairs of socks under my boots so (that) . . . .

□ **EXERCISE 35—ORAL/WRITTEN:** Using the given words, make sentences about yourself, your friends, your family, your classes, today's weather, current events in the world, etc.

1. now that
2. therefore
3. inasmuch as
4. as (meaning *because*)
5. consequently
6. so (meaning *therefore*)
7. since (meaning *because*)
8. as long as (meaning *because*)
9. in order to
10. so that
11. so . . . that
12. such . . . that
13. because
14. because of
15. due to
16. due to the fact that

8-12 REDUCTION OF ADVERB CLAUSES TO MODIFYING PHRASES: INTRODUCTION

In Chapter 6, we discussed changing adjective clauses to modifying phrases. (See Chart 6-13.) Some adverb clauses may also be changed to modifying phrases, and the ways in which the changes are made are the same:

(1) Omit the subject of the dependent clause and the **be** form of the verb.

    (a) ADVERB CLAUSE: *While **I was walking** to class, I ran into an old friend.*

    (b) MODIFYING PHRASE: *While **walking** to class, I ran into an old friend.*

(2) Or, if there is no **be** form of a verb, omit the subject and change the verb to **-ing**.

    (c) ADVERB CLAUSE: *Before **I left** for work, I ate breakfast.*

    (d) MODIFYING PHRASE: *Before **leaving** for work, I ate breakfast.*

An adverb clause can be changed to a modifying phrase ONLY WHEN THE SUBJECT OF THE ADVERB CLAUSE AND THE SUBJECT OF THE MAIN CLAUSE ARE THE SAME. *A modifying phrase* that is the reduction of an adverb clause *modifies the subject* of the main clause. No change is possible if the subjects of the adverb clause and the main clause are different.

    (e) CHANGE POSSIBLE: While **I** was sitting in class, **I** fell asleep.

                         While sitting in class, **I** fell asleep.

    (f) CHANGE POSSIBLE: While **Ann** was sitting in class, **she** fell asleep.

                         While sitting in class, **Ann** fell asleep.

    (g) NO CHANGE POSSIBLE: While **the teacher** was lecturing to the class, **I** fell asleep.*

    (h) NO CHANGE POSSIBLE: While **we** were walking home, **a frog** hopped across the road in front of us.

---

*"*While lecturing to the class, **I** fell asleep.*" means "*While **I** was lecturing to the class, **I** fell asleep.*"

8-13 CHANGING TIME CLAUSES TO MODIFYING PHRASES

(a) CLAUSE: ***Since Mary came to this country***, she has made many friends. (b) PHRASE: ***Since coming to this country***, Mary has made many friends.	Adverb clauses beginning with **after, before, while**, and **since** can be changed to modifying phrases.
(c) CLAUSE: ***After he (had) finished his homework***, he went to bed. (d) PHRASE: ***After finishing his homework***, he went to bed. (e) PHRASE: ***After having finished his homework***, he went to bed.	In (c): There is no difference in meaning between *After he finished* and *After he had finished*. (See Chart 1-17.) In (d) and (e): There is no difference in meaning between *After finishing* and *After having finished*.
(f) PHRASE: He went to bed ***after finishing his homework***.	A modifying phrase may follow the main clause, as in (f).

□ **EXERCISE 36:** Change the adverb clauses to modifying phrases if possible. Make no change if the subjects of the two clauses in the sentence are different.

1. While Joe was driving to school yesterday, he had an accident.
   → *While driving to school yesterday, Joe had an accident.*
2. While I was watching TV last night, the telephone rang. (*no change*)
3. Before I came to class, I had a cup of coffee.
4. Before the student came to class, the teacher had already given a quiz.
5. Since I came here, I have learned a lot of English.
6. After he (had) finished breakfast, he left the house and went to his office.
7. While I was living in Burma last year, I learned many things about Burmese customs.
8. Jennifer looked in the rearview mirror before she drove onto the main road.
9. Since he entered the Institute of Technology, Michael has begun to feel confident about his future.
10. While I was walking down the street, a car swerved to avoid a dog and almost drove onto the sidewalk.

□ **EXERCISE 37:** Change the adverb clauses to modifying phrases if possible. Make no change if the subjects of the two clauses in the sentence are different.

1. Before I went to Yellowstone Park last summer, I had never seen a black bear in the wild.
2. After she (had) completed her shopping, she went home.
3. Alex hurt his back while he was chopping wood.
4. You should always read a contract before you sign your name.
5. After the children get home from school, our house buzzes with their many activities.
6. The Wilsons have experienced many changes in their lifestyle since they adopted twins.
7. While I was trying to get to sleep last night, a mosquito kept buzzing in my ear.

8. Before the waiter came to our table, I had already made up my mind to order the fried shrimp.

9. Since I arrived here, I have found an apartment, registered for school, explored the city, and made some new friends.

10. After I heard Mary describe how cold it gets in Minnesota in the winter, I decided not to go there for my vacation in January.

11. While Susan was climbing the mountain, she lost her footing and fell onto a ledge several feet below.

12. Before you ask the librarian for help, you should make every effort to find the materials yourself.

8–14 EXPRESSING THE IDEA OF "DURING THE SAME TIME" IN MODIFYING PHRASES

(a) *While I was walking* down the street, *I* ran into an old friend. (b) *While walking* down the street, *I* ran into an old friend. (c) *Walking* down the street, *I* ran into an old friend. (d) *Hiking* through the woods yesterday, *we* saw a bear. (e) *Pointing* to the sentence on the board, *the teacher* explained the meaning of modifying phrases.	Sometimes *while* is omitted but the *-ing* phrase at the beginning of the sentence gives the same meaning (i.e., "during the same time"). (a), (b), and (c) have the same meaning.

8–15 EXPRESSING CAUSE AND EFFECT RELATIONSHIPS IN MODIFYING PHRASES

(f) *Because she needed* some money to buy a book, *Sue* cashed a check. (g) *Needing* some money to buy a book, *Sue* cashed a check. (h) *Because he lacked* the necessary qualifications, *he* was not considered for the job. (i) *Lacking* the necessary qualifications, *he* was not considered for the job.	Often an *-ing* phrase at the beginning of a sentence gives the meaning of "because." (f) and (g) have the same meaning. *Because* is not used in a modifying phrase. It is omitted, but the resulting phrase expresses a cause and effect relationship.
(j) *Having seen* that movie before, *I don't want* to go again. (k) *Having seen* that movie before, *I didn't want* to go again.	*Having* + *past participle* gives the meaning not only of "because" but also of "before."
(l) *Because she was unable* to afford a car, *she* bought a bicycle. (m) *Being unable* to afford a car, *she* bought a bicycle. (n) *Unable* to afford a car, *she* bought a bicycle.	A form of *be* in the adverb clause is often changed to *being*. The use of *being* makes the cause and effect relationship clear.

□ **EXERCISE 38:** Discuss the meaning of the following sentences. Which ones give the meaning of *because*? Which ones give the meaning of *while*? Do some of the sentences give the idea of both *because* and *while*?

1. Sitting on the airplane and watching the clouds pass beneath me, I let my thoughts wander to the new experiences that were in store for me during the next two years of living abroad.
2. Being a self-supporting widow with three children, she has no choice but to work.
3. Lying on her bed in peace and quiet, she soon forgot her troubles.
4. Having already spent all of his last paycheck, he does not have any more money to live on for the rest of the month.
5. Watching the children's energetic play, I felt like an old man even though I am only forty.
6. Having brought up ten children of their own, the Smiths may be considered experts on child behavior.
7. Being totally surprised by his proposal of marriage, Carol could not find the words to reply.
8. Driving to my grandparents' house last night, we saw a young woman who was selling flowers. We stopped so that we could get some flowers for my grandmother.
9. Struggling against fatigue, I forced myself to put one foot in front of the other.
10. Having guessed at the correct answers for a good part of the test, I did not expect to get a high score.
11. Realizing that I had made a dreadful mistake when I introduced him as George Johnson, I went over to him and apologized. I know his name is John George.
12. Tapping his fingers loudly on the desk top, he made his impatience and dissatisfaction known.

□ **EXERCISE 39:** Change the adverb clauses to modifying phrases.

1. Because he didn't want to hurt her feelings, he didn't tell her the bad news. → *Not wanting to hurt her feelings, he didn't tell her the bad news.*
2. Because the little boy believed that no one loved him, he ran away from home.
3. Because she was not paying attention to where she was going, she stepped into a hole and sprained her ankle.
4. Because I had forgotten to bring a pencil to the examination, I had to borrow one.
5. Because she is a vegetarian, she does not eat meat.
6. Because he has already flunked out of school once, he is determined to succeed this time.

☐ **EXERCISE 40:** Combine the two sentences, making a modifying phrase out of the first sentence, if possible.

1. The children had nothing to do. They were bored.
   → *Having nothing to do, the children were bored.*
2. I heard that Judy was in the hospital. I called her family to find out what was wrong.
3. The little boy was trying his best not to cry. He swallowed hard and began to speak.
4. I did not want to inconvenience my friend by asking her to drive me to the airport. I decided to take a taxi.
5. I was sitting on a large rock at the edge of a mountain stream. I felt at peace with the world.
6. John had run a red traffic light. The police officer arrested him.
7. I am a married man. I have many responsibilities.
8. I was reading the paper last night. I saw an article on solar energy.
9. I had not understood what he said. I asked him to repeat the directions.
10. I was watching the children fly their kites in the park. Suddenly the wind blew my hat off my head.
11. Ann was convinced that she could never learn to play the piano. She stopped taking lessons.

☐ **EXERCISE 41:** Change the adverb clauses to modifying phrases.

1. Before I talked to you, I had never understood that formula.
2. Because he did not want to spend any more money this month, Alfred decided against going to a restaurant for dinner. He made himself a sandwich instead.
3. After I read the chapter four times, I finally understood the author's theory.
4. Because I remembered that everyone makes mistakes, I softened my view of his seemingly inexcusable error.
5. Since he completed his Bachelor's degree, he has had three jobs, each one better than the last.
6. While I was traveling across the United States, I could not help being impressed by the great differences in terrain.
7. Before he gained national fame, the union leader had been an electrician in a small town.
8. Because we were enjoying the cool evening breeze and listening to the sounds of nature, we lost track of time.
9. Because she had never flown in an airplane before, the little girl was surprised and a little frightened when her ears popped.
10. Before he became vice-president of marketing and sales, Peter McKay worked as a sales representative.

8–16 USING *UPON* + *-ING* IN MODIFYING PHRASES

(a) ***Upon reaching*** the age of 21, I received my inheritance. (b) *When I reached* the age of 21, I received my inheritance.	Modifying phrases beginning with ***upon*** + ***-ing*** usually have the same meaning as adverb clauses introduced by ***when***. (a) and (b) have the same meaning.
(c) ***On reaching*** the age of 21, I received my inheritance.	***Upon*** can be shortened to ***on***. (a), (b), and (c) all have the same meaning.

☐ **EXERCISE 42:** Using the given information, make sentences with ***upon*** + ***-ing***.

1. When Tom saw his wife and child get off the airplane, he broke into a big smile.
   → *Upon seeing his wife and child get off the airplane, Tom broke into a big smile.*
2. When Tina crossed the marathon finish line, she fell in exhaustion.
3. When I looked in my wallet, I discovered I didn't have enough money to pay my restaurant bill.
4. I bowed my head when I met the king.
5. When Sam re-read the figures, he found that he had made a mistake.
6. When I got an appraisal of my coin collection, I was surprised how it had increased in value.
7. Mrs. Alexander nearly fainted when she learned that she had won the lottery.
8. When you finish the examination, bring your paper to the front of the room.
9. When the police found the thief, they also found the stolen merchandise.
10. When I was elected a member of the club, I found that the dues were more than I could afford.

☐ **EXERCISE 43:** Complete the following. Add commas where needed.

1. Before going to class _____
2. After coming home from the party _____
3. Having failed the entrance examination _____
4. Since arriving in this city _____
5. Driving home last night _____
6. Being new on the job _____
7. After traveling for four hours _____
8. Receiving no answer when he knocked on the door _____

9. Having been told that there were no more rooms available in the dormitory _____

10. Upon finishing this assignment _____

11. Being the largest city in the United States _____

12. Upon hearing a loud crash and feeling the house shake _____

☐ **EXERCISE 44—WRITTEN:** Complete the following. Punctuate carefully.

1. After having finished my . . . .
2. Before going to . . . .
3. Since coming to . . . .
4. Sitting in the park the other day . . . .
5. Having heard a strange noise in the other room . . . .
6. Being only four years old . . . .
7. Being disturbed by the noise from the neighbor's apartment . . . .
8. Upon discovering her car had been stolen . . . .
9. Not having read the directions carefully . . . .
10. Exhausted by the long hours of work . . . .
11. Upon reaching our destination . . . .
12. Before leaving on vacation . . . .

☐ **EXERCISE 45—ERROR ANALYSIS:** The errors in the following are adapted from student compositions. Test your skill by finding and correcting as many of the errors as possible.

1. The weather was such cold that I don't like to leave my apartment.

2. I have to study four hour every day because of my courses are difficult.

3. In the evening, I usually go downstairs for watching television.

4. On the third day of our voyage, we sailed across a rough sea before to reach the shore.

5. I can't understand the lectures in my psychology class, therefore my roommate lets me borrow her notes.

6. According to this legend, a man went in search of a hidden village, he finally found it after walk two hundred mile.

7. Because my country is located in a subtropical area, so the weather is hot.

8. I will stay at the united state for two more year. Because I want finish my degree before go home.

9. After graduating from college, my father wants me to join his business firm.

10. We were floating far from the beach, suddenly my mother cried out "shark! a shark is coming," we could see a black fin cutting the water and coming toward us, we are paralyzed with fear.

☐ **EXERCISE 46—WRITTEN:** Read today's newspaper. Find three articles—one on local news, one on national news, and one on international news—that you think are interesting. Read these articles several times, and then, without looking at the newspaper, summarize them. Use one paragraph for each summary. Be prepared to share your summaries orally with the rest of the class.

☐ **EXERCISE 47—PREPOSITIONS:** Supply appropriate prepositions.

1. I am grateful _____ you _____ your assistance.

2. The criminal escaped _____ prison.

3. Elizabeth is not content _____ the progress she is making.

4. Paul's comments were not relevant _____ the topic under discussion.

5. Have you decided _____ a date for your wedding yet?

6. My boots are made _____ leather.

7. I'm depending _____ you to finish this work for me.

8. Patricia applied _____ admission _____ the university.

9. Daniel dreamed _____ some of his childhood friends last night.

10. Mr. Miller dreams _____ owning his own business someday.

11. The accused woman was innocent _____ the crime with which she was charged.

12. Ms. Sanders is friendly _____ everyone.

13. Benjamin was proud _____ himself for winning the prize.

14. The secretary provided me _____ a great deal of information.

15. Ivan compared the wedding customs in his country _____ those in the United States.

☐ **EXERCISE 48—PHRASAL VERBS:** Supply an appropriate preposition for each of the following two-word verbs.

1. A: Who do you take _____ the most, your father or your mother?

   B: My mother, I think. I can see many similarities between the two of us.

2. A: Hey, cut it _____, you guys! I'm trying to sleep.

   B: What's the matter? Are we making too much noise?

3. A: Could I help you clean _____?

   B: Sure. Would you mind taking _____ the garbage?

4. A: Miss Ward, what seems to be the problem?

   B: Well, Doctor, for the last two days I haven't been able to keep any food down. Every time I try to eat something, I throw _____ soon afterward.

5. A: Where's my jacket?

   B: I hung it _____ in the closet.

6. A: Why are you going to see Professor Kelly?

   B: He called me _____ to talk about my research project.

7. A: Is that man's story true?

   B: Yes. A newspaper reporter checked _____ his story and found that it was true.

8. A: The city government is planning to redevelop a large section of the inner city.

   B: What's going to happen to the buildings that are there now?

   A: They are going to be torn _____.

9. A: Some people tried to crash our party last night.

   B: What did you do?

   A: We kicked them _____.

10. A: The test is about to begin. Please put _____ all of your books and notebooks.

CHAPTER *9*

Showing Relationships Between Ideas—Part II

9–1 EXPRESSING UNEXPECTED RESULT: USING *EVEN THOUGH*

(a) *Because* the weather was cold, I *didn't go* swimming. (b) *Even though* the weather was cold, I *went* swimming. (c) *Because* I wasn't tired, I *didn't go* to bed. (d) *Even though* I wasn't tired, I *went* to bed.	*Because* is used to express expected results. *Even though* is used to express unexpected results.
	Like *because*, *even though* introduces an adverb clause.

☐ **EXERCISE 1:** Complete the sentences by using either *even though* or *because*.

1. Tim's in good shape physically ___*even though*___ he doesn't get much exercise.

2. Jerry's in good shape physically ___*because*___ he gets a lot of exercise.

3. _____ Sue is a good student, she received a scholarship.

4. _____ Ann is a good student, she didn't receive a scholarship.

5. _____ it was raining, we went for a walk.

6. _____ it was raining, we didn't go for a walk.

7. This letter was delivered _____ it didn't have enough postage.

8. That letter was returned to the sender _____ it didn't have enough postage.

9. Susan didn't learn Spanish _____ she lived in Mexico for a year.

10. Joe speaks Spanish well _____ he lived in Mexico for a year.

11. A newborn kangaroo can find its mother's pouch _____ its eyes are not yet open.

12. Some people protest certain commercial fishing operations _____ dolphins, considered to be highly intelligent mammals, are killed unnecessarily.

□ **EXERCISE 2—ORAL (BOOKS CLOSED):** Use *even though*. Be sure to begin your response with either *yes* or *no*.

Example: It was raining. Did you go to the zoo anyway?
Response: Yes, even though it was raining, I went to the zoo.

Example: You studied hard. Did you pass the test?
Response: No, even though I studied hard, I didn't pass the test.

1. You weren't tired. Did you go to bed anyway?
2. The telephone rang many times, but did John wake up?
3. The food was terrible. Did you eat it anyway?
4. You didn't study. Did you pass the test anyway?
5. The weather is terrible today. Did you stay home?
6. You fell down the stairs. Did you get hurt?
7. You took a nap. Do you still feel tired?
8. You told the truth, but did anyone believe you?
9. You took an aspirin. Do you still have a headache?
10. You turned on the air conditioner. Is it still hot in here?
11. You mailed the letter three days ago. Has it arrived yet?
12. You have a lot of money. Can you afford to buy an airplane?
13. Your grandmother is ninety years old. Is she still young at heart?
14. (. . .) told a joke. You didn't understand it. Did you laugh anyway?
15. Your house burned down. You lost your job. Your wife/husband left you. Are you still cheerful?

9–2 SHOWING OPPOSITION (UNEXPECTED RESULT)

All of the following example sentences have the same meaning.		
ADVERB CLAUSES	*even though* *although* *though*	(a) ***Even though** it was cold*, I went swimming. (b) ***Although** it was cold*, I went swimming. (c) ***Though** it was cold*, I went swimming.
CONJUNCTIONS	*but . . . anyway* *but . . . still* *yet . . . still*	(d) It was cold, ***but** I went swimming **anyway**. (e) It was cold, ***but** I **still** went swimming. (f) It was cold, ***yet** I **still** went swimming.
TRANSITIONS	*nevertheless* *nonetheless* *however*	(g) It was cold. ***Nevertheless**, I went swimming. (h) It was cold. ***Nonetheless**, I went swimming. (i) It was cold. ***However**, I still went swimming.
PREPOSITIONS	*despite* *in spite of*	(j) I went swimming ***despite** the cold weather. (k) I went swimming ***in spite of** the cold weather.

☐ **EXERCISE 3:** Combine the ideas in the two sentences. Use the given words. Discuss correct punctuation. Use the negative if necessary to make a logical statement.

1. *We went to the zoo. It was raining.*
   even though
   but . . . anyway
   nevertheless
   in spite of
   because

2. *His grades were low. He was admitted to the university.*
   although
   yet . . . still
   nonetheless
   despite
   because of

☐ **EXERCISE 4:** Complete the following with your own words. Add commas where appropriate.

1. I had a cold but I _____ anyway.

2. Even though I had a cold I _____

3. Although I didn't study _____

4. I didn't study but _____ anyway.

5. I got an ''A'' on the test even though _____

6. Even though Howard is a careful driver _____

7. Even though the food they served for dinner tasted terrible _____

8. My shirt still has coffee stains on it even though _____

9. I still trust him even though _____

10. Even though he was drowning no one _____

11. Although I tried to be very careful _____

12. Even though Ruth is one of my best friends _____

13. It's still hot in here even though _____

14. Even though I had a big breakfast _____

☐ **EXERCISE 5:** Change the sentences by using *nevertheless*.

1. He wasn't tired, but he went to bed anyway.*
   → *He wasn't tired. Nevertheless, he went to bed.*

2. She wasn't hungry, but she ate two dishes of ice cream anyway.

3. Even though Jack wasn't feeling good, he went to class.

4. I still trust him even though he lied to me.

5. Sally was very sad, but she smiled and pretended to be having a good time.

6. George did not panic even though he was alone and lost in the woods.

7. Elizabeth is not a citizen of the United States, but she has to pay income taxes anyway.

8. Even though Henry Johnson is an honest politician, I would never vote for him because I do not agree with his positions on foreign policy.

9. The crime rate has continued to rise even though the local police department has implemented several new crime prevention programs.

10. Even though math has always been easy for him, he understands that it is not easy for everyone. As a result, he is a good teacher.

☐ **EXERCISE 6:** Give sentences with the same meaning by using *in spite of* or *despite*.

1. Even though her grades were low, she was admitted to the university.
   → *In spite of her low grades,*
   → *Despite her low grades,*   she was admitted to the
   → *In spite of the fact that her grades were low,*   university.
   → *Despite the fact that her grades were low,*

---

*Nevertheless and *but . . . anyway* have the same meaning: *but . . . anyway* occurs primarily in speaking, and *nevertheless* occurs primarily in writing.

2. I like living in the dorm even though it is noisy.
3. Even though the work was hard, they enjoyed themselves.
4. They wanted to climb the mountain even though it was dangerous.
5. Although the weather was extremely hot, they went jogging in the park.
6. He is unhappy even though he has a vast fortune.

□ **EXERCISE 7—WRITTEN:** Complete the following. Punctuate carefully. (Correct punctuation is not indicated in the given cues.) Capitalize as necessary.

1. I didn't . . . but . . . anyway.
2. He is very old yet he still . . . .
3. . . . nevertheless we arrived on schedule.
4. Even though she wanted . . . .
5. I wanted . . . however I . . . because . . . .
6. The teacher . . . even though . . . .
7. Although . . . only . . . years old . . . .
8. She never went to school however she . . . despite her lack of education.
9. Despite the fact that my . . . .
10. I have decided to . . . even though . . . .

9-3 SHOWING DIRECT OPPOSITION

ADVERB CLAUSES	*whereas* *while*	(a) Mary is rich, ***whereas*** *John is poor.* (b) Mary is rich, ***while*** *John is poor.* (c) John is poor, ***while*** *Mary is rich.* (d) ***Whereas*** *Mary is rich*, John is poor.	***Whereas*** and ***while*** are used to show direct opposition: "this" is exactly the opposite of "that." ***Whereas*** and ***while*** may be used with the idea of either clause with no difference in meaning. Note: A comma is usually used even if the adverb clause comes second.
CONJUNCTION	*but*	(e) Mary is rich, ***but*** John is poor. (f) John is poor, ***but*** Mary is rich.	In (e) through (j): As with ***whereas*** and ***while***, it does not make any difference which idea comes first and which idea comes second. The two ideas are directly opposite.
TRANSITIONS	*however* *on the other hand*	(g) Mary is rich; ***however***, John is poor. (h) John is poor; ***however***, Mary is rich. (i) Mary is rich. John, ***on the other hand***, is poor. (j) John is poor. Mary, ***on the other hand***, is rich.	

□ **EXERCISE 8:** Complete the following. Discuss other ways of expressing the same idea by moving the position of *whereas* or *while*.

1. Some people are fat, whereas . . . *others are thin. (Whereas some people are fat, others are thin.) (Some people are thin, whereas others are fat.)*

2. Some people are tall, whereas . . . .

3. Some people prefer to live in the country, while . . . .

4. While some people know only their native language, ...

5. A mouse is small, whereas . . . .

6. The climate at sea level at the equator is always hot, whereas the climate at the North and South poles . . . .

7. Some people . . . , while . . . .

8. Some countries . . . , whereas . . . .

□ **EXERCISE 9:** Give sentences with the same meaning by using *however* or *on the other hand*. Punctuate carefully.

1. Florida has a warm climate, whereas Alaska has a cold climate.

2. While Fred is a good student, his brother is lazy.

3. Sue and Ron are expecting a child. Sue is hoping for a boy, whereas Ron is hoping for a girl.

4. Old people in my country usually live with their children, whereas the old in the United States often live by themselves.

5. In the United States, gambling casinos are not legal in most states, while in my country it is possible to gamble in any city or town.

□ **EXERCISE 10—ORAL/WRITTEN:** What aspects of your country and the United States are in contrast? Use *while, whereas, however, on the other hand*.

1. Size?	6. Political system?
2. Population?	7. Economic system?
3. Food?	8. Educational system?
4. Time of meals?	9. Religion?
5. Climate?	10. Student life?

11. Coffee-tea?
12. Role of women?
13. Language?
14. Educational costs?
15. Medical care?

16. Family relationships?
17. Public transportation?
18. Length of history?
19. Dating customs?
20. Predictability of the weather?

9–4 EXPRESSING CONDITIONS IN ADVERB CLAUSES: "*IF* CLAUSES"

(a) *If it rains*, the streets get wet.	"*If* clauses" (also called *adverb clauses of condition*) present possible conditions. The main clause expresses results. In (a): POSSIBLE CONDITION = *it rains* RESULT = *the streets get wet*
(b) *If it rains tomorrow*, I will take my umbrella.	A present tense, not a future tense, is used in an "*if* clause" even though the verb in the "*if* clause" may refer to a future event or situation, as in (b).★

WORDS THAT INTRODUCE ADVERB CLAUSES OF CONDITION ("*IF* CLAUSES"):		
if	in case (that)	only if
whether or not	in the event (that)	providing (that)
even if	unless	provided (that)

*See Chapter 10 for uses of other verb forms in sentences with "*if* clauses."

☐ **EXERCISE 11**: Make sentences from the given possibilities. Use *if*.

1. It may be cold tomorrow.
   → *If it's cold tomorrow, I'm going to stay home.*
   → *If it's cold tomorrow, let's go skating.*
   → *If it's cold tomorrow, you should wear your wool sweater.*
   → *We can't go on a picnic if it's cold tomorrow.*
2. Maybe it will be hot tomorrow.
3. Robert will probably study for the test.
4. Maybe you will have some free time tomorrow.
5. The teacher may be absent tomorrow.
6. Maybe you won't do your homework tonight.
7. Maybe you will lock yourself out of your apartment.
8. Maybe the sun will be shining when you get up tomorrow morning.

9-5 ADVERB CLAUSES OF CONDITION: USING *WHETHER OR NOT* AND *EVEN IF*

WHETHER OR NOT (a) I'm going to go swimming tomorrow *whether or not it is cold*. (OR: *whether it is cold or not*.)	*Whether or not* expresses the idea that *neither this condition nor that condition matters*; the result will be the same. In (a): If it is cold, I'm going swimming. If it is not cold, I'm going swimming. I don't care about the temperature. It doesn't matter.
EVEN IF (b) I have decided to go swimming tomorrow. *Even if the weather is cold*, I'm going to go swimming.	Sentences with *even if* are close in meaning to those with *whether or not*. *Even if* gives the idea that a particular condition does not matter. The result will not change.
COMPARE: (c) *If* Ann studies hard, she *will pass* the exam. (d) *Even if* Mary studies hard, she *won't pass* the exam.	"*If* clauses" are followed by expected results, as in (c). CONDITION: *Ann studies* EXPECTED RESULT: *she passes the exam* "*Even if* clauses" are followed by unexpected results, as in (d). CONDITION: *Mary studies* UNEXPECTED RESULT: *she doesn't pass the exam*

☐ **EXERCISE 12:** Use the given information to complete the sentences.

1. *Usually people need to graduate from school to get a good job. But it's different for Ed. Maybe Ed will graduate from school, and maybe he won't. It doesn't matter because he has a good job waiting for him in his father's business.*
   a. Ed will get a good job whether or not . . . *he graduates.*
   b. Ed will get a good job even if . . . *he doesn't graduate.*

2. *Sam's uncle tells a lot of jokes. Sometimes they're funny, and sometimes they're not. It doesn't matter.*
   a. Sam laughs at the jokes whether . . . or not.
   b. Sam laughs at the jokes even if . . . .

3. *Maybe you are finished with the exam, and maybe you're not. It doesn't matter. The time is up.*
   a. You have to hand in your examination paper whether . . . or not.
   b. You have to hand in your examination paper even if . . . .

4. *It might snow, or it might not. We don't want to go camping in the snow, but it doesn't matter.*
   a. We're going to go camping in the mountains whether . . . or not.
   b. We're going to go camping in the mountains even if . . . .

5. *Max's family doesn't have enough money to send him to college. He would like to get a scholarship, but it doesn't matter because he's saved some money to go to school and has a part-time job.*
   a. Max can go to school whether or not . . . .
   b. Max can go to school even if . . . .

6. *Sometimes the weather is hot, sometimes the weather is cold. It doesn't matter. My grandfather always wears his gray sweater.*
   a. My grandfather wears his gray sweater whether or not . . . .*
   b. My grandfather always wears his gray sweater even if . . . .

7. *Your approval doesn't matter to me.*
   a. I'm going to marry Harry whether . . . or not.
   b. I'm going to marry Harry even if . . . .

Complete the following.

8. I'm really angry! Maybe he'll apologize and maybe he won't. It doesn't matter. Even if . . . , I won't forgive him!

9. I'm exhausted. Please don't wake me up even if . . . .

10. I'm not going to . . . even if . . . .

11. Even if . . . , I'm going to . . . .

12. I'm going to . . . whether or not . . . .

9–6 ADVERB CLAUSES OF CONDITION: USING *IN CASE (THAT)* AND *IN THE EVENT (THAT)*

(a) I'll be at my uncle's house **in case** *you (should) need to reach me.*	**In case that** and **in the event that** express the idea that something probably won't happen, but it might.*
(b) **In the event that** *you (should) need to reach me*, I'll be at my uncle's house.	**in case/in the event that** = *if by any chance this should happen* Notes: **In the event that** is more formal than **in case**. The use of **should** in the adverb clause emphasizes the speaker's uncertainty that something will happen.

In case that and *in the event that* introduce adverb clauses. *In case of* and *in the event of* have the same meaning, but they are prepositions followed by a noun object:
In case of trouble, call the police = In case (that) there is trouble, call the police.
In the event of rain, the picnic will be cancelled = In the event (that) it rains, the picnic will be cancelled.

☐ **EXERCISE 13:** Show the relationship between the ideas in the two sentences by using *in case* and/or *in the event that*.

1. You probably won't need to get in touch with me, but maybe you will. If so, I'll give you my phone number.
   → *I'll give you my phone number in case you (should) need to get in touch with me/in the event that you (should) need to get in touch with me.*

2. You probably won't need to see me, but maybe you will.
   If so, I'll be in my office tomorrow morning around ten.

3. I don't think you need any more information, but maybe you do.
   If so, you can call me.

4. You probably don't have any more questions, but maybe you do.
   If so, ask Dr. Smith.

5. You will probably be satisfied with your purchase, but maybe not.
   If not, you can return it to the store.

6. Jack probably won't call, but maybe he will.
   If so, please tell him that I'm at the library.

Complete the following.

7. I've told you all I know. In the event that you need more information, ...

8. It's a good idea for you to keep a written record of your credit card numbers in case . . . .

9. I think I'd better clean up the apartment in case . . . .

10. I have my umbrella with me just in case . . . .

11. In the event that the two countries agree to a peace treaty, ...

12. I'll try to be there on time, but in case I'm not, ...

13. According to the manufacturer's guarantee, I should return my new camera to the factory in the event that . . . .

9-7 ADVERB CLAUSE OF CONDITION: USING *UNLESS*

(a) I'll go swimming tomorrow **unless** *it's cold.* (b) I'll go swimming tomorrow *if it isn't cold.*	**unless = if . . . not** In (a): *unless it's cold = if it isn't cold* (a) and (b) have the same meaning.

□ **EXERCISE 14:** Make sentences with the same meaning by using *unless*.

1. I will go to the zoo if it isn't cold.
   → *I will go to the zoo unless it's cold.*

2. You can't travel abroad if you don't have a passport.

3. You can't get a driver's license if you're not at least sixteen years old.

4. If I don't get some film, I won't be able to take pictures when Ann and Rob get here.

5. You'll get hungry during class if you don't eat breakfast.

☐ **EXERCISE 15:** Complete the sentences.

1. Your letter won't be delivered unless . . . *it has the correct postage.*
2. I'm sorry, but you can't see the doctor unless . . . .
3. I can't graduate from school unless . . . .
4. . . . unless you put it in the refrigerator.
5. Unless it rains, ...
6. Certain species of animals will soon become extinct unless . . . .
7. . . . unless I get a raise in salary.
8. Tomorrow I'm going to . . . unless . . . .
9. The political situation in . . . will continue to deteriorate unless . . . .
10. Ivan never volunteers in class. He doesn't say anything unless . . . .
11. Unless you . . . .

9–8 ADVERB CLAUSES OF CONDITION: USING *ONLY IF* AND *PROVIDING/PROVIDED THAT*

(a) The picnic will be cancelled *only if it rains.* If it's windy, we'll go on the picnic. If it's cold, we'll go on the picnic. If it's damp and foggy, we'll go on the picnic. If it's unbearably hot, we'll go on the picnic.	*Only if* expresses the idea that there is only one condition that will cause a particular result.
(b) *Only if* it rains **will the picnic be cancelled**.	When *only if* begins a sentence, the subject and verb of the main clause are inverted, as in (b).
(c) *Providing/provided (that)* no one has any *further questions*, the meeting will be adjourned.	*Providing that* and *provided that* = *if* or *only if.*

☐ **EXERCISE 16:** Use the given information to complete the sentences.

1. *John must get a scholarship in order to go to school. That is the only condition under which he can go to school. If he doesn't get one, he can't go to school.*
   He can go to school only if . . . *he gets a scholarship.*
2. *You have to have an invitation in order to go to the party. That is the only condition under which you will be admitted. If you don't have an invitation, you can't go.*
   You can go to the party only if . . . .
3. *You have to have a student visa in order to study here. Unless you have a student visa, you can't go to school here.*
   You can attend this school only if . . . .

4. *Jimmy's mother doesn't want him to chew gum, but sometimes he chews it anyway.*
   Jimmy . . . only if he's sure his mother won't find out.
5. *If you want to go to the movie, we'll go. If you don't want to go, we won't go.*
   We . . . only if you want to.
6. *The temperature has to reach 32°F/0°C before water will freeze.*
   Water will freeze only if . . . .
7. *You must study hard. Then you will pass the exam.*
   Only if you study hard . . . .
8. *You have to have a ticket. Then you can get into the soccer stadium.*
   Only if you have a ticket . . . .
9. *My parents make me finish my homework before I can watch TV in the evening.*
   Only if my homework is finished . . . .
10. *I have to get a job. Then I will have enough money to go to school.*
    Only if I get a job . . . .

Complete the following.

11. Yes, John, I will marry you—but only if _____
12. I _____ only if _____
13. Only if _____

☐ **EXERCISE 17**: Give sentences with the same meaning by using *only if* and *unless*.

1. If you don't study hard, you won't pass the test.
   → *You will pass the test only if you study hard.*
   → *You won't pass the test unless you study hard.*
2. If I don't get a job, I can't pay my bills.
3. Your clothes won't get clean if you don't use soap.
4. I can't take any pictures if I don't buy some film.
5. I don't wake up if the alarm clock doesn't ring.

☐ **EXERCISE 18**: Complete the sentences.

1. I will come to the meeting at City Hall providing that . . . *I can get a ride with someone.*
2. Only students can apply for this low-cost health insurance policy. You are eligible for the insurance provided that . . . .
3. I will take the six-thirty flight to Atlanta providing that . . . .
4. You will be admitted to the university providing that . . . .
5. Provided that no one objects, ...

☐ **EXERCISE 19:** Using the given words, combine the following two ideas.

It may or may not rain. The party will be held inside/outside.

1. if → *If it rains, the party will be held inside.*
   → *If it doesn't rain, the party will be held outside.*

2. whether or not   6. unless
3. even if   7. only if
4. in case   8. providing that
5. in the event that   9. provided that

9–9 EXPRESSING CONDITIONS: USING *OTHERWISE* AND *OR (ELSE)*

(a) I always eat breakfast. *Otherwise*, I get hungry during class.	*Otherwise* expresses the idea "if the opposite is true, then there will be a certain result."
(b) You'd better hurry. *Otherwise*, you'll be late.	In (a): *otherwise* = *if I don't eat breakfast* In (b): *otherwise* = *if you don't hurry*
(c) I always eat breakfast, *or (else)* I get hungry during class.	*Or else* and *otherwise* have the same meaning.
(d) You'd better hurry, *or (else)* you'll be late.	*Otherwise* is a transition. *Or (else)* is a conjunction.

☐ **EXERCISE 20:** Make sentences with the same meaning by using *otherwise*.

1. If I don't call my mother, she'll start worrying about me.
   → *I am going to/should/had better/have to/must call my mother. Otherwise, she'll start worrying about me.*
2. If I don't wash my clothes tonight, I won't have any clean clothes to wear tomorrow.

3. If you don't leave now, you'll be late for class.

4. If you don't go to bed, your cold will get worse.

5. Unless you have a ticket, you can't get into the theater.

6. You can't enter that country unless you have a passport.

7. If Tom doesn't get a job soon, his family won't have enough money for food.

8. Mary can go to school only if she gets a scholarship.

9. Only if you speak both Japanese and Chinese fluently will you be considered for that job.

□ **EXERCISE 21—WRITTEN:** Complete the following. Punctuate correctly. (Correct punctuation is not indicated in the cues.) Use capital letters where appropriate.

1. I am going to . . . even if . . . .
2. We have no choice we have to . . . whether . . . .
3. I will go to . . . providing that . . . .
4. . . . is very inconsiderate he plays his record player even if . . . .
5. I can't . . . unless . . . .
6. Tomorrow I'd better . . . otherwise . . . .
7. You should . . . in case . . . .
8. I will . . . only if . . . .
9. I will . . . unless . . . .
10. . . . must . . . otherwise . . . .

9–10 SUMMARY OF RELATIONSHIP WORDS: CAUSE AND EFFECT, OPPOSITION, CONDITION

	ADVERB CLAUSE WORDS		TRANSITIONS	CONJUNCTIONS	PREPOSITIONS
CAUSE AND EFFECT	*because* *since* *now that* *as*	*as/so long as* *inasmuch as* *so (that)*	*therefore* *consequently*	*so* *for*	*because of* *due to*
OPPOSITION	*even though* *although* *though*	*whereas* *while*	*nevertheless* *nonetheless* *however* *on the other hand*	*but (. . . anyway)* *yet (. . . still)*	*despite* *in spite of*
CONDITION	*if* *unless* *only if* *even if* *whether or not*	*provided (that)* *providing (that)* *in case (that)* *in the event (that)*	*otherwise*	*or (else)*	*in case of* *in the event of*

☐ **EXERCISE 22:** Using the two ideas of *to study* and *to pass or fail the exam*, complete the following. Punctuate correctly. Add capital letters as necessary.

1. Because I did not study _____

2. I failed the exam because _____

3. Although I studied _____

4. I did not study   therefore _____

5. I did not study   however _____

6. I studied   nevertheless _____

7. Even though I did not study _____

8. I did not study   so _____

9. Since I did not study _____

10. If I study for the test _____

11. Unless I study for the test _____

12. I will pass the test providing that _____

13. I must study   otherwise _____

14. Even if I study _____

15. I did not study   consequently _____

16. I did not study   nonetheless _____

17. Inasmuch as I did not study for the test _____

18. I will probably fail the test whether _____

19. I failed the exam   for _____

20. I have to study so that _____

21. Only if I study _____

22. I studied hard   yet _____

23. You'd better study or else _____

☐ **EXERCISE 23:** Using the ideas of *to be hungry* (or *not to be hungry*) and *to eat breakfast* (or *not to eat breakfast*), complete the following. Punctuate and capitalize correctly.

1. Because I was not hungry this morning _____

2. Because I ate breakfast this morning _____ now.

3. Because I was hungry this morning _____

4. I did not eat breakfast this morning even though _____

5. Although I was hungry this morning _____

6. I was hungry this morning   therefore _____

7. I was hungry this morning   nevertheless _____

8. I was so hungry this morning _____

9. I was not hungry this morning but _____

10. I ate breakfast this morning even though _____

11. Since I did not eat breakfast this morning _____

12. I ate breakfast this morning   nonetheless _____

13. I was not hungry   so _____

14. Even though I did not eat breakfast this morning _____

15. I never eat breakfast unless _____

16. I always eat breakfast whether or not _____

17. I eat breakfast even if _____

18. Now that I have eaten breakfast _____

19. I eat breakfast only if _____

20. I ate breakfast this morning   yet _____

21. Even if I am hungry _____

22. I was not hungry   however _____

☐ **EXERCISE 24—ORAL:** Using the given words, combine the following two ideas. The time is *now*, so use present and future tenses.

(a) **to go (or not to go) to the beach**   (b) **hot, cold, nice weather**

1. because → *Because the weather is cold, we aren't going to go to the beach.*
    → *We're going to go to the beach because the weather is hot.*

2. so . . . that	13. since
3. so	14. but . . . anyway
4. nevertheless	15. unless
5. despite	16. therefore
6. now that	17. only if
7. once	18. nonetheless
8. although	19. in spite of
9. because of	20. even if
10. consequently	21. yet . . . still
11. as soon as	22. whether . . . or not
12. such . . . that	23. as long as . . . let's/why don't

☐ **EXERCISE 25:** Complete the following. Add necessary punctuation and capitalization.

1. While some people are optimists _____

2. Even though he drank a glass of water _____ still _____

3. Even if she invites me to her party _____

4. I have never been to Hawaii my parents however _____

5. I couldn't _____ for my arms were full of packages.

6. I need to borrow some money so that _____

7. The airport was closed due to fog therefore _____

8. _____ therefore the airport was closed.

9. As soon as the violinist played the last note at the concert _____

10. Since neither my roommate nor I know how to cook _____

11. I am not a superstitious person nevertheless _____

12. The crops will fail unless _____

13. Just as I was getting ready to eat my dinner last night _____

14. Now that she is married _____

15. We must work quickly otherwise _____

16. Some children are noisy and wild my brother's children on the other hand _____

☐ **EXERCISE 26—WRITTEN:** Complete the following. Punctuate and capitalize correctly.

1. According to the newspaper, now that . . . .
2. Ever since I can remember . . . .
3. Although my . . . .
4. The United States . . . whereas . . . .
5. I was tired however I . . . because . . . .
6. I . . . my friend on the other hand . . . .
7. You must . . . whether . . . .

8. Even though I . . . .

9. Since my apartment is very small . . . .

10. In spite of the fact that . . . .

11. . . . therefore I have decided to . . . .

12. . . . nevertheless I could not understand what . . . .

☐ **EXERCISE 27—ERROR ANALYSIS:** Try to find and correct the errors in the following.

1. Unless I study very hard, I will pass all of my exams.

2. My shoes and pants got muddy. Even though I walked carefully through the wet streets.

3. My neighborhood is quiet and safe however I always lock my doors.

4. Although I usually don't like french food, but I liked the food I had at the french restaurant last night.

5. Although my room in the dormitory is very small, but I like it. Because it is a place where I can be by myself and studying in peace and quiet.

6. Despite I prefer to be a history teacher, I am studying in the Business School in order for I can get a job in industry.

7. A little girl approached the cage however when the tiger shows its teeth and growls she run to her mother. Because she was frightened.

8. Many of the people working to save our environment think that they are fighting a losing battle. Because big business and the government have not joined together to eliminate pollution.

☐ **EXERCISE 28:** Complete the following.

1. If what he said _____

2. Because the man who _____

3. Even though she didn't understand what _____

4. Now that all of the students who _____

5. Since the restaurant where we _____

9-11 GIVING EXAMPLES

(a) There are many interesting places to visit in the city. **For example**, the botanical garden has numerous displays of plants from all over the world. (b) There are many interesting places to visit in the city. The art museum, **for instance**, has an excellent collection of modern paintings.	**For example** and **for instance** have the same meaning. They are often used as transitions.
(c) There are many interesting places to visit in the city, **e.g.**, the botanical garden and the art museum. (d) There are many interesting places to visit in the city, **for example**, the botanical garden or the art museum.	**e.g.** = *for example* (**e.g.** is an abbreviation of the Latin phrase *exempli gratia*.)* (c) and (d) have the same meaning.
(e) I prefer to wear casual clothes, **such as** jeans and a sweatshirt. (f) Some countries, **such as** Brazil and Canada, are big. (g) Countries **such as** Brazil and Canada are big. (h) **Such** countries **as** Brazil and Canada are big.	**such as** = *for example* (f), (g), and (h) have essentially the same meaning even though the pattern varies.**

*Punctuation note: Periods are used with **e.g.** in American English. Periods are generally not used with **eg** in British English.

**Punctuation note:
  (1) When the "**such as** phrase" can be omitted without substantially changing the meaning of the sentence, commas are used.
      Example: Some words, such as *know* and *see*, are verbs. (*Commas are used.*)
  (2) No commas are used when the "**such as** phrase" gives essential information about the noun to which it refers.
      Example: Words such as *know* and *see* are verbs. (*No commas are used.*)

☐ **EXERCISE 29:** Complete the following. Use **such as**.

1. You need a hobby. There are many hobbies you might enjoy, ___*such as*___ _ceramics or stamp collecting._

2. There are certain products that almost everyone buys regularly, _____

   _____

3. You should buy a small, economical car, _____

4. Medical science has made many advances, yet there are still serious

   diseases that have not been conquered, _____

5. Some countries, _____ and _____,

   are rich in oil.

6. I enjoy such sports _____

7. Such inventions _____ have contributed greatly to the progress of civilization. However, other inventions, _____ _____, have threatened human existence.

8. There are certain times when I wish to be alone, _____ when _____ or when _____.

9. Some subjects have always been easy and enjoyable for me, _____ _____. However, other subjects, _____ _____, _____.

10. In certain situations, _____ when _____ or when _____, my English still gives me a little trouble.

11. Numbers _____ are odd numbers, whereas numbers _____ are even numbers.

12. Some languages, _____ and _____, are closely related to English, while others, _____ and _____, are not.

□ **EXERCISE 30—ORAL (BOOKS CLOSED):** Use *such as* in the response.

Example: Give me some examples of sports you enjoy. (*I enjoy . . . .*)
Response: I enjoy sports such as (soccer and boxing).

(*To the teacher: Prompt the response with the words in parentheses only if necessary.*)

1. Give me some examples of places you would like to visit. (*I would like . . . .*)
2. Who enjoys watching television? Give me some examples of programs you enjoy. (*I enjoy . . . .*)
3. Do you like bright colors or dark colors? Can you give me some examples? (*I like . . . .*)
4. What are some examples of gifts that a woman likes to receive? (*A woman . . . .*)
5. And examples of gifts that a man likes to receive? (*A man . . . .*)

6. Give me some examples of problems a foreign student can easily overcome. (*A foreign student can easily overcome problems* . . . .)

7. Are there many sources of protein? Can you give me some examples? (*There are many* . . . .)

8. Give me some examples of emotions we all experience. (*We all* . . . .)

9. Should I buy a big car or a small car? For example? (*You should buy* . . . .)

10. What qualities do you appreciate in a friend? (*I appreciate* . . . .)

9–12 CONTINUING THE SAME IDEA

(a) The city provides many cultural opportunities. It has an excellent art museum. $\left\{\begin{array}{l}\textbf{\textit{Moreover,}}\\ \textbf{\textit{Furthermore,}}\\ \textbf{\textit{In addition,}}\end{array}\right\}$ it has a fine symphony orchestra.	*Moreover*, *furthermore*, and *in addition* mean *also*. They are transitions.
(b) The city provides many cultural opportunities. $\left\{\begin{array}{l}\textbf{\textit{In addition to}}\\ \textbf{\textit{Besides}}\end{array}\right\}$ an excellent art museum, it has a fine symphony orchestra.	In (b): *In addition to* and *besides** are used as prepositions. They are followed by an object (*museum*), not a clause.

*COMPARE: *Besides* means *in addition to*.
Beside means *next to*; e.g., *I sat beside my friend.*

☐ **EXERCISE 31:** Combine the ideas in the following by using *moreover, furthermore, in addition (to), besides*, or *also* where appropriate.

1. I like to read that newspaper. One reason is that the news is always reported accurately. It has interesting special features.

2. There are many ways you can work on improving your English outside of class. For example, you should speak English as much as possible, even when you are speaking with friends who speak your native language. You should read as many magazines in English as you have time for. Watching television can be helpful.

3. Along with the increase in population in the city, there has been an increase in the rate of crime. A housing shortage has developed. There are so many automobiles in the city that the expressways are almost always jammed with cars, regardless of the time of day.

4. Good health is perhaps one's most valuable asset. To maintain good health, it is important to eat a balanced diet. The body needs a regular supply of vitamins, minerals, protein, carbohydrates, and other nutrients. Physical exercise is essential. Sleep and rest should not be neglected.

□ **EXERCISE 32—WRITTEN:** Write a paragraph of approximately 100 to 150 words in which you give specific examples to support one of the following general ideas. Use connecting words such as *for example, for instance, such as, moreover, furthermore, in addition (to),* and *also.*

1. A newspaper contains a variety of articles to appeal to the different interests of its readers.
2. Some television programs are not suitable for viewing by children.
3. There are several things you should consider before you decide to get married.
4. There are several problems international students face when they first arrive in (the United States).

□ **EXERCISE 33—PHRASAL VERBS:** Supply an appropriate preposition for each of the following two-word verbs.

1. A: Guess who I ran _____ today as I was walking across campus.

   B: Who?

   A: Ann Keefe.

   B: You're kidding!

2. A: There will be a test on Chapters Eight and Nine next Friday.

   B: (Groan.) Couldn't you put it _____ until Monday?

3. A: You'd better put _____ your coat before you leave. It's chilly out.

   B: What's the temperature?

4. A: I smell something burning in the kitchen. Can I call you _____ in a minute.

   B: Sure. I hope your dinner hasn't burned.

   A: So do I! Bye.

   B: Good-bye.

5. A: I think that if I learn enough vocabulary I won't have any trouble using English.

   B: That's not necessarily so. I'd like to point _____ that language consists of much more than just vocabulary.

6. A: One billion seconds ago, World War II was being fought. One billion minutes ago, Jesus Christ was living. One billion hours ago, the human race had not yet discovered agriculture.

   B: How did you figure that _____?

   A: I didn't. I came _____ that information while I was reading the newspaper.

7. A: Your children certainly love the outdoors.

   B: Yes, they do. We brought them _____ to appreciate nature.

8. A: What forms do I have to fill out to change my tourist visa to a student visa?

   B: I don't know, but I'll look _____ it first thing tomorrow and try to find _____. I'll let you know.

9. A: How long were you in the hospital?

   B: About a week. But I've missed almost two weeks of classes.

   A: It's going to be hard for you to make _____ all the work you've missed, isn't it?

   B: Very.

10. A: Would you mind turning _____ the light?

    B: Not at all.

CHAPTER *10*

Conditional Sentences

10–1 SUMMARY OF BASIC VERB FORM USAGE IN CONDITIONAL SENTENCES

MEANING OF THE "*IF* CLAUSE"	VERB FORM IN THE "*IF* CLAUSE"	VERB FORM IN THE "RESULT CLAUSE"	
True in the present/future	*simple present*	*simple present* *simple future*	(a) If I ***have*** enough time, I ***write*** to my parents every week. (b) If I ***have*** enough time tomorrow, I ***will write*** to my parents.
Untrue in the present/future	*simple past*	***would*** + *simple form*	(c) If I ***had*** enough time now, I ***would write*** to my parents. (*In truth, I do not have enough time, so I will not write to them.*)
Untrue in the past	*past perfect*	***would have*** + *past participle*	(d) If I ***had had*** enough time, I ***would have written*** to my parents yesterday. (*In truth, I did not have enough time, so I did not write to them.*)

10–2 TRUE IN THE PRESENT OR FUTURE

(e) If I ***don't eat*** breakfast, I always ***get*** hungry during class.	In (e): The simple present is used in the result clause to express a habitual activity or situation.
(f) Water ***freezes (will freeze)*** if the temperature ***goes*** below 32°F/0°C.	In (f): Either the simple present or the simple future is used in the result clause to express an established, predictable fact.
(g) If I ***don't eat*** breakfast tomorrow morning, I ***will get*** hungry during class.	In (g) and (h): The simple future is used in the result clause when the sentence concerns a particular activity or situation in the future.
(h) If the weather ***is*** nice tomorrow, we ***will go*** on a picnic.	Note: The simple present, not the simple future, is used in the "***if*** clause."

10-3 UNTRUE (CONTRARY TO FACT) IN THE PRESENT/FUTURE

(i) If I **taught** this class, I **wouldn't give** tests.	In (i): In truth, I don't teach this class.
(j) If he **were** here right now, he **would help** us.	In (j): In truth, he is not here right now.
(k) If I **were** you, I **would accept** their invitation.	In (k): In truth, I am not you. Note: **Were** is used for both singular and plural subjects. **Was** (with *I, he, she, it*) is sometimes used in very informal speech but is not generally considered grammatically acceptable.

☐ **EXERCISE 1:** Complete the sentences with the verbs in parentheses.

1. If I have enough apples, I (*bake*) _____*will bake*_____ an apple pie this afternoon.

2. If I had enough apples, I (*bake*) _____ an apple pie this afternoon.

3. I will fix your bicycle if I (*have*) _____ a screwdriver of the proper size.

4. I would fix your bicycle if I (*have*) _____ a screwdriver of the proper size.

5. I (*make*) _____ a tomato salad for the picnic tomorrow if the tomatoes in my garden are ripe.

6. I (*make*) _____ a tomato salad for the picnic tomorrow if the tomatoes in my garden were ripe.

7. Jack would shave today if he (*have*) _____ a sharp razor.

8. Jack will shave today if he (*have*) _____ a sharp razor.

9. Sally always answers the phone if she (*be*) _____ in her office.

10. Sally would answer the phone if she (*be*) _____ in her office right now.

11. I (*not be*) _____ a student in this class if English (*be*) _____ my native language.

10–4 UNTRUE (CONTRARY TO FACT) IN THE PAST

(1) If you **had told** me about the problem, I **would have helped** you.	In (1): In truth, you did not tell me about it.
(m) If they **had studied**, they **would have passed** the exam.	In (m): In truth, they did not study. They failed the exam.
(n) If I **hadn't slipped** on the ice, **I wouldn't have broken** my arm.	In (n): In truth, I slipped on the ice. I broke my arm.
	Note: The auxiliary verbs are almost always contracted in speech. "If you'd told me, I would've helped you (OR: I'd've helped you)."

□ **EXERCISE 2:** Complete the sentences with the verbs in parentheses.

1. If I (*have*) _____ enough money, I will go with you.

2. If I (*have*) _____ enough money, I would go with you.

3. If I (*have*) _____ enough money, I would have gone with you.

4. If the weather is nice tomorrow, we (*go*) _____ to the zoo.

5. If the weather were nice today, we (*go*) _____ to the zoo.

6. If the weather had been nice yesterday, we (*go*) _____ to the zoo.

7. If Sally (*be*) _____ at home tomorrow, I am going to visit her.

8. Jim isn't home right now. If he (*be*) _____ at home right now, I (*visit*) _____ him.

9. Linda wasn't at home yesterday. If she (*be*) _____ at home yesterday, I (*visit*) _____ her.

□ **EXERCISE 3:** Complete the sentences with the verbs in parentheses.

1. It's too bad Helen isn't here. If she (*be*) _____ here, she (*know*) _____ what to do.

2. Fred failed the test because he didn't study. However, if he (*study*) _____ for the test, he (*pass*) _____ it.

3. An aerosol spray can will explode if you (*throw*) _____ it into a fire.

4. You should tell your father exactly what happened. If I (*be*) _____ you, I (*tell*) _____ him the truth as soon as possible.

5. If I (*have*) _____ my camera with me yesterday, I (*take*) _____ a picture of Alex standing on his head.

6. I'm almost ready to plant my garden. I have a lot of seeds. Maybe I have more than I need. If I (*have*) _____ more seeds than I need, I (*give*) _____ some to Nellie.

7. I got wet because I didn't take my umbrella. However, I (*get, not*) _____ wet if I (*remember*) _____ to take my umbrella with me yesterday.

8. I (*change*) _____ the present economic policy if I (*be*) _____ the President of the United States.

9. If the teacher (*be*) _____ absent tomorrow, class will be cancelled.

10. George has only two pairs of socks. If he (*have*) _____ more than two pairs of socks, he (*have to, not*) _____ wash his socks so often.

11. That sounds like a good job offer. If I (*be*) _____ you, I (*accept*) _____ it.

12. The cowboy pulled his gun to shoot at the rattlesnake, but he was too late. If he (*be*) _____ quicker to pull the trigger, the snake (*bite, not*) _____ him on the ankle. It's a good thing he was wearing heavy leather boots.

☐ **EXERCISE 4:** Supply the appropriate auxiliary verb.

1. I don't have a pen, but if I _____*did*_____, I would lend it to you.

2. He is busy right now, but if he _____*weren't*_____, he would help us.

3. I didn't vote in the last election, but if I _____*had*_____, I would have voted for Senator Anderson.

4. I don't have enough money, but if I _____, I would buy that book.

5. The weather is cold today, but if it _____, I would go swimming.

6. She didn't come, but if she _____, she would have met my brother.

7. I'm not a good cook, but if I _____, I would make all of my own meals.

8. I have to go to class this afternoon, but if I _____, I would go downtown with you.

9. He didn't go to a doctor, but if he _____, the cut on his hand wouldn't have gotten infected.

10. I always pay my bills. If I _____, I would get in a lot of trouble.

11. Helium is lighter than air. If it _____, a helium-filled balloon wouldn't float upward.

12. I called my husband to tell him I would be late. If I _____, he would have gotten worried about me.

☐ **EXERCISE 5—ORAL (BOOKS CLOSED):** Answer each question. Begin with ''No, but . . . .''

Example: Do you have a dollar?
Response: No, but if I did (No, but if I had a dollar), I would lend it to you.

1. Are you rich?
2. Do you have a car?
3. Are you a bird?
4. Are you in (*student's country/ hometown*)?
5. Do you live in an apartment? Dormitory? Hotel?
6. Are you the teacher of this class?
7. Do you have your own airplane?
8. Are you (*the President of the United States*)?
9. Are you tired?
10. Are you at home right now?
11. Are you married? Single?
12. Do you speak (*another language*)?
13. Is the weather hot/cold today?
14. Are you hungry?
15. Do you live in (*New York City*)?

□ **EXERCISE 6—ORAL (BOOKS CLOSED):** Begin your response with "But if I had known . . . ."

Example: There was a test yesterday. You didn't know that, so you didn't study.

Response: But if I had known (that there was a test yesterday), I would have studied.

1. Your friend was in the hospital. You didn't know that, so you didn't visit her.
2. I've never met your friend. You didn't know that, so you didn't introduce me.
3. There was a party last night. You didn't know that, so you didn't go.
4. Your friend's parents are in town. You didn't know that, so you didn't invite them to dinner.
5. I wanted to go to the soccer game. You didn't know that, so you didn't buy another ticket.
6. I was at home last night. You didn't know that, so you didn't visit me.
7. Your sister wanted a gold necklace for her birthday. You didn't know that, so you didn't buy her one.
8. I had a problem. You didn't know that, so you didn't offer to help.

□ **EXERCISE 7:** Change the following statements into conditional sentences.

1. I didn't buy it because I didn't have enough money. But . . . *I would have bought it if I'd had enough money.*
2. I won't buy it because I don't have enough money. But . . . .
3. You got into so much trouble because you didn't listen to me. But . . . .
4. The woman didn't die because she received immediate medical attention. But . . . .
5. Jack came, so I wasn't disappointed. But . . . .
6. Ann didn't pass the entrance examination, so she wasn't admitted to the university. But . . . .
7. We ran out of gas because we didn't stop at the service station. But . . . .
8. There are so many bugs in the room because there isn't a screen on the window. But . . . .

10–5 USING PROGRESSIVE VERB FORMS

Notice the use of progressive verb forms in the following examples. Even in conditional sentences, progressive verb forms are used in progressive situations. (See Chart 1-2 for a discussion of progressive verbs.)

(a) TRUE:	It *is raining* right now, so I *will not go* for a walk.
(b) CONDITIONAL:	If it *were not raining* right now, I *would go* for a walk.
(c) TRUE:	I *am not living* in Chile. I *am not working* at a bank.
(d) CONDITIONAL:	If I *were living* in Chile, I *would be working* at a bank.
(e) TRUE:	It *was raining* yesterday afternoon, so I *did not go* for a walk.
(f) CONDITIONAL:	If it *had not been raining*, I *would have gone* for a walk.
(g) TRUE:	I *was not living* in Chile last year. I *was not working* at a bank.
(h) CONDITIONAL:	If I *had been living* in Chile last year, I *would have been working* at a bank.

☐ **EXERCISE 8:** Change the following statements into conditional sentences.

1. It is snowing, so I won't go with you. But . . . *if it weren't snowing, I would go with you.*
2. The child is crying because his mother isn't here. But . . . .
3. You weren't listening, so you didn't understand the directions. But . . . .
4. Joe got a ticket because he was driving too fast. But . . . .
5. I was listening to the radio, so I heard the news bulletin. But . . . .
6. Grandpa is not wearing his hearing aid because it's broken. But . . . .
7. You were sleeping, so I didn't tell you the news as soon as I heard it. But . . . .
8. I'm enjoying myself, so I won't leave. But . . . .

10–6 USING "MIXED TIME" IN CONDITIONAL SENTENCES

Frequently the time in the "*if* clause" and the time in the "result clause" are different: One clause may be in the present and the other in the past. Notice that past and present times are mixed in the sentences in the following examples.

(a) TRUE:	I *did not eat* breakfast several hours ago, so I *am* hungry now.
(b) CONDITIONAL:	If I *had eaten* breakfast several hours ago, I *would not be* hungry now. *(past)* *(present)*
(c) TRUE:	He *is not* a good student. He *did not study* for the test yesterday.
(d) CONDITIONAL:	If he *were* a good student, he *would have studied* for the test. *(present)* *(past)*

□ **EXERCISE 9:** Change the following statements into conditional sentences.

1. I'm hungry now because I didn't eat dinner. But . . . *if I'd eaten dinner, I wouldn't be hungry now.*
2. The room is full of flies because you left the door open. But . . . .
3. You are tired this morning because you didn't go to bed at a reasonable hour last night. But . . . .
4. I didn't finish my report yesterday, so I can't begin a new project today. But . . . .
5. Helen is sick because she didn't follow the doctor's orders. But . . . .
6. I'm not you, so I didn't tell him the truth. But . . . .
7. I don't know anything about plumbing, so I didn't fix the leak in the sink myself. But . . . .
8. I received a good job offer from the oil company, so I won't seriously consider taking the job with the electronics firm. But . . . .

10–7   USING *COULD*, *MIGHT*, AND *SHOULD*

(a) If I *were* a bird, I **could fly** home.	In (a): **could fly** = *would be able to fly*
(b) If I **could sing** as well as you, I *would join* the opera.	In (b): **could sing** = *were able to sing*
(c) If I'*d had* enough money, I **could have gone** to Florida for vacation.	In (c): **could have gone** = *would have been able to go*
(d) If I *don't get* a scholarship, I **might get** a job instead of going to graduate school next fall.	In (d): **I might get** = *maybe I will get*
(e) If you *were* a better student, you **might get** better grades.	In (e): **you might get** = *maybe you would get*
(f) If you *had told* me about your problem, I **might have been** able to help you.	In (f): **I might have been** = *maybe I would have been*
(g) If John **should call**, *tell* him I'll be back around five.	In (g): **If John should call** indicates a little more uncertainty or doubt than **If John calls**, but the meaning of the two is basically the same.
(h) If there **should be** another world war, the continued existence of the human race *would be* in jeopardy.	In (h): **If there should be** indicates more uncertainty or doubt than **If there were**.

□ **EXERCISE 10:** Complete the following.

1. I could go ____*to Arizona over vacation if I had enough time.*____

2. I could buy _____

3. I would buy _____

4. I could have bought _____

5. I would have bought _____

6. If I could speak _____

7. You might have passed the test _____

8. If you should need to get in touch with me later _____

9. If it should rain tomorrow _____

10. I could have finished my work on time _____

10-8 OMITTING *IF*

(a) **Were I** you, I wouldn't do that. (b) **Had I known**, I would have told you. (c) **Should anyone call**, please take a message.	With **were**, **had** (past perfect), and **should**, sometimes *if* is omitted and the subject and verb are inverted. In (a): **Were I you** = *If I were you* In (b): **Had I known** = *If I had known* In (c): **Should anyone call** = *If anyone should call*

☐ **EXERCISE 11:** Give sentences with the same meaning by omitting *if* from the conditional sentences.

1. The other team committed a foul, but the referee didn't see it. If the referee had seen it, our team would have won the game.
   → *Had the referee seen it, our team would have won the game.*

2. Your boss sounds like a real tyrant. If I were you, I would look for another job.

3. You really should learn how to use a computer. If you had used a computer, you could have finished the work in half the time.

4. I'll be out of my office until 2:00. If you should need to reach me, I'll be in the conference room.

5. The factory was on the verge of bankruptcy. If it had gone out of business, hundreds of people would have lost their livelihood.

6. We would have won the game if Thompson had caught the ball.

7. If Thompson had not dropped the ball, we would have won the game.*

8. The artists and creative thinkers throughout the history of the world have changed all of our lives. If they had not dared to be different, the history of civilization would have to be rewritten.

---

*In the negative, *not* follows the subject. It is not contracted with the auxiliary verb:
CORRECT: *Had I not seen* it with my own eyes, I wouldn't have believed it.
INCORRECT: *Hadn't I seen* it with my own eyes, ...

9. If there should be a global nuclear war, some scientists predict that life on earth as we know it would end forever.

10. If Tom had told the truth about his educational background, he probably wouldn't have gotten the job with the accounting firm. I suspect his boss will figure it out and fire him one of these days.

11. I know you're getting discouraged and are planning to drop out of school. However, if you were to finish your education, many more career opportunities would be open to you.

12. I'm glad I went to the meeting. If I hadn't been there, my proposal probably would not have been accepted.

10–9 IMPLIED CONDITIONS

(a) I **would have gone** with you, but I had to study. (*Implied condition*: . . . **if I hadn't had to study**) (b) I never **would have succeeded** without your help. (*Implied condition*: . . . **if you hadn't helped me**)	Often the "*if* clause" is implied, not stated. Conditional verbs are still used in the "result clause."
(c) She ran; *otherwise*, she **would have missed** her bus.	Conditional verbs are frequently used following ***otherwise***. In (c), the implied "*if* clause" is: *If she had not run.* . . .

□ **EXERCISE 12:** Give sentences with the same meaning by using "*if* clauses."

1. I would have visited you, but I didn't know that you were at home.
    → *I would have visited you if I had known you were at home.*

2. It wouldn't have been a good meeting without Rosa.
    → *It wouldn't have been a good meeting if Rosa hadn't been there.*

3. I would have answered the phone, but I didn't hear it ring.

4. I couldn't have finished the work without your help.

5. I like to travel. I would have gone to Nepal last summer, but I didn't have enough money.

6. I stepped on the brakes. Otherwise, I would have hit the child on the bicycle.

7. Cathy turned down the volume on the tape player. Otherwise, the neighbors probably would have called to complain about the noise.

8. Jack would have finished his education, but he had to quit school and find a job in order to support his family.

☐ **EXERCISE 13:** Complete the sentences with the verbs in parentheses. Some of the verbs are passive.

1. If I could speak Japanese, I (*spend*) _____ next year studying in Japan.

2. Had I known Mr. Jung was in the hospital, I (*send*) _____ him a note and some flowers.

3. We will move into our new house next month if it (*complete*) _____ _____ by then.

4. How old (*be, you*) _____ now if you (*be*) _____ _____ born in the year 1900?

5. It's too bad that it's snowing. If it (*snow, not*) _____, we could go for a drive.

6. I was very tired. Otherwise, I (*go*) _____ to the party with you last night.

7. I'm broke, but I (*have*) _____ plenty of money now if I (*spend, not*) _____ so much yesterday.

8. That child had a narrow escape. She (*hit*) _____ by a car if her father (*pull, not*) _____ her out of the street.

9. I'm glad I have so many friends and such a wonderful family. Life without any friends or family (*be*) _____ lonely for me.

10. My grandfather is no longer alive, but if he (*be*) _____, I'm sure he (*be*) _____ proud of me.

11. If you (*sleep, not*) _____ last night when we arrived, I would have asked you to go with us, but I didn't want to wake you up.

12. Bill has such a bad memory that he (*forget*) _____ his head if it (*be, not*) _____ attached to his body.

13. According to one report, the average hen lays 247 eggs a year, and the average person eats 255 eggs a year. If hens (*outnumber, not*) _____ _____ people, the average person (*eat, not*) _____ _____ 255 eggs a year.

□ **EXERCISE 14:** Complete the sentences with the verbs in parentheses.

1. A: What would you be doing right now if you (*be, not*) _____ in class?

   B: I (*sleep*) _____.

2. A: Why were you late for the meeting?

   B: Well, I (*be*) _____ there on time, but I had a flat tire on the way.

3. A: How did you get to work this morning?

   B: I drove. I (*take*) _____ the bus, but I overslept.

4. A: Did you know that Bob got 100% on the test?

   B: Really? That surprises me. If I didn't know better, I (*think*) _____ _____ he cheated.

5. A: Boy, is it ever hot today!

   B: You said it! If there (*be*) _____ only a breeze, it (*be, not*) _____ quite so unbearable.

6. A: Why isn't Peggy Adams in class today?

   B: I don't know, but I'm sure she (*be, not*) _____ absent unless* she (*have*) _____ a good reason.

7. A: When did Mark graduate?

   B: He didn't.

   A: Oh?

   B: He had to quit school because of some trouble at home. Otherwise, he (*graduate*) _____ last June.

_____
*****unless** = **if not** (see Chart 9-7).

358 □ CHAPTER 10

8. A: Hi, sorry I'm late.

   B: That's okay.

   A: I *(be)* _____ here sooner, but I had car trouble.

9. A: Want to ride on the roller coaster?

   B: No way! I *(ride, not)* _____ on the roller coaster even if you paid me a million dollars!

10. A: Hi, Pat. Come on in.

    B: Oh, I didn't know you had company. I *(come, not)* _____ _____ *(know, I)* _____ someone was here.

    A: That's okay. Come on and let me introduce you to my friends.

11. A: How did you do on the test?

    B: Not so well. I *(do)* _____ much better, but I misread the directions for the last section.

12. A: Do you really mean it?

    B: Of course! I *(say, not)* _____ it unless I *(mean)* _____ it.

13. A: Are you coming to the party?

    B: I don't think so, but if I change my mind, I *(tell)* _____ you.

14. A: I hear Dorothy had an accident. Was it serious?

B: No. Luckily, she wasn't driving fast at the time of the accident. If she

(*drive*) _____ fast, I'm sure it (*be*) _____

_____ a more serious accident.

☐ **EXERCISE 15:** Complete the following. Add commas where necessary.

1. If it hadn't rained _____

2. If it weren't raining _____

3. You would have passed the test had _____

4. It's a good thing we took a map with us. Otherwise _____

_____

5. Without electricity modern life _____

6. If you hadn't reminded me about the meeting tonight _____

7. Should you need any help _____

8. If I could choose any profession I wanted _____

9. If I were at home right now _____

10. Without your help yesterday _____

11. Were I you _____

12. What would you do if _____

13. If I had the chance to live my life over again _____

14. Had I known _____

15. Can you imagine what life would be like if _____

☐ **EXERCISE 16—ORAL (BOOKS CLOSED):** Answer the questions.

Example: Suppose the student sitting next to you drops his/her pen. What
would you do?

Response: I would pick it up for him/her.

1. Suppose (pretend) there is a fire in this building right now. What would
you do?

2. Suppose there is a fire in your room or apartment or house. You have
time to save only one thing. What would you save?

3. Suppose you go to the bank to cash a check for twenty dollars. The bank
teller cashes your check and you leave, but when you count the money,
you find she gave you thirty dollars instead of twenty. What would you
do?

4. Same situation, but she gave you only fifteen dollars instead of twenty.

5. John was cheating during an examination. The teacher saw him. Suppose you were the teacher. What would you have done?

6. You go to a party. A man starts talking to you, but he is speaking so fast that you can't catch what he is saying. What would you do?

7. Late at night you're driving your car down a deserted street. You're all alone. In an attempt to avoid a dog in the road, you swerve to one side and hit a parked car. You know that no one saw you. What would you do?

8. Mary goes to a friend's house for dinner. Her friend serves a dish that Mary can't stand, doesn't like at all. What if you were Mary?

9. My friend John borrowed ten dollars from me and told me he would repay it in a couple of days, but it's been three weeks. I think he has forgotten about it. I really need the money, but I don't want to ask him for it. Give me some advice.

10. John was driving over the speed limit. A police car began to chase him, with red lights flashing. John stepped on the accelerator and tried to escape the police car. Put yourself in his position.

11. You are walking down the street and suddenly a large dog jumps in front of you. The dog doesn't look friendly. He is growling and moving toward you. If that happened . . . .

12. Suppose you are walking down the street at night all by yourself. A man suddenly appears in front of you. He has a gun. He says, "Give me your money." Would you try to take his gun away?

13. Suppose you go to (*Chicago*) to visit a friend. You have never been there before. Your friend said he would meet you at the airport, but he's not there. You wait for a long time, but he never shows up. You try to call him, but nobody answers the phone. Now what?

14. You are just falling asleep when you hear a burglar opening your bedroom window and climbing in. What would you do?

15. You ask a very special person to go to dinner with you. You like this person very much and want to make a good impression. You go to a fancy restaurant and have a wonderful meal. But when you reach for your wallet, you discover that it is not there. You have no money with you.

☐ **EXERCISE 17—WRITTEN:** Following are topics for writing.

1. If, beginning tomorrow, you had a two-week holiday and unlimited funds, what would you do? Why?

2. If you had to teach your language to a person who knew nothing about your language at all, how would you begin? What would you do so that this person could learn your language as quickly and easily as possible?

3. If you were Philosopher-King of the world, how would you govern? What would you do? What changes would you make? (A "Philosopher-King" may be defined as a person who has ideal wisdom and unlimited power to shape the world as s/he wishes.)

4. Suppose you had only one year to live. What would you do?

5. Describe your activities if you were in some other place (in this country or in the world) at present. Describe your probable activities today, yesterday, and tomorrow. Include the activities of other people you would be with if you were in this place.

10–10   VERB FORMS FOLLOWING *WISH*

	VERB FORM IN "TRUE" SENTENCE	VERB FORM FOLLOWING *WISH*	
A wish about the future	(a) She **will not tell** me. (b) He **isn't going to be** here. (c) She **can't come** tomorrow.	I *wish* (that) she **would tell** me. I *wish* he **were going to be** here. I *wish* she **could come** tomorrow.	**Wish** is used when the speaker wants reality to be different, to be exactly the opposite. Verb forms similar to those in conditional sentences are used. Notice the examples.
A wish about the present	(d) I **don't know** French. (e) It **is raining** right now. (f) I **can't speak** Japanese.	I *wish* I **knew** French. I *wish* it **weren't raining** right now. I *wish* I **could speak** Japanese.	
A wish about the past	(g) John **didn't come**. (h) Mary **couldn't come**.	I *wish* John **had come**.* I *wish* Mary **could have come**.	**Wish** is followed by a noun clause. The use of **that** is optional. Usually it is omitted in speaking.

*Sometimes in very informal speaking: *I wish John **would have come**.*

☐ **EXERCISE 18:** Supply appropriate completions in the following.

1. Our classroom doesn't have any windows. I wish our classroom

   _____ windows.

2. The sun isn't shining. I wish the sun _____ right now.

3. I didn't go shopping. I wish I _____ shopping.

4. I don't know how to dance. I wish I _____ how to dance.

5. You didn't tell them about it. I wish you _____ them

   about it.

6. It's cold today. I'm not wearing a coat. I wish I _____ a

   coat.

7. I don't have enough money to buy that book. I wish I _____

   enough money.

8. Martha is tired because she went to bed late last night. She wishes she _____ to bed earlier last night.

9. I can't go with you. I wish I _____ with you tomorrow.

10. My friend won't lend me his car. I wish he _____ me his car for my date tomorrow night.

11. Patricia isn't coming to dinner with us tonight. I wish she _____ _____ to dinner with us.

12. The teacher is going to give an exam tomorrow. I wish he _____ _____ us an exam tomorrow.

13. You can't meet my parents. I wish you _____ them.

14. Jerry didn't come to the meeting. I wish he _____ to the meeting.

15. I am not lying on a beach in Hawaii. I wish I _____ on a beach in Hawaii.

☐ **EXERCISE 19:** Supply an appropriate auxiliary in the following.

1. I'm not at home, but I wish I _____*were*_____.

2. I don't know her, but I wish I _____*did*_____.

3. I can't sing well, but I wish I _____*could*_____.

4. I didn't go, but I wish I _____*had*_____.

5. He won't talk about it, but I wish he _____*would*_____.

6. I didn't read that book, but I wish I _____.

7. I want to go, but I can't. I wish I _____.

8. I don't have a bicycle, but I wish I _____.

9. He didn't buy a ticket to the game, but he wishes he _____.

10. She can't speak English, but she wishes she _____.

11. It probably won't happen, but I wish it _____.

12. He isn't old enough to drive a car, but he wishes he _____.

13. They didn't go to the movie, but they wish they _____.

14. I don't have a driver's license, but I wish I _____.

15. I'm not living in an apartment, but I wish I _____.

10-11 USING *WOULD* TO MAKE WISHES ABOUT THE FUTURE

(a) It is raining. I *wish* it **would stop**. (*I want it to stop raining.*) (b) I'm expecting a call. I *wish* the phone **would ring**. (*I want the phone to ring.*)	**Would** is usually used to indicate that the speaker *wants* something to happen in the future. The wish may or may not come true (be realized).
(c) It's going to be a good party. I *wish* you **would come**. (*I want you to come.*) (d) We're going to be late. I *wish* you **would hurry**. (*I want you to hurry.*)	In (c) and (d): **I *wish* you *would*** . . . is often used to make a request.

☐ **EXERCISE 20:** Give the appropriate form of the verbs in parentheses to make wishes about the future.

1. Are you sure you won't be able to come with us? I wish you (*change*)

   _____ your mind.

2. Bob's mother doesn't like his beard. She wishes he (*shave*) _____

   _____ it off.

3. He needs some money. He wishes his parents (*send*) _____

   _____ him some.

4. The newspaper strike has been going on for two weeks. I wish it (*end*)

   _____.

5. My roommate is very messy. I wish she (*pick*) _____ up

   after herself more often.

☐ **EXERCISE 21:** Supply an appropriate form.

1. We need some help. I wish Alfred (*be*) _____ here now. If

   he (*be*) _____, we could finish this work very quickly.

2. We had a good time in Houston over vacation. I wish you (*come*) _____

   _____ with us. If you (*come*) _____ with

   us, you (*have*) _____ a good time.

3. I wish it (*be, not*) _____ so cold today. If it (*be, not*)

   _____ so cold, I (*go*) _____ swimming.

4. I missed part of the lecture because I was daydreaming, and now my

   notes are incomplete. I wish I (*pay*) _____ more attention

   to the lecturer.

5. A: Do you have enough money to buy that antique lamp?

   B: No, but I certainly wish I _____ .

6. A: Did you study for the test?

   B: No, but now I wish I _____ because I flunked it.

7. A: Is the noise from the record player in the next apartment bothering you?

   B: Yes. I'm trying to study. I wish he (*turn*) _____ it down.

8. A: What a beautiful day! I wish I (*lie*) _____ in the sun by a swimming pool instead of sitting in a classroom.

   B: I wish I (*be*) _____ anywhere but here!

9. A: I can't go to the game with you this afternoon.

   B: Really? That's too bad. But I wish you (*tell*) _____ me sooner so that I could have found someone else to go with.

10. A: How long have you been sick?

    B: For over a week.

    A: I wish you (*go*) _____ to see a doctor today. You should find out what's wrong with you.

    B: Maybe I'll go tomorrow.

11. A: I wish we (*have, not*) _____ to go to class today.

    B: So do I. I wish it (*be*) _____ a holiday.

12. A: He couldn't have said that! That's impossible. You must have misunderstood him.

    B: I only wish I _____, but I'm sure I heard him correctly.

☐ EXERCISE 22—ORAL (BOOKS CLOSED): Answer the questions. Use *wish*.

1. Where do you wish you were right now? What do you wish you were doing?
2. Are you pleased with the weather today, or do you wish it were different?
3. Look around this room. What do you wish were different?
4. Is there anything you wish were different about the place you are living?
5. What do you wish were different about this city/town?

6. What do you wish were different about this country?

7. What do you wish were different about a student's life? about a worker's life?

8. Just for fun, what do you wish were or could be different in the world? What about animals being able to speak? People being able to fly? There being only one language in the world? Being able to take vacations on the moon? Speed of transportation?

9. Where do you wish you could go on your next vacation?

10. Your friend gave you his phone number, but you didn't write it down because you thought you would remember it. Now you have forgotten the number. What do you wish?

11. John kept all of his money in his wallet instead of putting it in the bank. Then he lost his wallet. What does he probably wish?

12. You didn't eat breakfast/lunch/dinner before you came to class. Now you are hungry. What do you wish?

13. Mary stayed up very late last night. Today she is tired and sleepy. What does she probably wish?

14. Is there anything in your past life that you would change? What do you wish you had or had not done?

10–12 USING *AS IF/AS THOUGH*

(a) It looks *like* rain.	Notice in (a): *like* is followed by a noun object.
(b) It looks *as if* it is going to rain.	Notice in (b) and (c): *as if* and *as though* are followed by a clause.
(c) It looks *as though* it is going to rain.	
(d) It looks *like* it is going to rain. (informal)	Notice in (d): *like* is followed by a clause. This use of *like* is common in informal English but is not generally considered appropriate in formal English. *As if* or *as though* is preferred. (a), (b), (c), and (d) all have the same meaning.

"TRUE" STATEMENT	VERB FORM AFTER *AS IF/AS THOUGH*	
(e) He *is not* a child.	She talked to him *as if* he *were* a child.	Usually the idea following *as if/as though* is "untrue." In this case, verb usage is similar to that in conditional sentences. Notice the examples.
(f) She *did not take* a shower with her clothes on.	When she came in from the rainstorm, she looked *as if* she *had taken* a shower with her clothes on.	
(g) He *has met* her.	He acted *as though* he *had never met* her.	
(h) She *will be* here.	She spoke *as if* she *wouldn't be* here.	

☐ **EXERCISE 23:** Using the idea given in parentheses, complete each sentence with *as if/as though*.

1. (*I wasn't run over by a ten-ton truck.*)

    I feel terrible. I feel ___*as if (as though) I had been run over by a*___
    ___*ten-ton truck.*___

2. (*English is not her native tongue.*)

    She speaks English _____

3. (*His animals aren't people.*)

    I know a farmer who talks to his animals. _____

4. (*You didn't see a ghost.*)

    What's the matter? You look _____

5. (*His father is not a general in the army.*)

    Sometimes his father gives orders _____

6. (*I didn't climb Mt. Everest.*)

    When I reached the fourth floor, I was winded. I felt _____
    _____ instead of just three flights of
    stairs.

7. (*He does have a brain in his head.*)

    Sometimes he acts _____

8. (*We haven't known each other all of our lives.*)

    We became good friends almost immediately. After talking to each other

    for only a short time, we felt _____

9. (*A giant bulldozer didn't drive down Main Street.*)

    After the tornado, the town looked _____

10. (*I don't have wings and can't fly.*)

I was so happy that I felt _____

11. (*The child won't burst.*)

The child was so excited that he looked _____

12. *Note:* The following sentiments were expressed by Helen Keller, a woman who was both blind and deaf but who learned to speak and to read (Braille).

Use your eyes as if tomorrow you _____ become blind. Hear the music of voices, the song of a bird, as if you _____ become deaf tomorrow. Touch each object as if tomorrow you _____ never be able to feel anything again. Smell the perfume of flowers and taste with true enjoyment each bite of food as if tomorrow you _____ never be able to smell and taste again.

□ **EXERCISE 24:** General review of verb forms.

1. Some of the students (*speak, never*) _____ English before they came here last fall.

2. I wish I (*come, not*) _____ here last year.

3. It is essential that you (*be*) _____ here tomorrow.

4. Had I known Dan wouldn't be here, I (*come, not*)

_____.

5. My passport (*stamp*) _____ at the airport when I arrived.

6. My seventy-year-old grandfather, who owns his own business, (*continue, probably*) _____ to work as long as he (*live*)

_____.

7. I arrived here in September 1988. By September 1998, I (*be*) _____ _____ here for ten years.

8. Before (*go*) _____ to bed, I have to finish my homework.

9. (*Hear*) _____ that story many times before, I got bored when Jim began to tell it again.

10. Do you know that man (*sit*) _____ in the brown leather chair?

11. Many of the goods that (*produce*) _____ since the beginning of the twentieth century are totally machine-made.

12. The instructor said that she (*give*) _____ an exam next Friday.

13. I (*know*) _____ Beth for six years. When I (*meet*) _____ her, she (*work*) _____ in a law office.

14. If you (*be*) _____ here yesterday, you (*meet*) _____ my father and mother.

15. This evening the surface of the lake is completely still. It looks as if it (*make*) _____ of glass.

16. I don't know why the food service has to be so slow. We (*stand*) _____ here in the cafeteria line for over half an hour and there (*be*) _____ still a lot of people in front of us.

17. Sue says she can't come on the picnic with us. I wish she (*change*) _____ her mind and (*decide*) _____ to come with us.

18. My dog turned her head toward me and looked at me quizzically, almost as if she (*understand*) _____ what I said.

19. (*Be*) _____ an excellent researcher, Dr. Barnes (*respect*) _____ by the entire faculty.

20. Without the sun, life as we know it (*exist, not*) _____.

□ **EXERCISE 25:** General review of the verb forms.

1. Since (*come*) _____ to the United States six months ago, Maria (*learn*) _____ a lot of English.

2. Mrs. McKay (*give, already*) _____ birth to the child by the time her husband arrived at the hospital.

3. I recommended that he (*apply*) _____ to at least three universities.

4. Thank you for your help. I never (*be*) _____ able to finish this work without it.

5. Peggy told me she (*be*) _____ here at six tomorrow.

6. (*Sit*) _____ on a park bench and (*watch*) _____ the brightly colored leaves fall gently to the ground, he felt at peace with the world.

7. Why didn't you tell me about this before? I certainly wish I (*inform*) _____ earlier.

8. The large dormitory (*destroy, completely*) _____ _____ by fire last week. Since all of the students (*go*) _____ home for the holidays, there was no loss of life.

9. James blushed when his friend asked him an (*embarrass*) _____ _____ question.

10. Anna is grown up now. You shouldn't speak to her as if she (*be*) _____ _____ a child.

11. I asked all of the people (*invite*) _____ to the party to RSVP.

12. When the (*puzzle*) _____ student could not figure out the answer to the (*puzzle*) _____ problem, she demanded that I (*give*) _____ her the correct answer, but I insisted that she (*figure*) _____ it out for herself.

13. Ever since I can remember, mathematics (*be*) _____ my favorite subject.

14. The people (*work*) _____ to solve the problems of urban poverty are hopeful that many of these problems (*solve*) _____ within the next ten years.

15. It's a funny story. I'll tell you the details when I (*call*) _____ you tomorrow.

□ **EXERCISE 26:** Verb form review. The following is based on compositions written by students who were members of a multicultural class.

Next week, when I _____ _____ my final examinations, I
                    (*finish*)   (*take*)

_____ one of the best experiences I _____
(*finish, also*)   (*have, ever*)

_____ in my lifetime. In the last four months, I _____
                                                        (*learn*)

_____ more about foreign cultures than I _____
                                               (*anticipate*)

_____ before _____ to the United
                    (*come*)

States. _____ in a foreign country and _____
        (*Live*)   (*go*)

to school with people from various parts of the world _____
                                                          (*give*)

_____ me the opportunity _____
                                (*encounter*)

and _____ with people from different cultures. I
     (*interact*)

_____ to share some of my experiences and thoughts
(*like*)

with you.

When I first _____, I _____
              (*arrive*)   (*know*)

no one and I _____ all of my fingers _____
              (*need*)   (*communicate*)

_____ what I was trying to say in English. All of the

international students were in the same situation. When we _____
                                                            (*can, find, not*)

_____ the right word, we _____
                              (*use*)

strange movements and gestures _____ our meaning.
                                  (*communicate*)

_____ some common phrases, such as "How are you?"
(*Know*)

"Fine, thank you, and you?" and "What country are you from?", _____
                                                                (*be*)

_____ enough in the beginning for us _____
(make)

_____ friends with each other. The TV room in the

dormitory _____ our meeting place every evening after
(become)

dinner. _____ _____ our English,
(Hope)   (improve)

many of us tried to watch television and _____ what the
(understand)

people _____ on the screen _____
(appear)   (say)

_____, but for the most part their words were just a

strange mumble to us. After a while, _____ and a little
(bore)

sad, we slowly began to disappear to our rooms. I _____
(think)

that all of us _____ some homesickness. However,
(experience)

despite my loneliness, I had a good feeling within myself because I _____
(do)

_____ what I _____ to do for
(want)

many years: _____ and _____ in a
(live)   (study)

foreign country.

After a few days, classes _____ and we _____
(begin)   (have)

another meeting place: the classroom. _____ quite what
(Know, not)

_____ the first day of class, I was a bit nervous, but also
(expect)

_____. After _____ the right
(excite)   (find)

building and the right room, I walked in and _____ an
(choose)

empty seat. I _____ myself to the person _____
(introduce)   (sit)

_____ next to me, and we sat _____ for a few
(*talk*)

minutes. Since we _____ from different countries, we _____
(*be*)   (*speak*)

_____ in English. At first, I was afraid that the other

student _____ what I _____,
(*understand, not*)   (*say*)

but I _____ when she _____
(*surprise, pleasantly*)   (*respond*)

_____ to my questions easily. Together we _____
(*take*)

_____ the first steps toward _____ a friendship.
(*build*)

As the semester _____, I _____ out
(*progress*)   (*find*)

more and more about my fellow students. Students from some countries were

reticent and shy in class. They almost never _____ questions and
(*ask*)

_____ very softly. Others of different nationalities _____
(*speak*)   (*be*)

just the opposite: They spoke in booming voices and never _____
(*hesitate*)

_____ questions—and sometimes they _____
(*ask*)   (*interrupt, even*)

_____ the teacher. I _____ in a
(*be, never*)

classroom with such a mixture of cultures before. I learned _____
(*surprise, not*)

_____ by anything my classmates might say or do.

The time we spent _____ our ideas with each other and
(*share*)

_____ about each other's customs and beliefs _____
(*learn*)   (*be*)

valuable and fun. As we progressed in our English, we slowly learned about

each other, too.

Now, several months after my arrival in the United States, I _____

_____ (be)

able to understand not only some English but also something about different

cultures. If I _____ here, I _____
(come, not)   (be, not)

able to attain these insights into other cultures. I wish everyone in the world

_____ the same experience. Perhaps if all the people in
(have)

the world _____ more about cultures different from their own and
(know)

_____ the opportunity _____ friends with people
(have)   (make)

from different countries, peace _____ secure.
(be)

☐ **EXERCISE 27—WRITTEN:** Following are composition topics.

1. Summarize the major events that have occurred in your country and/or in the world in the past three or four months.

2. *For students who have been using this text in a multicultural class:*
   This class has given you the opportunity to meet and interact with students from countries other than your own. Describe your experiences and discuss any insights you might have made into other cultures.

3. *For students who have been using this text in a class where everyone has the same native language:*
   Discuss your experiences in this class, and give advice to people who are going to join this class in the future about how they can improve their English.

APPENDIX 1
Supplementary Grammar Units

UNIT A: Basic Grammar Terminology

A-1 SUBJECTS, VERBS, AND OBJECTS

S **V** (a) ***Birds*** ***fly.*** (NOUN) (VERB)	Almost all English sentences contain a subject (**S**) and a verb (**V**). The verb may or may not be followed by an object (**O**).
S **V** (b) The ***baby*** ***cried.*** (NOUN) (VERB)	**VERBS:** Verbs that are not followed by an object, as in (a) and (b), are called *intransitive verbs.* Common intransitive verbs: *agree, arrive, come, cry, exist, go, happen, live, occur, rain, rise, sleep, stay, walk.*
S **V** **O** (c) The ***student*** ***needs*** a ***pen.*** (NOUN) (VERB) (NOUN)	Verbs that are followed by an object, as in (c) and (d), are called *transitive verbs.* Common transitive verbs: *build, cut, find, like, make, need, send, use, want.*

S   **V**   **O**
(d) My ***friend***   ***enjoyed***   the   ***party.***
     (NOUN) (VERB)   (NOUN)
	Some verbs can be either intransitive or transitive.
	    intransitive: A student studies.
	    transitive: A student studies books.

	SUBJECTS AND OBJECTS: The subjects and objects of verbs are nouns (or pronouns). Examples of nouns: *person, place, thing, John, Asia, pen, information, appearance, amusement.*

A-2 PREPOSITIONS AND PREPOSITIONAL PHRASES

COMMON PREPOSITIONS				
about	before	despite	of	to
above	behind	down	off	toward(s)
across	below	during	on	under
after	beneath	for	out	until
against	beside	from	over	up
along	besides	in	since	upon
among	between	into	through	with
around	beyond	like	throughout	within
at	by	near	till	without

S   **V**   **PREP**   **O of PREP**
(a) The student studies *in the library*.
                                (NOUN)
 	
    S   **V**   **O**   **PREP**   **O of PREP**
(b) We enjoyed the party *at your house*.
                                 (NOUN)
	An important element of English sentences is the prepositional phrase. It consists of a preposition (**PREP**) and its object (**O**). The object of a preposition is a noun or pronoun. In (a): *in the library* is a prepositional phrase.

(c) We went *to the zoo* *in the afternoon*. (place) (time) (d) *In the afternoon*, we went to the zoo.	In (c): In most English sentences, "place" comes before "time." In (d): Sometimes a prepositional phrase comes at the beginning of a sentence.

□ **EXERCISE 1:** Find the subjects (**S**), verbs (**V**), objects (**O**), and prepositional phrases (**PP**) in the following sentences.

          S   **V**   **O**   **PP**

1. Jack put the letter in the mailbox.

2. The children walked to school.

3. Beethoven wrote nine symphonies.

4. Mary did her homework at the library.

5. Bells originated in Asia.

6. Chinese printers created the first paper money in the world.

A-3 ADJECTIVES

(a) Mary is an ***intelligent*** student.
            (ADJECTIVE) (NOUN)
(b) The ***hungry*** children ate fruit.
     (ADJECTIVE)(NOUN)
	Adjectives describe nouns. In grammar, we say that adjectives modify nouns. The word *modify* means "change a little." Adjectives give a little different meaning to a noun: *intelligent student, lazy student, good student.* Examples of adjectives: *young, old, rich, poor, beautiful, brown, French, modern.*

(c) I saw some ***beautiful*** pictures. *INCORRECT: beautifuls pictures*	An adjective is neither singular nor plural. A final *-s* is never added to an adjective.

A-4 ADVERBS

(a) He walks **quickly**.
        (ADVERB)
(b) She opened the door **quietly**.
                                (ADVERB)
	Adverbs modify verbs. Often they answer the question "*How?*"
	In (a): *How does he walk?* Answer: *Quickly.*
	Adverbs are often formed by adding **-ly** to an adjective.
	    adjective: **quick**
	    adverb: **quickly**

(c) I am **extremely** *happy*. (ADVERB) (ADJECTIVE)	Adverbs are also used to modify adjectives, i.e., to give information about adjectives, as in (c).
(d) Ann will come **tomorrow**. (ADVERB)	Adverbs are also used to express time or frequency. Examples: *tomorrow, today, yesterday, soon, never, usually, always, yet.*
MIDSENTENCE ADVERBS (e) Ann **always** *comes* on time. (f) Ann *is* **always** on time. (g) Ann *has* **always** *come* on time. (h) *Does she* **always** *come* on time?	Some adverbs may occur in the middle of a sentence. Midsentence adverbs have usual positions; they (1) come in front of simple present and simple past verbs (except **be**), as in (e); (2) follow **be** (simple present and simple past), as in (f); (3) come between a helping verb and a main verb, as in (g). In a question, a midsentence adverb comes directly after the subject, as in (h).

COMMON MIDSENTENCE ADVERBS
ever, always, usually, often, frequently, generally, sometimes, occasionally, seldom, rarely, hardly ever, never, not ever, already, finally, just, probably

☐ **EXERCISE 2:** Choose the correct word (*adjective* or *adverb*) in parentheses.

1. George is a (*careless, carelessly*) writer. He writes (*careless, carelessly*).
2. Frank asked me an (*easy, easily*) question. I answered it (*easy, easily*).
3. Sally speaks (*soft, softly*). She has a (*soft, softly*) voice.
4. I entered the classroom (*quiet, quietly*) because I was late.
5. Ali speaks English very (*good, well*). He has very (*good, well*) pronunciation.★

★The word **well** can be either an adverb or an adjective.
  (a) Don *writes well*. In (a): **well** = an adverb meaning "in a good manner." It describes how Don writes.
  (b) Mary was sick, but now she *is well*. In (b): **well** = an adjective meaning "healthy, not sick." It follows the verb **be** and describes the subject "she"; i.e., Mary is a *well person*, not a sick person.
NOTE: After the linking verb **feel**, either **good** or **well** may be used:
  (c) I *feel* **good**.
  (d) I *feel well*.
  (c) and (d) have essentially the same meaning. However, **well** usually refers specifically to health, whereas **good** can refer to one's physical and/or emotional condition.

□ **EXERCISE 3:** Identify the adjectives (**ADJ**) and adverbs (**ADV**) in the following sentences.

                                                 ADJ   **ADV**

1. Jack opened the heavy door slowly.
2. Chinese jewelers carved beautiful ornaments from jade.
3. The old man carves wooden figures skillfully.
4. A busy executive usually has short conversations on the telephone.
5. The young women had a very good time at the picnic yesterday.

□ **EXERCISE 4:** Put the adverb in parentheses in its usual midsentence position.

1. (*never*)   Erica has seen snow. → *Erica has never seen snow.*
2. (*often*)   Ted studies at the library in the evening.
3. (*often*)   Ann is at the library in the evening, too.
4. (*already*)   Fred has finished studying for tomorrow's test.
5. (*seldom*)   Jack is at home.
6. (*always*)   Does he stay there?
7. (*often*)   He goes into town to hang around with his buddies.
8. (*always*)   You should tell the truth.

A-5 THE VERB *BE*

(a) John *is*   **a student**.
     (BE)   (NOUN)
(b) John *is*   **intelligent**.
     (BE)   (ADJECTIVE)
(c) John *was* **at the library**.
     (BE) (PREP. PHRASE)
	A sentence with **be** as the main verb has three basic patterns:
	In (a): **be** + *a noun*
	In (b): **be** + *an adjective*
	In (c): **be** + *a prepositional phrase*

(d) Mary *is writing* a letter. (e) They *were listening* to some music. (f) That letter *was written* by Alice.	**Be** is also used as an auxiliary verb in progressive verb tenses and in the passive. In (d) *is* = *auxiliary*; **writing** = *main verb*

TENSE FORMS OF BE

	SIMPLE PRESENT	SIMPLE PAST	PRESENT PERFECT
	I am	*I was*	*I have been*
SINGULAR	*you are*	*you were*	*you have been*
	he, she, it is	*he, she, it was*	*he, she, it has been*
PLURAL	*we, you, they are*	*we, you, they were*	*we, you, they have been*

A-6 LINKING VERBS

(a) The soup *smells* *good*.
       (LINKING VERB) (ADJECTIVE)
 (b) This food *tastes delicious*.
 (c) The children *feel happy*.
 (d) The weather *became cold*.
	Other verbs like *be* that may be followed immediately by an adjective are called *linking verbs*. An adjective following a linking verb describes the subject of a sentence.★
	 Common verbs that may be followed by an adjective:
	     feel, look, smell, sound, taste
	     appear, seem
	     become (and *get, turn, grow* when they mean "become")

★COMPARE:
  (1) *The man looks angry.* → An adjective (*angry*) follows *look*. The adjective describes the subject (*the man*). **Look** has the meaning of "appear."
  (2) *The man looked at me angrily.* → An adverb (*angrily*) follows *look at*. The adverb describes the action of the verb. **Look at** has the meaning of "regard, watch."

☐ **EXERCISE 5:** Choose the correct form (*adjective* or *adverb*) in parentheses.

    1. This math problem looks (*easy, easily*). I'm sure I can do it (*easy, easily*).
    2. That chair looks (*comfortable, comfortably*).
    3. I looked at the problem (*careful, carefully*) and then solved it.
    4. I felt (*sad, sadly*) when I heard the news.
    5. Susan smiled (*cheerful, cheerfully*). She seemed (*cheerful, cheerfully*).
    6. I tasted the soup (*careful, carefully*) because it was hot. The soup tasted (*good, well*).
    7. The room got (*quiet, quietly*) when the professor entered. The students sat (*quiet, quietly*) at their desks.
    8. The sky grew (*dark, darkly*) as the storm approached.

A-7 PERSONAL PRONOUNS

	SINGULAR	PLURAL	

SUBJECT PRONOUNS	*I*
	 you
	 she, he, it
		we
		 you
		 they
			A pronoun is used in place of a noun. It refers to a noun. The noun it refers to is called the *antecedent*. *Examples:*
			     I read the **book**. **It** was good.
			 (The pronoun "it" refers to the antecedent noun "book.")
			     Mary said, "**I** drink tea."
			 (The pronoun "I" refers to the speaker, whose name is Mary.)

OBJECT PRONOUNS	*me* *you* *her, him, it*	*us* *you* *them*	

(continued)

POSSESSIVE PRONOUNS	*mine* *your* *hers, his*	*ours* *yours* *theirs*	Possessive pronouns are not followed immediately by a noun; they stand alone. *Example:* That book is **mine**. Those are **yours** over there.*
POSSESSIVE ADJECTIVES	*my* name *your* name *her, his, its* name	*our* names *your* names *their* names	Possessive adjectives are followed immediately by a noun; they do not stand alone. *Example:* **My** book is here. **Your** books are over there.

*Possessive nouns require apostrophes; e.g., That book is *Mary's*. (See Chart 5-3.) Possessive pronouns do NOT take apostrophes.
    CORRECT: That book is *hers*, and those books are *theirs*.
    INCORRECT: That book is *her's* and those books are *theirs'*.

☐ **EXERCISE 6**: Identify the pronouns and their antecedents in the following sentences.

    1. Jack has a part-time job. He works at a fast-food restaurant.

    (**he** = *a pronoun*; **Jack** = *the antecedent*)

    2. Many monkeys don't like water, but they can swim well when they have to.
    3. The teacher graded the students' papers last night. She returned them during class the next day.
    4. The cormorant is a diving bird. It can stay under water for a long time. In some countries, it is used by fishermen to catch fish for them.
    5. Tom took an apple with him to school. He ate it at lunch time.

☐ **EXERCISE 7**: Choose the correct word in parentheses.

    1. This is (*my, mine*) umbrella. (*Your, Yours*) umbrella is over there.
    2. This umbrella is (*my, mine*). The other one is (*your, yours*).
    3. Mary and Bob have (*their, theirs*) books. In other words, Mary has (*her, hers*) and Tom has his.
    4. A honeybee has two wings on each side of (*its, it's*) body.*
    5. (*Its, It's*) true that a homing pigeon will find (*its, it's*) way home even though it begins (*its, it's*) trip in unfamiliar territory.
    6. I have a pet. (*Its, It's*) name is Squeak. (*Its, It's*) a turtle. (*Its, It's*) been my pet for two years.

---

*COMPARE: **its** = a possessive adjective
         it's = a contraction of **it is** or **it has**

A-8 CONTRACTIONS

IN SPEAKING: In everyday spoken English, certain forms of *be* and auxiliary verbs are usually contracted with pronouns, nouns, and question words.

IN WRITING: (1) In written English, contractions with pronouns are common in informal writing, but not generally acceptable in formal writing.

(2) Contractions with nouns and question words are, for the most part, rarely used in writing. A few of these contractions may be found in quoted dialogue in stories or in very informal writing, such as a chatty letter to a good friend, but most of them are rarely if ever written.

In the following, quotation marks indicate that the contraction is frequently spoken but rarely if ever written.

	WITH PRONOUNS	WITH NOUNS	WITH QUESTION WORDS
am	*I'm* reading a book.	Ø	*"What'm"* I supposed to do?
is	*She's* studying. *It's* going to rain.	My *"book's"* on the table. *Mary's* at home.	*Where's* Sally? *Who's* that man?
are	*You're* working hard. *They're* waiting for us.	My *"books're"* on the table." The *"teachers're"* at a meeting.	*"What're"* you doing? *"Where're"* they going?
has	*She's* been here for a year. *It's* been cold lately.	My *"book's"* been stolen! *Sally's* never met him.	*Where's* Sally been living? *What's* been going on?"
have	*I've* finished my work. *They've* never met you.	The *"books've"* been sold. The *"students've"* finished the test."	*"Where've"* they been? *"How've"* you been?
had	*He'd* been waiting for us. *We'd* forgotten about it.	The *"books'd"* been sold. *"Mary'd"* never met him before.	*"Where'd"* you been before that? *"Who'd"* been there before you?
did	Ø	Ø	*"What'd"* you do last night? *"How'd"* you do on the test?
will	*I'll* come later. *She'll* help us.	The *"weather'll"* be nice tomorrow. *"John'll"* be coming soon.	*"Who'll"* be at the meeting? *"Where'll"* you be at ten?
would	*He'd* like to go there. *They'd* come if they could.	My *"friends'd"* come if they could. *"Mary'd"* like to go there, too.	*"Where'd"* you like to go?

☐ **EXERCISE 8—ORAL:** Read the sentences aloud. Practice usual contracted speech.

Example: The streets are wet. → "The streets're wet."

CONTRACTIONS WITH NOUNS:

1. My friend is here.
2. My friends are here.
3. Tom has been here since two.
4. The students have been here since one.
5. Bob had already left.
6. Bob would like to come with us.
7. Don will be here soon.
8. The window is open.
9. The windows are open.
10. Jane has never seen a ghost.
11. The boys have been there before.
12. Sally had forgotten her book.
13. Sally would forget her book if I didn't remind her to take it.

CONTRACTIONS WITH QUESTION WORDS:

14. Who is that woman?
15. Who are those people?
16. Who has been taking care of your house?
17. What have you been doing?
18. What had you been doing before that?
19. What would you like to do?
20. What did you do yesterday?
21. Why did you stay home?
22. When will I see you again?
23. How long will you be away?
24. Where am I supposed to go?
25. Where did you stay?

UNIT B: Questions

B-1 FORMS OF YES/NO AND INFORMATION QUESTIONS

A yes/no question	= a question that may be answered by *yes* or *no*.
	Yes/no question: Does he live in Chicago?
	Answer: Yes, he does. OR No, he doesn't.

An information question	= a question that asks for information by using a question word.
	Information question: Where does he live?
	Answer: In Chicago.

	QUESTION WORD	AUXILIARY VERB	SUBJECT	MAIN VERB		
(a) **She lives** there.		*Does*	she	*live*	there?	If the verb is in the simple present, use **does** (with *he, she, it*) or **do** (with *I, you, we, they*) in the question. If the verb is simple past, use **did**.
	Where	*does*	she	*live?*		
(b) **They live** there.		*Do*	they	*live*	there?	
	Where	*do*	they	*live?*		
(c) **He lived** there.		*Did*	he	*live*	there?	Notice: The main verb in the question is in its simple form; there is no final **-s** or **-ed**.
	Where	*did*	he	*live?*		
(d) **He is living** there.		*Is*	he	*living*	there?	If the verb has an auxiliary (a helping verb), the same auxiliary is used in the question. There is no change in the form of the main verb.
	Where	*is*	he	*living?*		
(e) **They have lived** there.		*Have*	they	*lived*	there?	
	Where	*have*	they	*lived?*		
(f) **Mary can live** there.		*Can*	Mary	*live*	there?	
	Where	*can*	Mary	*live?*		
(g) **He will be living** there.		*Will*	he	*be living*	there?	If the verb has more than one auxiliary, only the first auxiliary precedes the subject.
	Where	*will*	he	*be living?*		

(continued)

	QUESTION WORD	AUXILIARY VERB	SUBJECT	MAIN VERB		
(h) *John lives* there.	*Who*	∅	∅	*lives*	there?	If the question word is the subject, do not change the verb. Do not use *does*, *do*, or *did*.
(i) *Mary can come.*	*Who*	*can*	∅	*come?*		
(j) *They are* there.		*Are*	*they*		there?	*Be* in the simple present (*am*, *is*, *are*) and simple past (*was*, *were*) precedes the subject when *be* is the main verb.
	Where	*are*	*they?*			
(k) *Jim was* there.		*Was*	*Jim*		there?	
	Where	*was*	*Jim?*			

☐ **EXERCISE 9:** For each of the following, first make a yes/no question. Then make an information question using *where*.

> *Example:* They can stay there.
> 　　　　*Yes/no question:*　　Can they stay there?
> 　　　　*Information question:* Where can they stay?

1. She stays there.
2. She is staying there.
3. She will stay there.
4. She is going to stay there.
5. They stayed there.
6. They will be staying there.
7. They should stay there.
8. He has stayed there.
9. He has been staying there.
10. John is there.
11. John will be there.
12. John has been there.
13. Judy will have been there.
14. Ann and Tom were married there.
15. This package should have been taken there.

B-2 QUESTION WORDS

	QUESTION	ANSWER	
WHEN	(a) **When** did they arrive? **When** will you come?	Yesterday. Next Monday.	**When** is used to ask questions about *time*.
WHERE	(b) **Where** is she? **Where** can I find a pen?	At home. In that drawer.	**Where** is used to ask questions about *place*.
WHY	(c) **Why** did he leave early? **Why** aren't you coming with us?	Because he's ill. I'm tired.	**Why** is used to ask questions about *reason*.
HOW	(d) **How** did you come to school? **How** does he drive?	By bus. Carefully.	**How** generally asks about *manner*.
	(e) **How** *much* money does it cost? **How** *many* people came?	Ten dollars. Fifteen.	**How** is used with **much** and **many**.
	(f) **How** *old* are you? **How** *cold* is it? **How** *soon* can you get here? **How** *fast* were you driving?	Twelve. Ten below zero. In ten minutes. 50 miles an hour.	**How** is also used with adjectives and adverbs.
	(g) **How** *long* has he been here?	Two years.	**How** **long** asks about *length of time*.
	How *often* do you write home?	Every week.	**How** **often** asks about *frequency*.
	How *far* is it to Miami from here?	500 miles.	**How** **far** asks about *distance*.
WHO	(h) **Who** can answer that question? **Who** came to visit you?	I can. Jane and Eric.	**Who** is used as the subject of a question. It refers to people.
	(i) **Who** *is* coming to dinner tonight? **Who** *wants* to come with me?	Ann, Bob, and Al. We do.	**Who** is usually followed by a singular verb even if the speaker is asking about more than one person.
WHOM	(j) **Who(m)** did you see? **Who(m)** are you visiting? (k) **Who(m)** should I talk *to*? **To whom** should I talk? (*formal*)	I saw George. My relatives. The secretary.	**Whom** is used as the object of a verb or preposition. In spoken English, **whom** is rarely used; **who** is used instead. **Whom** is used only in formal questions. Note: **Whom**, not **who**, is used if preceded by a preposition.

(continued)

	QUESTION	ANSWER	
WHOSE	(1) **Whose book** did you borrow? **Whose key** is this? (**Whose** is this?)	David's. It's mine.	**Whose** asks questions about *possession*.
WHAT	(m) **What** made you angry? **What** went wrong?	His rudeness. Everything.	**What** is used as the subject of a question. It refers to "things."
	(n) **What** do you need? **What** did Alice buy? (o) **What** did he talk **about**? **About what** did he talk? (*formal*)	I need a pencil. A book. His vacation.	**What** is also used as an object.
	(p) **What kind of** soup is that? **What kind of** shoes did he buy?	It's bean soup. Sandals.	**What kind of** asks about the particular variety or type of something.
	(q) **What** did you **do** last night? **What** is Mary **doing**?	I studied. Reading a book.	**What** + *a form of* **do** is used to ask questions about activities.
	(r) **What countries** did you visit? **What time** did she come? **What color** is his hair?	Italy and Spain. Seven o'clock. Dark brown.	**What** may accompany a noun.
	(s) **What** is Ed *like*? (t) **What** *is* the weather *like*?	He's kind and friendly. Hot and humid.	**What** + **be like** asks for a general description of qualities.
	(u) **What** does Ed *look like*? (v) **What** does her house *look like*?	He's tall and has dark hair. It's a two-story, red brick house.	**What** + **look like** asks for a physical description.
WHICH	(w) I have two pens. **Which pen** do you want? **Which one** do you want? **Which** do you want? (x) **Which book** should I buy?	The blue one. That one.	**Which** is used instead of **what** when a question concerns choosing from a definite, known quantity or group.
	(y) **Which countries** did he visit? **What countries** did he visit? (z) **Which class** are you in? **What class** are you in?	Peru and Chile. This class.	In some cases, there is little difference in meaning between **which** and **what** when they accompany a noun, as in (y) and (z).

□ **EXERCISE 10:** Make questions from the following sentences. The words in parentheses should be the answer to your question.

1. I need (*five dollars*).
   → *How much money do you need?*
2. Roberto was born (*in Panama*).
3. I go out to eat (*at least once a week*).
4. I'm waiting for (*Maria*).
5. (*My sister*) answered the phone.
6. I called (*Benjamin*).
7. (*Benjamin*) called.
➤ 8. The boy has (*a ball*) in his pocket.*

9. "Deceitful" means ("*dishonest*").
10. An abyss is (*a bottomless hole*).
11. He went (*this*) way, (*not that way*).
12. These are (*Jim's*) books and papers.
13. They have (*four*) children.
14. He has been here (*for two hours*).
15. It is (*two hundred miles*) to New Orleans.

□ **EXERCISE 11:** Make questions from the following sentences. The words in parentheses should be the answer to your question.

1. She bought (*twelve gallons of gas*).
2. The doctor can see you (*at three on Friday*).
3. Her roommate is (*Jane Peters*).
4. Her roommates are (*Jane Peters and Sue Lee*).
5. My parents have been living there (*for three years*).
6. This is (*Alice's*) book.
7. (*The soap bubbles*) made her sneeze.
8. (*Fred and Jack*) are coming over for dinner.
9. Ann's dress is (*blue*).
10. Anne's eyes are (*brown*).
11. I was late (*because the traffic was heavy*).★★
12. (*Bob*) can't go on the picnic.
13. Bob can't go (*because he is sick*).
14. I didn't answer the phone (*because I didn't hear it ring*).

---

*A form of **do** is usually used in questions when the main verb is **have** (especially in American English but also commonly in British English); e.g., *Do you have a car?* Using **have** without a form of **do** is also possible but less common; e.g., *Have you a car?*
NOTE: Especially in British English but also in American English, the idiom **have got** is used to indicate possession instead of **have** alone; e.g., *Bob **has got** a car. **Have** you **got** a car?*

★★In informal spoken English, another way of asking **why** is **how come**. Usual question word order is not used with **how come**; instead, the subject comes in front of the verb.
    Example: John isn't here (*because he is sick*). → *Why isn't John here?*
                                        → *How come John isn't here?*

15. I like (*classical*) music.
16. I don't understand (*the chart on page 50*).
17. Janet is (*studying*) right now.
18. You spell "sitting" (*with two "t's." S-I-T-T-I-N-G*).
19. Tom (*is about medium height and has red hair and freckles*).
20. Tom is (*very serious and hardworking*).
21. Ron (*works as a civil engineer for the railroad company*).
22. Mexico is (*eight hundred miles*) from here.
23. I take my coffee (*black with sugar*).
24. Of Stockholm and Moscow, (*Stockholm*) is farther north.
25. (*Fine.*) I'm getting along (*just fine*).

□ **EXERCISE 12—ORAL (BOOKS CLOSED):** Make questions. Use question words.

Example: I bought a book.
Response: What did you buy?

1. It is fifty-five miles to (*Springfield*).
2. The fall semester begins on September 10th.
3. I bought the red pen, not the green one.
4. The secretary typed those letters.
5. I took four courses last semester.
6. "Rapid" means "fast."
7. (. . .) went to the library.
8. (. . .) telephoned me.
9. The post office is on Seventh Avenue.
10. It is three blocks to the post office.
11. I slept eight hours last night.
12. (. . .) gave a speech.
13. (. . .) talked about his/her country.
14. (. . .) talked about his/her family.
15. I need twenty-five dollars.
16. (. . .) lives on the fifth floor, not the fourth.
17. I will be in (*the United States*) for four years.
18. This is (. . .)'s pen.
19. I go to the library every day.
20. The next test is on Tuesday.
21. I have been studying English for ten years.
22. I laughed because (. . .) made a funny face.
23. (. . .) dropped his/her pen.
24. You should give that book to (. . .).
25. I didn't come to class yesterday because I wasn't feeling well.

□ **EXERCISE 13—ORAL (BOOKS CLOSED):** Make questions. Use question words.

1. I had a sandwich for lunch.
2. These are (. . .)'s books.
3. We are supposed to read Chapter Five, not Chapter Six.

4. I talked to (. . .).
5. I talked to (. . .) about the story in this morning's newspaper.
6. I fell asleep in class because I had only two hours of sleep last night.
7. That book belongs to (. . .).
8. "Request" means "ask."
9. It is 325 miles to (*Chicago*).
10. I can speak three languages.
11. (. . .) opened the window.
12. I didn't go to the party because I had to study.
13. I live in this house, not that one.
14. I hung my coat in the closet.
15. The letter is addressed to (. . .).
16. It took me three hours to finish my assignments.
17. Mr. Smith taught English in Japan.
18. You should be here at two o'clock.
19. I found (. . .)'s keys.
20. I visit my aunt and uncle twice a year.

B-3 NEGATIVE QUESTIONS

(a) ***Doesn't she live*** in the dormitory? (b) ***Does she not live*** in the dormitory? (*very formal*)	In a yes/no question in which the verb is negative, usually a contraction (e.g., *does + not = doesn't*) is used, as in (a). Example (b) is very formal and is usually not used in everyday speech. Negative questions are used to indicate the speaker's idea (i.e., what s/he believes is or is not true) or attitude (e.g., surprise, shock, annoyance, anger).
(c) Bob returns to his dorm room after his nine o'clock class. Dick, his roommate, is there. Bob is surprised. Bob says: "*What are you doing here?* ***Aren't you supposed to be in class now?***"	In (c): Bob believes that Dick is supposed to be in class now. *Expected answer:* **Yes.**
(d) Alice and Mary are at home. Mary is about to leave on a trip and Alice is going to take her to the airport. Alice says: "*It's already two o'clock. We'd better leave for the airport.* ***Doesn't your plane leave at three?***"	In (d): Alice believes that Mary's plane leaves at three. She is asking the negative question to make sure that her information is correct. *Expected answer:* **Yes.**
(e) The teacher is talking to Jim about a test he failed. The teacher is surprised that Jim failed the test because he usually does very well. The teacher says: "*What happened?* ***Didn't you study?***"	In (e): The teacher believes that Jim did not study. *Expected answer:* **No.**
(f) Barb and Don are riding in a car. Don is driving. He comes to a corner where there is a stop sign, but he does not stop the car. Barb is shocked. Barb says: "*What's the matter with you?* ***Didn't you see that stop sign?***"	In (f): Barb believes that Don did not see the stop sign. *Expected answer:* **No.**

☐ **EXERCISE 14:** Notice the examples in Chart B-3: Sometimes the expected answer to a negative question is *yes* and sometimes *no*. In the following dialogues, make negative questions from the words in parentheses and determine the expected response.

1. A: Why didn't you come to lunch with us? ___*Weren't you hungry?*___

    (*be hungry*)

    B: ___*No.*___ I had a late breakfast.

2. A: Did you give Linda my message when you went to class this morning?

    B: No. I didn't see her.

    A: Oh? _____ (*be in class*)

    B: _____ She didn't come today.

3. A: Do you see that woman over there, the one in the blue dress? _____

    _____ (*be Mrs. Robbins*)

    B: _____

    A: I thought so. I wonder what she is doing here.

4. A: It's almost dinner time and you haven't eaten since breakfast.

    _____ (*be hungry*)

    B: _____ I'm starving. Let's go eat.

5. A: You look tired this morning. _____

    (*sleep well last night*)

    B: _____ I tossed and turned all night.

6. A: You look pale. What's the matter? _____ (*feel well*)

    B: _____ I think I might be coming down with something.

7. A: Daddy, Tommy said that the sun rises in the west. _____

    _____ (*rise in the east*)

    B: _____, Annie. You're right. Tommy is a little mixed up.

8. A: See that man over there, the one in the green shirt?

    B: Yes. Who is he?

    A: _____ (*recognize him*)

    B: _____. Am I supposed to?

B-4 TAG QUESTIONS

(a) Jack *can* come, *can't he?* (b) Fred *can't* come, *can he?*	A *tag question* is a question added at the end of a sentence. Speakers use tag questions chiefly to make sure their information is correct or to seek agreement.★

AFFIRMATIVE SENTENCE + NEGATIVE TAG	→ AFFIRMATIVE ANSWER EXPECTED
Mary *is* here, *isn't* she?	Yes, she is.
You *like* tea, *don't* you?	Yes, I do.
They *have left*, *haven't* they?	Yes, they have.

NEGATIVE SENTENCE + AFFIRMATIVE TAG	→ NEGATIVE ANSWER EXPECTED
Mary *isn't* here, *is* she?	No, she isn't.
You *don't like* tea, *do* you?	No, I don't.
They *haven't left*, *have* they?	No, they haven't.

(c) *This/That* is your book, isn't *it?* *These/Those* are yours, aren't *they?*	The tag pronoun for *this/that* = *it*. The tag pronoun for *these/those* = *they*.
(d) *There is* a meeting tonight, *isn't there?*	In sentences with *there + be*, *there* is used in the tag.
(e) *Everything* is okay, isn't *it?* (f) *Everyone* took the test, didn't *they?*	Personal pronouns are used to refer to indefinite pronouns. *They* is usually used in a tag to refer to *everyone, everybody, someone, somebody, no one, nobody*.
(g) *Nothing is* wrong, *is* it? (h) *Nobody called* on the phone, *did* they? (i) You*'ve never been* there, *have* you?	Sentences with negative words take affirmative tags.
(j) *I am* supposed to be here, *am I not?* (k) *I am* supposed to be here, *aren't I?*	In (j): *am I not?* is formal English. In (k): *aren't I?* is common in spoken English.

★A tag question may be spoken:
    (1) with a rising intonation if the speaker is truly seeking to ascertain that his/her information, idea, belief is correct (e.g., *Ann lives in an apartment, doesn't she?*); OR
    (2) with a falling intonation if the speaker is expressing an idea with which s/he is almost certain the listener will agree (e.g., *It's a nice day today, isn't it?*).

□ **EXERCISE 15:** Add tag questions to the following.

    1. They want to come, _____*don't they*_____?

    2. Elizabeth is a dentist, _____?

    3. They won't be here, _____?

    4. There aren't any problems, _____?

    5. That is your umbrella, _____?

    6. George is a student, _____?

7. He's learned a lot in the last couple of years, _____?

8. He has* a bicycle, _____?

9. Joan can't come with us, _____?

10. She'll help us later, _____?

11. Peggy would like to come with us to the party, _____?

12. Those aren't Fred's books, _____?

13. You've never been to Paris, _____?

14. Something is wrong with Jane today, _____?

15. Everyone can learn how to swim, _____?

16. Nobody cheated on the exam, _____?

17. Nothing went wrong while I was gone, _____?

18. I am invited, _____?

☐ **EXERCISE 16—ORAL (BOOKS CLOSED):** Add tag questions.

Example: (*Carlos*) is a student....
Responses: ...isn't he?

1. That's (...)'s pen....
2. (...) is living in an apartment....
3. (...) lives on (*Main Street*)....
4. There isn't a test tomorrow....
5. (...) has his/her book....
6. You had a good time....
7. (...) has been invited to the party....
8. You didn't forget your key....
9. Your parents haven't arrived yet....
10. Turtles lay eggs....
11. (...) can't speak (*Arabic*)....
12. (...) is never late to class....
13. Something will be done about that problem right away....
14. These keys don't belong to you....
15. You used to live in New York....
16. There's a better way to solve that problem....
17. (...) is going to come to class tomorrow....
18. You should leave for the airport by six....
19. (...) doesn't have a car....
20. (...) sat next to (...) yesterday....
21. We have class tomorrow....
22. You've already seen that movie....
23. (...) will help us....
24. Nobody has told you the secret....
25. I am right....
26. Class ends at (*ten*)....

---

*A form of **do** is usually used in the tag when **have** is the main verb: *Tom **has** a car, **doesn't** he?* Also possible, but less common: *Tom **has** a car, **hasn't** he?*

UNIT C: Negatives

C-1 USING *NOT* AND OTHER NEGATIVE WORDS

(a) AFFIRMATIVE: The earth is round. (b) NEGATIVE: The earth is **not** flat.	**Not** expresses a *negative* idea.

AUX + *NOT* + MAIN VERB	**Not** immediately follows an auxiliary verb or *be*. (Note: If there is more than one auxiliary, **not** comes immediately after the first auxiliary: *I will not be going* there.) ***Do*** or ***does*** is used with **not** to make a simple present verb (except *be*) negative. ***Did*** is used with **not** to make a simple past verb (except *be*) negative.
(c) I *will* **not** *go* there. I *have* **not** *gone* there. I *am* **not** *going* there. I *was* **not** there. I *do* **not** *go* there. He *does* **not** *go* there. I *did* **not** *go* there.	

CONTRACTIONS OF AUXILIARY VERBS WITH *NOT*		
*are not = aren't** *cannot = can't* *could not = couldn't* *did not = didn't* *does not = doesn't*	*do not = don't* *has not = hasn't* *have not = haven't* *had not = hadn't* *is not = isn't*	*must not = mustn't* *should not = shouldn't* *was not = wasn't* *were not = weren't* *will not = won't* *would not = wouldn't*

(d) I **never** go there.
 I have **hardly ever** gone there.
 	
 (e) There's **no** chalk in the drawer.
	In addition to **not**, the following are negative adverbs:
	      never, rarely, seldom
	      hardly (ever), scarcely (ever), barely (ever)
	 No also expresses a negative idea.

COMPARE: *NOT* vs. *NO*	**Not** is used to make a verb negative, as in (f).
(f) I **do not have** any money. (g) I have **no money**.	**No** is used as an adjective in front of a noun (e.g., **money**), as in (g). Note: (f) and (g) have the same meaning.

*Sometimes in spoken English you will hear "ain't." It means *am not, isn't,* or *aren't.* "Ain't" is not considered proper English, but many people use "ain't" regularly, and it is also frequently used for humor.

☐ **EXERCISE 17:** Change the following into the negative in two ways: use **not . . . any** in one sentence and **no** in the other.

1. I have some problems. → *I don't have any problems. I have no problems.*
2. There was some food.
3. I received some letters from home.
4. I need some help.
5. We have some time to waste.
6. You should have given the beggar some money.
7. I trust someone. → *I don't trust anyone. I trust no one.**
8. I saw someone.
9. There was someone in his room.
10. She can find somebody who knows about it.

---

*In American English, **no one** is written without a hyphen. In British English, it is written either **no one** (without a hyphen) or **no-one** (with a hyphen).

C-2 AVOIDING "DOUBLE NEGATIVES"

(a) *INCORRECT: I don't have no money.* (b) CORRECT: I ***don't*** have ***any*** money. CORRECT: I have ***no*** money.	(a) is an example of a "double negative," i.e., a confusing and grammatically incorrect sentence that contains two negatives in the same clause.* One clause should contain only one negative.

*NOTE: Negatives in two different clauses in the same sentence cause no problems; for example:
    *A person who **doesn't** have love **can't** be truly happy.*
    *I **don't** know why he **isn't** here.*

☐ **EXERCISE 18—ERROR ANALYSIS:** Correct the following sentences, all of which contain double negatives.

1. I don't need no help.

2. I didn't see nobody.

3. I can't never understand him.

4. He doesn't like neither coffee nor tea.

5. I didn't do nothing.

6. I can't hardly hear the radio. Would you please turn it up?

7. The beach was deserted. We couldn't see nothing but sand.

8. Methods of horse training haven't barely changed at all in the last eight centuries.

C-3 BEGINNING A SENTENCE WITH A NEGATIVE WORD

(a) ***Never will I do*** that again. (b) ***Rarely have I eaten*** better food. (c) ***Hardly ever does he come*** to class on time.	When a negative word begins a sentence, the subject and verb are inverted (i.e., question word order is used).*

*Beginning a sentence with a negative word is relatively uncommon in everyday usage, but is used when the speaker/writer wishes to emphasize the negative element of the sentence.

☐ **EXERCISE 19:** Change each sentence so that it begins with a negative word.

1. We rarely go to movies. → *Rarely do we go to movies.*

2. I seldom sleep past seven o'clock.

3. I hardly ever agree with her.

4. I will never forget the wonderful people I have met here.

5. I have never known Pat to be dishonest.

6. The mail scarcely ever arrives before noon.

UNIT D: Articles

D-1   BASIC ARTICLE USAGE

<table>
<tr><td colspan="3" align="center">I. USING A or Ø: GENERIC NOUNS</td></tr>
<tr>
<td>SINGULAR
COUNT
NOUN</td>
<td>(a) A banana is yellow.*</td>
<td rowspan="3">A speaker uses generic nouns to make generalizations. A generic noun represents a whole class of things; it is not a specific, real, concrete thing but rather a symbol of a whole group.

In (a) and (b): The speaker is talking about any banana, all bananas, bananas in general. In (c), the speaker is talking about any and all fruit, fruit in general.

Notice that no article (Ø) is used to make generalizations with plural count nouns and noncount nouns, as in (b) and (c).</td>
</tr>
<tr>
<td>PLURAL
COUNT
NOUN</td>
<td>(b) Ø Bananas are yellow.</td>
</tr>
<tr>
<td>NONCOUNT
NOUN</td>
<td>(c) Ø Fruit is good for you.</td>
</tr>
<tr><td colspan="3" align="center">II. USING A or SOME: INDEFINITE NOUNS</td></tr>
<tr>
<td>SINGULAR
COUNT
NOUN</td>
<td>(d) I ate a banana.</td>
<td rowspan="2">Indefinite nouns are actual things (not symbols), but they are not specifically identified.

In (d): The speaker is not referring to "this banana" or "that banana" or "the banana you gave me." The speaker is simply saying that s/he ate one banana. The listener does not know nor need to know which specific banana was eaten; it was simply one banana out of that whole group of things in this world called bananas.</td>
</tr>
<tr>
<td>PLURAL
COUNT
NOUN</td>
<td>(e) I ate some bananas.</td>
</tr>
<tr>
<td>NONCOUNT
NOUN</td>
<td>(f) I ate some fruit.</td>
<td>In (e) and (f): Some is often used with indefinite plural count nouns and indefinite noncount nouns. In addition to some, a speaker might use two, a few, several, a lot of, etc. with plural count nouns, or a little, a lot of, etc. with noncount nouns. (See Chart 5-8.)</td>
</tr>
<tr><td colspan="3" align="center">III. USING THE: DEFINITE NOUNS</td></tr>
<tr>
<td>SINGULAR
COUNT
NOUN</td>
<td>(g) Thank you for the banana.</td>
<td rowspan="2">A noun is definite when both the speaker and the listener are thinking about the same specific thing.

In (g): The speaker uses the because the listener knows which specific banana the speaker is talking about, i.e., that particular banana which the listener gave to the speaker.</td>
</tr>
<tr>
<td>PLURAL
COUNT
NOUN</td>
<td>(h) Thank you for the bananas.</td>
</tr>
<tr>
<td>NONCOUNT
NOUN</td>
<td>(i) Thank you for the fruit.</td>
<td>Notice that the is used with both singular and plural count nouns and with noncount nouns.</td>
</tr>
</table>

*Usually *a/an* is used with a singular generic count noun. Examples:
> *A window is made of glass. A doctor heals sick people. Parents must give a child love. A box has six sides. An apple can be red, green, or yellow.*

The is sometimes used with a singular generic count noun (not a plural generic count noun, not a generic noncount noun). "Generic *the*" is commonly used with, in particular:
- (1) species of animals: *The whale is the largest mammal on earth.*
  > *The elephant is the largest land mammal.*
- (2) inventions: *Who invented the telephone? the wheel? the refrigerator? the airplane?*
  > *The computer will play an increasingly large role in all of our lives.*
- (3) musical instruments: *I'd like to learn to play the piano.*
  > *Do you play the guitar?*

D-2 GENERAL GUIDELINES FOR ARTICLE USAGE

(a) **The sun** is bright today. Please hand this book to **the teacher**. Please open **the door**. Jack is in **the kitchen**.	GUIDELINE: Use **the** when you know or assume that your listener is familiar with and thinking about the same specific thing or person you are talking about.
(b) Yesterday I saw *some dogs*. **The dogs** were chasing *a cat*. **The cat** was chasing *a mouse*. **The mouse** ran into *a hole*. **The hole** was very small.	GUIDELINE: Use **the** for the second mention of an indefinite noun★; in (b): first mention = *some dogs, a cat, a mouse, a hole* second mention = *the dogs, the cat, the mouse, the hole*
(c) *INCORRECT: The apples are my favorite fruit.* 　　CORRECT: **Apples** are my favorite fruit. (d) *INCORRECT: The gold is a metal.* 　　CORRECT: **Gold** is a metal.	GUIDELINE: Do not use **the** with a plural count noun (e.g., *apples*) or a noncount noun (e.g., *gold*) when you are making a generalization.
(e) *INCORRECT: I drove car.* 　　CORRECT: I drove **a car**. 　　I drove **the car**. 　　I drove **that car**. 　　I drove **his car**.	GUIDELINE: Do not use a singular count noun (e.g., *car*) without: (1) an article (**a/an** or **the**); OR (2) **this/that**; OR (3) a possessive pronoun.

★**The** is not used for the second mention of a generic noun. COMPARE:
　(1) What color is **a banana** (*generic noun*)? **A banana** (*generic noun*) is yellow.
　(2) Tom offered me **a banana** (*indefinite noun*) or an apple. I chose **the banana** (*definite noun*).

☐ EXERCISE 20: In the following dialogues, try to decide whether the speakers would probably use *a/an* or *the*.

1. A: I have ___*an*___ idea. Let's go on ___*a*___ picnic Saturday.

   B: Okay.

2. A: Did you have fun at ___*the*___ picnic yesterday?

   B: Sure did. And you?

3. A: You'd better have _____ good reason for being late!

   B: I do.

4. A: Did you think _____ reason Jack gave for being late was believable?

   B: Not really.

5. A: Where's my blue shirt?

   B: It's in _____ washing machine. You'll have to wear _____ different shirt.

6. A: I wish we had _____ washing machine.

   B: So do I. It would make it a lot easier to do our laundry.

7. A: What happened to your bicycle? _____ front wheel is bent.

   B: I ran into _____ parked car when I swerved to avoid _____ big pothole in the street.

   A: Did you damage _____ car?

   B: A little.

   A: What did you do?

   B: I left _____ note for _____ owner of _____ car.

   A: What did you write on _____ note?

   B: My name and address. I also wrote _____ apology.

8. A: Can you repair my car for me?

   B: What's wrong with it?

   A: _____ radiator has _____ leak, and one of _____ windshield wipers doesn't work.

   B: Can you show me where _____ leak is?

9. A: Have you seen my boots?

   B: They're in _____ closet in _____ front hallway.

☐ **EXERCISE 21:** Complete the sentences with *a/an*, *the*, or Ø.

1. ____Ø____ beef is a kind of ____Ø____ meat.

2. ____The____ beef we had for dinner last night was excellent.

3. Jack is wearing ____a____ straw hat today.

4. Jack likes to wear _____ hats.

5. _____ hat is _____ article of clothing.

6. _____ hats are _____ articles of clothing.

7. _____ brown hat on that hook over there belongs to Mark.

8. Everyone has _____ problems in _____ life.

9. My grandfather had _____ long life.

10. That book is about _____ life of Helen Keller.

11. Tommy wants to be _____ engineer when he grows up.

12. The Brooklyn Bridge was designed by _____ engineer.

13. John Roebling is _____ name of _____ engineer who designed the Brooklyn Bridge. He died in 1869 from _____ infection. He died before _____ bridge was completed.

14. _____ people wear _____ jewelry to make themselves more attractive.

15. _____ jewelry Diana is wearing today is beautiful.

16. Mary is wearing _____ beautiful ring today. It is made of _____ gold and _____ rubies. _____ gold in her ring was mined in Canada. _____ rubies came from Burma.

17. One of the first things you need to do when you move to _____ new city is to find _____ place to live. Most _____ newspapers carry _____ advertisements (called "want ads") for _____ apartments that are for rent. If you find _____ ad for _____ furnished apartment, _____ apartment will probably contain _____ stove and _____ refrigerator. It will also probably have _____ furniture such as _____ beds, _____ tables, _____ chairs, and maybe _____ sofa.

18. My wife and I have recently moved to this city. Since we're going to be here for only _____ short time, we're renting _____ furnished apartment. We decided that we didn't want to bring our own furniture with us. _____ apartment is in _____ good location, but that's about the only good thing I can say about it. Only one burner on _____ stove works. _____ refrigerator is noisy, and _____ refrigerator door won't stay closed unless we tape it shut. _____ bed sags in the middle and creaks. All of the rest of _____ furniture is old and decrepit too. Nevertheless, we're still enjoying living in this city. We may have to look for _____ another apartment, however.

APPENDIX 2
Preposition Combinations

Appendix 2 contains two lists of preposition combinations. The first list consists of preposition combinations with adjectives and verbs. The second list contains phrasal verbs.

These lists contain only those preposition combinations used in the exercises in the text and in the accompanying workbooks.

PREPOSITION COMBINATIONS WITH ADJECTIVES AND VERBS

A *be* absent from
    accuse of
    be accustomed to
    be aquainted with
    be addicted to
    be afraid of
    agree with
    be angry at, with
    be annoyed with
    apologize for
    apply to, for
    approve of
    argue with, about
    arrive in, at
    be associated with
    be aware of

B believe in
    blame for
    be blessed with
    be bored with

C *be* capable of
    care about, for
    be cluttered with
    be committed to
    compare to, with
    complain about
    be composed of
    be concerned about
    be connected to
    consist of
    be content with
    contribute to
    be convinced of
    be coordinated with
    count (up)on
    cover with
    be crowded with

D decide (up)on
    be dedicated to
    depend (up)on

be devoted to
be disappointed in, with
be discriminated against
distinguish from
be divorced from
be done with
dream of, about
be dressed in

E *be* engaged to
be envious of
be equipped with
escape from
excel in
be excited about
excuse for
be exposed to

F *be* faithful to
be familiar with
feel like
fight for
be filled with
be finished with
be fond of
forget about
forgive for
be friendly to, with
be furnished with

G *be* grateful to, for
be guilty of

H hide from
hope for

I *be* innocent of
insist (up)on
be interested in
be involved in

J *be* jealous of

K *be* known for

L *be* limited to
look forward to

M *be* made of, from
be married to

O object to
be opposed to

P participate in
be patient with
be polite to
pray for
be prepared for
prevent from
prohibit from
protect from
be provided with
be proud of
provide with

R recover from
be related to
be relevant to
rely (up)on
be remembered for
rescue from
respond to
be responsible for

S *be* satisfied with
be scared of
stare at
stop from
subscribe to
substitute for
succeed in

T take advantage of
take care of
be terrified of
thank for
be tired of, from

U *be* upset with
be used to

V vote for

W *be* worried about

PHRASAL VERBS (TWO-WORD AND THREE-WORD VERBS)

The term *phrasal verb* refers to a verb and preposition which together have a special meaning. For example, ***put + off*** means "postpone." Sometimes a phrasal verb consists of three parts. For example, ***put + up + with*** means "tolerate." Phrasal verbs are also called *two-word verbs* or *three-word verbs*.

SEPARABLE PHRASAL VERBS (a) I **handed** *my paper* **in** yesterday. (b) I **handed in** *my paper* yesterday.	A phrasal verb may be either *separable* or *nonseparable*. With a separable phrasal verb, a noun may come either between the verb and the preposition or after the preposition, as in (a) and (b).
(c) I **handed** *it* **in** yesterday. (*INCORRECT: I handed in it yesterday.*)	A pronoun comes between the verb and the preposition if the phrasal verb is separable, as in (c).
NONSEPARABLE PHRASAL VERBS (d) I **ran into** *an old friend* yesterday. (e) I **ran into** *her* yesterday. (*INCORRECT: I ran an old friend into.*) (*INCORRECT: I ran her into yesterday.*)	With a nonseparable phrasal verb, a noun or pronoun must follow the preposition, as in (d) and (e).

Phrasal verbs are especially common in informal English. Following is a list of common phrasal verbs and their usual meanings. This list contains only those phrasal verbs used in the exercises in the text. The phrasal verbs marked with an asterisk (*) are nonseparable.

A ask out . . . . *ask someone to go on a date*

B bring about, bring on . . . . *cause*
bring up . . . . *(1) rear children; (2) mention or introduce a topic*

C call back . . . . *return a telephone call*
call in . . . . *ask to come to an official place for a specific purpose*
call off . . . . *cancel*
*call on . . . . *(1) ask to speak in class; (2) visit*
call up . . . . *call on the telephone*
*catch up (with) . . . . *reach the same position or level*
*check in, check into . . . . . *register at a hotel*
*check into . . . . *investigate*
check out . . . . *(1) take a book from the library; (2) investigate*
*check out (of) . . . . *leave a hotel*
cheer up . . . . *make (someone) feel happier*
clean up . . . . *make clean and orderly*
*come across . . . . *meet by chance*
cross out . . . . *draw a line through*
cut out . . . . *stop an annoying activity*

D do over .... *do again*

   *drop by, drop in (on) .... *visit informally*

   drop off .... *leave something/someone at a place*

   *drop out (of) .... *stop going to school, to a class, to a club, etc.*

F figure out .... *find the answer by reasoning*

   fill out .... *write the completions of a questionnaire or official form*

   find out .... *discover information*

G *get along (with) .... *exist satisfactorily*

   get back (from) .... *(1) return from a place; (2) receive again*

   *get in, get into .... *(1) enter a car; (2) arrive*

   *get off .... *leave an airplane, a bus, a train, a subway, a bicycle*

   *get on................. *enter an airplane, a bus, a train, a subway, a bicycle*

   *get out of............. *(1) leave a car; (2) avoid work or an unpleasant activity*

   *get over .... *recover from an illness*

   *get through .... *finish*

   *get up .... *arise from bed, a chair*

   give back.............. *return an item to someone*

   give up................ *stop trying*

   *go over................ *review or check carefully*

   *grow up (in) .... *become an adult*

H hand in .... *submit an assignment*

   hang up............... *(1) conclude a telephone conversation; (2) put clothes on a hanger or a hook*

   have on .... *wear*

K keep out (of)........... *not enter*

   *keep up (with) .... *stay at the same position or level*

   kick out (of) .... *force (someone) to leave*

L *look after............. *take care of*

   *look into .... *investigate*

   *look out (for).......... *be careful*

   look over .... *review or check carefully*

   look up .... *look for information in a reference book*

M make up .... *(1) invent; (2) do past work*

N name after, name for .... *give a baby the name of someone else*

P *pass away .... *die*

   pass out .... *(1) distribute; (2) lose consciousness*

   pick out............... *select*

   pick up .... *(1) go to get someone (e.g., in a car); (2) take in one's hand*

   point out .... *call attention to*

put away .... *remove to a proper place*
put back .... *return to original place*
put off .... *postpone*
put on .... *put clothes on one's body*
put out .... *extinguish a cigarette or cigar*
*put up with .... *tolerate*

R *run into, *run across .... *meet by chance*
  *run out (of) .... *finish a supply of something*

S *show up .... *appear, come*
  shut off .... *stop a machine, light, faucet*

T *take after .... *resemble*
  take off .... *(1) remove clothing; (2) leave on a trip*
  take out .... *(1) take someone on a date; (2) remove*
  take over .... *take control*
  take up .... *begin a new activity or topic*
  tear down .... *demolish; reduce to nothing*
  tear up .... *tear into many little pieces*
  think over .... *consider carefully*
  throw away, throw out ... *discard; get rid of*
  throw up .... *vomit; regurgitate food*
  try on .... *put on clothing to see if it fits*
  turn down .... *decrease volume or intensity*
  turn in .... *(1) submit an assignment; (2) go to bed*
  turn off .... *stop a machine, light, faucet*
  turn on .... *begin a machine, light, faucet*
  turn out .... *extinguish a light*
  turn up .... *increase volume or intensity*

APPENDIX 3
Guide for Correcting Writing Errors

To the student: Each number represents an area of usage. Your teacher will use these numbers when marking your writing to indicate that you have made an error. Refer to this list to find out what kind of error you have made and then make the necessary correction.

1	SINGULAR-PLURAL	He (1)have been here for six (1)month.
		He has been here for six months.
2	WORD FORM	I saw a (2)beauty picture.
		I saw a beautiful picture.
3	WORD CHOICE	She got (3)on the taxi.
		She got into the taxi.
4	VERB TENSE	He (4)is here since June.
		He has been here since June.
5+	ADD A WORD	I want (5+)∧ go to the zoo.
		I want to go to the zoo.
5−	OMIT A WORD	She entered (5−)to the university.
		She entered the university.
6	WORD ORDER	I saw (6)five times that movie.
		I saw that movie five times.
7	INCOMPLETE SENTENCE	I went to bed. (7)Because I was tired.
		I went to bed because I was tired.

8	SPELLING	An accident occured.⁽⁸⁾ *An accident occurred.*
9	PUNCTUATION	What did he say.⁽⁹⁾ *What did he say?*
10	CAPITALIZATION	I am studying english.⁽¹⁰⁾ *I am studying English.*
11	ARTICLE	I had a accident.⁽¹¹⁾ *I had an accident.*
12?	MEANING NOT CLEAR	He borrowed some smoke.⁽¹²⁾ *(? ? ?)*
13	RUN-ON SENTENCE*	My roommate was sleeping, we didn't want to wake her up.⁽¹³⁾ *My roommate was sleeping. We didn't want to wake her up.*

---

*A run-on sentence occurs when two sentences are incorrectly connected: the end of one sentence and the beginning of the next sentence are not properly marked by a period and a capital letter or by a semicolon. (See Charts 8-3 and 8-9.)

Index

Able to, 107, 109, 112 *(Look on pages 107, 109, and 112.)*	The numbers following the words listed in the index refer to page numbers in the main text.
Be, A4 *(Look in the back part of this book on the fourth page of the Appendixes.)*	The index numbers preceded by the letter ''A'' (e.g., A4) refer to pages in the Appendixes, which are found in the last part of the text. The main text ends on page 374, and the appendixes immediately follow. Page 374 is followed by page A1.
Continuous tenses, 3*fn.* *(Look at the footnote on page 3.)*	Information given in footnotes to charts or exercises is noted by the page number plus the abbreviation *fn.*